Praise for *Mommy Millionaire*

"Lavine's human and authoritative story makes this one of the most engaging and useful resources available for readers hoping to convert their passion into a healthy company—any man who perceives her lessons as gender-specific will lose out on a rare gem."   —*Publishers Weekly* (starred review)

"Lavine has good tips for anyone interested in launching a home-based business."   —*Library Journal*

"*Mommy Millionaire* is an inspiring gift and road map to success for anyone who's ever had a dream."   —Barbara De Angelis, Ph.D., #1 *New York Times* bestselling author of *How Did I Get Here*

"Kim Lavine's memoir-cum-business-primer breaks new ground in the crowded field of startup sagas. By seamlessly blending the epiphanies that she gained through launching a business with practical lessons, Lavine has packaged a core set of new-venture tenets into something fresh and relevant. . . . Lavine's book is worth reading."   —*Strategy and Business Magazine* (chosen as one of the best business books of 2007)

MOMMY MILLIONAIRE

M⬤MMY
MILLIONAIRE

How I Turned My Kitchen Table Idea into a
Million Dollars and How You Can, Too!

Kim Lavine

President of Green Daisy, Inc.

 St. Martin's Griffin ⋈ New York

www.stmartins.com

Library of Congress Cataloging-in-Publication Data

Lavine, Kim.
    Mommy millionaire : how I turned my kitchen table idea into a million dollars and how you can, too! / Kim Lavine.
        p. cm.
    ISBN-13: 978-0-312-35471-8
    ISBN-10: 0-312-35471-1
    1. New Business enterprises. 2. Entrepreneurship. 3. Businesswomen. I. Title.

HD62.5.L385 2007
658.1'1—dc22

                                                                    2006051001

10   9   8   7   6   5   4   3   2

For David, my hero, and Dylan and Ryan,
my special angels from heaven whom God sent me

CONTENTS

ACKNOWLEDGMENTS

I would like to extend my sincere gratitude to the following individuals for the invaluable contributions they made to this book:

My business mentor, Dave Sayers, whose support and expert advice made this journey possible, guiding me successfully through every challenge along the way.

My editor, Diane Reverand, whose unrivaled talent, vision, and dedication were poured into these pages.

My agent, Jim Levine, a true Master of the Universe, whose incomparable energy and ability for putting together people and ideas made this book happen.

Dave Hathaway and all my angel investors, grand and otherwise, who taught me how to discern opportunity in places very few can and under whom I am still a willing and grateful apprentice.

LETTER TO THE READER

Dear Reader,

This book is for you.

This book is for every woman in America, particularly all the moms in America who are in search of the "perfect part-time job"—you know, the one we all dream about finding, which offers personal and career fulfillment without compromising the very heart and soul of our lives: our family.

This book is for every woman who ever had a dream. A dream of taking control of her own destiny. A dream of finding financial independence. A dream of finding work that leaves her satisfied and fulfilled at the end of the day. A dream of a workplace that doesn't penalize her for being a mom.

This book is for every woman who came up with an idea, an idea for making the world a better, or prettier, or kinder, or easier place, and didn't know what to do to turn her idea into a reality. Simple ideas, big ideas, ideas that can change the world, discovered at their kitchen tables, in between making peanut butter sandwiches for lunch and helping kids with homework after school.

This book is for every woman who is facing challenges. Challenges to keep her family healthy and her house clean, to pay the bills, to advocate for her kids, to stand up for herself. This book is for the women who are pushing through challenge, facing down prejudice, and standing up to those who would underestimate them, cutting a swath wide enough for the rest of us to follow.

This book is for every woman who ever loved. Who is passionate about her ideas. Who has a desire to make her life better for herself and her family. Who boasts unapologetically about her kids and her husband. Who fights to keep her family her number-one priority. Who isn't afraid to be enthusiastic when the whole world is telling her she is crazy. And for the women who find the courage to follow their dreams.

Everything begins with a search for something better—a dream, an idea, the courage to face a challenge, and the passion to get it done. You can do it. Believe in yourself. Change the rules. Join the revolution.

Kim Lavine
Grand Haven, Michigan
www.mommymillionaire.com

MOMMY
MILLIONAIRE

INTRODUCTION

"How did you turn that kitchen table idea of yours into a million dollars?" It's a question I hear everywhere I go as I tour the country on business as president of Green Daisy, Inc. Whether I'm at trade shows in cities across the United States or at lectures I give to women's and community groups, everyone wants an answer to that question!

It became clear to me that there was a real need for a *How to Make a Million Dollars* book. You don't need to be the next Bill Gates or Steve Jobs to make a million dollars on the next big thing. Becoming a millionaire is not about luck, being a genius, or having any special talents. You don't have to be selling the next high-tech invention to get rich. You can do it with something as simple as a Wuvit! What's a Wuvit? A simple little gift I made at my kitchen table that I turned into a million dollars in just over three years.

There has been no shortage of books in the last few years telling you how to think like a millionaire, but just thinking like a millionaire is not enough. The truth is, people only learn to think like a millionaire by becoming one. Read this book, and you'll see step by step how I went from a stay-at-home mommy to a Mommy Millionaire, and every lesson I learned along the way.

It's About Time Someone Wrote This Book!

This book is not just about how to become a millionaire; it's about how to become a millionaire while putting your family first. Being a mommy entrepreneur is a lot like being Ginger Rogers—doing everything Fred Astaire did, but "backwards in high heels," while making it look effortless. My workday as president of Green Daisy, Inc., is routinely interrupted by numerous requests from my kids, like "Can I have chocolate milk?" and "Can I buy a BB gun?" And you know what? That's a good thing! Seeing my children's smiling faces throughout the workday is one of the perks of being a Mommy Millionaire.

This is the twenty-first century. Technology has empowered us in new and liberating ways, which will radically transform the nine-to-five workday world. Never before has it been so distinctly possible for us, as women, to have it all.

Before you get it all, you're going to need some handy rules to keep you sane and focused on what's really important—your family—that I carved out from years of first apologizing for my kids, then celebrating them. Before these rules, I'd routinely shush my kids when a business call came in, running into the bathroom while they cried and pleaded on the other side of the door. Now, anyone who calls me during business hours will likely have the privilege of hearing my six-year-old, home from morning kindergarten, scream that he wants "a peanut butter and jelly sandwich" while I have a phone meeting. For a complete list of all my Mommy Millionaire Rules, designed to make your life a whole lot easier and less stressful as you chase down your million dollars, keep reading.

Debunking the Myth

It's true that a few successful woman entrepreneurs, Mommy Millionaires like Martha Stewart, have gone before, paving the way for those who would follow, while creating an unrealistic image of a supersuccessful mom, to which many of us aspire. From the outside, these women appeared to have achieved success effortlessly, baking, sewing, or "make-*overing*" their way to million-dollar empires. In fact, part of the illusion is deliberately creating a brand that makes it appear that their success was but a happy coincidence of motherhood, stumbled upon by accident while hosting dinner parties, sewing pajamas up as a lark after having a baby, or helping friends with makeup tips in the privacy of their own homes. I, however, discovered that becoming a millionaire like Martha Stewart had a lot less to do with being a perfect stay-at-home mom and a lot more to do with Herculean workloads, grassroots marketing tours, and the deft manipulating of smoke and mirrors to create an image of a "perfect mom and homemaker" as a means to sell product, something commonly referred to as "lifestyle marketing." I meet many women across America who have a great idea that could be "the next big thing" but have no idea what it really takes to grow an idea to a million dollars. I'm here to debunk the myths of Mommy Millionaire to which I succumbed and to show those of you who have one "good idea" and want to turn it into "the Next Million-Dollar Idea" how to accomplish your goal while still attending PTA meetings and school parties and gazing into the adorable, smiling faces of your kids throughout each day.

The Next Women's Revolution

New census data tell us that there is a dramatic new trend: women turning in historic numbers to the option of entrepreneurship.

- There are an estimated 11 million women-owned companies in the U.S., which is nearly half of all privately held firms, according to the Center for Women's Business Research, and by 2025 the U.S. Census Bureau projects the number to rise to 55 percent.
- Women are starting businesses today at two times the rate of men, and the growth rate of women-owned firms regularly outpaces overall business growth, according to the National Foundation for Women Business Owners.

This is an extremely exciting time for women entrepreneurs, who are entering the business world in record numbers. Women are forging into the uncharted domain of woman entrepreneurship with a new spirit of freedom and independence, bettering their lives and the economic well-being of the entire country. No doubt we'll change a few rules along the way about work and family during this revolution as we did about sex and gender roles in the seventies.

The Rise of the Woman Entrepreneur

The fact is, more mommies than ever are entering the world of entrepreneurship. And why not? Who knows better what America's consumer culture needs next than the ultimate consumers—mothers, usually women in their thirties who control most of a household's buying decisions and power the American economy with their spending habits. Women are just starting to penetrate the world of entrepreneurship in significant numbers. Sure, there were a few pioneering figures before us, Martha Stewart being the most famous of all—vilified for her determination, perfectionism, drive, and singular devotion to work, which, by the way, are indispensable attributes you'll surely need to make a million. The sheer number of women choosing to become entrepreneurs is remarkable. According to the U.S.

Census Bureau, the number of women-owned businesses grew 20 percent between 1997 and 2002, twice the national average for all businesses. The nearly 11 million women-owned businesses generated more than $940 billion in revenue, up 15 percent from 1997.

Why Are All These Women Starting Their Own Businesses?

There are many different reasons, but the desire to spend more time with their kids than a nine-to-five job in the corporate world would allow is no doubt number one. This became most apparent to me when I was standing "outside the gates" at QVC at a national cattle call they call a "New Product Search," in Orlando, Florida, when I heard a woman in line say, "I wish there was a book telling us how these moms you hear about make millions on their ideas, not just *that* they did it, but *how* they did it, every little detail about what it took to turn their little kitchen table idea into millions!" Standing before me were hundreds of entrepreneurs, men, women, old and young, some dressed in suits, some in cut-off shorts and flip-flops, all taking their turn in a long line that snaked around the elegant hotel's mezzanine, waiting for their golden moment of opportunity when they would stand before a QVC buyer and have ten precious minutes to pitch their product. This was my second trek across the country in pursuit of what most considered the *American Idol* of retailing, and I, unlike the other itinerant "millionaires in the making," felt some ease knowing what would be expected of me once the line had fed me into that brightly lit room filled with long rows of tables, each row broken up into ten six-foot sections on which to present your product. I considered the woman who had made the plea for a guidebook on how to become a Mommy Millionaire and wanted to answer her right then and there, "Just give me a few months to write it!" But it was her turn to forge into that brightly lit room, her shot at becoming an "overnight success," as so many of these budding entrepreneurs believed was the promise being held before them, and she tidied her wheeled apparel rack of prototype drawings and rolled it into the room before I could steel her with one word of advice.

What was it about QVC that brought out all the dreamers, all the cash-strapped inventors, all the "get rich quick" idealists, all the moms—waiting in line with their cute matching costumes and bright feather boas, serving up homemade cookies, doll clothes, and hand-painted shoes while pushing their kids in strollers? What made people drive or fly across the country with nothing but an invention still just on paper or a passed-down family recipe for fudge with dreams of selling out in record time as "Today's Special Value," checking into hotels with their parents' credit cards? According to QVC's own Marilyn Montross, it was because a few could go virtually overnight from "somebody with a product and a dream to somebody with a very large company." Case in point, Jeanne Bice, founder of the Quacker Factory, who appeared on QVC the first time eleven years ago with two embellished T-shirts, and who now makes regular appearances showcasing entire collections at least four times a year, accomplishing millions of dollars of sales. It's easy to be seduced by the success stories, but the truth is that QVC can break you just as fast as it can make you. Only a very small percentage of the thousands of products that "try out" are chosen for on-air presentation, and even fewer result in Bice's success. I personally know more entrepreneurs who have faced financial crisis taking back returned product, which they may have custom-manufactured to fill QVC Purchase Orders, than I know who have experienced success. Getting on air is one thing; selling out of your product is a whole other. If indeed you don't record resounding sales success in your first three minutes of airtime, you could be sent home without a second chance, with all the product you shipped in advance of your appearance returned. In many cases, QVC requires a guaranteed sale, which means that they won't pay for your product unless you sell it all. For every one person I know who has made a pile of cash on QVC, I know ten who have not. It's a lottery and for that lucky one-in-a-million product can deliver a jackpot. You actually have much better odds at success with the nation's conventional retailers than on QVC. Still, QVC persists in the minds of everybody just starting out as the end-all and be-all of retailing. Go after it, that's for sure, but if they don't select you, don't think that's the end. In fact, their rejection marked just the beginning for me.

To learn more about how to get your product on QVC, including how to successfully participate in a Product Search event or how to find an independent marketing representative specializing in QVC, read chapter 9 and visit QVC's Web site, www.qvcproductsearch.com.

. . . .

QVC PRODUCT SEARCH—THE *AMERICAN IDOL* OF RETAIL

- In total, products discovered by QVC have generated more than $1 billion in sales since 1995.
- QVC reaches over 87 million homes in the United States.
- The four cardinal criteria for a successful QVC product:

    1. Is the product unique?
    2. Does it demonstrate well?
    3. Does it save time or solve a problem?
    4. Is it timely or topical?

. . . .

The "How to Make a Million Dollars" Instruction Manual

Everything happens for a reason. That is one of the most essential and surest rules of business that I have distilled from my experience on the roller-coaster ride that is entrepreneurship. The plea by a stranger for an instruction manual on how to turn her kitchen table idea into a million dollars uttered out loud seemed providential. *That was me, two years ago,* I thought. I, too, was once seduced by the lure of quick success that QVC seemed to represent to mommies all over the U.S. Someone had to stop this insanity! Someone had to write the instruction manual this woman demanded.

If you're one of millions of budding entrepreneur moms every year who have made the choice to stay at home with their young children—or are thinking of leaving careers to do so—and you're looking for a book that tells you every step to turning your great idea into a million dollars, filled with practical business advice, you came to the right place. This is a business book for mommy or even daddy wannabe entrepreneurs, full of real-life savvy that nobody else will tell you, knowledge that other successful "lifestyle marketers" definitely don't want you to know. *Mommy Millionaire* is full of inside secrets on how to:

- Write a business plan.
- Develop and fund your idea.
- Get on QVC.
- Break down the doors of big retailers.
- Take it to the streets—launching your product into the national marketplace.
- Develop the power of a story and the will to drive it.
- Get free publicity.
- Devise and execute an exit strategy that will net you millions upon the sale of your company just years after start-up.

In these pages, you will find step-by-step directions on how not to fail and, more important, how to succeed.

Free Money! Where Is It and How Do I Get It?
The Untold Secrets About Getting Free Money for Start-up

This information alone is worth the price of this book. Take it from me, I've been there and done this! There is more to this story than meets the eye. *But wait, there's more! Mommy Millionaire* will tell you the essentials of running a business that you can't learn in schools, explaining once and for all what mommies and daddies alike need to know about entrepreneurial success.

SECRETS TO DOING BUSINESS NO ONE WILL TELL YOU

- Why you never pay anyone in thirty days.
- How to fund your business with personal credit cards.
- The secrets of marketing.
- The tricks to using numbers to your advantage.
- How to create your own "B.S. Detection Machine" and run everything through it first to avoid being scammed.
- Secrets of doing business with big retailers.
- How to create a killer Web site for almost no money and with no knowledge of HTML.
- Trade-show secrets nobody will tell you that will save you thousands of dollars!

There are also a few indispensable rules that I've put together from my own experience, designed to help you take shortcuts to your own success.

TEN RULES FOR DOING BUSINESS

1. Don't apologize for being a mom.
2. When dealing with someone in business, always ask yourself, *What's in it for them?*
3. Pay your attorney for advice only. Most of the paperwork you can do yourself (including setting up your corporation, registering your trademarks, and even writing your own patent).
4. Find a mentor. Having someone who's "been there and done that" can really help you get through tough times and understand it's part of the territory.
5. Remember that nobody ever got rich by spending money, and understand what overcapitalization is and how to avoid it.
6. Have a story. Everybody loves a good story.

7. Create a pitch and cold-call! Nothing has been more effective for me than cold-calling *major* accounts.
8. Realize that everything happens for a reason. Accept challenge, conquer it, and learn from it.
9. Learn the "$20,000 Rule": what it really takes to fund even the smallest business start-up.
10. Believe in yourself!

My Story, in a Nutshell

My own odyssey began nearly three years ago when my husband was laid off. He was running out of unemployment benefits in a job market that was decimated. I had to find a way to support our family! I was making a novel little product I had invented at my kitchen table and that people were crazy about. After giving it as a Christmas present to my kids' teachers, I found myself inundated with phone calls from strangers who wanted one, eventually selling hundreds of them off the back of my truck wherever I went: to the bank, the YMCA, my kids' schools, my neighborhood pool. My husband took the product to a local gift store without telling me and asked the owner if she would try selling them on consignment. She did and sold out of them in a week. I like to say "the rest is history," and unfortunately, that is what most successful woman entrepreneurs would want you to believe, attaching market value to their "Mommy Millionaire Mystique," but the reality is that what followed was years of stunning success, exciting and challenging hard work, and the narrow escape from bankruptcy. Unfortunately, narrowly escaping bankruptcy or the near collapse of your business is frequently not the exception but the rule.

. . . .

BUSINESS 101

Current research shows that the cold, hard facts about starting a business are brutal and inescapable. One-third of new businesses will fail in two years. Fifty-six percent will fail in four years. *Everyone obviously needs all the help they can get! Mommy Millionaire* will show wannabe millionaire entrepreneurs everywhere the approach that is necessary for a business to survive and thrive. This is my own real-life account that will tell you exactly what it takes to succeed as an entrepreneur, both physically and emotionally.

. . . .

Who Needs to Read This Book?

Whether you're a seasoned entrepreneur or just starting out, you'll find the story of how I took my funny-sounding product to millions of dollars in sales an inspiration, including how I successfully launched my product into the national retail landscape by adopting a grassroots marketing approach and personally traveling to stores across the country to do in-store Demo Events. You'll get all the details, including how I:

- Invented a million-dollar product at my kitchen table on a free sewing machine.
- Created my own brand.
- Registered my own trademark.
- Drafted my own patent.
- Built my own Web site.
- Turned my funny-sounding product into a national brand "overnight."

What It Really Takes to Think Rich

Having millionaire mentors is what taught me to see opportunity—to think rich—and to recognize the tough choices and smart decisions that led to their financial success. How many of you have millionaire friends for mentors? If you do, how many of those millionaires are willing to tell you every single secret they learned the hard way for free—including all the stuff nobody wants to admit? *Mommy Millionaire* will. I'll reveal the missing steps between wanting success and achieving it, between desiring a million dollars and getting it.

You Need to Read This Book

I go beyond the myth of the overnight millionaire to the reality to show the blood, sweat, and tears behind the creation of a Mommy Millionaire. With useful lists of resources that offer help to owners and prospective owners of new businesses and my own account that gets to the heart of what it takes to succeed as an entrepreneur, *Mommy Millionaire* is necessary reading for those fascinated by business and eager to create their own million, or anyone interested in a personal story of risk, hardship, and personal and financial transformation.

THE IDEA:
MY OWN INCREDIBLE
STORY

Discerning opportunity in the day's mundane moments is the instinct necessary to entrepreneurial survival; having the courage and the ability to act upon opportunity is what essentially separates those who succeed from those who fail.

Risk Equals Reward—Big Risk Equals Big Reward

How do you turn your kitchen table idea into a million dollars? How do you become a successful entrepreneur? There are many books that detail all the abilities and strengths that need to be brought to the task, but it's not so much a question of competence as one of entrepreneurial character. You could bring with you every word of wisdom and degrees from venerable Ivy League colleges on how to succeed to the threshold as an entrepreneur, but without the necessary willingness to take a calculated risk, you could not take the first step toward that exciting and mysterious frontier of risk and reward.

There is no reward without risk, and the bigger the risk, the bigger the reward.

KEY CHARACTERISTICS OF THE SUCCESSFUL ENTREPRENEUR

- Persistent
- Goal-oriented
- Willing to take a calculated risk
- Possessing strong vision
- Competitive
- Self-confident
- Creative

Don't worry if you don't have all of these characteristics starting out—I didn't!

To some people—a couple of whom will no doubt be family members—the willingness to embark upon a path of risk will be perceived on one day as courage, on the next as foolish abandon, and on another as insanity. At the very beginning, I was walking in the darkness of faith and not the light of reason. There was no way I could communicate my expectations to friends and family—I just had a gut feeling that I would be successful and I had to follow my gut. Many told me I would fail. Let's face it; vision is a gift of the dreamer, and not everyone was born to dream. People had been laughing at dreamers for aeons before I came along. I'm sure a lot of people laughed at Bill Gates when he dropped out of college to pursue some little business he had going on in his garage.

I Was No Bill Gates

The little project on the side I was working on in my basement was laughably simple. In fact, no one took me seriously, and why should they have? It was literally a bag of corn! The whole invention itself was a complete accident. I was a stay-at-home mom with two boys, aged two and four, who was just looking for something clever to give to her kids' teachers for a Christmas present. My husband was feeding deer in the backyard of our sprawling tree-lined suburban neighborhood. What did we know? We were city kids with our first official house with a certified yard! I saw a fifty-pound bag of corn he had left standing upright next to my sewing machine and a lightbulb went off in my head. I had heard of rice in socks, surely corn would be better: It had a bigger grain that would hold on to heat longer. I put the corn in a hastily sewn pillowcase, heated it up in the microwave for a couple of minutes, then took it out and held it against my chest. I was blown away by the wave of soothing moist heat that enveloped my body.

The Eureka Moment: When Inspiration Meets Invention

I was overtaken by something that can only be described as a fever. I was possessed during the next three days by a tireless need to work on this thing only. Sewing different-sized pillowcases like an automaton, I experimented with different weights and fills, dragging my screaming, uncooperative kids through blinding whiteout snowstorms to every fabric store within thirty miles, looking for the perfect fabric, the perfect print, the perfect welt cord. I used a hundred-dollar sewing machine I had gotten for free with my credit card points, jamming my fingers under the needle occasionally—I was a lousy sewer—and produced pretty pillowcases with tiny little bloodstains on them where I had sewn over my finger as I tried to turn a tight corner on the cheap, lumbering machine.

- -

DO YOU HAVE A MILLION-DOLLAR PRODUCT?

To evaluate your product, ask yourself the following questions:

- Is there a need for my product?
- Does a market exist to buy it?
- How big is that market?
- Do I have the capacity to meet the need?
- Am I willing to learn how to knock down doors to take it to market?

- -

The Next Big Thing: Evaluating Trends and Countertrends

Some of the nation's biggest retailers employ full-time trend spotters, who do nothing but look in their crystal balls of research, intuition, and popular culture to come up with the next big thing. This is actually more of a predictable science than you would think. Hallmark, with more than forty-two thousand stores nationally, employs a professional trend forecaster, Marita Wesely-Clough, whom the magazine *American Demographics* identified as one of the top five trend spotters in the nation, to keep its retailers ahead of the consumer curve. To read her current forecasts, type "Hallmark trends" into your Google Search bar. She predicts that the next five years will give birth to a new entrepreneurial age, in which young companies will produce ingenious products and devise new strategies to take their products direct to consumers as retailing giants experience temporary stasis from their megamergers, including Sears and Kmart, Federated (Macy's) and May Company, Belk and Proffitt's. So brush off your idea for the next big thing you've been sitting on for years and ask yourself these questions:

- **Do you have a great idea?** What is a good idea? Generally speaking, it's anything that will wake you up in the middle of the night or keep you up. I experienced this same inexplicable passion about my quaint little invention soon after I made it, seeing opportunity that made me so excited I couldn't sleep. Whether you're investing your precious time or money in a product or a service, there are a few key elements to what defines a "great idea."

- **Have you identified an underserved niche?** Every successful entrepreneur is always on the hunt for their next unexploited market. Once you find a customer base that has previously been ignored in the marketplace, it is easier to design your product's features and benefits around it. One of the most successful examples of this in the last decade was Tommy Hilfiger's almost accidental connection with the rap and hip-hop community. Until Tommy, almost nobody was making clothes for this image-conscious and sometimes affluent group of consumers, and they practically made his empire overnight. My product's success identified a niche by merging home decorator accent with spa therapy; consumers could buy a microwaveable moist heat pillow that no longer looked like a medical device, a sock, or a doughnut. It would look great in their homes or as a gift. Other features that distinguished it from similar products in the marketplace included a superior heat source, removable washable pillowcase, no smelly herbs, and upscale designer fabrics. You don't have to reinvent the wheel. Everyone is always looking for something "hot and new," and so my product found its way into every retail environment there is!

I woke one morning to the tune of *2001: A Space Odyssey* playing in my head. What had I made? Why was I so possessed? What would I call it?

After all, this was just corn in a bag. "A very pretty bag," I would years later joke with my chief financial officer. After at least two dozen different prototypes, I had finally sewn the perfect pillow, with a finished size of ten by sixteen inches, complete with a removable, washable pillowcase, featuring a contrasting fabric-covered welt cord trim and an envelope-style closure on the back. Inside was a very nicely sewn pillow of cotton muslin filled with my ingenious thermodynamic heating element, feed corn. Later this internal heating element would be upgraded to expensive seed corn.

I recognized my dilemma instantly: How could I possibly express in a name the superiority and comfort of something so deceptively simple? How would I put into words the indescribable feeling of soothing relief that I felt when I held this heated bag against my chest, allowing its waves of healing warmth to pulse into my heart, making me distantly recall the embrace of my mother when I was a child? How could I communicate to tense, overtaxed modern consumers the release of a deep sigh that this product would deliver to their cold, weary bodies after heating it for only two to three minutes in the microwave? I stood in my kitchen, a Michigan snowstorm raging outside in the deep woods that surrounded our suburban development, as two troublemaking, mischievous toddlers ran around my house with abandon and glee, breaking, spilling, crying, and laughing like Thing One and

Thing Two in Dr. Seuss's *Cat in the Hat*. Impervious to the chaos, I thought about the solace provided by my simple little product, which made me feel, for one peaceful moment, that all was right in the world.

Trademark 101: Crazy Is Good

How do you put that into words?! I want to say the name Wuvit instantly came to my mind, but that would just be subscribing to the myth of the Mommy Millionaire, which I am trying to dispel here. The real story is that I held it next to my chest and whispered in a childlike voice, "I love it." "Love It. Luvit. Hmmmmm." I raced down to the computer—first popping a videotape of *Rugrats* into the VCR and shoving a box of cereal at my still pajama-clad toddlers—went to the United States Patent and Trademark Office Web site, www.uspto.gov, and just started searching trademarks. Damn! "Luvit" was already taken by a brand of toilet paper. What a waste of a great name! Who *luvs* toilet paper? I had a job before I was a mommy, in marketing at a Fortune 500 pharmaceutical company. I still possessed some creative brain cells that weren't destroyed by two years of pregnancy and four years of an almost total and complete lack of sleep. I had to use them.

WHY YOU NEED A TRADEMARK

- A trademark provides legal protection in the marketplace for the name of your product or business name and is defined as any word, name, symbol, or device used to identify and distinguish a producer's goods from others. A service mark provides legal protection for a service instead of a product.
- A trademark is a key piece of intellectual property (IP) that is critical to the future success of your product in the marketplace, as well as a valuable asset to your company.
- You need to protect your product's name right at the beginning, before you introduce it to the marketplace, or you may risk losing the name later to someone who may contest your ownership rights because you didn't register it.
- Another reason you need to register your trademark right at the beginning is to make sure that you're not impinging on anyone else's trademark rights, which you'll discover with a search on the USPTO's Web site, www.uspto.gov. You could be sued if you do so.
- It can take up to a year to have your trademark formally approved by the USPTO, at which time you will be legally allowed to use the

registered trademark symbol ®. Until then, you need to use the symbol ™ behind your product's name to let the public know that you're claiming it as your mark.

What was the next best name after Luvit? Wuvit! Why, that was brilliant! I guessed that nobody could have possibly registered that as a trademark, and I was right. I only had to fill out a simple online form with line-by-line directions provided by the USPTO and charge $325 on my credit card and I could own this trademark in a year. As a former marketing professional, I knew that creating a unique, nonsensical brand name would get the instant attention of the consumer in a brand-crowded marketplace. Look at Kleenex. That was marketing genius. The latest to join the crazy name ranks is Google, after only seven years valued at over $100 billion. You know you've created gold when your brand becomes so distinct and unforgettable that it comes to represent the generic product itself and becomes part of the language, like Kleenex. What consumer would ever be able to walk by a product called Wuvit in the marketplace without at least stopping to find out what the heck it was?

THREE TYPES OF INTELLECTUAL PROPERTY

1. Trademarks
2. Patents
3. Copyrights

All are registered and controlled by the USPTO (www.uspto.gov) or the U.S. Copyright Office (www.copyright.gov).

- To search for a trademark, start by logging on to www.uspto.gov and click on the Trademarks tab on the left navigation bar. Select Main tab. Read under Basics, you'll find "Where Do I Start?" (www.uspto.gov/web/trademarks/workflow/start.htm).
- Beneath the Trademarks navigation link, click on Search Trademarks. You will be directed to Tess, the Trademark Electronic Search System. Click on "New User Form Search" and follow the specific directions.

HOW TO REGISTER A TRADEMARK

1. Take the TEAS (Trademark Electronic Application System) Tutorial, a free service of the USPTO, which explains step-by-step how to fill out

your electronic trademark application online. (www.uspto.gov/teas/eTEAStutorial.htm).

2. Determine what mark you want to register.

3. Use Tess to search the USPTO database to determine whether a similar mark is already registered or whether an application for a similar mark has been filed for related goods and/or services.

4. If you didn't find any similarly confusing marks in your search of Tess, check the Trademark Application and Registration Retrieval (TARR) system to see if there are any other potential conflicts.

5. If not, it's time to file your application online, which will require you to submit a payment of $325 by credit card. This is a nonrefundable fee, so make sure you do your homework first. If they turn down your application because a similar mark already exists, you will not get your money back.

6. If your mark consists of any original artwork, you'll need to convert it first to a jpeg file so that it can be electronically attached with your application.

7. Once you file your application, you'll immediately receive e-mail acknowledgment of your filing. Save this, because it will have important information, including your filing date and case number. You'll need to have this handy when an examining attorney calls from the USPTO to discuss your application.

What's the Difference Between ™ and ® and How Do I Protect My Trademark?

Use ™ to identify your brand in the marketplace while awaiting the acceptance of your trademark application from the USPTO. This gives fair warning to all competitors that you are claiming this mark as a brand. You may only use ® when your request for a trademark has been formally granted and it is accepted as a registered trademark.

Scam Alert—Trademarks

Every time I file a trademark, I will get numerous letters in the mail looking very official with an invoice inclosed for anything from $200 to $2,000, offering to "record" my trademark application in their database. This is an unnecessary expense. They are counting on your inexperience to cause you to send them a check for a useless service. Some of these scammers will go to great lengths to make their correspondence look like it came from an official U.S. government source. Be careful and read the fine print.

Office Essentials

There are few tools more essential to running a successful business than a good phone system and an Internet cable modem. In addition to my cable modem, I have always had at least three phone lines operating out of my home office, one for business, one dedicated fax line, and one line that my customers can call toll-free. If you're still using a dial-up modem, stop. Enter the twenty-first century and invest in a technology that will make your work infinitely easier and happier. Since cable modems provide Internet access over cable, they are much faster than modems that use typical phone lines. I still know many holdouts who refuse to spend the extra cash for a cable Internet connection, and I feel that their stubbornness on this small front will contribute to their ultimate failure as successful businesswomen. Believe me, there will be hundreds of phone conversations you'll have with million-dollar clients while you seamlessly surf through Web sites tracking down critical, deal-closing information as you speak. If you have to wait for three minutes for Web pages to load through your dial-up connection or you miss an important call from a customer who has to listen to an annoying busy signal or voice mail while you comb the Web researching the names of buyers, you might as well not be in business.

> ### HOW TO DOWNLOAD THE FREE GOOGLE TOOLBAR
>
> Go to toolbar.google.com and follow the directions. With the Google toolbar, you'll also get the PageRank display. This is a bar graph that shows you how many clicks a particular Web site gets, broadly indicating its popularity.

Google—Cost to Investors: $2.7 Billion; Cost to You: Free

Since you're doing all this sophisticated searching, download the Google toolbar right now so that you have the best tool for the job. Doing so will insert a little toolbar in your browser window, from which you should initiate every search. Google is so far ahead of everyone else with their features—including the critical PageRank display that tells you how important each Web site you visit is—that you're operating at a disadvantage without it. It's *free* and easy!

Non-negotiable Hardware Must-Haves

Resist every temptation there is to go out and spend a lot of money at start-up on things you don't absolutely need, like fancy office furniture and expensive multiline phone systems. However, you really can't run the most basic business successfully without the following:

- Laptop computer with a wireless modem
- Cable modem with a wireless router
- Color printer/scanner/copier
- Dedicated fax line with multifunction fax machine
- Digital camera
- Professional e-mail server. This is defined as any POP3 server that functions with Microsoft Outlook, preferably using your domain name as the e-mail extension, like name@greendaisy.com. If you want to look professional, don't use any of the popular personal free e-mail servers like Yahoo and defintely not like Hotmail.
- Land telephone line for your toll-free customer service number.

· ·

GETTING A TOLL-FREE PHONE NUMBER

Having a toll-free number buys you instant legitimacy with your customers and costs relatively little. There are dozens of companies nationally that sell toll-free numbers with varying degrees of services attached to them. Talk to your current telephone service provider or do a search for "800 numbers" for a listing of providers. The cost can be as low as ten dollars a month. Eight-hundred numbers can only be linked to land lines—not a VoIP, or Voice over Internet Protocol, provider or a cell phone.

· ·

If you're not computer literate and don't know how to use the Internet to access resources, you probably should reconsider starting a business at all. Today's businesses are driven by e-commerce, and all the tools mentioned in this book are directly available to you through Internet access, saving you countless hours of work and precious amounts of money with the simple download of a template or the online application of a trademark. If you haven't mastered the basic computer skills demanded of the twenty-first century, you are either a relic holdout fighting a losing battle or a Master of the Universe who because of your success is so rich and so well supported by a team of assistants that you don't have to turn on a computer, because someone else will do this menial and demeaning task for you. I have certain accomplished business associates who brag about this unique ability in today's modern world. If you're not one of them, get yourself to a community college and get some basic skills now. You really have to master Microsoft Word, Outlook, and Excel spreadsheets at the bare minimum. If you really want to succeed, learn everything you can about PowerPoint and the ultimate Holy Grail, QuickBooks. Knowledge of QuickBooks alone could save you twenty to thirty thousand dollars! QuickBooks is the only universally used accounting software I know and recommend for small businesses. It is maddeningly complex, but it is an essential component to managing every aspect of your business and once mastered is an invaluable tool for your success. Don't try to tackle this at first unless you have serious accounting skills—leave it to a professional.

NON-NEGOTIABLE SOFTWARE MUST-HAVES

- Microsoft Word
- Excel
- PowerPoint
- Outlook
- QuickBooks—the Holy Grail!
- Adobe Acrobat Reader

Adobe Acrobat Reader is a program designed for reading PDF files. These are files that have been created in another application, like Photo-Shop, then saved with a .pdf extension using Adobe Acrobat, so that they can be viewed by anyone, regardless of whether they have the software the files were created in or not. Go to www.adobe.com to learn more. For all the features of Adobe Acrobat you have to buy the full program, but you can download the Reader program for free from their Web site.

Some programs on your computer, like graphic design and photo programs, allow you to save the files you create in a .pdf format. Use a PDF file to send flyers and price lists to customers. It is a uniform way of presenting information on all computer formats. Also, PDFs can't be changed unless the recipient has the full Acrobat program.

Internet Domain 101

Nowadays, just years later, I would recommend you do a domain name search before you register your trademark. Owning the rights to an Internet domain name to your brand is essential, and even with all the .biz and .nets out there, I still think it's best to own a .com domain. If I were to advise anyone today on creating a brand, I would tell them to start searching the Internet before searching the USPTO. You have to own the rights to both.

What Is a Domain Name?
This is the name or "address" of your Web site, like greendaisy.com. A domain name is uniquely yours and can only point to your Web site. Some domain names have been registered for e-mail purposes, like kimlavine @greendaisy.com, even though they may not have an official Web site. You can have several different domain names "point" to the same Web site, like www.wuvit.com points to www.greendaisy.com.

Technically a domain name is the text name that corresponds to a numeric Internet Protocol address of a server on the Internet. Also called a URL, or Uniform Resource Locator, it is preceded with http://www or Hyper Text Transfer Protocol (http) and World Wide Web (www).

How to Search for and Register an Internet Domain Name
Log on to any of the popular domain registration sites in the box below and type in the domain name you are looking for. You'll instantly learn if it's available and, if it isn't, who owns it. You may contact these owners to see if they would be interested in selling it, though this can be pricey.

For as little as five dollars a year you can retain ownership of your domain by keeping your registration current. If you let your registration lapse even for a day, someone else can buy it, so opt for the long term. Some of these services offer e-mail accounts, Web site building tools, and even e-commerce.

You can register any domain name for your business ending in *.com, .biz,* or *.net* and *.info.* Nonprofits and educational institutions can register using *.org* and *.edu.*

POPULAR DOMAIN REGISTRATION WEB SITES

- www.namesecure.com
- www.godaddy.com
- www.register.com

Opening Your Online Storefront

Today every business must have an online presence to conduct commerce and display Web pages, as well as to serve as a front door to the operation. Use any popular domain search engine to register the available name you want; then you can move later to selecting your hosting service and get to building your Web site. You would be smart to register several domains, one for your primary brand and one for each product you may make, like www.greendaisy.com and www.wuvit.com.

How Do I Get a Domain Name?

It is relatively inexpensive to register names, costing as little as eight dollars a year for a no-frills setup. As a valuable insurance policy against others who may want to hijack a name you left unregistered, think about just adding an "s" to your company or product name and registering that, too. You may be tempted to sign up for a lot of extra services with your registration provider, like e-mail addresses, but resist this until you've gone out and really shopped around for Web site hosting packages. The only advice I can give you now is to forget any e-mail service you can buy that doesn't utilize Microsoft Outlook. This is the single most valuable software application I use on a daily basis. Outlook is your e-mail platform, database manager, calendar, and organizer all rolled into one. You can synchronize it with countless sophisticated database management programs that will integrate even with your QuickBooks customer list. Trust me, all this information will be invaluable to you sooner than later, and anything that can help you organize and manage it is a critical tool.

What About My Web Site?

Now that you've registered your domain name, you will need to start shopping around for Web site packages. But first you have other, more important things to do. Read chapter 5 for everything you need to know about building your Web site for almost no money and with no knowledge of HTML.

Brand Building 101: How to Stand Out in the Marketplace

I had the brand; now I needed the name of the company. I went back to searching domain names on the Internet and, after many hits and misses, just started brainstorming ideas that would capture my corporate culture. I just started writing words that I liked about things that I liked, "flowers" and "nature" and "fun" and "happy." I had about twenty words, ten in one column, ten in another, and I just started putting them together in random order and searching for available domain names. After a couple of thwarted attempts I hit upon Green Daisy after just taking the word "green" out of one column and "daisy" out of the other. *That's brilliant,* I thought. *It's about being green and all that green means, including healthy, natural, verdant, modern. And who can argue with "daisy" for fun?* Again, I encountered this overwhelming feeling of being possessed, and I picked up a pen and drew my company logo fully formed on a piece of scrap paper on the desk in front of me. It was a simple six-petaled green daisy graphic with a pink center and a circle around it. The minute I drew it, I felt as if I had been waiting my whole life to do it.

I didn't know it at the time, but I had created the key elements of a successful brand in the hour it took for my kids to watch Rugrats. I had created a logo and a company name complete with fonts and colors and identified my company's image with fun and natural products.

· ·

KEY ELEMENTS OF A SUCCESSFUL BRAND, A COMPANY'S MOST VALUABLE ASSET

Image or Personality: What do you want your company to be known for? Fun? Integrity? Quality?

Associations: All the other intellectual property that makes up your brand, including logos, colors, taglines, and fonts.

Story: A written document twenty-five to one hundred words long describing the unique values and benefits of your product or brand. For example: "Green Daisy is a company featuring fun, natural products for a happy life, including our Wuvit. What's a Wuvit? It's a warm, moist hug, the next big thing, and your new best friend. A Wuvit is *wuv*! Get a Wuvit, America, and feel good!"

· ·

Creating the Perfect Logo: The Basics for Getting Started

What makes a perfect logo? Keep it simple and make it memorable. Keep reading and you'll learn from a master what makes a good logo in chapter 9. For now, a great logo is anything you can see once, close your eyes, and see in your mind. An example may be the retailer Target's logo, which not only is visually effective but also expresses the name of the company itself, as does Green Daisy's. Once you've created an effective logo, you can eventually use it to brand an infinite list of products, which you may or may not make. This is where the real value of your company may be hiding, in its intellectual property. Much more on this later; for now, stick to the basics:

PMS Colors: Short for Pantone Matching System colors, these numbers represent a standardized ink color system used in the printing industry. Once you create your logo, go to a local printer and match your colors to their PMS chart and write them down so you can make sure all your advertising collateral matches, regardless of the printer or application.

The Importance of Typeface: The typeface you select can communicate a lot about your image. You can find hundreds of free typefaces available to download on the Internet, or you can purchase the newest and best.

Tagline: A very short advertising slogan, such as "fun, natural products for a happy life.™"

Business Cards: These can be had very cheaply. Order a lot; you can give hundreds away at one trade show alone. Don't use the free ones you can get on the Internet.

Letterhead: Invest in some quality letterhead if you want to be taken seriously.

Clip Art: You can find tons of free images on the Web to use for your company logo, but I wouldn't recommend using this if you have any hopes of your company having a national presence. In the end, intellectual property like logos, taglines, typefaces, and PMS colors may be the most valuable assets your company has to sell.

It can cost up to thousands of dollars to have a logo designed. If you can afford it, hire it out, but make sure you're very clear about what you want. I designed and executed my own in PowerPoint and was able to save it in a format all of my printers could use.

The Best Ideas Come in the Shower, or Why God Made Videotape!

I went upstairs to make sure my two little boys hadn't killed each other—which is all I promised my husband as a wife and mother nowadays, that his kids would still be alive when he came home from work every day. They were such demanding, diaper-filling, chaos-creating, labor-intensive, giggling, drooling, adorable babies that coming home to a relatively clean house with dinner on the table was just a bonus for him. Getting a shower in and keeping toddler boys from accidental death or killing each other was my sole objective at this point in our lives. Thank God for videotapes and DVDs! I popped in another tape and went upstairs to take a shower at three o'clock in the afternoon, with the slogan "fun, natural products for a happy life" coming fully formed from my shampoo-covered head.

In the span of less than a week, I had created a product, a brand, which I registered with the USPTO, a registered domain name, a company name, and a slogan. I didn't set upon this path with a master plan. I wasn't looking to become a millionaire or an entrepreneur. I was a stay-at-home mommy, savoring every second of my opportunity as a precious gift from God. As I said before, everything happens for a reason. As an entrepreneur, I've learned that every physical and mental capacity you command will be called upon and tested in your business-building odyssey. You have to bring every lesson you've ever learned anywhere to the job, along with tireless energy, passion, curiosity, fearlessness, kindness, grit, but, most important, instinct. I can look back now and see the providence in this fateful week of my life when I was possessed by this impulse to invent a product, complete with branding! It was that Eureka moment that inspires every inventor or entrepreneur, the most critical moment perhaps when a product or idea is born, along with a fire of excitement and ambition that will fuel you through the challenge of bringing that idea to fruition in the marketplace. I was sitting on top of the world! How could I possibly have known that even with all that I had, an invention, a brand, a marketing foundation, what I had was less than 5 percent of the process of turning my idea into a million dollars. Perhaps it was better that I didn't know. Sometimes you just have to go for it. When the heart and head have worked over a problem without an answer, it is always time to do a gut check.

The voices of the world will drown out the voice of God and your intuition if you let them. And most people are directed by voices outside themselves.

—Oprah

Everything I Need to Know I Learned from My Millionaire Mentors

Every millionaire I know has had a Eureka moment. Every millionaire I know when making the decision to start a business took an unreasonable risk based on his or her gut. It helped that I had as friends a married couple who had recently become millionaires, selling the business that they had grown over the course of nine years. When I first met them, they lived in an extremely modest home, driving modest cars, working together like mad while juggling the demands of two little babies only a year apart in age, living a life much like mine. Just years after I met them, they sold their company and retired at forty-five, enjoying their young children, their homes on the water, and I looked at them and thought, *If they can do it, I can do it, too!* It was so helpful to have had these mentors along my own odyssey. I learned that all the seemingly Herculean tasks I was encountering were part of the territory. They described the fifteen-hour workdays; they explained how waking up with a jerk of anxiety in the middle of the night could be handled by keeping a piece of paper and pen by the bed to free my mind of a nagging demand till the morning by writing it down; they even warned me of the day when I would wake up and not be able to move at all, paralyzed by the scope and quantity of the demands of my business. I had already heard of the emergency second and third mortgages they had to take out on their modest home just to make payroll. All of this taught me one very valuable lesson: Short-term pain equals long-term gain. The greatest inspiration was seeing them rewarded for their work when they banked their big earn-out bonuses, flew to Philadelphia, and formally turned over the ownership of their business to fly home with a big check, rich, retired, and happy. Even then they weren't extravagant. Their richness was in time and freedom. You would never know they had millions—not a fancy car to be found. That was the complete paradox of becoming a millionaire: Once you've worked hard enough to earn a million, you didn't need the money to make you feel good. Your self-esteem no longer is defined by the car you drive, the size of your home, or your jewelry. Instead you had come to understand through all your trials and accomplishments, through rising to every new challenge and conquering it with energy, ingenuity, and attitude, that the virtue of all success is victory over all personal shortcomings in oneself. That was a feeling money just couldn't buy.

You Don't Have to Find the Cure for Cancer or Accomplish Cold Fusion

How can I possibly be waxing so philosophical about a bag of corn? How could I possibly have had a Eureka moment over something so ordinary and quaint? I mean, it wasn't like I had discovered the Internet, or wireless phone communication, or anything remotely related to software, or blogs, or search engines. It would have been a lot easier on my friends and family if I were hawking something elusive defined by ever-evolving tech-speak, instead of a Wuvit. At least then they probably wouldn't have come out and told me right to my face I was crazy. Indeed, every person I know, at one point in my journey, questioned my sanity—even me!

I was, in fact, probably one of the last to be truly converted. I gave my precious little Wuvits out for holiday presents that Christmas, to friends, teachers, neighbors, and family, and these bags of corn took on a life of their own. Apparently, my experience that all was right in the world when I held my warm Wuvit against my chest was something others appreciated, too. Some people joked, asking me if Elmer Fudd had anything to do with naming my product. The majority of people who had received them loved them and called me to ask for more. In our small town strangers can look your name up in the phone book and have no problem calling you. Suddenly that was what was happening. People I didn't know were calling asking if I was the "Wuvit Wady." Apparently, their children's teacher/coach/neighbor had one they had tried and they wanted a Wuvit of their own.

One day a teenage boy showed up at my front door in the middle of a snowstorm, looking over his shoulder as if to ensure he wasn't being observed visiting the "Wuvit Wady's" house, and asked if I could sell him one. He was a high school hockey player, and one of the kids on his team used a Wuvit heated or frozen for sprains and strains. I recognized this teenage boy represented the toughest, most inscrutable market demographic to sell to. If he was willing to suffer the risk of humiliation of being seen at the Wuvit Wady's house, other people would take less risk to get one, too.

"You're Going to Be a Millionaire!"

I may be crazy, but I'm not stupid. I started hearing the recurrence of the phrase "you're going to be a millionaire" coming out of people's mouths. These were smart people making upward of six figures annually, including my neighbor, a pilot who flew a big commercial jet that guaranteed to turn him into a millionaire with salary. Here was a millionaire in the making, who would have gladly traded his job for my opportunity. Was he nuts? He quizzed me weekly with jealous glee about how my Wuvit business was developing, admitting that he was an inventor and entrepreneur at heart, in search of his own personal Eureka moment.

Winter was beginning to melt into spring, and my days were filled with shuttling kids to preschool and play dates, planning elaborate parties, gardening, and decorating a brand-new three-thousand-square-foot home in a large subdivision that can only be described as the Garden of Eden, complete with towering oaks, creeks, and acres of wilderness preserve. We spent our afternoons at a neighborhood pool and clubhouse, and the sound of musical tree frogs filled up the night around us. I had probably sewn at least three hundred Wuvits on my rickety sewing machine by then, producing pretty pillowcases with traces of my DNA hidden in their beautiful floral patterns. My husband, seeing opportunity where I did not, took a dozen Wuvits without telling me to our town's best gift store, asking the store's owner if she would be interested in testing them out on consignment for a week or two. I was selling them for fifteen dollars each off the back of my truck, and they both agreed she could charge up to five dollars more. There would be no risk to her, he promised; she didn't have to pay for them until she sold them, and if she didn't sell them, she could just give them back. She tried one and became an instant convert, admitting later that her husband went as far as to buy a microwave for the bedroom just to heat his up in. She took the dozen on consignment, selling out of them in a week. It was then that a neighbor's father, a former marketing executive with a national high-end retailer based in Detroit, pulled me aside at a spring graduation party for his grandson and said, "You've got something here. You have to take it to the market in a big way!"

And the Rest Is History—NOT!

In the myth of the Mommy Millionaire, this is where the story would end, with a "the rest is history, and they all lived happily ever after." I would create this elaborate persona of suburban domestic bliss, while in reality I worked with a single-minded obsession to make my product a success alongside dozens of legal and illegal Mexican immigrants in a hundred-year-old factory where the only language understood was Spanish—to make my product a success. Where the story ends publicly, it begins in earnest.

The fairy tale came to a crashing halt when my husband came home that week with news that he was without a job. His whole industry was in dire straits, and eight out of ten of his peers were losing their jobs right alongside him. Not only did he not have a job any longer, but the prospects of getting another one were not good. I woke up from my gentle dream with what felt like a slap in the face, recalling those infamous words uttered by Cher to the lovesick character played by Nicolas Cage in the movie *Moonstruck:* "Snap out of it!" and looked at my quaint little hobby project in a whole new light. With two small children and no regular income, I had to decide to make a leap of faith and risk our life savings to invest in a product that many people were still laughing at. I took a deep breath, did a gut check, and risked that first step onto the path of entrepreneurship.

THE BIRTH OF A BUSINESS

I was trying to put together the foundations of a business selling a product most people laughed at, while shuttling two- and four-year-old boys to attorneys, insurance agents, and uncountable fabric stores, spending every precious dime on fabric and sewing supplies, while all the time doubting the whole financial viability of such an undertaking. *Let's face it,* I kept reminding myself. *This is just corn in a bag.* Still, I couldn't deny that some of the best products were the simplest, the ones you would smack your forehead over and say, "Jeez, why didn't I think of that!" I started to understand that sometimes the simplest ideas are the best. In sales, any kind of sales, it's a numbers game: The more people you can appeal to, the more likely you are to make more sales. And there was certainly something about a Wuvit that appealed to everybody. With almost 300 million bodies in the U.S., even if I only sold to 1 percent of them, that was 3 million Wuvits. At twenty-five dollars each, that equaled potential revenues of $75 million. To be honest, I wasn't thinking these thoughts as I waited in line at another fabric store with our children, spending money from savings on materials to make Wuvits, as we depended on unemployment to keep us in house and home. More often than not, I wasn't thinking millionaire; I was feeling guilt and doubt.

Later, when you are building your business plan or looking for investors, be very careful about making claims of potential sales to investors, because they just might hold you to it, even suing you if you don't produce. Con-

---

HOW TO CALCULATE YOUR PRODUCT OR SERVICE'S POTENTIAL MARKET

1. Research any available statistics and demographics.
2. Project possible volume in total units.
3. Convert numbers of units into sales revenues by factoring *retail* price.

ventional wisdom in calculating market share now usually involves portraying the total market for a product and service in terms of demographics and total potential revenues and letting the investors draw their own conclusions about the percentage of penetration.

Building Your Corporate Culture

About this time, winter turned to spring, and I was selling dozens of Wuvits a week off the back of my truck. All those people who had gotten one for the holidays were starting to talk, and my reputation began to precede me. I learned to keep a basket with me at all times, because people would stop me everywhere I went and tell me they wanted to buy one for a gift or for themselves. The basket I hauled Wuvits around in soon became so closely identified with the product that it was key to the unique personality of my brand. At this point, with only one retailer, I still hadn't felt the need to refine my Point of Purchase (P.O.P.) merchandising strategy. Heck, I didn't even know what that meant then! All I knew was that having an attractive wicker basket in my car that held at least ten Wuvits at a time was not only a convenient way to carry them into the bank or the YMCA on my daily errands, but it looked good, too! Necessity is the mother of invention and soon the basket became a critical image of my corporate culture, an identifying element of my fledgling company that would help define and promote it in the marketplace. Just as Google used such accoutrements as LAVA lamps, large rubber exercise balls, and sawhorse desks to express its culture of fun, high-

. . . .

CORPORATE CULTURE: WHAT IS IT?

A company's distinctive personality, distinguished by its core values, work environment, and guiding principles. An example of a corporate culture that is key to identifying and promoting its unique brand in the marketplace is Google, where, for example, Googlers (employees) work at the Googleplex (headquarters), where everyone is encouraged to celebrate their self-consciously nerdy culture by casually talking about computer games or algorithms in their Google Café lunchroom. Corporate culture can be a very powerful tool when recruiting top talent to work for you. If your culture is one of stylish offices with a relaxed work environment and flexible hours that focus on family, employees may choose to work for you over another company that pays more.

. . . .

density productivity and small-company feel, I realized that wicker baskets filled with homemade gifts carried by a mom with two small children in tow had a magical and marketable charm all its own.

I Was No Google

I didn't need to go out and create cold fusion or launch a billion-dollar technology IPO, or Initial Public Offering, of a stock to be traded publicly to make a million dollars. All I had to do was sell comfort and warmth to at least a very small percentage of 300 million tired and cold bodies who just wanted to come home from the daily grind, sit on the couch with their kids, and hold a warmed Wuvit to their chests or their necks while they watched TV. That was precisely what I was selling. People were not just buying the product; they were also buying the concept of feeling good, taking time for themselves, and being happy for the twenty minutes to an hour that they relaxed with their special reward.

The idea is only 5 percent of a product's success; the other 95 percent is passion and marketing.

Wow, the product really was only 5 percent of its success; what I was really selling was so much more than a simple bag of corn! I was selling comfort, warmth, and feeling good. Back to the drawing board!

I had to find a way to express to the consumer the promise of feeling good behind my product. Once I had created my Wuvit, I hadn't spent much time thinking about packaging for it. It was a soft, fluid pillow that presented unique packaging challenges I wouldn't think about earnestly for months. When I was still in the invention phase and feeling rushed to get the recently perfected prototypes out as gifts to the kids' teachers in time for the holidays, I had picked up a few pieces of raffia I had lying around the house from a previous craft project and threaded it through a Wuvit tag I had created in PowerPoint and printed off my own computer. Folding the Wuvit pillow in half, I tied a very rustic and charming bow around the pretty fabric. *There, it looks like a present,* I remember thinking, *a present you don't have to open.* When I gave them away the first comment was, "What's a Wuvit?" then, "It's so pretty!" I didn't know then that such a simple and inexpensive packaging solution would significantly contribute to my product's future marketing success.

On the little card, I had printed copy to describe the features, benefits, and use of a Wuvit to a browsing shopper in two seconds. I focused on copy elements that put all the features in a nutshell:

1. Fun-sounding company name: Green Daisy
2. Logo, bright and eye-catching
3. Product name: "What's a Wuvit?"
4. Tagline: "Fun, natural products for a happy life"

Potential buyers would be interested already!

What's a Wuvit?

A Wuvit is your own personal spa therapy designer pillow. Just heat in the microwave two to three minutes for up to hours of moist heat. Or freeze overnight for icy relief. A Wuvit is a warm, moist hug, a full body massage, one degree away from heaven, the next big thing, and your new best friend. A Wuvit is *wuv*!

Saving Money by Designing and Printing Your Own Tags

I hadn't begun to think about creating a product tag to sell my product in the marketplace. Up until that point I was printing my own tags from my printer, which I cut with a straightedge and an X-Acto knife, from a simple

---

DESIGN AND PRINT YOUR OWN PRODUCT TAGS INEXPENSIVELY ON YOUR COMPUTER, OR PAY A PRINTER

PowerPoint Basics: You don't need to be an expert at this to create a product tag. There are so many templates available for you to use that it's remarkably easy.

Card Stock: You can buy quality card stock at any office supply store. Run it through your printer, making sure to trim it with a straightedge and an X-Acto knife.

Digital Printers: With advances in printing technology, a new breed of printing business exists that can produce top-quality print runs with small minimums at competitive pricing. Look around; these printers are usually the little guys instead of the big. This is an extremely competitive market, so shop hard.

design I had created myself in PowerPoint. With just the name Wuvit on the front of the tag with my Green Daisy logo and my slogan "Fun, natural products for a happy life" and the directions for use on the back, I had come up with the concepts in one afternoon—saving myself thousands of dollars in branding fees. I punched a hole in the corner with an ordinary hole puncher to hang on my raffia bow. Months later I would sit around with a brilliant graphic designer for hours, unable to improve on this basic concept, which eventually took me all the way to Saks Incorporated.

I took my product all the way to Saks Incorporated on a tag I originally printed on my own printer in PowerPoint! In fact, when given the choice, my buyer preferred its homey simplicity to the slickness of a more professional version.

Writing Ad Copy: What Is It and How Do I Do It?

I had to write ad copy. I had to flesh out my marketing message on my product tags if I had any hope of communicating with consumers from store shelves across the country. Though I had yet to learn the term for it—"shelf talking"—I had to make my product speak for itself from the shelf to the consumer, competing in an already crowded space filled with hundreds of other products, all attempting to capture the precious two seconds of atten-

WHAT IS AD COPY OR MARKETING COLLATERAL?

Any material used to market a product or service usually includes an advertiser's name, sales message, trademark, or slogan. Different copy is produced for different purposes:

- Product tags
- Product brochures
- Catalog (most catalog companies will write the copy that accompanies your product themselves)
- Web sites (sometimes called content)
- Spec sheets: usually a sheet that outlines all the technical features and benefits of a product to a potential buyer
- Product shots: stock photographs of your product produced professionally for the purpose of placing in ads or for publicity

tion a passing shopper would typically spare. Most retailers can't afford to hire expensive sales personnel to explain your product, so it's critical that your product or service effectively explains itself. How did I explain the features, benefits, and use of a Wuvit to a browsing shopper in two seconds without spending a ton of money on expensive signage and P.O.P. displays? By focusing on key copy elements to capture all the feelings I wanted to communicate: my company name, Green Daisy; my logo, bright and eye-catching; the product name, "What's a Wuvit?" my tagline, "Fun, natural products for a happy life"—they're interested already.

I already knew the name Wuvit would stop them in their tracks long enough to ask themselves, *What's a Wuvit?* The odds were on my side that they would walk over to the shelf to read the product tag to answer their question, rather than walk away and be plagued by it for a lifetime. I couldn't waste that precious opportunity with a long, boring narrative on how to use my product. I had to ambush them with a feeling message that expressed what it was that I was really selling: feeling good, taking time for themselves, and being happy.

EXERCISE FOR WRITING AD COPY

- Focus on the big picture of what you are selling.
- Brainstorm—there is no right or wrong!
- Free-associate—let your mind go to say anything.
  Describe:
- Key features
- Key benefits
- Key feelings
- Key demographics

  Don't be afraid to be different!

EFFECTIVE SHELF TALKING

- It's a reality that most retailers can't afford to hire expensive sales personnel to explain your product, so it's critical that your product effectively explains itself.
- Two seconds: That's how much time you can expect to get to make a first impression on a shopping consumer. Don't squander it by saying something boring. Say something interesting, funny, provocative, or emotional.
- Don't say something when you can make them feel something.

I had a half hour to come up with my ad copy before my kids would storm the office looking for cookies or a monopoly on my attention. I got out my trusty notepad, warmed up a Wuvit, then closed my eyes and held it to my chest, asking myself, *What's a Wuvit?* and letting answers come to me uncomplicated by too much thinking.

I just started out writing down the words that floated up from my unconscious: "warm," "moist," "*wuv*," "comfort," and "*warm-being.*" I started to think of all the instances in which I really loved to use my Wuvit, like when I came home from a cold and windy day of grocery shopping and I had a chill I just couldn't get rid of, or when I was really stressed out from a day of refereeing toddler mayhem. I pared down the thoughts I was receiving into two-second messages that if I could, I would say directly to a consumer. Before I knew it I had a whole page of good ideas:

- A warm, moist hug
- A full body massage
- One degree away from heaven
- The next big thing
- Your new best friend
- *A Wuvit is wuv*

I loved all of them. I pasted them together in a line, separated only by semicolons, and stuck it on the back of my tag, along with the directions for use. What was not to *wuv*?!

I still had left all those more lengthy descriptions of how I loved to use my Wuvit. My strategy was, once the customer stopped, flipped over my tag, she would get the two-second messages in bold green font. I laid it out in PowerPoint on my own computer—no expensive design or printing fees yet, even though I had sold hundreds of Wuvits worth thousands of dollars—so that "What's a Wuvit?" was the question on top and the answer on the bottom of the tag was, "A warm, moist hug; a full body massage; one degree away from heaven; the next big thing; your new best friend. A Wuvit is *wuv*." In the middle was all the rest of the information they would need printed in simple black type, including the directions for use along with the washing instructions. This very same tag I started out with, tied to a piece of raffia from a shelf in my basement, is the exact same packaging that took my Wuvits all the way to the nation's biggest retailers. I could have printed them off my printer if I hadn't needed so many of them. Since then, I've observed thousands of consumers encountering my product for the first time in the marketplace. Usually they quickly walk by, stop, go back, pick up the Wuvit, ask themselves *What's a Wuvit?* as they flip over the tag, then stand there reading the description. Mission accomplished! I had no idea that soon people across America would be asking themselves, *What's a Wuvit?*

The lesson: Don't say something when you can make them feel something. The surest way to a consumer's wallet is through their heart, not their head.

Selling Comfort, Warmth, and Feeling Good

It was June; I had sold thousands of dollars' worth of Wuvits without investing anything but my time, the cost of raw materials, and a few miscellaneous office supplies. Keeping in mind the old adage that it takes money to make money, I started to imagine what could happen if I started to invest money in this amazing product. Maybe it's a good thing that my husband was without a job. I resisted by necessity every temptation to overcapitalize up front that a start-up business usually falls prey to. This is the number-one reason most start-ups fail: They spend too much money to make too little money. Most businesses won't "make money" until the third year. I know everyone goes into business thinking they are the exception to that rule— including me—but I'm here to tell you that you aren't. I make it a rule not to even talk to people about their "great idea" unless they've written a business plan and have a minimum of $20,000 of personal cash that they are willing to invest in their business. There are all kinds of ways to raise capital—money—to fund your business, but if you aren't willing to risk $20,000 in non-negotiable cold, hard cash of your own, chances are no bank and no group of investors will be willing to risk theirs.

The $20,000 Rule: **It will take a minimum of $20,000 of cold, hard personal cash to start up any business or fund any product development.**

Even without a job, my husband and I possessed the single most valuable asset a small business owner can have: an excellent credit rating. If you don't have stellar credit, don't start a business till you do. Use these tips to clean up your credit rating today, so that you can tap into hundreds of thousands of dollars of cash credit later. The Fair Credit Reporting Act (FCRA) requires each of the nationwide consumer reporting companies—Equifax, Experian, and TransUnion—to provide you with a free copy of your credit report, at your request, once every twelve months.

HOW TO CLEAN UP YOUR CREDIT RATING

- Obtain a free copy of your credit report from each of the three reporting companies at www.annualcreditreport.com.
- Go over it with a microscope. You'll be amazed at how closely you need to police this report every year. You might find erroneous reports of outstanding debt on credit cards you forgot you had years ago.
- Once you find errors, contact the creditor directly to dispute the errors. The Fair Credit Reporting Act requires the credit agency to correct all errors and send a notice of correction to anyone who has requested your report in the last six months.
- If you have reason to dispute something on your credit report (perhaps you were the victim of identity theft), file a written explanation to be distributed to everyone who requests one.
- Cancel and close all credit card accounts you have and don't use. Having a lot of available credit, even if you have no credit card debt, will lower your score, because there exists a risk that you could quickly run up a lot of debt.
- Don't open any of those credit cards that every retailer offers you for discounts on merchandise you buy that day. Even if you cancel them immediately, too many credit inquiries can lower your score, too.
- If you have a lot of credit card debt and you aren't able to make minimum payments in a timely manner, call up the credit card company directly and work hard to negotiate a payment plan with reduced interest rates. You'll be amazed at how willing they will be to work with you if they think it's the only way they'll get paid.
- You need at the minimum two years to clear up records of delinquent payments, so start working today. Use that time to design, prototype, and test-market your idea.
- Finally, get rid of any expensive luxuries you don't need, like that $50,000 SUV lease. This just hurts your debt-to-income ratio, making it difficult to secure good, revenue-generating debt.

Overcapitalization Up Front: One of the Top Reasons Small Businesses Fail and How You Can Avoid It

My grandfather and all his brothers emigrated from Russia with a few dollars in their pockets and eventually turned themselves into self-made millionaires. They had a favorite saying that I still love to quote: "Nobody ever

FOR BUSINESS CREDIT REPORTS

You can do the same thing to check your business's credit rating, but don't expect to get these reports for free. Just like individuals, businesses have credit ratings, too, which indicate whether you make your payments on time, how much debt you have, and if you're a good credit risk. The business credit reporting agencies are:

Dun & Bradstreet
Business Information Reports
99 Church Street
New York, NY 10007
800-TRY-1DNB

Experian
The Credit Bureau, Inc.
P.O. Box 596
Pittsburgh, PA 15230
888-397-3742

got rich spending money." They always had the most spartan offices and warehousing. Most of the millionaires I know think the same way.

I've personally seen great businesses fail because they borrowed too much money up front to fund expensive investments in offices and equipment. You might think that getting as much money as possible right at the beginning is a good thing, but it just burdens you with unnecessary debt service, which can put you out of business fast if you don't generate the sales revenues to pay it.

You should resist every temptation possible to sign expensive leases on warehouse and office space at start-up. Forget about fancy office furniture until you can pay cash for it. Some founding Googlers are still working on the same sawhorse desks they started out with! Work out of your basement or garage for as long as possible. If it's good enough for Bill Gates, it's good enough for you.

The most successful businesses are lean and mean. Everybody I know who saddled themselves with expensive buildings that looked good at one time regretted it in the long run.

Funding Your Business Start-up with Credit Cards

Our credit rating was so good that we received daily invitations by phone and by mail to open credit cards with $25,000 limits and no interest. Of course, we had always thrown away the dozens of offers we received each month. We didn't have many credit cards and had no credit card debt, so they wanted us. When I made a neat pile of the preapproved offers, I soon discovered that we had up to $100,000 worth of credit/cash available to us for little or no interest and no annual fees. Money with 0 percent interest is free money. We filled out every application for each card we got and took all those beautiful shiny pieces of plastic and filed them away neatly in a locked metal filing cabinet drawer for a rainy day. We didn't see it coming then, but there was a massive storm rumbling on the distant horizon in the form of a first cash crisis, which I only discovered much later is an inevitable event for every business.

THE COST OF MONEY: HOW TO RAISE CAPITAL AND HOW MUCH DOES IT COST?

Credit Cards: Look for cards that offer introductory rates of little or no interest for a period of time. This is as close to free money as it gets.

Small Business Association (SBA) Loans: These loans are negotiated by the lender and borrower, but subject to SBA maximums tied to prime, which is the interest rate banks charge their most steady, credit-worthy customers. The rate will depend on how good your credit score is. Anywhere from prime plus 2.25 percent to prime plus 4.75 percent is typical.

Conventional Financing: This is dependent on your credit rating and your debt-to-income ratio. Shop around.

Home Equity Loans: Taking out a line of credit on your home equity may be the easiest way to raise capital after credit cards. Rates are very competitive. You can be approved for an amount you borrow against only when you need it.

Venture Capital: Typically, venture capitalists get a percentage of the capital they raise for you, anywhere from 5 percent to 10 percent, depending on what you negotiate and how much you are raising. This is a onetime, front-end cost, and you don't have to pay it unless they get the money. The investors then usually take an equity position in the company, which usually means that they are stockholders.

Angel Investment: Angels will almost always trade stock or shareholder stakes in your company in exchange for capital or cash that they bring to fund its growth. Sometimes investors will guarantee a loan to your company with an annual interest rate of 7 or 8 percent. This is negotiable, and they don't always expect to be paid the interest.

The Cost of Money

I remember the first time I heard this expression, thinking how funny it sounded. It costs more money to borrow money than it's worth? You bet it does! You have to figure the cost of borrowing money right into your net profit or bottom line when figuring the cost of your product or service. For instance, if it costs 8 percent interest to borrow the money to make a product that costs you $10, that's $.80 in "cost of money" costs alone. This is quite a chunk of money that will need to be factored in when trying to come up with what to charge for your product or service.

First Cash Crisis: Not a Question of If but When

An acute shortage of cash is "business as usual" for most companies on a daily basis. If lesson number one in starting your own business is "Cash is King," then lesson number two surely has to be that your first cash crisis is inevitable and crisis, believe it or not, is something you will eventually get used to.

Even the most financially solvent businesses I knew, which by the way are almost always "service businesses," were victims of cash crises. A service business is one that usually just sells the time of a professional rather than a product. As a result, a service business doesn't have the overhead associated with manufacturing, warehousing, and inventory. My millionaire mentors, the couple I had met years before whom I had watched trade their regular cash crises eventually for a multi-million-dollar buyout upon the sale of their company, had a great service business model. They hired high-priced professionals with experience in older mainframe computers, high-level complex computers sometimes the size of a room used by corporations to run their whole system, and leased them out to major corporations across the U.S. for a multiple of their salary. It turns out major corporations couldn't afford to keep these pricey professionals on the salary books for the occasional demands of mainframe maintenance. They also couldn't afford to divest themselves of the millions they had invested in their mainframe systems. A dwindling generation of mainframe professionals, who were there at the dawn of computers in the business world, were billing out at a premium, flying their private planes from their remote ranches and estates to distant airports where they would work for a few weeks or months. They only needed a couple of these jobs a year to prosper.

My mentors only needed to go out and sell their services and secure a contract to have a working business. They would recruit and hire the contract labor to do the job once they had a contract. They had to develop valuable relationships over years, cultivating respect and trust with human resource "gatekeepers," but they only had the monthly operating expenses of a modest home office, insurance, and their own salaries. Still, there were numerous occasions in their nine-year history that caused them to take out emergency second and third mortgages on their modest personal residence just to make payroll, before they made their millions and had multiple homes.

THE DIFFERENT TYPES OF BUSINESSES

Service Businesses: Businesses for which little or no capital is required to set up; examples include staffing services, event/wedding planner, computer trainer, accountant. Pluses include low risk, little overhead, little capital investment; negatives include lower cash-outs at sale.

Product Businesses: Businesses for which significant capital is required to produce, manufacture, market, and distribute a product in a national retail marketplace. Pluses include the building of a valuable national brand, the forging of channels of distribution, the development of critical intellectual property, high likelihood of significantly greater financial reward on cash-out at sale. Negatives include high overhead, risk of overproduction, capital outlay to build and fund infrastructure.

Franchises: Businesses that are traditionally established in the marketplace, for example, Starbucks and Curves, which sell you the right to sell or distribute their goods or services in a particular area. Pluses include reduced risk, proven market, and corporate sales and training support. Negatives include lower cash-outs at sale. Start your own franchise concept for maximum reward.

Direct Sales: Businesses for which you sell direct to the consumer, like Avon, Tupperware, Alitcor, formerly Amway. Pluses include low overhead and little risk; negative is that financial return may be limited.

What Is a Franchise?

A franchise is a business in which the owner of a product or service (franchisor) gains distribution of that product or service through independent operators, or franchisees. The franchisor, in exchange for a fee, grants a license to market and sell its brand, while offering help in organization, merchandising, and management, frequently in an exclusive territory. In exchange, the franchisees agree to uphold certain quality standards and practices critical to the integrity of the product and brand.

Buying or Selling a Franchise
Use these popular Web sites to research and educate yourself on franchising:

www.franchise.org: This is the official Web site of the International Franchise Association. Visit this Web site for the best free resources and information available on the business of franchising.

www.aafd.org: The American Association of Franchisees & Dealers is a national nonprofit trade association dedicated to defining and promoting quality franchising practices.

www.franchisee.org: Here free information is provided by the American Franchisee Association for everything you need to know about successfully operating a franchise.

www.business.gov: Visit the federal government's business home page and type in "franchise" in the search bar for important resources.

www.franchise.com and www.franchisedirect.com: At these sites you can search available franchise opportunities.

If Not Now, When?

My husband's search for a new job was going nowhere fast. The clock was ticking on our unemployment benefits. My prospects, after having been a stay-at-home mommy for five years, for finding a job that paid a salary that could sustain our standard of living were nonexistent.

THE NEXT WOMEN'S REVOLUTION, OR WHY GOD INVENTED THE INTERNET, FAX MACHINES, AND E-MAIL

Why the corporate world penalizes the mommy with a fast track to career dead end is something I won't go into here. Don't get mad—get even! Join the next women's revolution! Start your own business and talk business on the phone with your toddler screaming in the background without apologizing; wipe cute baby noses and butts while working out of your home office; schedule in PTA meetings and school parties without guilt and apology. Help free all of humanity—including men—from the outdated and family-unfriendly culture of the archaic nine-to-five corporate world.

I'll never forget the exact moment I decided fear wasn't enough to keep me from living. I was at a final interview for a marketing position. It was my last chance for a decent job that could carry us, and things were looking good. I just had one more test to take. In the middle of test taking, people started running all over the place. I looked up just in time to see the second plane fly into the World Trade Center live on TV. I freaked out, like everyone in America, and blew the test and the interview. I drove home screaming at myself and crying—crying for the lost opportunity to support my kids, crying for the tragedy I had witnessed, crying because I didn't know what to do next.

After the shock subsided, I decided America really needed a Wuvit and fear wasn't enough to keep me from selling it to them. I asked myself, *If not now, when?* I realized that life is short and to look back with regrets was not an option. I accepted my destiny as an entrepreneur and got to work, pushing doubt and fear aside.

When people tell me now that they're scared when starting their business, I respond by saying, "Heck, the most critical element of my success was finding the courage to get up every morning for the first year and just do what had to be done!"

The most critical element of my start-up success was finding the courage to get up every morning for the first year and just do what had to be done.

The Business Plan—A Non-negotiable Must-Have

You must have a business plan! A good plan is instrumental to any business's success, yet I am still surprised to discover that most businesses start up without one. Without a business plan, how are you ever going to have the unique and unparalleled experience of having a millionaire angel investor tear up your business plan and throw it in your face? That actually happened to me!

Don't just write a business plan for your banker or your investors. Do yourself a favor and write a business plan for you. Writing up a business plan may seem like an onerous task, but working on a plan will reveal questions that will help you find your focus and direction. Many people come to me and ask questions that they could easily answer themselves if they had only written a business plan.

Fortunately, writing a business plan is easier than you would think. This may seem dauting at first, but it's really just a simple matter of answering a series of questions on a form, or business plan template. You can get these templates for free from a variety of sources off the Internet. A business plan is essentially a blueprint for operating your business on a daily basis. Don't rush this. It can take several weeks to complete. Many of the questions asked will require you to do some homework. But don't worry. These templates will help you anticipate every detail of running a business that you never would have thought of without their help. Even if you've never seen a business plan before, you will produce a polished product by just following these formats.

WHERE TO DOWNLOAD FREE BUSINESS PLAN TEMPLATES

- **SCORE:** Service Corps of Retired Executives (www.score.org/ template_gallery.html)
- **SBA:** Small Business Administration (www.sba.gov/starting_business/ planning/writingplan.html)
- **WBDC:** Women's Business Development Center (www.wbdc.org/tools/ develop/develop.asp)

What Is a Business Plan and Why Do You Need It?

You need a business plan first and foremost for personal planning purposes. You may also choose to write a plan for participation in a business plan competition. These are events held by universities and corporations where entrepereneurs come together throughout the year to present their plans to a panel of experts, as well as an audience. The experts will choose a winning plan based on its business model viability and may award cash prizes to help entrepreneurs fund their ideas. All conventional financing requires a business plan. Suppliers of alternative financing, including venture capitalists and angel investors (see chapter 14), won't even talk to you unless your business plan is absolutely polished.

Where to Get Free Help Writing Your Business Plan

These agencies exist to give you information and to connect you with valuable free resources. One of the best excuses you have to visit them right away is to get free assistance writing your business plan. I missed this step, because I wasn't aware that it existed, and my business suffered for it in the long run. There is just no substitute for getting good advice early in the process.

Service Corps of Retired Executives (SCORE): Visit www.score.org for more information or make an appointment with a SCORE volunteer counselor to review all of your documents for free by calling 1-800-634-0245.

Small Business Development Center (SBDC): What's a Small Business Development Center? It's a free program administered by the Small Business Administration (www.sba.gov), available in all fifty states and usually based at a major university. It is your one-stop resource for all the management assistance and resources you could possibly need, staffed by *real-life* experienced private-sector business professionals. Visit www.sba.gov/sbdc to find your local office.

Your Local College or University: You can frequently enlist the help of a business graduate student to assist you in exchange for college credit, from writing or perfecting your business plan to doing market research. Contact your local college or university's school of business.

If You Have a Great Idea and Great Credentials, Your Business Plan Could Be a Cash Machine

I have seen individual business plans that were written by graduate student entrepreneurs with no business experience raise up to a million dollars in start-up capital. These aren't your ordinary business plans. They are the absolute best of the best. To prepare yourself fully for this opportunity, attend any of the many business plan competitions conducted across the U.S. each year by major universities and corporate institutions. What you will learn is invaluable.

Visit your counselor at your local SBDC to find out where these business plan competitions are held in your area. They may also help you write your plan to prepare for the competition or find a graduate business student to help you in exchange for college credit.

The Executive Summary: Most Important Part of Any Business Plan

This is the first and most important part of any business plan. The irony is that you can't write your Executive Summary until you've completed all the other detailed and exhaustive sections. The E.S. is exactly that: an executive summary condensing in what should be a maximum page and a half all the lengthy work you did that follows. It is conventional wisdom that almost nobody reads anything *but* the E.S. I saw this firsthand when my banker skimmed it, then turned immediately to the second most important part of the business plan, the financials. (Keep reading to learn what is essential about your financials.) When I told her I felt cheated that she ignored everything in between, she assured me that *nobody* reads it. Nobody at a bank will read it, but expect other serious investors to scour it from top to bottom.

It was my personal experience that the only person who read my business plan from front to back was the person responsible for doing due diligence on my company for the purpose of selling a portion of it to a group of angel investors years later. (What's due diligence? Check out chapter 17.) But I didn't necessarily do things right. The moral is your business plan can be as simple or as complex as you choose; the only non-negotiable caveat is *have one*!

Everything I Need to Know I Got for Free on the Internet

Well, almost everything. The fact is, the Internet is a wonderful thing. Never before has doing business been so easy and so cheap, and it's largely attributable to your easy access to free information on the Web that you formerly had to pay an attorney or some other professional big dollars to get. Sure, pay an attorney for advice, because that's important, but you can still do much of the legwork in advance, if not most of the paperwork, saving yourself thousands!

A wannabe daddy entrepreneur recently cornered me for advice. His business associate had created and printed many documents off the Web and he was concerned that these were just "papers printed off the Internet."

FREE BUSINESS TEMPLATES AVAILABLE FOR DOWNLOAD THROUGH SCORE (WWW.SCORE.ORG/TEMPLATE_GALLERY.HTML)

- Business Plan for a Start-up Business
- Business Plan for an Established Business
- Balance Sheet (Projected)
- Bank Loan Request for Small Business
- Breakeven Analysis
- Cash Flow Statement (12 Months)
- Competitive Analysis
- Financial History & Ratios
- Loan Amortization Schedule
- Nondisclosure Agreement
- Opening Day Balance Sheet
- Personal Financial Statement
- Projected Balance Sheet
- Profit and Loss Projection (12 Months)
- Profit and Loss Projection (3 Years)
- Sales Forecast (12 Months)
- Start-up Expenses

There is nothing wrong with that! The list of documents on page 46 is critical to starting a business. Just follow the links to the templates available at www.score.org and fill in the blanks. Then, make an appointment with a SCORE volunteer counselor to review all of your documents for *free* by calling 1-800-634-0245.

Don't Freak Out

The message here is don't get overwhelmed. Nobody's going to expect you to master all these documents right at the beginning. This is a gradual process that your SBDC counselor will be happy to assist you with. If you got a great idea, nothing will keep the marketplace from discovering it with a little enthusiasm and work from you. It would be great if you had a Master of Business Administration (MBA) degree and knew exactly what all of these documents listed earlier were. You've been too busy being a mommy the last five to ten years, plus you've probably lost a lot of brain cells with all those extra hormones and sleep deprivation. Ironically, being awake most of the time has made you smarter. You don't have time to waste! You're the definition of a multi-tasker! And your work—mommy, incorporated—is more important than anything anyone is doing on Wall Street right now. Someday you'll be rich and will be able to hire this work out. Until then, believe in yourself and your product or service, and take it to the marketplace with all the passion you can muster. The truth is, just about anyone can be taught how to create a twelve-month Cash Flow Statement in Excel. What are really valuable are ideas—visionary ideas and passion. Ask any seasoned investor what the single most important factor in their decision to invest in a company is, and they will almost always tell you that it comes down to the person who's running it, a person who has vision and passion. That's something you just can't teach.

Becoming a millionaire means learning to value passion and vision, where others only value degrees and job titles.

I wrote my business plan and learned to answer all the questions that that pesky template kept asking me. I hadn't known all the free resources that were available to me at that time, so my plan wasn't perfect. I didn't have any business counselor review it; I didn't have the benefit of a graduate business student perfecting its form and content; I didn't have any business experience at all. The usual business terms and spreadsheets were a mystery to me. Still, the plan I prepared was good enough to get a loan through the Small Business Administration, after working with my local banker. You'll find more details in chapter 7.

Do As I Say, Not As I Do

My millionaire mentors urged me for years to go to the local office of the SBDC, and I ignored them because I didn't understand how valuable a resource this was and I didn't think I had the time to go. What a mistake! Enough can't be said about the quantity and quality of the free expert advice and resources I got when I finally, in desperation and near bankruptcy, caved in and made an appointment. My business counselor there is probably the most critical element of my business's success. He not only connected me with the angel investors who eventually funded my company, but he also introduced me to the banker who financed the whole enchilada! *Did I mention it was free?*

Do yourself a favor and don't ignore good advice. Get as much help as possible at start-up, because it will save you a lot of time, money and heartache later down the line. Once you have a top-notch business plan, you can move on to the next critical step with ease and confidence—getting money!

What Is a Good Banker and How Do You Find One?

Go to the local businesses in your town and ask them who their banker is and if they like them. You will discover that everyone who owns a business has an opinion on this—they either love or hate their banker. You'll soon hear the name of the banker who earns the most love come up repeatedly.

Now that you know that banker's name:

1. Go to their bank branch and open an account.
2. Make sure you stop and introduce yourself. Sit down at the banker's desk and tell that you have the greatest idea for the next big thing. No matter how distant your dream is on the horizon, everybody loves a good story and an underdog, and they'll surely love you. Try to establish a good professional relationship with this banker—you're going to need it.
3. When you start to bring in revenues, never use the drive-through to make deposits. Always physically walk into the bank and let your banker see you making deposits. Glad-hand and lick their boots as much as possible while times are good, because they can decide to help you when times are bad based on your personal relationship with them alone.
4. Resist any temptation or advice you may get to go to another city that might be bigger, with more banking resources. Banking locally is probably one of the most important things you can do at start-up. This is a relationship business.

It Takes Money to Make Money

Once I wrote the business plan, I began to determine a path forward that was nicely summed up in my business plan like a detailed shopping list. I had goals to execute every day. My business plan became my friend, like having a personal coach encouraging me daily to succeed, to do what had to be done. I soon became focused on the "to-do" list rather than the fear.

It was time to get serious and ante up the cash: $20,000, to be exact. My husband and I had $20,000 in cash we were willing to invest in the business. We could have used the credit cards we had put away for a rainy day, but at that time we were still of the mind that all debt was a bad thing, especially credit card debt. These cards remained safely stashed away, awaiting that impending rainy day.

I decided to take my product to market, and the best way to do that is to attend a trade show. Since I live just hours outside Chicago, I decided my first trade show would be there, at the famous Chicago Merchandise Mart, (www.merchandisemart.com), where there were different markets on a weekly basis—including the Chicago Gift and Home Market—selling everything from high-end office furniture to Beanie Babies. I didn't know it then, but the Mart, as it is called, is the biggest commercial building in the world, twenty-five stories high and two blocks long, filled with ultraluxe showrooms displaying some of the most exclusive home furnishing and design elements in the world.

Attending a trade show can cost thousands of dollars at the very least. Before I blew $2,000 of my $20,000 budget, I had to do my homework. It was October, and I noticed after visiting the Mart's Web site that they not only had an upcoming gift show in January, but they also offered some free "How to Exhibit" seminars. I signed up for a seminar, drove to Chicago for the day, and found myself walking through the hallways of the massive, intimidating building, filled with home furnishings I could only have dreamed about before, wondering just who could afford them besides maybe Celine Dion and Oprah. Obviously there were rich people in the world, and none of them were telling me how to become one. I was on my own.

Actually, I wasn't. I got up to the seminar room and found at least twenty other first-time entrepreneurs—most of whom were mothers—just as nervous and scared as I! We sat through an informative session on how to get the most from every precious dollar you invested in a trade-show "booth" at the Mart. This was a venue where you sold your product wholesale, direct to retailers who were looking for interesting new products for their stores, and there was a lot to be learned about this other side of retail. When we went out to the hallway during breaks, we guardedly hinted to each other what our big idea was. Everyone was nervous and possessive of their concept, a trait I later learned is common to those just starting out. Eventually you learn that having a great idea is one thing, making it happen is another thing. I took a walk through the Mart, through a cash-and-carry trade show event that happened to be going on in its cavernous resources, taking in with amazement the absolutely beautiful, ingenious, and cheap ways people had come up with to display their product in their ten-foot-by-ten-foot booths. I was inspired!

$18,000 and Counting

I'd done my homework. Investing $2,000 for the trade show was definitely a good idea. I didn't have much information to go on, but I was forecasting that I could sell up to 2,000 Wuvits in the remaining months of 2001 and into January of 2002. Though I had sewn hundreds of Wuvits myself on my rickety sewing machine, I knew I couldn't go on that way. I had to find a sewing contractor to start to sew all the Wuvits I hoped to possibly sell at this trade show. I was already selling a ton of product off the back of my truck for fifteen dollars each; I knew a retailer could get at least twenty dollars for each Wuvit.

ThomasNet 101

How would I go about finding an industrial sewing contractor? I had no clue. My husband made me aware of an industrial resource I had never heard about: the Thomas Register, or ThomasNet.

. . . .

THOMASNET (WWW.THOMASNET.COM)

ThomasNet is the most comprehensive resource for industrial information, products, and services on the Web. Use it to source manufacturers and suppliers in the U.S. and worldwide through Thomas Global Register, listing 700,000 suppliers in twenty-eight different countries. And it's free! Well, mostly.

. . . .

How to Use the Thomas Register

The concept is simple. You type in the product, service, or even brand name of any commodity you want to source in the search bar and press enter. Voilà! You have instant results. You can narrow your search by typing in the state you want results in. Once you have those results, you can click on the links they provide directly to the company's own Web site. A couple of clicks here and there, and you have effectively weeded out the companies that aren't a good match. You have produced a list complete with contact info to start your phone calling. You can search for products, including brand names, materials, and even contract services.

Sourcing 101

I thought it was a little pretentious at the time to call this exercise sourcing, but that's exactly what it was. Sourcing can be a full-time job and is definitely one of your most important tasks at start-up.

Sourcing can be defined as a process of searching for and qualifying potential vendors of services or supplies essential to the operation of your business, then negotiating with them to create a successful and profitable working relationship.

• •

WHAT IS A VENDOR?

A vendor can be anyone who provides a service or supply critical to the operation of your business, from the person who manufactures your product in China to your local office supply store where you buy your envelopes.

• •

This is where you really have to go to work on price. Everything is negotiable. Part of your job is to sell yourself. If you're still an unknown, then you have to sell your prospects. Negotiating is always about leverage. You can't expect to get a good price on anything if the supplier doesn't perceive any benefit from doing business with you. Though some people underestimate the task of sourcing, there isn't a better way to invest your precious time than in finding the right vendors, because your success is also theirs. The most effective sourcing involves making your vendors invest in your long-term success by impressing them with your vision and passion.

Sourcing: The Word and the Deed

I produced a list of possible sewing contractors located within an hour of my home I found on ThomasNet and proceeded to call them all, weeding them out until I came up with a short list of two. On a phone call one of them seemed to be exactly what I was looking for: They not only would sew my product; they would package it and warehouse and ship it, too, if I needed those services. Talk about one-stop shopping! I set up an appointment to visit.

Time for the Nondisclosure Agreement

As inexperienced as I was, even I knew I had to protect myself if I was going to start telling everybody about my plans to launch the next million-dollar idea. I knew my husband had had to sign Nondisclosure Agreements in his jobs, prohibiting him from revealing sensitive technical information to potential competitors. If it worked for him, surely it would work for me. If I knew then what I know now, I would have gone online to download a boilerplate NDA from one of the many legal resource Web sites that exist. An NDA is a legally enforceable contract that prevents anyone who signs it from disclosing or even discussing your idea with other parties and thus grants you certain protections in the marketplace while you go out and float your concept, look for a manufacturer, or even to attempt to sell your concept outright to a big company.

I wasn't about to walk into the place of business of a potential vendor, who already had in place the means to manufacture my product and effectively deliver it in large numbers across the U.S., without an NDA in hand. Not when I had the next big thing under my hat.

I was in the market for an attorney who could help me with all the paperwork involved with setting up my business, so I made an appointment for an initial no-charge consultation with one who specialized in business issues. Be certain to select an attorney who specializes in your particular area of concern. Don't just take the first attorney you meet. Having a bad attorney can cost you more in the long run than paying the fees for a good attorney. When it comes to lawyers, it's true that you get what you pay for; that's why I had some of the most expensive attorneys in my area—even when I was broke. You just need to know how to use their time wisely. Don't pay them for anything but advice; the paperwork you can almost always do yourself. They will usually charge you their hourly rate in fifteen-minute increments for every phone call you make—something I didn't know at first—so be prudent when it comes to calling them. In addition, incidental costs will be billed to you, like the costs for copies and postage.

At this point in my business, I have no fewer than three different attorneys at three different firms:

- My patent attorney, who specializes in just patents
- My general business attorney, who handles all kinds of general paperwork including the management of my corporation papers, et cetera

- My IP attorney, who does nothing but manage and protect my trademarks, copyrights, and domain registrations

But at the beginning I was really too broke and too cheap to pay an attorney for something I could easily do myself.

TIPS ON FINDING THE RIGHT ATTORNEY FOR YOUR NEEDS

- Find an attorney in a practice that specializes in your particular need, whether it is an IP firm to help you with your patent or a business-oriented practice that can help you draft a term sheet, which is a nonbinding agreement setting forth the basic terms under which investors would purchase part of your company.
- Ask business associates whom they have successfully used in the past. Don't assume because certain lawyers helped them with tax issues they can help you with your IP concerns.
- Don't ever consult with a family practice attorney for any of your business needs, even if he is your brother-in-law.
- Don't count on a lawyer referral service to do anything but give you the name of an attorney who is paying them for the referral. You can find many of these services on the Web, which appear to offer a free service to help you find a good attorney in your needed specialty. In reality, most of these do not qualify the attorneys listed in any way.
- Call your local SBDC office; they no doubt have names of attorneys with whom their clients have successfully worked in the past.

Using a Nondisclosure Agreement, or NDA

An NDA is a legally enforceable contract that prevents individuals from disclosing confidential trade secret information you may present to them regarding the product or service you are developing. The main purpose of an NDA is to keep people with whom you discuss your ideas from ripping them off by making the products themselves. An NDA will outline specifically what the nature of the information disclosed is, for example, a software product or concierge franchise, and will outline a specific time period for confidentiality. Hire an attorney to draft a general NDA for you, or visit www.nolo.com for some affordable templates. You don't need to reinvent the wheel every time. Keep a copy on your computer and just change the name and date as needed. You shouldn't pay an attorney more than a couple of hundred of dollars at the most to draft an NDA. It is always best, but not necessary, to hire an attorney to do this. Make sure you ask everyone, from potential manufacturers to sales agents, to sign an NDA before you show them anything, every time, without exception. Scrupulously keep all copies of these on file. A dentist friend of mine gave a lot of proprietary information to someone he assumed was a business partner without an NDA. The other party took the information he received over weeks and used it to develop his own product, without any remuneration to my friend, who thought he was part owner of a start-up he was helping to form. By the time he went to an attorney, too late. If you're in a meeting and one of the participants advises you that you're under a verbal NDA and you agree, that's the same as signing a document. You still have a legal obligation to confidentiality and noncompetition. Even if you're just exchanging information and not showing products or prototypes, you still need an NDA. Sometimes information is your most important asset. If someone uses your information, ideas, or prototype to develop a similar concept of their own, you can use the NDA in court to sue for damages.

Red Flags Everywhere

I met with an attorney who had been referred to me by our financial planner and let him use the hour of his free consultation to sell himself to me. I asked as many probing and pointed questions as possible about a Nondisclosure/Noncompete Agreement, and he answered all of them in great detail. I was just about to sign on the dotted line when I asked him the single most important question you can ask an attorney: "What do you spend most of your billable hours doing?" When he told me that it was doing bill collection on open invoices for the other attorneys in his office, a big red flag went up. I didn't want an attorney who did the grunt work for the busy attorneys in his office. I went home and decided to use all the information he had given me for free and, with a little more Web surfing, found plenty of good Web sites that offered free or cheap templates for very good NDAs for less than $20. This particular attorney billed out at $165 an hour! And he would have charged me a minimum of an hour to draft a contract.

Nolo.com: The Only Legal Web-Based Resource You Need

There are a lot of sites on the Web offering legal resources, but for my money, the only one you need for now is Nolo.com (www.nolo.com). In my experience, it is the best single location for almost all the issues that concern a start-up business, from registering your own corporation to writing and filing your own patent. Most of the information is free, and if not, the technical legal templates and software you can purchase or download with the click of a button are bargains.

I used all the free information I could get from my Web research and put it together with the documents my husband had previously signed for his

---

ONE-STOP LEGAL SHOPPING: WWW.NOLO.COM

Everything you need to know at one site.

- Patent
- Trademark
- Copyright
- Corporation
- Wills

---

jobs, along with all the information the attorney I consulted with had volunteered, and drafted a strong NDA, then drove off with it in hand to my first vendor sourcing meeting, nervous that they were going to steal my million-dollar idea.

"Don't Get Too Excited; We See Dozens of People like You Every Day Who Don't Go Anywhere"

I met with the manufacturing company's team—the owner, the office manager, and the production supervisor—in their employee lunchroom, in a hundred-year-old four-story warehouse in which the dominant language spoken was Spanish. I sat with my invention tucked away secretly in a bag, knowing that I had to take it out and show them every single detail of manufacturing but dreading it at the same time.

"Would you mind signing this Nondisclosure Agreement?" I asked, springing it upon them without any forewarning. Good thing to do, because they immediately agreed to sign it without much more than a cursory consideration. I was relieved to have gotten that out of the way! I later found out that no matter how uncomfortable you are with this, it is standard operating procedure for most vendors, and they're used to signing NDAs.

Somewhat comforted by the small protections this agreement offered but still terrified that I was about to give away a million dollars to people who were going to take my idea and beat me to the marketplace with it, I opened my bag and presented to them—the Wuvit!

The office manager looked at me in response with a bored look on her face, and said, "Don't get too excited; we see dozens of people like you every day who don't go anywhere."

That wasn't what I was expecting from someone who wanted my potential millions of dollars' worth of business. A lesser person would have been crushed by this pronouncement, but I had two little boys and a husband to feed, plus I had $20,000 of cold, hard cash committed to this product. I wasn't going to give up because a cynical office manager thought I was crazy. She was only the first of uncountable many who told me I was going nowhere fast. The irony is, that same office manager later became not only my product's biggest enthusiast but also my sales manager.

Rejection Number 1: NEXT!

Not satisfied with just one put-down, I decided I had to stay true to my crazy vision of a Wuvit in every home, so I moved on to Rejection Number 2: my patent attorney.

The manufacturer with whom I had met with ironically agreed to manufacture my 2,000 Wuvits at a price we had worked out that day at the employee lunchroom table. I had no idea at that time whether it was a good price. I was yet to discover all the costs of doing business, but I had very little overhead. The company could make them, and I could store and ship them out of my garage. I had a computer. What other expense was there besides the upcoming trade show? Plenty!

I knew my NDA would only get me so far with vendors; it offered me no protection in the general marketplace. For that I needed a patent. I was getting ready to take my product to a major trade show in one of the biggest U.S. cities, where thousands of people would see it. There was no better time to start working on my patent than now!

After my experience with my first lawyer I decided to do some homework and get a prominent attorney for my patent work. I called and clicked around and found the biggest, the best, the most prestigious, and most likely the most expensive patent attorneys within a hundred miles of me. I made a phone call and was transferred against all odds to one of the firm's senior partners, no doubt because I could sell my opportunity to even a telephone receptionist at a law firm. I went to my first "no charge" consultation with him just days later. I could see the incredulity in his eyes when I pulled out my humble little Wuvit and told him I wanted to patent it.

Ten Thousand Dollars, Please

This was a prominent lawyer. He wasn't going to tell me to get lost, that he'd seen dozens of people like me come and go already, that I was throwing good money after bad, only to fail. He billed out at $285 an hour, and if I wanted to pay him that, that was my business. He proceeded to do me one of the biggest favors anybody's ever done for me in business. He advised me to write my own patent, allowing me to save a lot of money that would have to be spent up front before I knew whether my product would be a hit in the marketplace. I unfortunately know too many people who got bogged down in this process right at the beginning. Don't let this happen to you. Always consult an attorney, no matter what. If you can afford having them write your patent, that is always the safest bet. But if you can't, save yourself as much money as possible by working with your attorney to do as much of the thankless, time-consuming legwork as possible, and let your attorney worry about the really important parts of the patent.

Patent 101

You can answer all these questions in detail at the USPTO Web site (www .uspto.gov). Click on the Patents tab, then the About Patents navigation link.

What is a patent? A patent grants an owner a twenty-year property right to an invention. There are three types of patents: design, utility, and plant.

What are the key elements of a patentable idea? Not everything can be patented, and of those items that can, they must show useful, nonobvious, and novel features distinguishing them from things that have gone before. Do your homework; then consult with an attorney.

What does it cost? A patent written and filed exclusively by an attorney can cost you anywhere from $10,000 to $40,000. With a little effort, you can save yourself money, sometimes a lot of it, by doing some of the legwork yourself.

How can you save money? Consult with an attorney and ask how you can work with them to save money. One way is to draft your own patent, using one of the many downloadable templates available on the Internet.

When do you need an attorney, and when can you get by without one? You always need to consult with an attorney. The easiest and most cost-effective way to file a patent is with a Provisional Patent Application, or PPA. This allows you to claim patent-pending status for up to one year while you test the waters to see if your idea has got legs.

What is a patent really worth? In the real world, a patent isn't worth anything if you don't have the money necessary to protect it in court through litigation. My philosophy is to take your product to market patent-pending as hard and fast as possible, so you can generate the revenues necessary to defend the patent.

What does patent-pending mean? This is a means of notifying the public that you have applied for a patent on the item you are selling, thus giving any competitors fair warning that you are entitled to compensation as well as damages if they should reproduce a product similar to yours and your patent is granted.

How long does it take to get a patent? This depends a lot on the complexity of the invention. It can take months to draft a Nonprovisional Patent Application, and then it goes to the USPTO, where it is assigned an examining attorney. Depending on that particular attorney's caseload, it could take months more for them to examine it and comment, which usually means your attorney has to respond again. Once this process is complete, the application has to be submitted for public comment and dispute, which takes a year at best. Better file a PPA right away.

THE THREE TYPES OF PATENTS

- **Utility:** Applies to new and original inventions related to a process, machine, article of manufacture, or compositions of matters, like genetic material.
- **Design:** Applies to a new, original, and ornamental design for an article of manufacture.
- **Plant:** Applies to any distinct and new variety of plant.

Search on Your Own

It doesn't make sense to go to all the time, trouble, and money of filing a patent application if somebody already has a patent for the same product. You need to do a search of existing patents to make sure that there is no "Prior Art" in existence in a prior patent that would predate your patent application. "Prior Art" refers to subject matter or technology that was previously published in connection with an existing patent. If you find existing Prior Art that is critical to your invention in the USPTO database of patents for other inventions, you may not be able to patent yours. You can search patents at the USPTO Web site, www.uspto.gov. Log on to the Patents link, then choose Search. It can take a little patience getting around through the search process. Start broad, then eliminate everything that is not related. Each patent that comes up in your search will be assigned a number; make a note of all the patent numbers that you find that are similar to your idea so that your attorney can reference them. You can save hundreds of dollars doing your own patent search. If you need the attorney, they will gladly take all the information you found and apply it to the search, saving you money. Don't be disappointed if you find something very similar to your product. I did and my heart sunk, but my attorney told me "no worries," for those impossible-to-understand attorney reasons.

HOW TO SEARCH PATENTS

Learn how to search existing patents by logging on to the USPTO Web page and clicking on the Help link under the Search Patents tab (www.uspto.gov/patft/help/help.htm).

I would strongly advise you to pay an attorney to search for Prior Art or existing patents, which may or may not limit your very ability to apply for a patent. This should be discussed at your initial consultation with your attorney.

Register Your Business Name or File a DBA (Doing Business As)

Before you invest a lot of money printing letterhead and business cards, you need to make sure your company name isn't already being used by someone else by checking with the appropriate state and/or local agency, like the county clerk. In the case of corporations, limited partnerships, and limited liability corporations, you may have to contact your state's division of corporations.

Maybe you already have a business and you want to start a new venture that operates as a subsidiary of your current business. Then you'll need to file a DBA.

DBA

- Short for "Doing Business As"
- A registration of your business, usually at the county level
- Ensures that nobody else is currently using the same name
- Allows your company to use more than one name if desired

See About Licensing and Permits

Some businesses and services require licenses and permits. Check with your county clerk, city clerk, and state licensing board to make sure you have completed all necessary licensing.

See If You Need an EIN

An Employer Identification Number (EIN), also known as a Federal Tax ID Number, is a number the IRS assigns to most business entities. You need to get an EIN if your business has employees or operates as a corporation or partnership. An EIN is kind of like a Social Security number for your business. To apply for an EIN, go to www.irs.gov, search forms, and look for Form SS-4.

EIN

- Short for "Employer Identification Number"
- Nine-digit number assigned to businesses by the IRS
- Like a Social Security Number for your business
- Sometimes called your Federal Tax ID Number
- Use Form SS-4 to apply for one
- Go to www.irs.gov and search forms or call IRS at 1-800-829-4933

Get a State Tax ID

A state tax ID number is just like an EIN: a number assigned by the state's department of revenue to keep track of your business and its taxes. In my experience, the state tax ID number is the same as the federal EIN. Most states have two such numbers, one for state income tax and one for state sales tax, frequently called a Reseller Certificate.

Write Your Own Patent

You can go to many resources on the Web and actually download templates for writing your own patent for as little as fifty dollars, much like the template you downloaded for writing your own business plan. You don't need to have a "published" patent to be afforded protection in the marketplace. All you need is the designation of "patent-pending" to warn everyone that you will have the opportunity to sue them for damages if they should try to rip you off—enough of a big stick to scare off most of the ripper-offers.

The problem with patents is they're time-consuming. The review process by the USPTO can take six months, and then there is a period of a year after formal acceptance of your application for it officially to "publish," which means that anyone who might have an existing or similar claim can file opposition to your patent being granted.

The solution is the provisional patent. The provisional patent was created by Congress as a way to grant inventors temporary protection of their ideas, while buying them time to file a regular patent application. Basically, it allows you to claim "patent-pending" status for your product for a year, for only an eighty-dollar filing fee. If you're not comfortable with a NDA with a potential manufacturer or if that manufacturer is unwilling to sign it before you show them your invention, make sure you file a PPA. It's relatively easy and quick. All you need is a detailed description of your invention, an informal drawing of it, and a one-page cover sheet.

WHAT IS THE PROVISIONAL PATENT APPLICATION (PPA)?

A PPA is a shortcut to twelve months of patent-pending status, involving a fraction of the work normally required of a nonprovisional patent. It protects inventors by serving as a formal record of filing date while they continue to pursue product development, manufacturing, or marketing.

WHAT MAKES UP A PPA?

- Cover sheet
- Detailed description of how you make your invention and how you intend to use it
- Informal drawing
- Eighty-dollar filing fee

The Nonprovisional Patent Application (NPA)

If after you file your PPA your invention looks like it is marketable, you should file an NPA. You have a year after you file your PPA to file your NPA to take advantage of the initial filing date of your PPA for patent protection. On the one hand, a PPA allows you to file for patent protection without making a formal claim or providing more specific technical information. On the other hand, an NPA must include a specification sheet, claims, and detailed drawings. A PPA will automatically become abandoned within a year if you don't file an NPA.

HOW TO FILE YOUR OWN PATENT APPLICATION ONLINE

You can use the Electronic Filing System (EFS) of the USPTO to write and file your PPA online. EFS can be used to file both utility patents and provisional applications. You cannot currently file design or plant patents online.

Log on to uspto.gov, click on File under the Patents tab, then the navigation link How to File, and follow the detailed step-by-step directions.

Beyond the Provisional Patent Application

After a year, you need to convert your PPA into a Nonprovisional Patent Application. This means adding essential elements including a summary, claims, a Patent Application Declaration, and an Information Disclosure

Statement. But don't worry, you can still do most of this work yourself, writing your own patent application.

The advantage to writing your own patent is that a lot of time and expense can be saved. Instead of educating your attorney about your product, which nobody knows better than you, you can write all the details down and let your attorney massage it. I wrote 90 percent of my own patent following the template I had downloaded. When I presented it to my attorney, he commented that it was better written than some of his junior attorneys' work. The one element of the patent that you should always, unequivocally, leave to your attorney is the "claims" section.

INVALUABLE FREE INVENTORS' RESOURCES

The United States Patent and Trademark Office, www.uspto.gov: The most important resource you will ever use, it will help you do everything from searching patents to filing your own online.

The Inventors Assistance Center through the USPTO provides patent information and services to the public. Staffed by former USPTO examining attorneys. 1-800-PTO-9199.

Patent and Trademark Depository Library Association, www.ptdla.org.

Invention Dimension at Massachusetts Institute of Technology, web.mit .edu/invent/invent-main.html, features a free downloadable Inventor's Handbook with step-by-step instructions on how to protect and commercialize your idea.

The United Inventors Association, www.uiausa.org: This excellent Web site helps you find the services you need as well as information on how to avoid getting ripped off by scam marketing groups that prey on inventors.

The National Business Incubation Association, www.nbia.org: Information, education, advocacy, and networking resources are provided here for entrepreneurs and inventors.

- -

INVENTORS BEWARE!

Be very careful with your ideas. Don't turn them over to just any inventor Web site or TV direct-marketing company that promises to make you a lot of money. Many of these can be unscrupulous, preying on your inexperience with fraudulent and costly offers to evaluate and patent your invention. Do everything you can to protect yourself. To learn more about inventor fraud schemes and how to avoid becoming a victim, visit the Federal Trade Commission's fact page on invention promotion firms at www.ftc.gov/bcp/conline/pubs/services/invent.htm.

- -

PATENT CLAIMS: THE MOST CRITICAL COMPONENT
OF ANY PATENT APPLICATION

Critical element of any patent detailing the unique, novel, and nonobvious features and benefits of your invention not already used in the marketplace, demonstrating why it deserves patent protection. Definitely not a "do-it-yourself" job. Leave this to your attorney. The whole success of your patent relies on the careful crafting of this language, which only a patent attorney understands.

How to Get Your Product Manufactured

Can you believe filing for a patent was the easy part? Manufacturing, selling, and distributing the product is where the real work is. Now that you have successfully searched and filed that patent application, you need to find someone to manufacture it.

METHODS OF MANUFACTURING, SALES, AND DISTRIBUTION

1. Manufacture and sell your product yourself.
2. License your idea to a company that already manufactures, sells, and distributes.
3. Sell your rights to your invention outright through an Assignment.
4. Pay someone else to manufacture your product while you focus on sales and marketing.

Manufacture and Sell Your Product Yourself

In my experience, nobody actually makes their own product at start-up. Who could afford it? The idea of starting a company, then investing in all the capital required to manufacture that product, including machinery, warehousing, forklifts, expensive employees, computers, desks, coffeemakers, paper clips, before you even know if it's going to sell, is not reasonable.

License Your Idea to a Company That Already Manufactures, Sells, and Distributes

If you're an inventor who is willing to make a small profit from your idea— anywhere from 2 percent to 10 percent of net or gross, depending on what you negotiate—then you should seriously consider licensing. The downside is, 2 percent to 10 percent of net or gross is not a lot of money. You're going to need a lot of products if you're going to become a millionaire. You'd better do a lot of homework on the person or company to which you license your rights; getting stuck with an ineffective manufacturing and sales partner means no money. In that case, 2 to 10 percent of nothing is still nothing.

· ·

CAUTION REQUIRED

Be very careful at this stage. There are many scam artists making a lot of money on overwhelmed and intimidated inventors and entrepreneurs, offering them what looks like a shortcut to a million dollars, while actually paying little or no profits by hiding their own profits in the "cost of doing business." In fact, they're counting on you being overwhelmed and intimidated so that they can offer you too-good-to-be-true scenarios of how they're going to make your life easy while they make you rich. Generally, signing any kind of deal in which your royalty is figured on a percentage of their net profits and not gross profits should really be passed through the "B.S. Detection Machine" I will outline in chapter 8. At the very least, hire an attorney to do a smell test on this deal before you sign anything. Or better yet, make an appointment with your business counselor at the SBDC.

· ·

Sell Your Rights to Your Invention Outright Through an Assignment

When it comes to an outright sale of all your rights in the form of an assignment, some of the same advice applies. The good thing is that you get a lump sum payment up front that is not contingent on any future revenues. You also are spared all the worries that go along with nursing your product along to sales momentum in the marketplace. Before you do this, consult with an attorney who specializes in licensing. If you go this route, you're really an inventor and not an entrepreneur and you're probably not reading this book anyway.

Pay Someone Else to Manufacture Your Product While You Focus on Sales and Marketing

I know the conventional wisdom is that you open a factory and start making widgets the day you file your PPA, but that just isn't the way things work— especially nowadays! I know this idea dies hard. I kept dreaming for the first years of the day I would have my own building, with my own sewing machines, and my own office where my kids would do their homework while I planned holiday parties for all of those expensive employees I was going to hire, who worked at those expensive machines I bought. Now with a little experience and a lot of perspective, I break out in a cold sweat just thinking about the health-care costs of those imaginary employees on a monthly basis.

The truth is, for better or worse, not a lot of people are paying anybody to make anything in America anymore. Go to your average trade show and look at the thousands upon thousands of products exhibited, ask enough questions of those exhibiting them, and you'll soon realize that most of the products are being manufactured by subcontractors hired by the company selling the products, either domestically or internationally. More and more of that manufacturing is being done internationally every day, particularly in China and the Pacific Rim nations.

When to Start Looking for a Manufacturer

Looking for a manufacturer for your product should be one of the first things you do. You need to determine the marketability of your product right at the beginning, and the only way you can do that is to find out how much it is going to cost to make. You might have a great idea, but if you can't find anyone to make it at a price the consumer is willing to pay, or that you can make money at while selling it, you're setting yourself up to fail. I had already tested the marketability of my product by making it myself and successfully selling it. I knew what the consumer was willing to pay and knew what price I had to get my product manufactured at to make a reasonable profit. Before you even attend your first trade show to sell your product, you should have done all the homework necessary to make sure you can adequately manufacture and deliver your product at the price you're going to sell it for.

How Do You Find an International Manufacturer?

The best way to find someone to manufacture your product outside the U.S. is to attend a trade show in your industry featuring international sourcing resources. Manufacturers from all over the world set up booths for no other reason than to meet prospective customers like you. Almost all of the shows that offer international sourcing are in either New York or Las Vegas. At the shows, make sure to stop and talk to everyone and collect their business cards. If you don't find someone already making a product like the one you want to make, ask them if they can refer you to another manufacturer they might know. Also, make sure to call up the organizers of any trade show you want to attend in your industry and ask them if they have any international sourcing resources for you. The show organizers have a wealth of information.

Alibaba.com

I've seen a lot of books out there that refer to Alibaba.com as a good source for finding offshore manufacturing. Alibaba.com is a network of Chinese manufacturers who use this portal to connect with American businesses looking to source products and manufacturing overseas. I've never personally found it to be effective at sourcing any manufacturing or products.

Basically, it is a Web site that claims to connect you to over 100,000 Chinese manufacturers and suppliers in every product line known to man. You are asked to first register, then contact the vendors by e-mail. In my experience, none of the vendors I've contacted by e-mail have ever responded. Instead, I now receive a constant stream of e-mails from Chinese manufacturers selling things I am not interested in like marine valves, quartz tubes, and auto parts.

I think it is a grave mistake for anyone to assume that such an undertaking as sourcing products and services from a country halfway around the world, with such a formidable language and cultural barrier, would be as easy as that. Maybe it is for some people. But all I'm saying is that it would be a mistake to assume so.

. . . .

HOW TO FIND INTERNATIONAL SOURCING TRADE SHOWS

Log on to www.globalsources.com and click on their trade-show link to get a listing of all the various shows offered around the world.

. . . .

Another way to find someone to help you is to find a sourcing agent. This is not always easy. Some of the bigger international manufacturers employ Americans to be their contact in the States. This is effective because the American representatives make sure you understand how the process works and keep you going in the right direction on time. Freelance sourcing agents can help you make the connection in their particular industry, and sometimes handle the customs, duty, and brokerage of the shipment. Try conducting an Internet search, listing your product with "Sourcing Agent," and see what you can find. This is how I eventually found the person who put me in contact with the company in Hong Kong that brought Cabbage Patch Kids into the country for Mattel.

Working with sourcing agents will be more expensive than working with the manufacturer directly, but it is probably worth it to make sure you do it right.

HOW TO FIND AN INTERNATIONAL MANUFACTURER

- Visit globalsources.com and search trade shows.
- Attend a trade show with international sourcing resources.
- Call trade-show management and ask them if they have any sourcing references.
- Search for "Sourcing Agent" with your product or industry type on the Internet.
- Visit your local office of the SBDC and ask for references.
- Visit your local office of the U.S. Commerce Department and ask them for references.
- Call up U.S. manufacturers in your field who don't represent direct competition and ask them. This assumes you have some talent for schmooze.
- Ask everybody you know and meet. It's amazing what a small world this is!

U.S. Department of Commerce—Invaluable Free Resource

Before you do anything with an international manufacturer, you need to visit your local U.S. Commerce Department office. What you learn here will be invaluable in pursuing any international sourcing and manufacturing you are going to do. Don't assume manufacturing in another country, working with people who don't even speak your own language, is going to be easy. You're going to earn every dollar you save. Just dealing with customs and duties alone can make you break out in a sweat. My local Commerce Department is located at a university near me, along with the branch of the SBDC, my other dependable resource. What happened to me on my first visit scared me out of the idea of manufacturing abroad for at least a good year. The message to take away from this story is "Be Careful!"

At my first appointment with the Commerce Department, I met the office director, who had been to China with a contingent of local U.S. businessmen interested in finding manufacturing resources there. (This was a couple of years ago, so things may have changed.) Upon their arrival in provincial China, they met with the local governor of that area, who showed them into a conference room. They spoke for about ten minutes with significant difficulty, because of the language problem. After ten minutes the governor got up and brought four factory owners into the room, assigning one to each of the Americans by pointing his finger. The American businesspeople had no choice. They had to work with the factory owners they were assigned by the Chinese governor. The American contingent assumed that he was getting a payoff for making sure these factories got the business.

The short story is that only two of the U.S. businessmen received products that looked good upon visual inspection, while the other two received goods that were not of good enough quality to be sold. In one case the pen that came in a notepad gift set didn't work. They ended up with a whole container of product that wasn't sellable. As if to underscore his story, the Commerce Department official took a book the size of two New York City phone books from his shelf and dropped it on the table in front of me with a bang. The book was filled with all the various tariff codes. I think he felt it was his job to keep all manufacturing in the U.S. by using fear.

- -

FREE RESOURCE: U.S. DEPARTMENT OF COMMERCE, WWW.COMMERCE.GOV

Purpose: "to foster, promote, and develop the foreign and domestic commerce" of the United States. Visit a local office to discuss all logistics involved in manufacturing and importing or exporting before you send your first Purchase Order across the ocean, including customs and duty costs. You can find an office in most big cities, staffed with professionals who give you not only book knowledge on the business of importing and exporting but also real-world experience and insight into how this complicated process works. The message is BEWARE, in big capital letters. The major roadblocks to smooth trade continue to be quantity, quality, reliable delivery, and culture.

- -

Custom Brokers—What You Need to Know

If you continue to persist despite the horror stories people will inevitably share with you—usually the result of them not doing due diligence or overseeing the manufacturing or inspection process closely enough—and find someone to make your product abroad, it is essential to hire a customs broker to make sure your product gets delivered on time. These people will handle the customs, duty, and brokerage of any shipment but most of the time won't handle the actual shipping logistics, which are your responsiblity. You arrange for the container to be shipped, usually through Maersk when you're just starting out (www.maersk.com); customs brokers take care of all the formidable paperwork that provides the proper documentation for the U.S. government when your container hits U.S. soil for a fee. The general rule of thumb is to add anywhere from 10 to 20 percent onto your manufacturing cost as "factor costs," which include all incidental costs of customs, duty, freight, brokerage, boxes, labeling, warehousing, and miscellaneous shipping expenses. Twenty percent is considered extremely high, but that's how my husband likes to work, anticipating worst-case-scenario costs.

As you can see, you really need to start at the U.S. Commerce Department. Some TV pundits might bash any company that manufacturers internationally, driving American jobs to other countries, but the reality is that the world is becoming one big global economy faster and faster every day. In business, you have to adapt or die. This can be a good thing, as long as we capitalize on the strengths that are unique to America: innovation, design, cultural exportation. We need to develop foreign markets and export our products to emergent countries around the world that are hungry for anything American. Even a small- to medium-sized business can do this because of today's technology.

A lot of manufacturing is moving from China to South and Central America and developing Pacific Rim countries like Cambodia. Even some of my business associates in heavy manufacturing tell me that Eastern Europe is now where the real growth is. The world is becoming full of niche manufacturers: For cut-and-sew on roller print fabric, it's China; for custom weaves of synthetic and natural fabrics with cut-and-sew, it's Colombia—and that's just my industry. My brother works with steel, designing and manufacturing overhead crane systems for everybody from Boeing to Kimberly-Clark. He won't touch Chinese steel. According to him, it can't begin to approximate the quality of American steel. His explanation is that twenty or thirty years ago, when China was building its steel manufacturing infrastructure, the emphasis was on the quantity of factories and not the quality. They have more than a billion people needing employment. As a result, they built many small foundries and no big ones, which means that they can't generate the heat necessary to forge top-quality steel. This isn't going to change any time soon.

Stay focused on developing your American market, using American manufacturing if you can for its quality and reliability. As you grow, look at these international challenges as an exciting opportunity to grow and learn. It's a time of great possibility, and you can be part of it!

WHY YOU SHOULD MANUFACTURE YOUR PRODUCT IN THE USA

1. **Quality:** Quality you can depend on, quality you can take to the bank.
2. **Short turnaround time:** Almost no start-up company can afford to carry hundreds of thousands of dollars on the books for up to 180 days through the manufacturing, shipping, and collection process of working overseas.

MANUFACTURING 101: CHINA OR THE U.S.—IT'S NOT AS BLACK-AND-WHITE AS YOU THINK IT IS!

Before you try to find a manufacturer in China, stop, take a deep breath, and consider a few facts:

- Unless you are simply reselling a product that is already manufactured in large quantities in China, you're going to have a tough time getting anyone interested in making anything but full container loads of anything for you. How much is a container load? A container is roughly twenty feet long and ten feet wide and ten feet high.
- Manufacturing a whole container load of product for something you're just starting to market is going to cost you a good deal of money! That's something most start-up businesses do not have.
- Best-case scenario, it takes ninety days from the moment you send a Purchase Order and pay half the total cost of a production run of a full container of product until that product leaves for the United States, when you'll be expected to pay the other half of the cost of a production run of a full container worth of product—double gulp!
- For ninety days you're out, let's say, $50,000, and you haven't even collected your first payment from any vendor to whom you've made a sale. If you have been lucky enough to sell the entire container, you have to wait another thirty to ninety days to be paid by your customers.
- There exists the distinct possibility that you have been delivered an entire container full of product that you can't sell because it was made so poorly, because you don't have the connections, expertise, and leverage necessary to ensure your product gets made correctly in the first place.
- And at least a million other things can and will go wrong.

With U.S. manufacturers, you can actually manufacture and ship product, which you may not have to pay for for sixty days, while customers pay within thirty days. Also, you can develop, prototype, and deliver products in half the time those manufacturing abroad can, which gives you competitive advantages in the marketplace.

3. **Reduced risk:** You probably just put every dime you had into this business. Why would you want to expose yourself to more unnecessary risk, which could put you out of business during this time of baby steps faster than I could change a diaper.

4. **Costs:** You won't have to pay duties of up to 20 percent or expensive freight costs or brokerage fees.

Carry Your Product with You Wherever You Go

The reason you want to carry your product everywhere is to learn. The world is one big testing ground filled with knowledgeable, astute consumers who will give you terrific free information about how to make your product better every day. Listen to them and don't resist it. Don't be disappointed when they tell you you're crazy.

For every one person who told me I was crazy, ten people told me I was going to be a millionaire after trying my product. And all the "you're crazy" people came at me at this delicate, scary, risky time of start-up, where most people would have given up.

The End of a Very Long Week

It was indeed a tough week, being told that I "wasn't going anywhere" by my new contract sewer and seeing the incredulity in the eyes of my new patent attorney as I showed him my "invention." It wasn't just a coincidence that, as I was leaving my attorney's office, the same receptionist I had spoken to on the phone to schedule my appointment stopped me and asked to see this Wuvit I had told her about. Ten minutes later I was walking back to my truck, having sold her six Wuvits on the spot that I had in my convenient little wicker basket, with a whole new sense of renewed confidence and intuition that I was really on to something.

3

THE BUSINESS ENTITY

Making It Legal

I had been in business unofficially for a couple of weeks and had managed to dodge some big expenses by consulting with attorneys but committing to doing all the grunt work myself, from creating an NDA to drafting my own patent. I still wasn't a business officially with either the state or the U.S. government until I filled out some mandatory forms that seemed overwhelming at first but, once I moved down the checklist provided by my state, were taken care of quickly and painlessly. You can find your particular state's requirements for starting a business either by contacting the local SBDC or by calling or logging on to your state's official governmental Web site and searching the Department of Revenue, Treasury, or Taxation. Almost all of them have Small Business Resource links. You're going to find there are hundreds of free useful forms, templates, downloadable books, and checklists of what to do to register your business there officially.

There is no central agency where all businesses must register. Depending on the legal structure you choose, you may be required to register with the county clerk's office as well as the state and federal governments. Since every state, city, township, and county is different, it is mandatory that you call all government offices—including city, township, county, state, and federal—to ensure you've completed all the necessary forms and registrations to their satisfaction.

- -

FREE RESOURCE: SMALL BUSINESS RESOURCE GUIDE

The guide, created by the IRS and the SBA, can be ordered free from the IRS by calling 1-800-829-3676. It provides critical info for small businesses, including forms, instructions, and publications.

- -

Registering a Business

This chapter covers just a few of the steps that you're going to need to take to register your business. They're going to come at you fast and furious. Don't freak out. It's time to get down to the paper-pushing part, registering, licensing, insuring, and Dun & Bradstreetizing.

Determine Your Business's Legal Structure

This is just not smart to do by yourself, without an attorney's expert advice. Basically the four choices available to you are:

• Sole Proprietorship
• Partnership
• Corporation
• Limited Liability Corporation, LLC

Each structure offers its own particular benefits and protections. You need to discuss all of them with an experienced business attorney who specializes in just this. They will help you determine which structure is best by evaluating the risks and liabilities of your business, the paperwork and expense involved in managing it, your income tax needs, and your investment needs.

Don't worry if you start out as one entity and change to another one just weeks later. I started out as a sole proprietorship, filing the papers online myself, but after a visit with my next attorney was convinced by him of the tax-sheltering and product liability benefits of an "S" corporation. An "S" corporation is one that is granted special tax status by the IRS. The corporation itself pays no income tax; rather, the income is passed through the corporation to the individual shareholders, usually resulting in earnings being taxed at a lower rate than "C" corporations. In "C" corporations, earnings are taxed first on the corporate level, then again as income when they pass through to the shareholders. There are very complex laws governing corporation law; consult an attorney.

Attorney Number 3!

I was only in business for a few weeks, and I was already looking for my third attorney! I asked my millionaire mentors whom they had used, and they sent me to a lawyer specializing in taxation and corporate structure, who helped them sell their business for millions of dollars.

I'll never forget this meeting. I had an appointment at his office, an hour's drive from my home, and my babysitter called at the last minute to tell me she couldn't come. *Crisis,* I thought, *important meeting, child care falls through. How many millions of times does this happen to mothers every day? What do I do?!* My husband was out of town, and I had no family living within two hundred miles of me, and it was too short notice to call any friends.

My four-year-old, Dylan, was in afternoon preschool, and my two-year-old, Ryan, was still at home with me full-time. With an hour drive there and an hour drive back, I had an exact window of an hour to meet with the lawyer between dropping my older son off at school and picking him up—a schedule that didn't allow the slightest bit of flexibility. If I were even just a few minutes late, he'd be all alone sitting in the principal's office by the time I got there, four years old and crying. I was already stressed out, and I hadn't even gotten on the road!

I had to take Ryan with me. Ryan is a special kid. He can at one minute be the most challenging, at the next, the most precious kid God put on earth. In a nutshell, Ryan is a riddle, wrapped in an enigma, wrapped in a conundrum. At this point, everybody was using the word "autistic" to describe him. I was just beginning an incredible odyssey of doctors and specialists, bringing me to tears of stress, exasperation, gratitude, and love on a daily basis. Starting my business while caring for Ryan presented another layer of challenge and difficulty that no man I knew had to consider when plopping down at his desk every day. I had a husband with no job, a kid everyone told me was autistic, *and* I was starting a business based on a product people were not only laughing at but outright telling me was going to fail. Don't tell me you're too afraid to do this!

I dropped Dylan off at school and started my hour drive to my appointment, Ryan drifting off to peaceful sleep in his car seat in the back. I didn't know what I was going to do with him once I got there. I pulled into the parking lot, very secure and quiet, hidden in a grove of peaceful trees in a very upscale neighborhood, and turned around to look at the angelic face of a sleeping two-year-old and agonize over waking him up.

I'm not proud of what I did next, but it changed my life and my attitude forever. I was still apologizing everywhere I went for having kids. One just didn't bring kids to an attorney's office, all sedate with leather chairs, black shelves, and dusty books, where everyone crept around hushed corridors. Mommies and their kids were unwelcome guests in such stuffy environs, where even receptionists spoke to you crisply.

If I woke Ryan up to take him into the meeting, he would most likely shut their operation down in fifteen minutes. Ryan was inscrutable. He could walk into any strange place, instantly assess the place's vulnerabilities and locations of key computers, go to them like lightning, opening every door and drawer along the way, then proceed to paralyze the place despite my best attempts, while people stood around stunned as he crashed their computers. Believe me, I tried to rein him in. This was just Ryan—he possessed an incredible energy, restlessness, and curiosity that some people would call brains and other people would call autism.

I left him sleeping alone in the car while I went into my meeting. I told you I'm not proud of this. I waited in the waiting room for five minutes till my attorney was ready to meet with me, checking Ryan's sleeping silhouette in the car every minute. I went back to my attorney's office in the farthest, deepest reaches of the cavernous offices and could hardly hear the words he said over the voice in my head screaming at me that Ryan was sleeping, no, he was waking, no, someone was stealing him, no, he was choking!

Boss Mom

What the hell was wrong with me? I finished my meeting quickly, bowing out in just over a half hour instead of the hour I had scheduled, asking myself that question. I was paying this guy $200 an hour! He should be apologizing for not having a first-class toddler play area in not only his lobby but also his office! What was wrong with this world, after all, when you had to apologize for having kids? Or pretend you didn't have them? Or be ashamed of being a lowly mommy while simultaneously paying these rich attorneys' salaries?

I went out into the parking lot to find Ryan awake and screaming, all red faced and teary. That was it. I resolved from that moment on that I would never apologize for having kids, never refrain from bringing them to meetings with people to whom I was paying exorbitant amounts of money, never shush them from speaking when I was on the phone—because I was the boss! Boss Mom! I for once was the one in charge. I had nobody to answer to or apologize for. If there wasn't room for my kids in this new journey I was embarking upon, where I was the president of a company that I founded and funded, I wasn't going.

I'm Mad As Hell, and I'm Not Going to Take It Anymore!

I cleaned my precious angel up, changed a diaper, and fed him his lunch in his car seat, kissing him all over as I sat in the backseat with him, promising to never leave him alone again. I looked around the parking lot at all the sleek black BMW sedans that belonged to the attorneys inside. I realized that it was people like me—sitting in my aging but paid-for Mercury Mountaineer—who had paid for those cars. I was mad as hell and I wasn't going to take it anymore. I was no longer going to be corralled and beaten down by the impossible, silly, and outdated prejudices against moms and their kids in the workplace.

MOMMY MILLIONAIRE: THE RULES

1. **Don't apologize for having kids!** Children are special angels from heaven whom God sent you. What's wrong with this world when you have to apologize for having children beside you as you work? You're Superwoman. You can manage kids, find your husband's car keys, and close million-dollar deals at the same time. Be proud of yourself!

2. **Remember that when you are conducting business over the phone with other mommy entrepreneurs, it is proper and allowable to out-yell your kids, while I out-yell mine!** Just like Murphy's law, Mommy's Law says that the minute you get on the phone while at home with young children they will immediately retaliate by demanding your full attention with capricious and unnecessary demands screamed in the most whiny, abrasive voices they can muster. Ignore this! This is a tactic on their part to make you feel guilty. You sat in a La-Z-Boy watching endless reruns of *Teletubbies* for ten hours of nursing for three months—you deserve the right to a lousy phone call! Don't run and hide in the garage with the cordless, or make crazy gestures to silence them. Stand your ground and scream over them! I can't believe how this simple ground rule transformed my life.

3. **Don't freak out over what your kids do while you are on the phone yelling over them.** As long as your house is childproofed, they probably aren't in any peril of dying while you ignore them for fifteen minutes. The worst that can happen is your two-year-old will empty your fireplace of all the ashes onto your off-white rug, or you'll find them sitting behind your $5,000 "do not touch" sofa in your "do not enter" living room, on your "do not walk on with shoes" ecru carpet sharing a half-gallon of melted chocolate ice cream. It's happened to me! Sternly reprimand them while trying not to burst into tears as you take pictures, reminding yourself that someday this will be really funny.

4. **Never forget that if you're going to be a Mommy Millionaire, you must accept the fact that you will have to burn down your house and build another one after ten years.** This is especially true if you are the parent of young boys. The first thing that is going to go in your unbelievably busy schedule is housework. Just try to keep your kids from bringing live wild animals, running hoses, and five screaming friends into the house to build tents with every sheet off every bed as they write secret Indian codes they make up in permanent marker on your walls. Don't scoff—all this has happened to me at one time while I was on the phone doing business!

5. **When your child care unexpectedly falls through at the last minute, take your toddlers to your attorney's office for that important meeting without guilt and apology.** You're paying your attorney $200 an hour. They should

change their diapers, too, for that! Don't feel the need to be the perfect mom—throw the Hot Wheels you brought on their floor and do not be distracted as your kids make loud car-crashing and wheel-squealing sounds. Your attorney is on your time, and you're Boss Mom!

6. **Accept the fact that SEX SELLS.** God gave you enlarged mammary glands in exchange for your popping out multiple children in quick succession. Having bigger breasts is definitely an upside to being a mom. Push them up high like Erin Brockovich and prepare to do battle. You will have instant mastery over any man as you stand apart from all the drab dark suits that surround him in the sexless business environment. You will immediately get a businessman's attention, and he will grant you any request, including a trip to the Bahamas—which you could probably take if wasn't for those pesky kids of yours—while he stands helplessly mesmerized by your all-powerful feminine assets.

7. **Keep in mind that children are in reality evil geniuses.** Even the smallest toddler understands the power of guilt and can use it effectively to render you instantly under their control and gain material possessions galore. They possess a prescient ability to know when you are under the most pressure to complete the largest assignment on the tightest deadline and will assert their dominance over you by bugging you with the most maddening and redundant requests until you will do anything for an hour of uninterrupted work time, including rushing out and buying them that new Nintendo GameCube game that very minute.

8. **Don't feel guilty for rushing out to buy your kid that new Nintendo GameCube game if it gives you one day of guiltless uninterrupted work time.** You only get to use this rule sparingly—once a year per child. After all, your first job is to raise good kids.

9. **Know that in the business world the conventional wisdom is that you are considered a non-entity as a mommy.** Use this rule right out of the classic Zen *Art of War* to your advantage as you stalk your enemies under the detection of their radar until you surprise them with your brilliance. Understand that their underestimation of you is a critical power that drives you on to greater successes.

10. **Remember we're all equal in the eyes of God and our kids' teachers.** Just because you're the president of your own company doesn't mean God or your child's teacher is going cut you any slack when it comes to being a good person or a good parent. If you're not doing these jobs well, it doesn't matter what kind of money you're bringing into the home. No amount of money can replace waking up to a bright and happy child who is excited to go to school, so stay focused on what's important.

. . . .

From then on, there was no going back. I came up with a list of Mommy Millionaire Rules to keep me and all the other women entrepreneurs out there sane
as we chased down our own million-dollar empires.

Structuring a Business

This business lawyer had radically changed my perspective on what type of
business entity I should become for tax and product liability purposes. You
can pick up books and download forms that tell you how to do the actual
paperwork to incorporate in your state for little or no money. These books
never adequately explained whether to incorporate and which form of corporation to file. Once I had been advised by my attorney about the best
structure for my business, it was easy enough to go online to the Michigan
Corporation Division, download the correct forms, fill them out with the
help of a state employee over the phone, and submit them, with the knowledge and "blessing" of my attorney.

Find Insurance—A Whole 'Nother Opportunity for Rejection

*It's not a question of if you'll get sued; it's a question of when you'll get
sued.*

—My attorney

If you make any product used by consumers, you can just about count on
being sued in this litigious society. Run, don't walk, to find good product liability insurance. There are innumerable types of insurance that your company may need, from Worker's Compensation to Errors and Omissions.
The only way to find out the scope of what you need is to find a good insurance agent. Use the same strategy outlined earlier for finding a good banker.
I didn't at first, and I went to a big agency that was referred to me by a crony
friend of one of the insurance agents. Mistake! I made an appointment that
week, this time taking my kids without any apology. No play area again. I
was expecting it at least in an insurance agent's office.

Having a Play Area for Mommies' Kids Will Go a Long Way Toward World Peace

Mommies live in a whole different universe than other people. One minute
of time spent trying to keep a two-year-old under control in a business of-

fice's waiting room without a play area is equal to an hour at a nine-to-five desk job. We're busy! We got jammies to wash, noses to wipe, chocolate ice cream to clean off our carpets, and car keys to find for our husbands! Making me wait unnecessarily for twenty minutes while you stand around the watercooler gabbing away—I can hear you—is only going to make me cranky. And everybody knows, if mommy's not happy, nobody's happy!

When I finally was ushered into his office I could tell I was again an unwelcome guest. It was apparent that this agent thought the evidence of me being stupid was my two children. He couldn't have been more patronizing if he said to me, "Now you go home and bring your husband back and we'll talk to you about this prod-uct li-a-bil-i-ty insurance." I could tell I was going nowhere fast, so I asked him to fax me a quote, which he did only after I called to follow up with his secretary twice. His quote was—gulp—$10,000 a year! I called him in disbelief and he basically told me, "Good luck; you're not going to find any better rates anywhere else."

I got out the phone book and started paging through it, looking for another insurance agent to call. I found what looked like a supersuccessful guy; he had two offices in different towns, and he sold securities as well as insurance. Here was a multi-tasker I could relate to. I called him up and made an appointment, bringing with me not only a sample Wuvit for him, but also one for his nice receptionist, with whom I had spoke on the phone.

This agent was certainly higher up on the food chain than the previous insurance agent. He was smart, wore a suit and tie to meet with me, and had won several sales and service distinctions on a state level, the evidence of which he had all over his office. And he didn't make me wait, either. He was extremely professional, but I could tell he, too, thought I was at least a little nuts, taking the complimentary Wuvit I left him with all the politeness and appreciation he could force himself to exhibit. I left there with not much hope, thinking, *Oh, well, let's see what he comes up with.*

He called me first thing the very next morning with good news and bad news.

"Wow," he said. "I can't believe this product! This is incredible! This is awesome! You really have something here!" I couldn't believe my ears. "I checked rates for liability insurance on this," he went on, "and the best I can do for you is an annual premium of ten thousand dollars."

"Ten thousand dollars!" I said, unable to control myself. *Ten thousand dollars,* I thought. *Jeez, my business is over before I begin! I can't afford that!*

"I know that's a lot," the agent was saying over the phone. "And then you'll need insurance on the warehouse and inventory your manufacturer will be making for you. Make sure you get your raw materials insured during transit. To tell you the truth," he finished into the phone, "I really don't care if you buy insurance from me or not. I'm just glad to say I was there on the ground floor when this product was introduced! It's great!"

There was no way I could afford $10,000 cash-on-the-barrelhead for insurance. My prospects for going on seemed dim, especially since I got two quotes that confirmed each other. I was crushed.

Now another person might have said, "That's it; I quit." But I had kids to feed. That's when I went to my great banker and asked her for a recommendation. It turns out she knew a former great banker, who was now selling insurance. I went to my third agent and told him I needed a good rate and I needed it now! I could tell he was a winner, because he didn't have time for water cooler chat. He had two computers going, a headset to answer his land line, and a cell phone that kept on ringing, which he very respectfully didn't answer. Here was a guy who understood the value of time—mine and his! He got his underwriter on the phone and worked hard applying all the ideas and leverage he could to find me a good rate, which turned out to be a fraction of the other two quotes.

Persistence in the face of resistance brings success. Just about any problem will go away if you work hard enough.

I learned a valuable lesson that day that I have carried with me during my entrepreneurial journey. Don't give up, and keep looking for solutions until you find one. I was proud of myself. I had averted crisis and had tackled the big issues involved in starting my business.

Dun & Bradstreet

Shortly after I applied for my EIN, I got a call from Dun & Bradstreet, a company that provides credit reports of corporations to whoever wants to buy them. In the world of business, when you're seeking to get payment terms of thirty to sixty days from vendors, or credit, those vendors will usually look you up with Dun & Bradstreet and get a credit score on your company. If it's good, you'll get good credit; if it's bad, you may get no credit and have to pay cash or by credit card for everything you purchase, which can really put a damper on your growth. Just like your personal credit score, you want to do everything possible to maintain a good D&B credit score.

How to Get and Maintain a Good Credit Score with Dun & Bradstreet

When you're first starting out as a business, you will probably have no commercial credit history to score. It's just like starting out with your first credit cards in college. It's the old catch-22: No credit is just as bad as bad credit. You need to entice vendors to extend you credit that you pay back on time, so that you can get a good commercial credit rating that will make other vendors extend you credit.

Step 1 is to provide Dun & Bradstreet with the most in-depth, accurate, and positive background on your company as possible. As soon as you register for an EIN, Dun & Bradstreet will likely call you and ask questions like:

- Who are the owners, shareholders, and board members of your corporation?
- What are their educational backgrounds?
- Who are their former employers, and do they have any significant accomplishments under their belts?

Dun & Bradstreet will then take this information and craft a short narrative that any prospective vendors can read. The more elaborating detail you can give about all the positives that you bring to the table, the more interested people will be in doing business with you and extending you credit. Don't worry if you don't have an MBA or even a college degree or if you have no board members. A lot of the most successful entrepreneurs I know are college dropouts. Just focus on those great tenets that underlie your corporate culture and sell those instead.

Maintaining Your Dun & Bradstreet Credit Report

As soon as you get listed with Dun & Bradstreet you will be assigned a number by them. Keep this handy; you will use it a lot. After that they will start calling you regularly to sell you their various credit-reporting programs. This is good, but not necessary. Just remember, they're in the business to make money through selling credit reports, including yours to you. Try not to spend your precious limited resources on services that are not necessary as you start out, and don't be alarmed by "sudden changes" they report that, when looked into in depth, may actually be good.

However, you may need to look at your credit report occasionally just to make sure everything is correct, just as you should do with your personal credit report. Dun & Bradstreet is very respectable, and they only let the best national companies provide information that would characterize your credit as good or bad. That means, when Joe Blow, who may or may not have a legitimate credit claim against you, threatens to "report you and ruin your credit rating," he can't. This actually happened to me, and I called Dun & Bradstreet just to make sure small-time operators can't file nuisance claims against you.

Scam Alert

Besides Dun & Bradstreet getting your newly filed corporation notice, scam artists get it, too. First evidence of this was a bill for $160 that was faxed to me for a listing in a yellow pages phone book somewhere I had never heard of. I called the number on the faxed bill and asked where this ad they were claiming I took out was listed and who gave them authorization to place it. The guy on the other end told me that someone at *Daisy Green* had authorized it and that if I didn't pay it he would file a complaint with Dun & Bradstreet. I instantly knew he was lying, because there is no Daisy Green. Somehow these scammers had gotten my company's name off a hotlist which transposed the two words of my company, Green Daisy. This was only the first of scams directed toward Daisy Green. When I told him no one had authorized such a bill and that I wouldn't pay it and I wasn't afraid of him "ruining my credit rating," he just gave in and said, "Okay. Most people pay it," then hung up.

What Do You Call Yourself?

When Dun & Bradstreet calls, they're going to want to know your title. This was one of the most difficult and exciting dilemmas I had when starting out: What do I call myself?

It seemed really presumptuous to call myself president or chief executive officer at the time. I called my millionaire mentors and asked them what titles they used. "President" was suggested, and I went with it. Don't shy away from giving yourself a great title right at the beginning: You're going to earn it in no time.

How to Establish Business Credit

You need to establish business credit, and the fastest way to do that is to apply for business credit cards. These are different from personal credit cards in that they are debt secured against your business assets and not your personal. When you apply for these cards, they're going to want your Federal Tax ID Number—your EIN—instead of your personal Social Security number. Make sure you make every payment on time and in full if possible. Especially at the beginning when you can still afford it. Though not my first choice, it's perfectly okay to carry a balance on your business card, because this is good debt, not bad debt.

Good Debt Versus Bad Debt

Incurring good debt for your business usually means giving up bad debt in your personal life. You have to ask yourself if you are willing to adjust to a lower standard of living for you and your family, and risk family assets in the short term for long-term reward. The key words in the preceding sentence are "short term" versus "long term." When you start making money, you'll start to realize very quickly what the value of each dollar truly is. Every day and every dollar you put into your business is an investment in building your business machine. You're trading in your weekly paycheck for a big machine that you own, that will need money to run on, one that will start to generate revenue and build value on its own. Now you earn another dollar; what do you do? Do you take that dollar and buy a revenue-consuming machine like a fancy car that depreciates a third of its value the minute you drive it off the lot, or do you put that dollar into your big revenue-generating machine where it will only grow the machine bigger and generate more revenue? Of course you know the answer. To your neighbors, who will see you working twelve-hour days, driving a car that's paid for and is over four years old while they trade their expensive leases in every two years for a new, bigger vehicle, it will appear that you are adjusting to a lower standard of living, but you'll know better. Just keep on minding your own business while they eke out their livings at nine-to-five jobs many of them hate, building colossal bad debt as you keep building more and more good debt.

Getting Credit from Your First Vendor

Though I had found a manufacturer for my product, I still had to find a supplier of fabric. I had been dragging my kids to every fabric store within fifty miles, but that had to end. They were starting to revolt, crying, "Not another fabric store, Mom!"

During my trips, I began to write down all the information from the bolts of fabric I liked, including the manufacturers and their style numbers. I went to Switchboard.com and looked up the phone numbers for all these fabric suppliers, then just called them up.

Rejection Again

I can laugh about this now, but it was not at all funny at the time. I called up a major fabric manufacturer in New York City and was transferred to a salesman named George. I told him I was interested in buying fabric wholesale.

"Sure," he responded to my inquiry, he'd sell me fabric. "What are you going to make with it?" he asked out of curiosity.

"Wuvits," I answered, about to launch into my explanation of what a Wuvit is.

"What?!" he interrupted me.

"Wuvits," I began again.

Click.

Yes, that's right. He hung up on me.

Guess people in New York don't have much of a sense of humor, I thought. But I was used to rejection at this point. I'd better have a sense of humor if I was going to sell a product named Wuvit. I called George in New York right back. I really wanted that fabric!

The minute I got George back on the phone, I laughed off his hanging up on me—"We must have been disconnected"—and launched into an explanation of what a Wuvit was. New Yorkers love people with moxie. He didn't give a damn about any Wuvit, but he obviously was impressed enough because I had the courage to call him back that he didn't hang up on me again. He was going to sell me some fabric, but I was going to have to pay with credit card the first time out and fax him a credit sheet for his factor for any thirty-day terms.

"Factor? What's a factor?" I asked him.

"A factor!" he practically shouted.

I was too embarrassed to admit then that I didn't know what a factor was, let alone ask what a credit sheet was. I asked him to please send me some fabric samples, and he told me to pick out the ones I wanted and send him a Purchase Order with my credit card number attached.

"Purchase Order," I repeated, not letting on again that I had no idea how to write a purchase order.

"This is the price," he quoted. "F.O.B. New York."

"F.O.B.?" What this meant I couldn't even guess, but I had to know, because it meant money. I could hear the exasperation in his voice on the other end when I asked him.

"Freight On Board!"

I did my research and discovered that a commercial factor is like a bank that provides businesses with lending solutions like credit and Purchase Order financing.

Factoring 101

Factoring, I've since learned, is when a company sells its account receivables to a bank or financial institution, which purchases them at a discount of anywhere from 1 to 10 percent typically. The advantage is that the company selling the account receivables gets their cash in one day instead of thirty or sixty, freeing up cash flow while taking the worry and administration out of collecting bills, while the financial institution that buys them makes interest. A lot of companies use factors, and a lot of them use the same big factors, so if your credit goes bad at one account, it will go bad at them all. The good thing is that once you get approved for a credit line, you can use that line with other vendors.

PURCHASE ORDERS

A Purchase Order is a written authorization to purchase goods or services at an agreed-upon price, which is a legally binding contract. The only recommended way to write a Purchase Order is through QuickBooks or your accounting system.

CREDIT SHEET

A standard sheet providing critical company information for the purpose of obtaining credit terms from potential suppliers. Non-negotiable information includes company name, shipping and billing addresses, legal entity such as a corporation and in what state, EIN, DUNS number, and at least three credit references from whom you get credit, including company name, address, contact person, and fax and phone numbers. Also required is your banking information with the name and telephone number of your business banker. Don't worry; nobody can check your bank credit without a written authorization from you each and every time.

Keep a copy of your credit sheet handy at all times so you can fax it at a moment's notice. You will provide potential suppliers with this information who may set you up with credit through their factor or may use it to request that their factor call you directly in order to establish credit.

F.O.B.: FREIGHT ON BOARD

Freight On Board is the point at which a customer assumes possession of goods from a supplier. It's usually used in referring to a price of goods, telling you that you will be expected to pay freight from the F.O.B. delivery point.

The Biggest Mistake I Ever Made

I had done just about everything to prepare for my big national debut in Chicago, just months away. I had only one thing left on my list, and that was to meet with a Certified Public Accountant (CPA) to whom my banker referred me, to discuss setting up my QuickBooks.

I was never so nervous meeting a professional as I was meeting this woman. I had no head for detailed numbers, so I was simultaneously in awe and scared of someone who was expert at it. She charged $180 an hour. I was absolutely tormented at our first meeting by how slowly she talked and how long it took her to make a point. She might as well have been speaking a foreign language. I looked at my watch and realized we had been sitting there for two hours and we hadn't even scheduled the QuickBooks session.

This woman single-handedly scared me away from CPAs for two years. As a consequence of meeting perhaps the worst CPA a multi-tasking mommy could have possibly met, I made the biggest mistake I ever made. I decided not to have a CPA set up my QuickBooks.

Trust me here. You need to hire a QuickBooks professional to set up your books from day one. You need to sit next to that professional and learn everything he or she does, because QuickBooks can be either your best friend or your worst enemy on a daily basis. I unfortunately chose worst enemy by default. Don't make the same mistake. You don't need to hire a CPA to set up your books. You can hire other accounting professionals who are well versed in QuickBooks and who charge a fraction of what CPAs charge. Or you can go back to your invaluable and free pal at the SBDC, who's helped you with everything else up to this point.

QuickBooks can be either your best friend or your worst enemy on a daily basis. I unfortunately chose worst enemy by default. Don't make the same mistake. Hire a professional to set up your books properly right at the beginning.

I was still running this operation out of my basement! I was so afraid of paying someone $5,000 to set up my books that I didn't even look for alternative resources. Don't make this mistake. QuickBooks is the only truly manageable accounting system there is for small business owners. There are other choices, but don't even bother. When you finally do have the money to hire the CPA, or the part-time chief financial officer, and the part-time bookkeeper, you won't find anybody who knows those other systems. QuickBooks is the gold standard that almost every accounting professional can instantly plug into. Unfortunately, setting up QuickBooks is not a do-it-yourself option, unless you have serious accounting skills. Once it's correctly set up, you can use it yourself in the daily operations of your business with adequate training—strongly recommended!

QuickBooks: The Gold Standard of Small Business Accounting

Here is what you absolutely must know about working with it:

1. Hire a professional to set up your business accounting system. This is not a do-it-yourself job.
2. If possible, and you can afford it, find a QuickBooks Pro Advisor in your area to set your books up. You can search for one at quickbooks.intuit .com. Type "ProAdvisor" into the search bar on the Intuit Web site. These people are CPAs, accountants, bookkeepers, and consultants certified in QuickBooks setup, payroll, reporting, and other day-to-day QuickBooks functions.
3. Shop around. You can find people to set up your QuickBooks at the cost of anywhere from $15 to $200 an hour. I eventually hired a bookkeeper at $15 an hour who knew more than a certified QuickBooks Advisor I hired at $50 an hour. She straightened out our QuickBooks after a CPA had made a total mess of them.
4. Take a class and learn as much about QuickBooks as you possibly can. You're going to need it!
5. Use your invaluable free resource the SBDC and see if they have tools to help you, including referrals to QuickBooks professionals, free assistance with setting up your books, or any classes on how to use them.

Mission Accomplished: NEXT!

I'd done everything I knew how to do to get the business set up, glancing down my checklist and seeing that everything had indeed been handled. I had to trust that I had done everything required to ensure that I had complied with every federal, state, county, city, and township rule. *If I didn't,* I thought to myself, *I'm sure they'll find me.*

With that done, all the deadlines for my upcoming trade-show debut in Chicago were looming. I had to design a trade-show set. I had never done anything even remotely like this before, and I was excited and terrified at the same time.

LAUNCHING, OR TRAVELING THROUGH THE VALLEY OF SHADOW

I created the business—now what? It was time to make sales. I had no sales experience and no sales training. I had just climbed one mountain—registering my trademarks, drafting my patent, setting up my business, sourcing my vendors—only to find a whole mountain range waiting for me on the other side.

Preparing for My First Trade Show

I had filled out the six-page application to exhibit at the Chicago Merchandise Mart and mailed it in with my deposit. I had received a huge volume of paperwork in the mail, including an exhibitor's manual that I pored over. I was having weekly conversations with the market rep who had sold me my space. Still, no one could help me with the problem that was the most daunting: the design of my trade-show set.

My advice to all those people who call me now about trade shows is to go walk the particular show in which you are interested before you plunk down thousands of dollars to exhibit. What you learn can make or save you thousands of dollars.

Building the Perfect Trade-Show Set
I really was glad that I had had an opportunity to see a trade show in action when I visited the Merchandise Mart several months earlier. I learned a lot about how to make the best use of my ten-foot-by-ten-foot space from studying all the exhibitors and observing how the buyers reacted firsthand to each booth.

$15,000 and Counting
I was already out $5,000 for all the previous business expenses I've described, and I hadn't made a dollar yet—not counting any of the usual sales

· ·

TRADE-SHOW FACTS 101

- You can find a trade show for every industry to sell your product or service. To find a trade show specific to your industry, go to www.tradeshowweek.com and click on the navigation link on the left called Tradeshow Directory.
- Trade shows are simply one of the most cost-effective ways to reach qualified buyers.
- Trade shows generate more leads and require less effort to close than a typical business call in person or on the phone.
- Trade shows are a great way to meet both existing and new customers, building critical personal relationships that will fuel your business's growth.
- Trade shows will also give you a great opportunity to study the market and your potential competition. Be very, very careful here. Read "Tradeshow Etiquette" later in this chapter to make sure you know the best way to protect yourself, while respecting the rights of your competitors.

· ·

off the back of my truck. I had to pay for all the materials and production costs of my run of 2,000 Wuvits, so that left me with very little to spend on a trade-show set.

I panicked. I called my market rep and begged for ideas. She did her best: "Try finding material with daisies on it [Green Daisy] and drape it as a backdrop." No. "Blow up a giant picture of corn kernels [Wuvit filling] and put your product in front of it." Good, but too expensive, I thought.

The booth space that comes standard is different in every trade-show venue you visit. Some of it is "pipe and drape," or just flimsy pipes holding up white curtains, or "hard-wall," which are walls made of wood or sometimes metal, white unless you spend a ton of money to have them painted in advance.

Booth Design: Keep It Simple

I've seen it a hundred times. People get carried away on expensive trade-show displays, which do nothing but distract from their product or service. Having a set, made up of the furniture, fabric, signs, easels, design elements, and products, that tries too hard to make a good impression on buyers is always the kiss of death. The new exhibitors who win the "Best New Booth Display" at every trade show I have attended are never seen or heard from again. They wasted too much money buying expensive props, shipping antique furniture, purchasing slick vinyl signs, or paying for expensive booth customization packages available from the show organizers. They've invested so much money in the show, there's practically no way they can get a justifiable return with sales. Buyers walk by their booths giving them the typical two- to five-second once over, wondering just what is being sold in all that overdone design.

Buyers are looking for fresh products or services that are different from everything else out there. The first time you go to a trade show, you will be amazed at the thousands, even hundreds of thousands, of things you will see for every part of your life from every country in the world. Once you've gone back to the same show twice a year for two years, you'll see a lot of what's on display is the same old stuff that's been there year after year. Buyers who walk these shows at cities all over the country for years upon years have precision radar focusing on hot and new! You have no idea of the opportunities that await you when you bring your fresh new ideas for the next big thing into this tired environment.

. . . .

BOOTH DESIGN DO'S

Here are some examples of the best booth designs I've seen that put the most attention where it belonged—on the product—for the least amount of money:

Product: Handmade leather writing journals

Presentation: Each book hung from nearly invisible fishing line, from a series of supports that spanned the ten-foot-wide booth. The books appeared to be floating in air, and everybody stopped to look in amazement.

Cost: Almost nothing

Product: Kitschy Christmas ornaments

Presentation: A tiny booth only four feet wide, stuffed with all kinds of various products from all different vendors. The ornaments, supposedly handmade, were unique—a really wacky combination of cheap plastic doll heads and crochet— an *In Style* magazine editor was snapping pictures galore and interviewing the booth owner for an article, while store window merchandisers from the biggest retailers across the country were snapping the ornaments up like hotcakes.

Cost: Nothing but the table that came with the booth and a tablecloth to throw over it

---

Product: A major national brand of 100 percent natural skin care products

Presentation: Another tiny booth filled with black wire shelves for display and a life-size cardboard cutout of the company's eccentric founder—nothing else.

The booth was so packed with buyers it was impossible to see any other design independent of the simply shelved product. This was a major national brand, so they had established customers. Still, it taught me a valuable lesson: Less is more. Maybe it's that philosophy that made them a major national brand.

Cost: A blow-up photo display of the company's founder and a vinyl banner

---

Product: A fresh, new line of greeting cards and stationery, featuring hand drawings and witty quips

Presentation: Christmas lights strung from a center point over the booth like a circus tent, and hand-painted canvas cloths covering the walls, featuring some of the adorable illustrations on the cards, which hung on strings and clothespins

Cost: Lights and canvas, strings, and clothespins

BOOTH DESIGN DON'TS

Here are some examples of the worst booth designs I've seen—not because they weren't beautiful, but because they took all the attention away from the product or because they just cost too much!

Product: I really don't know, the booth design was so weird. It was some sort of bath and body line.

Presentation: I just couldn't get past the real sod that had been laid out like a carpet in a huge wooden frame that was ten feet by fifteen feet.

Problem: Where do I start?! First, it was messy and dirt was everywhere. You had to step up over the boundary of board holding it all in, which created a psychological barrier keeping customers from entering the booth. For the brave who did, women's heels sank into the dirt, getting stuck and making it impossible to walk. And the grass was totally brown halfway into the show. I never saw them at any show again.

Product: Custom-blended luxury bath salts

Presentation: Way too much! The exhibitors shipped their entire living room, complete with antique furniture, including a huge seashell-encrusted armoire that broke, to exhibit only four very large apothecary jars of salt, in an enormous ten-foot-by-fifteen-foot space. They won Best Booth Design, though nobody knew what they were selling. I never saw them again, either.

• •

The Importance of Good Lighting

If you have to drop big bucks on a trade show, better budget enough money to light your product adequately. Every major trade show offers these services at a premium, including electricians installing floodlights that spotlight your product that you can rent for the show. Or you can always bring your own lights. Check with show management to make sure you understand what their requirements are. I still always rent my lights from the show management, though it's probably not the most economical choice.

Focus on Your Product

Sticking to the philosophy of keeping it simple, I took out my pen and paper and started brainstorming again. "Green Daisy" meant that I had to be green, fun, funky, and natural. I got in my truck and drove three hours to the nearest Ikea in Chicago, where I knew I could find fun, funky, and natural, in addition to cheap.

Schlepping 101

While everything up to this point had been academic, what followed shortly was all physical. At least having an unemployed husband meant not having to worry all the time about child care. I drove to Ikea in Chicago and wandered the cavernous self-serve aisles for four hours, looking for anything for my trade-show set. I bought two inexpensive collapsible shelving units, green stain for them, yards and yards of a forest green raw-linen fabric, and a big bunch of six-foot-tall osier sticks, very dramatic straight tree branches tied with a jute cord, that I just had to have. I stopped at a home improvement store on my ride home to buy a microwave for heating up Wuvits and two cute folding chairs.

I set up a space ten feet by ten feet in my basement and practiced setting up the stuff I bought until I had the right feel. I ordered a fake fireplace log insert from a catalog, just a lightbulb inside some birch logs, with something that made a crackling sound, and stuck it in the middle of the tepee I made

---

MISCELLANEOUS TRADE-SHOW ITEM CHECKLIST

1. Order forms
2. Brochures or catalogs
3. Business cards
4. "Toolbox" comprised of tape, scissors, glue gun, staple gun, hooks, pens, calculators, et cetera

of the six-foot-tall osier sticks. It looked like a big campfire, and people could not keep themselves from stopping to stare at it in amazement. I made a hand-lettered sign for every word of my slogan, "Get a Wuvit, America, and feel good," and framed them with a thick border of natural moss, with raffia ties glued on the back for hanging. I had all my friends come over and check it out, and they all proclaimed, "You're ready!"

The Most Scared I've Ever Been in My Life

I'll never forget this day. I was possibly the most scared I have ever been in my life. Okay, I need to qualify this. The most scared I've ever been in my life was when my first child almost died at birth. On a scale of 1–10 on scared, 10 being the scariest, my son almost dying was a 100, while this only rated your normal 10. I had loaded up my truck with my entire trade-show set and all the Wuvits I could pack in and driven off to Chicago very early in the morning to get in line with all the other trucks and vans waiting at the Mart to get their merchandise unloaded onto the show floor.

I was all alone, doing something I had never done before, in a place I had never been before. I looked at all the other vehicles and saw friends, family, work associates talking and laughing as they waited, while I sat in my truck, worrying about my kids, blaming my husband for doing this to me, and praying to God to give me the strength and courage to get through this, whatever it was. Besides not knowing anything about what to do in a situation like this, the thing that scared me most was not knowing what people would think of my incredibly simple product with the crazy name.

I was trembling as I walked onto the floor where my booth was. I didn't know quite what had to be done, but I started doing it. I just broke down all my boxes the Teamsters had brought up on big floats and began at the beginning by taking out my curtains that I had made from the green fabric I had bought for booth backdrops, reading carefully the show guidelines that limited me from using anything but "S" hooks to hang them. I did what the guidelines told me and thought the curtains looked pathetic. Obviously, a fellow exhibitor thought so, too, as he came up and handed me his staple gun, saying "Here, kid, use this."

"But I'm supposed to use these 'S' hooks. It says so in the exhibitor's manual."

"Screw the exhibitor's manual. I've been doing this for ten years, and I use a staple gun."

I stapled up my curtains and they looked much better. Exhibitor's Manual: 0, Experienced Exhibitor: 1. I set up the rest of my booth in a way that I thought looked great, using at least a million staples out of the guy's staple gun.

Trade-Show Tips

1: The Best Backdrop
Booth customization through painting is expensive and is only good for one use. If you get inexpensive fabric for drapery, not only is it much cheaper, but also you can reuse it indefinitely. Once you get all your product or people in front of it, nobody will see it anyway.

2: Be Nice to Your Fellow Exhibitors; You're Going to Need Them!
It's a good thing another exhibitor had been so generous. I felt like a stranger in a strange land and was too scared to even talk to anybody. Surely they could tell I didn't know what I was doing. This man's kindness broke the spell. I could admit it was my first time doing a trade show, and I benefited in the next four days from the valuable advice and friendly companionship of seasoned exhibitors all around me. The truth is, you're going to be sharing a lot of time with these people during a period of four to seven days, so getting off on the best foot is imperative, if for nothing else than to keep you amused and smiling. I've met many different exhibitors in many different cities across the U.S. and found that people who weren't nice didn't have good show karma, meaning they didn't write many orders and make a lot of money. This isn't scientific, but the nicer the people, the more orders I saw them writing—so be nice! I got a red Buddha at the dollar store, hid him somewhere on my trade-show set, and rubbed his belly throughout the show for luck.

After I was done setting up my small set, I wandered down the maze of aisles and hundreds of booths that surrounded me, a chaos of noise, broken-down boxes, and strewn-out packing peanuts. There seemed to be an infinite array of products piled high on teetering pallets clogging the aisles everywhere. Teams of people worked hard and fast setting up complex displays and artistic vignettes, listening to loud music, pounding Diet Coke, and laughing. I looked at my simple set with my one product, sold by one person, and felt a wave of sadness, overwhelmed by my smallness.

I arrived at my set early the next morning, ready to go for the first day of my first show. The chaos of the previous evening had transformed into booths of abundant order and stunning design. As for my booth, what it lacked in size it certainly made up for in originality. Besides my two shelves loaded with Wuvits, I had a table with the microwave on it, my tepee of osier twigs with the crackling "fire" inside, and the chairs I had bought for all those buyers to sit on while I wrote their orders. I stood there smiling, thinking it looked good. Boy, was I wrong.

3: Put Your Product Right Up Front Where Everybody Can See It!
I was there for no more than the first half hour of the first day of the show before the exhibitor across the way from me—a seasoned "master rep" who was selling a line of scrapbooking supplies and stickers—could take it no more. She introduced herself, then commanded me to change my whole setup while she stood there supervising. In five minutes, she had my product-filled shelves moved from the sides of my ten-by-ten-foot booth to right up front where the passing buyer couldn't help seeing them and wonder what a Wuvit was in the precious two to five seconds of their attention I would get as they strolled by. In ten minutes, she had me standing next to them right up front asking everyone who passed, "Do you want to try a Wuvit?"

4: Offer a Show Special
"What's your show special?" she asked me.

"What's a show special?" I answered.

Everybody had to have a show special, I learned. It was a special incentive, she explained, that you extended to buyers at shows to induce them to order. People want to feel as if they're getting a deal, and the better the deal, the more likely you are to get an order.

"What about free shipping?" I offered.

"You never offer free shipping!" she admonished me. "Shipping is almost always more costly than free product! You have to remember that free product is more valuable for a number of reasons: You give it away at cost, they get it at wholesale, and then they sell it at retail. So it's cheaper to you than wholesale, and it's worth more to them than wholesale!" I later learned to exploit this formula to the absolute best returns possible. My special was always "Buy a dozen, get one free."

"What's it cost to ship a box of Wuvits?"

"I don't know," I answered. "I've never shipped any! This is my first show!" Out of all the things I had thought of to do, researching shipping costs was one thing that had totally escaped my attention.

5: Require a Minimum Opening Order
"Well, what's your minimum opening order?" she asked.

"What's a minimum opening order?" I answered.

I could almost hear her thinking to herself, *I got my work cut out with her!* "A minimum opening order is either a minimum dollar amount or quantity, which the customer needs to order of your product," she explained. "You need minimum opening orders for a couple of reasons. Number one: to keep people from the street coming in here to just buy their Christmas presents at wholesale. Number two: to make retailers buy enough of your product to ensure a merchandising presence in their stores."

"What do you recommend?" I asked.

"You're just starting out, so I would say a dozen pieces or $100–$150 minimum. You need to make sure the retailer can make keystone on the sale of your product though, in order for them to order anything."

6: Offer a Minimum of Keystone Markup to Small Retailers

"What's a keystone?" I asked.

"Oh, honey. You've got a lot to learn!" she laughed. I was thinking right about now how happy I was that I was so nice to her when we were busy setting up the night before. "A keystone is the standard minimum markup a retailer needs to keep the lights on, or 100 percent. So if you sell your product wholesale for ten dollars, the retailer needs to sell it for twenty dollars to make a keystone. Nowadays though, a lot of retailers are coming to expect 125 percent markup. Anything is possible if they're going to buy enough of what you're selling."

I realized how much I didn't know about this business. Even though I had spent a month working tirelessly to prepare for this show, I had failed to prepare myself in critical ways I couldn't have even known about. I've come light-years in the few years that have passed since this first trade show. Offering a keystone markup is the minimum small retailers can expect to get, but big retailers work on a whole different formula. Nobody told me about this until a buyer for a major national retail chain practically screamed it at me in all caps in an e-mail. Understanding the necessary markup for each industry to which you're selling is critical not only to pricing your product correctly in the retail marketplace but also to understanding your own bottom-line costs and necessary margins.

7: Understand the Difference Between Small-Retail and Big-Retail Markup Formulas

Once you read this book and skip all the time-consuming mistakes I made, you'll be going from 0 to 70 mph in one show flat. Big retailers have to shop just like small retailers. They're always on the prowl for anything "hot and new" to drive new profits on their cutthroat competitive floors. Don't be surprised if you find yourself talking to a DMM (Divisional Merchandise

Manager) for a major retail chain of over 2,000 stores at your first trade show. Don't panic! Read this book and don't quote any prices on the floor except for your normal wholesale price list. Get her business card, offer to send her samples, and study this formula to understand the difference between margin formulas for Mom & Pop Pharmacy in Podunk, PA, and Mega–Department Store Merger in New York, NY.

. . . .

MARKUP FORMULAS FOR BIG RETAILERS VERSUS SMALL RETAILERS

Small retail: usually figures a keystone equal to 100 percent markup. Example: Ten dollars wholesale, with a suggested retail price point of twenty dollars, equals ten dollars profit or 100 percent markup.

Big retailers use the following formula: Retail price point (R), minus the cost of wholesale (W), equals X, divided by retail price point (R). $R - W = X/R$. So, for example, a twenty-dollar retail price point, minus ten dollars wholesale cost, equals ten dollars, divided by twenty dollar retail, equals a 50 percent markup! "What?! I thought you just said the same profit represented one hundred percent?" Nope, whole different animal!

Most big retailers will demand more than a 50 percent markup. The sweet spot markup for big retail is 60 percent. A lot of retailers operate on anywhere from 30 percent to 60 percent typically.

. . . .

8: Think Like a Retailer

My whole set had been remerchandised by a seasoned exhibitor. I had my Wuvits warmed up and ready for buyers to try. I had blank order forms I had bought at my local office supply store. I wasn't experienced enough at this point to have some personalized order forms printed. And I had little trifold brochures I had printed out from my computer with product information and pricing, ready to hand out to customers. All I needed was the customers.

I had no idea what I was going to say to anyone I could get to stop and look at my product. You need to get in front of customers in the beginning to see what they have to say about your product or service. Find out what the key selling features are by watching their response to what you are offering, and sell those features. These people are experts. They've seen and evaluated thousands of products and services. They're on the front line daily, interacting with consumers, monitoring trends, gathering critical sales data. Listen to them. Ask them questions. If they're not interested in your product, ask them why. Don't take it personally—it's just business. Maybe your idea is just not right for their store. Ask them about their stores. What do they sell? What makes them money? Learn to think like a retailer, which means one thing:

Show Them the Money!

The key difference between selling to an individual consumer and selling to a retailer is that the consumer is primarily interested in the product and the retailer is primarily interested in the profit. I learned very quickly on the first day of my first trade show that I needed to master a few key points in selling:

1. **Know Your Demographic:** In any kind of sales, it's a numbers game. The more types of people you can appeal to, the more likely you are to make a sale. I improvised my sales pitch and let them know that just about anybody who walked in their store would be interested in a Wuvit, whether a man or a woman, a senior or an athlete, a spa lover or a chronic pain sufferer. I even talked about the teenage boy who showed up at my doorstop in a snowstorm. Their eyes lit up, as they recognized, as I did, that this was the toughest consumer group to make a sale to. If you don't have a product or service with wide appeal, that's okay. Just focus your marketing on smaller niche trade shows that capture your customers more effectively.

2. **Know Your Key Features:** Why should a retailer want to buy your product? You have to give them the knowledge necessary to sell your product's key features to consumers by identifying and explaining them in your brief presentation and on paper.

3. **Know Your Retail Price Point:** Educate yourself on whether your product represents a good value to the consumer by checking out other products that may be similar in the marketplace. If you can convince a buyer that your product is worth more money or is a better value than another successful product in the marketplace, you're halfway to making a sale.

4. **Know How to Merchandise Your Product:** Come up with interesting ways to show retailers how to merchandise your product or how to arrange it in their stores easily and with appeal. Retailers don't have a lot of money to spend on this. Recognizing that each foot of floor space needs to generate a certain amount of revenue in the form of sales will earn you points toward a sale. I didn't know it at the time, but my exceedingly simple packaging—a raffia string tied around my simple fabric pillow—was merchandising genius.

Retail Price: What's a Product Worth?

At this time I still hadn't gotten a good grasp on the cost of doing business. I had very little overhead and so didn't even know how to anticipate future costs. It's very hard, when you're starting out, even to guess what some of the costs of doing business are, like EDI, or Electronic Data Interchange, until you get to the point when you need to use them. In my experience, as you grow bigger, the number of individual costs increase, while typically costs as a whole decrease because of quantity discounts and greater productivity. So don't even worry about them at the start. The price I had arrived at for my Wuvit was a retail one, which I casually just calculated from my costs. It seemed to work, because people were really buying them. How do you find out what a product is really worth in the marketplace after you've done all your homework on existing products that may be competitors? By test-marketing!

Determining Retail Price Point

How do you find the true value of anything? Fair market value is determined by what anybody is willing to pay for it on the open market at any time. The only way to arrive at that figure is through test marketing.

You need to arrive at a fair retail price point on your product before you even proceed to selling it. I know some people who start at their costs first, then add on their margins, when it should be the other way around. If their cost at start-up is too high and they add on their margins, they have a retail price that just is too high, ultimately dooming the success of their product. You need to do whatever it takes to find out what a fair retail price for your product is before you spend a dollar on manufacturing. I had already indirectly test-marketed my own product by first selling it directly to consumers, then having my husband take it to a local retailer and offer it on consignment.

· ·

What is gross profit? The percentage of every dollar earned that can be used to pay general and administrative expenses such as utilities, advertising, rent, et cetera. Sales minus Cost Of Goods Sold.

What is Cost Of Goods Sold (COGS)? The amount of money you spend to manufacture the products you sell. Usually figured as a percentage of a selling price. For example, if an item costs you five dollars to make and you sell it for ten dollars, you have a 50 percent COGS.

· ·

TEST MARKETING: INEXPENSIVE STRATEGIES TO DETERMINE THE MARKETABILITY OF YOUR PRODUCT

Focus Groups: This is a standard way corporate America operates, hiring expensive marketing firms to gather up consumers and pay them for their opinions in double-blind tests. You don't need to drop big bucks for the opinion of a focus group. All you need to do is invite all your friends, family, kids' teachers, kids' friends—everyone you meet—to give you their opinion. My neighbors were constantly giving me feedback on every new incarnation of a product I ever produced: I knew that each one of them—the pilot with a lot of disposable income, the working family with three teenage kids all getting ready to go to college—represented a particular market segment that spoke for thousands, if not millions. Ask them what they think of your product or service and what they would be willing to pay for it. Write down all the information you get, scrupulously breaking it down into price, willingness to buy, et cetera, then average it out between those who gave you high retail price suggestions and those who gave you low. You'll be amazed at how good a snapshot this provides of your potential market!

Mall Marketing: Just about every mall in America has dozens of kiosks or carts in the public space of the mall. Most of these kiosks are rented heavily by the fall, in time for holiday retailing. But they can be empty, without tenants, for long periods of time. Call the mall leasing manager and ask if you can lease a cart for a weekend to conduct a test marketing of your product or service. I actually did this, and it led to my first million dollars! (Read chapter 7 to find out how I did this.) Technically you can't do this without at least registering your business with the state and getting a tax ID number so that you can collect sales tax. You probably shouldn't do it without insurance, either.

I paid $350 to put my product on the cart for a full weekend, Friday through Sunday, selling it cash or check only. The sales, though significant, weren't the full story. I learned invaluable information from putting my product directly in front of the consumer, including price sensitivity, top-selling designs, consumer bias, et cetera. I kept a journal, recording the number of shoppers who stopped, what their age and sex was, whether they bought, if they thought the price was too high or too low, and what they would want to see improved if they could. Some of the ideas and suggestions given to me that weekend were critical to making my product a million-dollar product.

Test Consignment: This is a great way to find out what impartial consumers would be willing to pay for your product. Find a retailer who you think offers merchandise similar to yours. Start with a small, independent one—but even Wal-Mart will participate in local test marketing of your product. Go in and ask for the manager and discuss it with them. Never visit a retailer on a Monday. After the weekend's sales, they are busy with tons of paperwork. If you call in advance, you can sometimes find out that retailers set aside one day a week to meet with reps and vendors, often a Tuesday. Ask politely if you can stop by to show them your great new product. If you can adequately demonstrate its demographic, key features, retail price point, and merchandising, or its packaging and the way it displays on the shelf, you just might convince them to give you a test. Consignment means that they don't pay you anything unless they sell it, which means there is no risk to them. They don't want to just put anything on their floor, though, because their reputation is at stake, so you still have to work to get them to do this. Give it to them for a limited period of time, like a week; you don't want it sitting there indefinitely. Then go back in a week and see how you did. If you don't sell any or if you don't even get a test, don't worry. Just ask them why. Was it price? Was it features? Was it appearance? Merchandising? Design? Take what you learn and use it to make your product better. The drawback here is that you can't actually know firsthand what the consumer thinks, because you're not there.

Trade Shows: Trade shows are the most expensive of all these options, but you definitely get what you pay for. If you're trying to decide whether you want to ante up the minimum $20,000 necessary to launch a million-dollar venture, spending a couple grand on a trade show could save you a lot of heartache and expense.

Selling Your Product from a Prototype Alone: You can use a trade show to market a product you haven't even produced, based on just a prototype. Believe it or not, many products are actually launched this way. There is nothing wrong with going to a trade show, showing a prototype, and telling customers that it will be delivered in four months. People do it all the time. When I was at my two separate visits to QVC at their New Product Search, at least one-quarter of the exhibitors there trying to sell product were selling it from prototypes alone. One, lodged in my memory because we shared a table to present on, was an in-home airbrush tanning system. Two guys in suits had brought along an airbrush, which you can buy in any art supply store, and a cosmetic case they had picked up at Walgreens on the way there. The buyer for QVC practically bought the concept on the spot. She would have, in fact, if they answered the basic questions of demographic, key features, price, and merchandising adequately. They had spent so little time putting this concept together they couldn't answer these questions as the buyer asked them. If they had spent more time preparing, they could have become the next "Today's Special Value," with the possibility of becoming "instant millionaires." I don't know what happened to them. They should have gone home, worked out the kinks, called the buyer, and sat on QVC's step until she met them again. But I doubt they did. That's how easy it can be to make a million dollars! And that's how some people just blow it, by not doing simple homework or recognizing opportunity.

Would You Like to Try a Wuvit?

I realized that the only way I was going to sell Wuvits at the trade show was to make people try Wuvits. Approach total strangers and ask them to try a Wuvit for four days? I thought about my unemployed husband at home, having his own personal nervous breakdown, my two little boys, just turned three and five—worrying if they were eating anything besides cookies while I was gone—and my $200,000 mortgage, and just sucked it up. I wasn't naturally good at this. I had no sales background. I didn't even like talking to strangers. But sometimes a mommy has just gotta do what a mommy's gotta do.

It amazes me to this day when people tell me they could never do this. They comment on how confident I am. How much they admire me for doing these things that they could never do. I have to laugh. I am probably one of the most anxious people you will ever meet, the product of a dysfunctional family upbringing that has screwed up my self-esteem irrevocably for life. I can be squirming inside, beating myself up, second-guessing and doubting, but I have the innate ability to hide this behind a mostly impenetrable shield of composure. If you pretend long enough to be something, you actually start to become it. Maybe it's a cheap alternative to therapy. The more I pushed myself to do things that were terrifying, mortifying, physically and emotionally challenging, the stronger I became.

Since the early days, I've met a lot of rich and powerful people. A lot of the self-made millionaires were just like me. They weren't confident, flashy entrepreneurs who easily glided from their fraternity, to their country club, to their condo in Boca Raton. They were real human beings with something to prove, some need to redeem themselves, or some unstoppable drive to fix something in themselves that was broken, that money just couldn't buy. Don't ask them to tell you what it was. They're always too busy trying to forget about it, or hide it, or bury it. So don't tell me you can't do this.

Being a flawed human being is actually an asset when it comes to becoming a millionaire.

I stopped everybody I could and asked each one if they would like to try a Wuvit. To my surprise, this was easier to do than I had expected. People would stop, look at me in total bewilderment, and ask, "Would I like to try a what?!" "A Wuvit," I would answer with a smile. The genius in the name Wuvit became immediately apparent to me. These people had no idea what it was I was selling. They couldn't reference it to anything else in the marketplace. Almost invariably they said yes. Once I got a warm one on their shoulder my job was essentially over. The product sold itself. And what was not to *wuv*?

All I had to do was explain the features, benefits, and price, while they stood there like zombies, oohing and aahing in a zone all their own. This was a phenomenon that would later be called the dead raccoon effect by a jealous exhibitor. I didn't get it until she explained the analogy to me. According to her, it was like being near the dead raccoon on the side of the road. All the drivers were braking to look at the roadkill. Next thing you knew, there was a traffic jam of people all rubbernecking to see what everybody else was looking at. Soon I was talking loud enough to be heard by a crowd. The exhibitors around me just stood speechlessly watching as people, after trying my product, or stopping to gawk, or occasionally even ordering it, moved on without even one glance at their booths. *The dead raccoon effect.* When this phenomenon was named by this frustrated exhibitor, I had a lot of fun with it. I went to the plush toy vendors section and found a couple of stuffed raccoons. I borrowed them long enough at my booth to ask a couple of unsuspecting buyers wandering past in the aisle if they would like to try a Wuvit, offering them the raccoon instead. Everyone broke up.

I couldn't believe it. I was writing orders! People liked me. They really, really liked me! Before I had left for the show, I had called credit card companies and asked for an imprint machine and some credit card receipt forms, and I was imprinting their credit cards for payment.

How to Set Up Your Business with a Merchant Account to Accept Credit Cards

A merchant account is an account established through a bank or merchant business that allows you to accept and process credit cards for payment online or by phone through a processing terminal you can either lease or buy. These are more expensive than you would think. On average, $1,000 if you buy them and up to $70 a month if you lease them. Be careful of buying terminals on eBay, or anywhere for that matter. Almost all of them come with expensive contracts for providing your processing services. So don't assume an inexpensive terminal is necessarily inexpensive till you evaluate processing fees. You must apply for this account and be accepted. If you've had problems with bad credit, you may not be approved for a merchant account or may be forced to pay higher transaction fees.

Merchant account fees vary widely. Make sure you get the entire picture. Ask for an explanation of every charge related to a merchant account, usually including an application fee, a minimum monthly fee, a monthly statement fee, and a transaction fee. In addition, you will have to pay a discount rate, which is a percentage of the transaction ranging anywhere from 1.8 to 5 percent, straight to the credit card companies. There are sometimes even more hidden fees, like batch fees or extra charges for cards that aren't physically swiped, using their magnetic strip to conduct the transaction. You need a merchant account if you are going to be a serious entrepreneur. Just remember that everything is negotiable, particularly in the highly competitive merchant banking business. If you have good credit, take them to the mat. If your credit is poor, you may have to endure higher processing fees until you can get it cleaned up. Then go back to negotiate.

Try to open your merchant account through your bank to keep things simple. The more business you do with your bank, the more they'll value you as a customer. Once you have a merchant account, you can shop for a terminal. You have a choice of either leasing or buying a terminal. Most terminals come with contracts for service, so don't make a decision based on the price of the terminal alone until you factor in all the costs.

You Got the Orders; How Do You Get Paid?

I've been in the trade-show business for years now, and I still am just writing down credit card numbers on order forms. I even ditched the imprinter. I don't have time. We're too busy writing orders. I know some people bring along a credit card terminal to the show, but that is mostly impractical for just about every kind of wholesale business. First, if you use a terminal, you need to rent a telephone line from the show management. This is expensive.

Every retailer has a different need: They want a later ship date—maybe months away when they are stocking up for the holidays—or they have six stores and they need the exact order of thirty-six pieces for all six stores. You just don't have time to figure that all out while they wait, and they don't have time to wait. Since you won't be shipping for weeks at best, charging their credit card immediately is just wrong. You should never charge a credit card until the very day you ship. Anything else is unethical and illegal. The retailers know the drill. They'll hand you their credit card while you jot down the numbers on their order form, then take it back with a carbon copy of the line sheet or order form you just filled out with their order.

* *

CREATING A LINE SHEET

A line sheet is a form used for the purpose of ordering, preferably in carbonless triplicate. It should be something a buyer can take away to fill in the necessary information to fax an order to you. It should include:

- Your company letterhead and all your contact information, including your e-mail address, Web site address, fax number, and toll-free number if you have one.
- Area for information to be filled out by the buyer asking for:
  Company name, address, phone, fax, and e-mail
  Contact person
  Bill-to address and ship-to address
  Credit card information, including type of card, number, expiration date, and security code
- Line-by-line listing of all your products. Don't worry if it's only one. You will need to assign each product an Item Number, which you can determine for your own purposes. If you have a UPC code assigned to that item, put that in, too. You don't need UPC codes at the beginning. Keep reading to find out how and when to get one. On each line you will need a short written description of each item, like "Sleepy-head Fred Children's Wuvit."
- A place for the buyer to sign and date. You should have each buyer sign every order form or line sheet you fill out, particularly if they're using a credit card. Rip off the third NCR copy of the form and give it to the buyer with any literature you might have so that they remember just what they ordered.

* *

When I was just starting out I only accepted MasterCard and Visa from customers, because American Express and Discover seemed too expensive. I was writing an order six months later at my very next trade show and a woman pulled out an American Express Platinum card and handed it to me. I was writing a $2,000 order for her six stores. I told her I didn't take American Express, and she told me, "Honey, you almost just lost this sale! I don't use any other card. If you're serious about being in business, you'd better take American Express." Needless to say, I went home and signed up for it immediately.

Extending Credit to Customers: Just Say No

At my first trade show I was writing orders. I was so grateful, I was practically giving the product away. Customers were asking me for credit, and I said, "Sure," thinking this was business as usual, because everyone was asking for it. That is, until my neighbor the master rep senior exhibitor who had put me through my paces heard this. She stormed right over and put an end to that immediately. "You can't give credit to customers!" she scolded me. I learned then that credit is something that everybody wants, but few deserve. And I learned it again the hard way, when I got back from the show and shipped a $750 order I had taken before I stopped giving credit—meaning the buyers got thirty days to pay for product. I was burned by a deadbeat customer, whom I had to chase down for months for pennies on the dollar. Nobody should get credit from you except for any public institution or nonprofit. This category includes hospital gift stores, museums, libraries, zoos, schools, et cetera. These accounts usually don't have credit cards to use. They have to be billed through a central office. The good thing is, they pay on time every time. These people will always come with a credit sheet, much like the one you made for your vendors, with all your company information, including Federal Tax ID Number, a billing address, and a banking reference with a contact number. Also, some people will demand credit, and they will deserve it, including family-owned chains, which may have up to ten stores.

My policy always was, credit card for first purchase, thirty-day terms for any order after that with approved credit. Which meant I checked their banking references.

C.O.D.—Don't Do It!

You should never offer C.O.D., or Cash on Delivery. C.O.D. means that a customer doesn't have to pay for anything you ship them until they get the invoice at the door when it is delivered. Most major national shipping companies offer you a C.O.D. option for an extra cost. I agonized over doing C.O.D. at the beginning and was told by an acquaintance that I had to do it if I was going to be in business. Wrong! This is just another opportunity to lose lots of money. People will give the UPS delivery person a check when they show up with their package, but in my experience it's almost always been a rubber check.

How to Check the Credit of Potential Customers

I was alone at this show for four days, and certain bodily functions had to be met. The downside was that my booth was unattended for those times I had to get something to eat or go to the bathroom, but they provided me with a few minutes here and there to see what booths were selling and what booths were selling a lot. One, filled with kitschy country tchotchkes, was doing a lot of business. The woman selling handed me a credit application and asked if I wanted to fill it out. I thought, *No, but I'll take it, since you put so much work into it, and adopt it for my own use as a credit application for my customers.* I did, and use it to this day.

But the only really critical information on credit applicatons is bank information. To get that, you need customers to sign not only a credit application but also a Bank Authorization Form, which allows you to fax their bankers to check if your customers have accounts in good standing, for how long, and what the average balances are. You can ask for references from other vendors, but nobody's going to give you that information. Everything you need to know about a potential customer can be had from their banker. In my years of doing business, I would say that fewer than 1 percent of my customers haven't paid me, for whatever reason. That's remarkably good.

On my way back from the bathroom, I got lost! I thought about all those customers waiting and possible sales I was losing as I tried to find my way through the maze of aisles that led to my booth. I knew I was in aisle D—I even knew my booth number was just like a street address in numerical order—but I kept running into dead ends as the aisle was broken up by elevator shafts and bathrooms. After ten minutes of wandering I stumbled upon my own booth by accident and found a buyer waiting for me there, whom I had demonstrated my product to earlier.

"It's the *Wuvit Wady!*" she almost screamed, a happy, funny type. I loved her, and I loved the moniker. It's been with me ever since. "I've been looking all over this place for you!" the woman went on. "I want to order some of those Wuvits. It took me forever to find you again, and I had been here already!"

I learned that not all booths in an exhibit space are the same—even though you pay the same square footage fee for them. The difference between having a good location on a floor and a bad location, I would later learn, could be tens of thousands of dollars for one show. I was definitely in what you would call a bad location. I didn't know how to evaluate a floor plan back when I signed my contract and saw my first one. Good locations are in the highest-traffic areas near escalators, entrance doors, or elevators. You also may want to be near a big, established brand that brings a lot of buyers to its booth by reputation. Bad locations are generally in faraway corners. You can sometimes mitigate the effects of bad locations by putting ads in the show directories, inviting customers to your booth with some kind of promotion. Most shows reserve prime space on corners or prominent aisles

Credit Application

FOR OFFICE USE ONLY   *Account #:* _____   *Date:* _____

Name of Firm or Individual	Years at This Address
Address	Area Code/Phone No.
City, State, Zip	Area Code/Fax No.

Type of Ownership:
☐ Corporation   ☐ Partnership   ☐ Individual   ☐   EIN _____

Name of Principal(s)	Address, City, State, Zip	Social Security No.	Area Code/Phone No.

Bank Name	Account #
Address, City, State, Zip	Area Code/Phone No.

REFERENCES

Business Name	Street Address	Area Code/Phone No.
Contact Name	City, State, Zip Code	Area Code/Phone No.
Business Name	Street Address	Area Code/Phone No.
Contact Name	City, State, Zip Code	Area Code/Phone No.
Business Name	Street Address	Area Code/Phone No.
Contact Name	City, State, Zip Code	Area Code/Phone No.

(over)

Terms & Conditions of Agreement

The undersigned and [Your Company's Name, *YCN*] hereby agree that the following terms and conditions will govern all extensions of credit by *YCN* to the applicant named on the reverse. This agreement shall be effective only when signed by the applicant and accepted by *YCN*.

1. Provided this agreement is then in effect, and is not in default, *YCN* will extend credit to applicant for the purchase of products from *YCN* in such amounts as shall be determined by *YCN* in its sole discretion. All extensions of credit shall be subject to the credit policies as may be established by *YCN* from time to time. Applicant represents that applicant's purchases, and the credit extended hereunder, are for business purposes only.

2. The information provided by the applicant on the reverse is true and *YCN* is authorized to investigate the references provided by the applicant. So long as this agreement is in effect, applicant will notify *YCN* of any material changes in such information. *YCN* is also authorized to furnish information regarding the applicant's performance on this account to proper credit reporting agencies and others who may properly receive such information.

3. The applicant agrees to pay all amounts owed *YCN* in full within 30 days from the invoice date. Failure to pay within that time period may result in a finance charge being assessed on the outstanding balance at the rate of 1.5% per month, or the highest interest rate allowed by law, whichever is less. If there are any past due amounts owed by applicant to *YCN*, no additional extensions of credit will be given to applicant until applicant's account is paid in full. Failure to pay any amount when due, including any finance charge, can also result in the termination of this agreement.

4. The applicant shall be considered in default of this agreement if the applicant fails to pay *YCN* any amount when due. Upon any default, *YCN* may place the applicant's account with an attorney or debt-collection agency for collection. The applicant agrees to pay all collection costs including reasonable attorney fees and collection agency fees should this account be placed in collection. The applicant waives notice of default and notice on nonpayment.

5. I certify that the information in my application in complete and true. I authorize *YCN* to investigate my credit, banking, and employment history, obtain credit reports, and release information about their credit experience with me.

6. The applicant agrees to pay $20.00 for any check or other instrument given in payment of the account if such check or instrument is not honored by the institution upon which it is drawn for any reason. This amount may be changed by *YCN* from time to time as *YCN* may determine.

7. The applicant agrees to notify *YCN* of any ownership changes in the applicant's business by written notice to *YCN* accompanied by payment in full of all amounts owed by applicant to *YCN*, whether or not then due. Upon receipt of such notification, this agreement will automatically be terminated and no further extensions of credit will be allowed. All amounts owed *YCN* by applicant will be due in full upon receipt of the notification by *YCN*.

8. This agreement can be terminated by the applicant only by written notice to *YCN*. The applicant further agrees that notification of termination shall include payment of all amounts owed to *YCN* on its account at the time of termination including finance and collection charges if any. Acceptance of payment in full and receipt of the written termination notification shall constitute *YCN*'s acknowledgment of termination of this agreement.

9. This agreement shall be governed by the law of the state of Michigan. Any notice to be sent under the terms of this agreement shall be sent by United States Certified mail, return receipt requested to the address of the parties appearing on the reverse side of this Application. This agreement contains the entire and only understanding between the applicant and *YCN*. No provision of this agreement can be waived, amended, modified, or renewed except by a duly authorized representative of *YCN*.

Applicant:

Name_____ Company or Business_____

Signature_____ Title_____ Date_____

Bank Information Release Form

Date_____

Account Name_____

Contact Name & Title_____

Address_____

Phone/Fax_____

Dear Customer:

Please provide us with the name and address of your bank, your bank account number, and your signature in the designated space below, and **return this form with your credit application and a copy of your resale tax certificate** to our Credit Department at the above address.

Bank Name_____ Contact Name_____

Bank Address_____

Bank Account Number_____

Authorized Customer Signature
to Release Bank Information_____

For Bank Use Only

Dear Bank:

Your customer is requesting an Open Account with our company. Please provide us with the following information regarding the above account, which will be held in strict confidence. Please return this form to our Credit Department at the fax number listed above.

Date Account Opened_____

Average Monthly Figure: High (5-figure)_____ Medium (4-figure)_____ Low (3-figure)_____

Rating: Satisfactory_____ Fair_____ Poor_____

Problems: Overdrafts_____ Returned Checks_____

Other Remarks_____

Bank Service Representative Signature_____

Should you have any question, please do not hesitate to contact our credit department at _____.

Thank you very much for your assistance.

for big companies, who have national brands and have been around for years. You're able to negotiate better locations in higher-traffic areas usually by being a "senior exhibitor" or coming back regularly. In theory, this is the way it is supposed to work, but it doesn't. It's all about politics, schmoozing, and your booth design.

THE SECRETS OF TRADE SHOWS NO ONE WILL TELL YOU!

- Everybody exaggerates sales. Don't feel bad when someone tells you she's doing ten times the amount of business you are. Don't contribute to this by exaggerating yourself. Just tell everyone you're doing great!
- Show management will often inflate attendance figures. Nobody's on the floor, nobody's writing orders, all the exhibitors are complaining, and the show management—who are responsible largely for selling booth space—will walk the floors and tell everyone that the show is the best they've ever seen historically. In some venues, the worse the show is, the more you'll see show management telling you it's not them, it's you.
- Certain popular trade shows are famous for claiming they have a waiting list stretching years. This is just a convenient way to weed out people whom they don't want and people who don't want it bad enough. The truth is, if you have something that is hot and new, they'll find a place for you, no matter how long the waiting list is.
- One show salesperson desperate to get me—or any warm body—to their show once misled me about the desirability of a booth location and my prospect for making money, making me believe a large bank of doorways on the floor plan was in use when it wasn't.
- In my industry, any venue on the West Coast is largely regional, mostly attracting small retailers exclusively attending as buyers. New York and Atlanta are just about the only two places to meet national accounts, and New York, on a scale of 1–10 is a 10, while Atlanta is anywhere from a 2 to a 5, depending on what industry you're in. Chicago is an extremely important market for certain industries. Other industries, like furniture, depend on High Point, North Carolina. Las Vegas becomes more important every year. The largest trade-show venue in the world is in Frankfurt, Germany, where Europe comes to shop.
- There are two types of shows: writing shows and contact shows. At writing shows you can count on writing large quantities of mostly smaller short-term "cash" orders. At contact shows you collect business cards from major national retailers, where you will eventually make

contacts that will lead to big long-term business. Most contact shows are in New York.

- Some people go to trade shows just to steal your ideas. The more experience you have with trade shows, the more obvious these people will become. Be suspicious of any international "buyer" who walks the show alone and only looks—frequently staring—and never talks. Also be suspicious of any recent-college-graduate-looking buyer who works for a major discount national retailer. You can't stop these people from looking, but don't volunteer any information you don't feel completely comfortable giving away. Some exhibitors even keep their product brochures behind counters, giving them only to people whom the exhibitor qualifies with a conversation.

TRADE-SHOW ETIQUETTE

- Don't ever go into a direct competitor's booth. You wouldn't want them in yours. It is perfectly acceptable to ask any competitor who enters your booth to leave immediately. If they persist, tell the show management. There are usually rules prohibiting this, and they can lose their right to exhibit at future shows.
- Don't waste other exhibitors' time or money by browsing through their booths, sampling their free product, eating their free food, drinking their free wine, taking their free giveaways. All of this costs money, and you don't deserve any of this unless you're buying. Besides, you belong in your own booth—selling.
- Don't ever walk the floor of a trade show and deliberately "flip your badge," or turn it over so exhibitors can't immediately tell if you're a buyer or an exhibitor. Big retail buyers are notoriously guilty of doing this. If any exhibitor sees a flipped badge, they might assume you're the jackpot buyer they've been waiting for. If anyone walks into your booth with a flipped badge, you are within your rights to ask who they are.
- Don't ever leave the trade-show floor early, whether it's minutes or even days. You never know when the million-dollar account will walk in. It hurts the quality and integrity of the show if exhibitors leave.
- Don't ever enter any other exhibitor's booth after the show closes to look at merchandise or exhibits.
- Don't ever take an exhibitor's expensive marketing materials, unless offered.
- Don't eat in your booth in front of customers. If you have to eat in your booth, be discreet.
- Don't sit down in your booth unless you have to. Always be standing,

available, and ready to talk to customers. (Be sure to wear comfortable shoes!)

- Don't ever take any pictures of anyone's booth or product besides your own.
- Always be positive. Never engage in negative gossip or complaining, no matter how bad the show is. Negativity breeds more negativity, which translates into fewer sales and bad karma. Just smile and go get a cappuccino.

HOW TO GET THE MOST OUT OF A TRADE SHOW

Make up a press kit, pore through the exhibitor manual before the show, and find the names of any press people who cover the show. Send these people a press kit along with samples of your product and your booth number at least a week before the show. This has gotten me press in national trade magazines twice!

Take five to ten additional press kits to the show. Every good show has a press room. Make sure you take your press kits to the press room before the show starts and leave them in the spot designated for this. Do a nice job, or the show organizers may not let you leave your material. While you're there, check out the other press kits. You can't look through them unless you're press, but the covers are frequently works of marketing art.

Advertise in show directories. This has always been a very cost-effective way of reaching customers and important press contacts. *The Market,* the show directory at AmericasMart, gets mailed to more than 200,000 registered retail buyers across the U.S.! Circulation numbers are very important, but any show directory in New York will usually reach the right important people. Hire a graphic designer to do a first-rate ad. Some shows even offer these services to you at a cost.

ANATOMY OF A PRESS KIT

Presentation Cover: Make this eye-catching. Use your imagination and come up with something different but uncomplicated, hitting them with your brand, company name, and logo. At this point in my business, mine was a simple folder made of corrugated white craft paper with a window cut-out that said: "You're gonna Wuvit." Tied with a raffia bow, it was irresistible to press, who had to find out what a Wuvit was.

Company Bio on Letterhead: Make this short, one page maximum, outlining who you are, what your company is about, who your customers are, and what your mission statement is.

Press Release on Letterhead: Announce your participation in the show. Try to find a link to your product and service and any current news angle or trend that a reporter can use as a hook. Quote yourself in third person saying something interesting.

Clippings: If you have any press clippings, put them in. If you don't have any clippings, try to get something done on you before the show by your local newspapers. As a former stringer, I know reporters are starving for news and feature stories on local entrepreneurs. Send them a press release announcing the birth of your business along with a sample of your product and any marketing collateral you have.

Product Brochures: Include any marketing materials you have developed.

Miscellaneous: If your product has been featured in a catalog or store circular, put a copy of that in along with a press release explaining when and where it was featured. If you've won any awards or earned any distinctions prior to starting your new business, put that in in the form of a press release.

How to Write a Press Release

Press releases follow a standard format that you should adhere to:

- The words "For Immediate Release"
- Your company logo
- Contact information, including your name, company, phone, and e-mail address
- Headline that grabs the attention of the reader and summarizes the press release
- Place line identifying town, state, and date
- Lead paragraph answering the five questions of Who, What, Where, When, and Why
- Body of press release, two to four additional paragraphs, with additional quotes from you or other involved parties to make it more interesting
- Boilerplate: information that goes on every press release briefly describing the company, products, location, and operation and giving a mission statement

GREAT PRESS RELEASE RESOURCES

You can get help writing press releases at these Web sites, then submit them over the wire where press agencies around the world can pick them up:

- www.prweb.com
- www.prnewswire.com

TRADE-SHOW COUNTDOWN

What follows is a list of what you need to do and when in order to get the most out of your trade-show dollar:

Twelve Months to Go: If possible, pick the show you're interested in and go walk it before you exhibit. You'll absorb a lot, including what the best locations are and what is hot.

Six Months to Go: Talk to the show staff about becoming an exhibitor. Make sure you understand all costs and pricing for extra services, and study available locations on a floor plan. Most advertising opportunities sponsored by the show need to be reserved by this point, with artwork due for any ads only one month later. Advertising in trade-show directories can be your best value, reaching up to hundreds of thousands of retailers across the U.S. Plus, most buyers at national chain retailers read these market guides, helping to establish your brand in the marketplace.

Three Months to Go: Work on your booth design. Check your exhibitor's manual and record all the important deadlines for freight, electrical, and telephone services on your calendar. Using the show's exhibitor travel service, make your hotel and travel reservations now for the best discounts.

Two Months to Go: Set up your trade-show "set" in a space the size of your booth. Make sure all the pieces flow together to make an attractive presentation and that you're making the best use of limited space. Put together a tool kit for everything you could possibly ever need, including tape, scissors, staple gun, glue gun, tools, paint, hangers, hooks, et cetera. Hire and train the staff you need to man your booth. Make sure you have all product catalogs designed and printing by now.

One Month to Go: Confirm your travel reservations. Ship your freight. Register for all your employee badges. Make up and print your carbonless triplicate order forms. Buy comfortable clothes and comfortable shoes! Get ready to work your butt off!

I'm So Glad That's Over

My first show was winding to a close. I had tested my product in the marketplace outside of just my friends and neighbors, and it was a success. I gathered up my neat little stack of order forms, all the business cards I could collect from the people who stopped and didn't buy—including one from a premier national home fashions fabric brand representative who wanted to talk to me about making Wuvits with his fabric—and showed them with glee to my friend and confidant the master rep.

"Pretty good, kid," she observed, "considering you're showing your product in the wrong season."

"Wrong season?" I asked. "It's Chicago, and it's January. How much colder does it get? If people aren't interested in buying Wuvits now, when would they be?"

"You're not thinking right, again. Think like a retailer. These people just got through the holiday retailing season. You have an item that is perfect for holiday gift giving. They're thinking four to six months ahead! They're looking for fresh, bright items to put on their floor for spring. Considering that, you did really well, judging by your stack of orders."

"Four to six months ahead?" I asked, stunned that I hadn't thought of this, either. "That means I have to be here in July to get them to buy it for the holidays!"

"Right."

"Yikes!" I said out loud, thinking about the 2,000 Wuvits I had promised to start manufacturing with my contract sewer as soon as I got back from the show. I was six months off on my production schedule. I assumed I was going to sell those Wuvits in the next three months. I got a sick feeling in the pit of my stomach, the first of what would be many to come. How could I have made such a critical error on such an expensive proposition of manufacturing? Every dollar was precious to me. The pit in my stomach started feeling like fear again. My work was just beginning. I had to find a way to sell 2,000 Wuvits—fast!

I started packing up my set and realized that this was the first time I had spent any amount of time away from my kids. I had been too busy and too nervous to think much about it. I actually couldn't bring myself to talk to them on the phone at night from the hotel, because I would cry. I didn't know what was worse, crying or missing them, so I just ignored the whole thing. I had to pack up my whole set, wait hours for the Teamsters to load up my truck, then drive the three hours home in the night. I was already starting to get weary, just thinking about it, until I saw Master Rep across the way crying. She was such a pillar of strength, it literally shook me to see her openly and uncontrollably crying. I immediately went over and asked her what in the world was happening.

"My daughter got a liver," she said, tears pouring down her face, pointing to the very thin and pale teenage girl who sat at the table with her occasionally at the booth during the show. "I just got the phone call."

"Your daughter? I didn't know she was sick," I admitted, embarrassed, having thought she was just your normal anorexic, sullen teenager.

"We've been waiting years for a donor match. They said she'd die in months without it."

Suddenly my silly, stupid problems were nothing. I drove home alone with a grateful heart and crept into the darkened bedrooms where my kids slept after arriving home late, staring into their beautiful healthy faces and thanking God for every breath they took, every smile, every "Mommy!" screamed with glee at seeing me, every cute, naughty, funny thing they did. With every challenge that would be levied on me in the next couple of years, this was the one thing that I treasured, comforting myself in troubled times with the realization that this pure joy and happiness was something no amount of money could buy—or lack of money could take away.

ENTREPRENEURS
—AND MILLIONAIRES—
AREN'T BORN; THEY'RE MADE

I got out of bed the next morning, not knowing exactly what to do, but resolving to do whatever it was that needed to be done. I remember wondering just how I was going to sell 2,000 Wuvits. I had a choice: lie here and worry or get up and find a way to get it done. This simple decision alone was the key to my company's eventual success. I know some entrepreneurs who never got past this point. They never resolved consciously to do whatever had to be done and instead focused on every problem, paralyzing themselves in fear and inaction.

I had sold about $3,000 of Wuvits at the trade show. Not a bad launch, but I didn't make money, because the trade show cost me at least $3,000 with booth costs, travel expenses, set design, and all the other miscellaneous costs. Nobody expects to go to their first trade show and make money. "Making money," I've since learned, has many definitions to many people.

Since the contract sewer would not manufacture my product in a quantity less than 2,000 units, I bit the bullet and told them to proceed. *You have to start somewhere*, I reminded myself. The remaining inventory of 1,700 units needed to be converted into revenue, so I decided it was time to start cold-calling any retailer I could think of. I used the Web to search tourist town gift stores in Michigan and called them up.

I had never made a cold call before in my life. I remembered how my fabric vendor had hung up on me when I mentioned I sold something called Wuvits, and figured I really had my work cut out for me. The only thing that stood between me and actually making the phone calls was fear, and a complete lack of comfort. I began to think that if only I got rid of emotions, this entrepreneur thing would be a snap. You can't get rid of emotions, but you can learn the simple mechanics of asking for a sale.

The Mechanics of Asking for the Sale

How to make a sale—it is obviously something not being taught in today's institutions of higher learning. The world of sales making has definitely changed with the advent of voice mail and e-mails, with a whole new book of rules and business etiquette that requires the salesperson to speak faster, get to the point quicker, and just show the buyer the money already!

The modern world has succeeded in making us all busier, with ever-shortening attention spans and ever-lengthening to-do lists. The mommy entrepreneur has to understand the new and as of yet unwritten rules of doing business in a world where your wandering e-mail or droning voice mail can be deleted with one sigh of exasperation and a simple push of a button. Send an e-mail in all capital letters; voilà, you're instantly deleted. Ramble on in a conversational tone as if to one of your girlfriends in a voice mail, your voice disappears from the harried buyer's full voice-mail box.

If you're going to succeed as a Mommy Millionaire, you're going to have to master a few of the basic pitches for doing business. All of them present separate challenges and protocols, which, when mastered, will return you heart-racing success and million-dollar prospects.

- The handshake
- The elevator pitch
- The cold-call pitch
- The e-mail pitch
- The trade-show pitch
- The voice-mail pitch
- Even the airplane pitch

The Handshake

Shaking hands is a skill especially in need of teaching to women, who are relatively new to this old-boy formality. You can't move on to the elevator pitch until you perfect your handshake, so practice this with your husband until you get it right. The first thing to do when greeting a new business acquaintance is to extend your hand with the statement, "Hi, I'm Kim Lavine. It's nice to meet you." Look them in the eyes and smile. Make sure your hand is far out in front of you and your voice is prominent, so it's clear that you are in the lead and demand a response—don't ever wait until someone offers his or her hand first unless you are being formally introduced by a third party. The more confident person is always the person who extends the greeting first. Push your hand firmly into the other person's hand until your thumbs lock, grasp the hand with enough of a squeeze to imply confidence and self-assurance, then shake it up and down counting, *One thousand one, one thousand two.* Disengage and move on to the next person, asserting your presence with a big smile to each member of the group until you've mastered them all. Make sure you squeeze their hand with confidence while holding it. Don't ever give a limp-wristed woman handshake you reserve for your girlfriends at scrapbooking parties. The rule of how hard to squeeze is just short of "too hard." If you can feel the other's grasp while grasping yourself, it's probably just about right. Don't ever give them the "Clinton," which is accompanied by the other hand on the back or arm, unless you're in Bill Clinton's class of schmoozing, of which he is the undisputed king.

The Elevator Pitch

Here's a handy and indispensable rule with which to start your pitch practice. The rule is simple and the analogy is obvious. Imagine you bump into a prospect in an elevator and you have only the time it takes to get from the ground floor to their office on the seventh floor to tell them all they need to know about the money you're going to help them make. This pitch is basic to all pitch making and once mastered can be used in a multitude of situations, including introducing yourself at business meetings to answering your curious neighbor's or doctor's inquiries as to, "What is it that you do?"

This pitch should never be more than thirty seconds long. Try timing yourself while speaking, and you won't believe how short thirty seconds is and how few words you'll get to utter before your microwave timer beeps. Remember you have to start with the handshake, so there go five of your thirty seconds. In the remaining precious seconds, always finagle a business card out of your day planner *while* seamlessly speaking your twenty-five-second pitch.

It should go something like, "Hi, I'm Kim Lavine, president of Green Daisy, manufacturer of the newest retailing phenomenon, the Wuvit, two million dollars in retail sales in just over two years on a product I made as Christmas presents for my kids' teachers! Could I please have your card? I'd love to send you some samples!"

Mission accomplished. You introduced yourself, exuded confidence while firmly shaking their hand, showed them the money, and asked for the sale, all in the time it took to ride the elevator up to the seventh floor.

No matter that they don't know what it is you actually sell at the moment, they're mesmerized and impressed by your confidence and will hand you their card and start asking more questions, which you'll have to be prepared to answer. Don't worry if you haven't done $2 million in sales yet. Retail buyers are trained to respond to the magic words "hot" and "new" like

Pavlov's dog. Even if you're just starting, you can introduce yourself by saying, "Hi, I'm Taffy Goldman, president of When Pigs Fly, maker of this holiday season's hot and new gift phenomenon, the Manhandler, an ingenious idea I came up with after spending twenty-four hours a day with twin two-year-olds. Could I please have your card? I'd love to send you samples."

Non-negotiable must-haves of the elevator pitch include having the confidence of calling yourself president or CEO when just starting out and getting the all-important business card. It doesn't matter if the card belongs to the kid who runs the mailroom; that business card is gold, which can lead you to the e-mail addresses of everyone in that organization once you understand the "syntax" of their company's e-mail addresses. Before you know it, just putting a period, a hyphen, or an underscore between people's names you get from cold calling will turn them into million-dollar prospects.

The Cold-Call Pitch

Here is the real art of the deal. I have gotten million-dollar accounts from cold calling. Cold calling is defined as picking a major retailer out of a hat on any given day, looking up their corporate office phone number by searching either www.hoovers.com, www.switchboard.com, or Google, and calling to request the name of the appropriate buyer to contact regarding your hot and new product and their address, phone number, and e-mail address, all gotten with the offhand comment of, "By the way, before you transfer me, could you please give me all this information?"

Now that you have the contact number of the switchboard operator, you need to put together your cold-call pitch. This is an upgraded version of your elevator pitch, spun with a lot of old-fashioned charm, hereafter defined as schmooze. Since you are not face-to-face, you have to improvise new techniques to establish a personal connection with that busy switchboard operator on the other end of the phone who may or may not be having a good day. You have to get their attention and get them to give you precious information, usually within a minute's worth of time, maximum. Fortunately for you, the operator's familiar with this process. You're not the first person to cold-call Macy's after all. Whether you succeed where others have failed all depends on how good your pitch is. Read "The Art of the Pitch" later in this chapter to see what works for me.

The E-mail Pitch

If you're lucky enough to get somebody's e-mail address, don't waste it by writing a long, boring e-mail. The most important element of any e-mail pitch is the subject line, which the recipient sees displayed in their in-box. Most buyers get countless numbers of e-mails a day. You have to make yours stand out and provoke the recipient enough to open yours and read it. Show them the money, while saying something clever. When writing the body of the e-mail, never make it longer than what you see displayed on your screen. Try to use bullet points or bold typeface to focus the attention on the key things you want to emphasize. Always end your e-mail by asking for the sale. An example might be, "What would it take to bring this great product to your stores for a test?" At the very least, ask if you may send a product sample. Never send an invoice with any samples. Buyers are never expected to pay for samples.

The Trade-Show Pitch

At a trade show, you have willing buyers who are standing before you, with whom you have only a few minutes to make the sale. You have to skip all the personal introductions and fluff and focus solely on the facts. "May I show you a Wuvit? Two million dollars in retail sales in just over two years. They're sold in every retail environment there is. They're the perfect gift-giving idea that everybody loves, all at a retail price point of twenty-five dollars. If you order our minimum opening order of a dozen at the show, you get one free, a twenty-five dollar retail value." If you can demonstrate your product or service, make sure you do it while giving them your pitch. If they don't order there, make sure to give them an order form with your booth number, so they can come back later, as well as your contact information so they can call or fax an order in.

The Voice-Mail Pitch

This is a world dominated by voice mail, so you have to perfect this pitch. Rule number 1: It can't be more than thirty seconds long. Nobody likes to hear long voice mails that drone on repeating the same information. Rule number 2: Make sure you introduce yourself first by name, along with the name of your company and your phone number, said slowly enough that the buyer can actually write it down. One of my pet peeves is people who say their phone number so fast I have to replay a message three times to get it. In fact, never talk to anybody on the phone without first introducing yourself with your name and your company's name. Leave your short message, using your elevator pitch as the basis, then repeat your name, company, and phone number again at the end so that they can write down the information they may have missed the first time.

The Airplane Pitch

I was once on a flight to New York, sitting next to a man whom I had ignored the entire time. It was only after we had landed, when we were getting

ready to get off the plane, that someone casually asked him what he was doing in New York.

"Oh, I manage a capital investment firm," he answered. "We're pretty
big, based in Westchester County, New York."

I immediately took out my business card and gave him my ten-second
pitch while he stared in amazement, taking out one of his cards at my request and handing it to me. "That was the best pitch I've ever heard in my
life," he said. "I gotta hand it to you. On an airplane—never had that happen to me before. I specialize in life sciences exclusively. But if I didn't, we'd
definitely be talking." Believe it or not, there were even bigger fish whose
cards I would soon extract using the same stealth mode.

- -

HOOVER'S: INVALUABLE RESOURCE FOR MAKING SALES

You need to be creative when doing your research on finding the right phone
number to initiate your conversation. The best place to start on the Web is at
www.hoovers.com. Hoover's, Inc., is a company that maintains a database of 12
million companies and provides "market intelligence" with in-depth coverage of
40,000 of the world's top businesses. Much of the information, especially on the
bigger companies, is free, including company profiles, in-depth financials, executives' names, and competitors.

Most big retailers have several different nameplates, with many different divisions located across the country, so just finding the corporate headquarters can
be a real challenge. Go to Hoover's and type in "Macy's" in the search window,
and you'll soon discover that the name of the company is really Federated Department Stores. In addition, you'll get the location of each one of its five buying offices across the country and their phone numbers, from which you can start
your cold-calling exercise.

I would suggest you click on the Fact Sheet option for each division and print
it off. Then you can start a folder with all the information you need at hand to
call, while logging your phone successes as you move through the inevitable line
of contacts you'll encounter as you search for "the right buyer" for your particular product.

- -

QuickBooks Customer Manager

You're going to need a good database management tool to keep track of all
your correspondence when you're cold-calling twenty to thirty companies,
which you'd better be if you want to make a million dollars. It can be confusing to keep track of who said what when and when you need to follow
up. For my money QuickBooks Customer Manager is the best tool for the

job. It's relatively affordable, has an easy learning curve, and integrates with both QuickBooks and Outlook, so you don't have to duplicate all that data. Finding the right buyer is sometimes more of an art than an exact science.

The Art of the Pitch

First thing you need to do is develop your pitch by writing it down. Focus on the same elements as the elevator pitch: introduce yourself, show them the money, then ask for the sale or, in this case, the contact information necessary to make the sale. Write your pitch down and practice saying it in a friendly way until you can repeat it by heart without having to refer to a piece of paper you're obviously reading off of. This will come in handy later, when someone actually does answer a phone, instead of it going to voice mail, and you're stunned to find yourself unexpectedly communicating with a real person; the pitch will come out automatically.

My pitch goes like this: "Hi, my name is Kim Lavine and I own a company called Green Daisy. We make a hot and new gift item called the Wuvit. We've done over two million dollars in retail sales on it in just a few years, and went from 40 Saks Inc. stores—no test—to 239 stores in four months, selling them twenty-five thousand units in five months. Could you possibly give me the contact information for the correct buyer for this product at your store? I'd really appreciate it."

I pause and listen for the response, which is usually, "What's a Wuvit?" which is all part of my brilliant brand strategy, come up with a funny-sounding name that gets their attention, stops them dead in their tracks, and makes them engage in further conversation with you. I laugh warmly, which is as close to a smile you can get on the phone, and tell them, "Yeah, I'm otherwise known as the Wuvit *Wady*." They love that I can make fun of myself and make them laugh, too. "A Wuvit is your own personal designer spa therapy pillow," I explain. "You heat it up in the microwave two to three minutes, and it stays hot up to hours! Or you can freeze it overnight for icy relief! We sell it in every retail environment there is, from golf and tennis pro shops, hospital gift stores, home decor, general gift, spas, and salons—nobody doesn't *wuvit*!"

Usually, after I mention that we rolled out from 40 Saks Inc. stores—no test—to 239 stores in four months, selling them 25,000 units, the person on the other end of the phone transfers me complete with contact information to a Divisional Merchandise Manager or vice president, because that's a serious accomplishment, akin to hitting a grand slam in the World Series. I'm talking their language, showing them the money in fifteen seconds, and they know in retail parlance that I didn't roll out to 239 stores in four months without selling product! I didn't start out that way, though. You can still get this information without these stats. Write your pitch remembering to (1) introduce yourself, (2) show them the money, and (3) ask for the sale or contact info.

"Hi, I'm Taffy Goldman, president of When Pigs Fly, maker of this holiday season's hot and new gift phenomenon, the Manhandler, an ingenious idea I came up with that I know consumers will love. We're taking calls from all over the country on this, and I know it would be perfect for Macy's! Could I please have the contact information for the appropriate buyer to send samples to? I would really appreciate it!"

Who could turn you down? Especially when you add how much you would appreciate it if they helped you out.

THE "DO'S" OF COLD CALLING

- *Do* stand up when talking, it adds energy to your voice.
- *Do* smile when you're speaking. People can sense it on the other end of the phone.
- *Do* think positively that you're going to get this information, and you will, it's magic!
- *Do* know that this buyer is always on the lookout for a hot and new product to bring new revenues on the floor with and is truly interested in seeing what you have.
- *Do* stick to your scripted pitch without rambling on.
- *Do* remember that they're busy and can't evaluate your product until they see it, so get off the phone in a few minutes tops, unless you discover your mothers are second cousins.
- *Do* say "have a great day" like you mean it. This just makes people feel good.

THE "DON'TS" OF COLD CALLING

- *Don't* ask them, "Is this a good time to talk?" It's never a good time!
- *Don't* stop after you introduce yourself and say something like, "How are you?" Unless you already know them, it's disingenuous.
- *Don't* use a manner of addressing them that is too formal and business-speak, keep it light and conversational so you can make that personal connection.
- *Don't* ramble on or act too familiar; buyers appreciate brevity.
- *Don't* ever be demanding, short, or rude.

Be Prepared for What Happens Next

They will give you the information you want, because you were nice to them and they know you're a hardworking mom just trying to make a buck, and hey, even someone like you, an underdog, has their day, and everyone loves an underdog and wants to see them hit one out of the ballpark, so it might as well be you today, "good luck, honey!"

Have Your Pen Ready

They will probably transfer you to the buyer's voice mail directly, but you'll want to stop them first and ask one more favor:

• "Before you transfer me, could you please tell me the buyer's name and correct spelling?"
• "Can I also please have their direct dial phone number?"
• "Would it be possible to get their e-mail address, too?"
• "Can you confirm that the mailing address is the same as I have here?" as you read from your Hoover fact sheet.
• "Thank you!"

If you get the e-mail address, consider yourself a master. That is the last thing that anyone will ever give to you, so don't get discouraged if you don't. You can go to their vendor portal later and, as long as you have the correct spelling of the first and last name, can click around long enough to find out that company's particular e-mail syntax.

You're now being transferred to the buyer. It's more than likely that you'll get voice mail, but just in case you don't and a real person picks up the phone, you'll have to be prepared to do your cold-call pitch all over again! If it's voice mail, use the same script you've just read with the following additions:

• "I was referred to you by Macy's Corporate as being the appropriate buyer to contact regarding this great, new product!"
• "I'm going to send you out a sample today along with a press kit."
• "I'll call you to follow up soon after."
• "I know you're gonna love it!"
• "Thank you and have a great day!"

WHAT IS A VENDOR PORTAL, HOW DO I FIND IT, AND HOW DO I USE IT?

A vendor portal is the business back end of a retailer's Web site that they use to conduct business with their vendors. The most important piece of information you'll find in a vendor portal is their standards manual. This can be called different things by different retailers, but its purpose is the same, to provide trading partners with all the specific and technical information necessary for doing business with a national retailer, from hanger specifications, to shipping and routing guides, to EDI service providers.

You use a vendor portal to become set up as a vendor with a retailer once you get the first Purchase Order from them. This can be a very complicated process, as you create relationships with their various departments from shipping, to distribution, to advertising, to accounts payable. There are certain approval processes that you need to submit to. This is complicated, but everybody is there to help you learn and succeed.

Click around any big retailer's business end of their Web site long enough and you'll find a link to their vendor portal. Some of them require a password to log in with, which you can only get as an approved vendor. This is an unbelievable wealth of information, giving you an insight into what it takes to work with the big boys. Once you get this down, you'll understand that it's all designed to make everything easier instead of harder.

Working with Reps

The winter of 2001 had quickly turned into the spring of 2002. I had one son, just turned five, enrolled in half-day kindergarten and a three-year-old son who was undergoing every kind of medical testing, neurological evaluation, and special education available. In the midst of all of this, I managed to put together two solid hours every day for the purpose of doing nothing but making sales calls.

My manufacturer was cranking out Wuvits I had to sell, and I couldn't turn off the voice in my head of the master rep telling me retailers just wouldn't be interested in my product in the spring. But I had no choice. I picked up the phone and prepared myself for rejection on an even larger scale. After five calls with responses ranging from yelling and hanging up on me to polite invitations to send information about my crazy-sounding product, I sat at my desk thinking I had come to the absolute end of the road. Boy, was I wrong! I look back at those days now and have to laugh. What I thought were insurmountable problems then were really just blips on the radar screen in the big picture.

Here's an unspoken rule of business that only seasoned entrepreneurs know: Just when you think you're licked, something comes along to pick you up and inspire you with a whole new sense of purpose.

You can pretty much rely on it. In fact, one of my fellow entrepreneurs, who was my part-time chief financial officer for a while, used to joke about it. "You're really down and think you're at the end? You know that means something good is going to happen!" And he was right. Just when I thought I was not going to make any sales that day, two people asked if they could rep me.

When I was at the trade show I had gotten a glimpse into the opportunities offered by road reps, like the master rep who counseled me at my trade show in Chicago, and wondered just how I went about getting someone to rep me— not knowing at the time how to use the trade show effectively to accomplish this. As a master rep, she supervised several road reps who had contacts with retailers across the state or even country, who called on them regularly offering new products and taking orders for existing lines they represented. It doesn't matter, I discovered, what you're selling, from collectible gifts to automotive parts, from a service to a franchise, there is a representative who is in the business to get you business, as a service rep or a manufacturer's rep.

THE BENEFITS OF USING SALES REPS OR OUTSOURCING SALES

- No expensive employee salaries
- Immediate market penetration
- Experienced sales force
- Established relationships in your industry
- Opportunity to learn through market intelligence
- Paying only for results
- Predictable costs or commissions

If I could have cried as I sat at my desk after five calls and five rejections, I would have. One of the upsides of a dysfunctional childhood was an innate toughness that I built up, that just didn't allow tears to come anymore, except for those that resulted from love and joy. Put me in a boardroom with a bunch of hardball-playing investors beating me up for power; you'll never see the slightest trace of any tear. However, put me ten minutes later at my kids' school assembly for their Christmas pageant while I watch them

REP RESOURCES AVAILABLE ON THE INTERNET

U.S. Department of Labor, Bureau of Labor Statistics, www.bls.gov. For a big picture overview, read "Sales Representatives, Wholesale and Manufacturing" online at www.bls.gov/oco/ocos119.htm.

Manufacturers' Agents National Association, www.manaonline.org. According to their Web site, "MANA's mission is, through a major emphasis on education, to aid in the development and promotion of mutually profitable relationships, ethical standards of behavior and interdependence among multi-line, outsourced sales and marketing entrepreneurs, their principals and their joint customers."

Manufacturers' Representatives Educational Research Foundation, www.mrerf .org. All kinds of great information about the function of outsourcing sales.

HIRA (Health Industry Representatives Association), www.hira.org. "Focuses on promoting the manufacturers' rep function within the health care industry."

Manufacturers' Agents Association for the Foodservice Industry, www.mafsi .org. Check out their Reading Room link for important insight into the world of the rep.

If I haven't mentioned your particular area here, just go to Google and type in your industry coupled with the word "rep" and see if you can find a resource on your own.

---

sing loud and off-key the lyrics to "Rudolph, the Red-Nosed Reindeer"— which I can do because I'm now Boss Mom—and I'm bawling uncontrollably like a newly crowned Miss America contestant.

After having made five cold calls with five rejections, I took my kids to the YMCA for their Dinky Dunkers basketball game. I scooped them up and made the usual mad dash, standing on the sidelines watching them play as at least three people came up, recognizing me as the Wuvit Wady and asking if they could buy Wuvits.

I went out to my truck to get the basket of Wuvits I kept there at all times and brought it into the Y for the three people who had wanted to buy some. Another mommy stopped me on the way, asking what was in my great-looking basket filled with beautiful fabrics, and wanted to buy some. Halfway down the hallway to the gym, I had sold more! By the time I got to the gym, I was bubbling over with enthusiasm for the opportunity Wuvits offered for any rep. I remembered master rep's advice: "Show them the money!"

Hallelujah! My days of making cold calls were over, I thought. A neighbor of mine, who loved the product so much, wanted to come work for me on commission only. How could I go wrong with that? That's the beauty of reps, and can also be the problem: You don't have to pay them unless they produce. It's easy to find yourself giving lots of expensive product samples, brochures, and catalogs to as many reps who ask you because you think it's not costing you anything but the samples. I learned a lesson almost a year later that showed me that perhaps working with reps—believe it or not— was the most expensive decision I could make at start-up.

At the moment, reps looked like the answer to all my problems. Anybody who could take away the pain of cold calling from me was welcome in my book. The other person interested in repping me was an established rep in the gift industry. I told him excitedly about my trade show in Chicago, which by all accounts was a resounding success for a first time out in a horrible location, and about how I had already sold thousands of dollars' worth of Wuvits off the back of my truck, including sixty dollars' worth on my walk through the Y. I was enthusiastic about my product and realized it was my job to transfer that enthusiasm to him so that he could effectively sell. I tried to impress him, and he tried to impress me by mentioning the names of really big retailers at which he had some kind of "in," making me think that all this was the beginning of easy street.

"How much do you charge for your product?" was the first question he asked as our kids waved at us from the court, sensing we were talking business and so needing to interrupt. I told him what the wholesale cost was and what the Manufacturer's Suggested Retail Price (MSRP) was.

"That's gotta change," he said. "You have to add on your fifteen-percent rep commissions."

"But that raises the cost of Wuvits thirty percent at retail," I observed, "if I'm going to give retailers keystone."

"Yup. That's what you need to charge."

I didn't know about raising my pricing by 15 percent to the wholesale customer, and thus by 30 percent to retail customers. Still, if anyone could relieve me of the dreaded task of cold calling, it was worth giving it a try. He had a regional gift show coming up in a week and was going to a show at his permanent showroom in Detroit the week after. He would need product for all seven of his road reps, enough product for a display at the regional gift show, and product along with a permanent display fixture for his showroom in Detroit, all in five days.

Money still was too tight for me to buy anything, so I decided I could make a collapsible display fixture for about twenty dollars that I saw in a trade-show furnishings catalog for $150. I sawed, cut, and painted, delivering him the display with thirty Wuvits to display on it, as well as thirty-five additional Wuvits, five for each of his seven reps, displayed in beautiful wicker baskets like I was used to carrying, and another thirty Wuvits for his gift show. I had given him a total of ninety-five Wuvits, worth close to $1,000 wholesale and $2,400 retail, if you used his math. He loaded up his van and promised me a fantastic show with lots of orders upon his return.

I received about $250 worth of sales from him over a period of six months. He never returned any of my samples or the permanent fixture I made. Two years later, I discovered that many of my Wuvits were given as Christmas gifts to all his kids' teachers. Believe it or not, I did this a number of times—as almost everybody does, seduced by the lure of people who promised me sales, with the very same results, before I finally screamed, "Stop the insanity!"

REPS, THE GOOD, THE BAD, AND THE UGLY: THE SECRETS ABOUT WORKING WITH THEM THAT NOBODY WILL TELL YOU

- Standard commission for reps is 15 percent; however, this is negotiable, especially on very large volumes, or if you are getting pressured to deliver a discounted price.
- Reps usually want to be assigned exclusive territories, which means that only they are allowed to sell your product or service in sometimes up to a five-state area.
- Once they are assigned exclusive territories, you may have to pay reps a commission on all sales in that territory, whether the reps generate the sales or you do. Be very careful at the beginning and make sure you reserve existing customers and exempt trade-show sales from commissions. Someday you will have that $100,000 trade show, and paying a rep who may or may not have even been there a $15,000 commission is distressing.
- Allowing reps to service your existing customers in exchange for commissions can be a good thing, because reps will touch base with those customers regularly and keep a foot in the door.
- Reps are expected to help you at trade shows in their territory for no compensation beyond commissions. These commissions are negotiable and can be for a reduced percentage on the show's entire sales or their standard percentage on the sales they write exclusively. Don't offer to pay them in excess of commissions.
- Reps are expected to cover all their own operating expenses from their home office or while on the road. Any other forms of compensation, like mileage or office expenses, are thought to be covered by their commission and are negotiated on a case-by-case basis.

- Most reps with whom I've worked are at best effective for a short period of time and at worst not effective at all. Before you sign a contract, check their references from other manufacturers or clients they represent. Ask if you can contact one or two of the retailers or clients they call on to sell. Make sure you have a clause that allows you to terminate their contract at will with an appropriate notice, no more than thirty days. Make sure that you specify the return of all samples to you upon termination.
- A great way to find reps in your area and in your industry is to go to retailers or customers directly and ask them what reps they recommend. Retailers are happy to do this, because having professional, reliable reps, who keep them abreast of fresh new products or services, makes their own work easier.
- Be very careful about the quantity of product you give to reps for free. Many of these people are in the business simply to collect free product samples, which they resell at craft shows or even trade shows.
- Keep an inventory of the product you give to reps. Make sure they can account for it. You don't want them to sell your product directly and keep the money, which has been known to happen.
- Most of a rep's income should come from commissions. If not, you have probably found a rep with whom you don't want to work. Reps have a dozen other ways to ask you for money, from requiring you to pay for booth space at their trade shows or their permanent showrooms to even hitting you up for business cards and advertising expenses. This in itself can be a racket. Keep reading to see how I was stung on this scam.
- Having a rep who doesn't produce sales is not a bargain, even if you're only paying a commission on sales. They're limiting your ability to become successful in their territory, and they're either inflating the price of your products to buyers with their 15 percent commission or cutting 15 percent into your margins. You'd better have reps who produce if you're willing to charge 15 percent more for your product to everybody, regardless of whether a rep sold it or you did at a trade show.

AN ALTERNATIVE: DISTRIBUTORS

- Have a contract agreement granting them, as a third party, an exclusive right to sell your product or service in a specific geographical location
- Typically pay you for the right to distribute your product
- Buy the product up front, taking responsibility for all sales and adding a markup to cover their costs
- Maintain their own inventory

My other rep offer that day turned out to be much more productive. She was another stay-at-home mommy, but instead of needing to work, she just wanted to find something interesting to do besides her volunteer work at school and church. She *wuved* Wuvits, was absolutely passionate about them, and wanted to work beside me turning my mission statement into a reality: a Wuvit in every home. Here was someone who believed in my dream. Maybe I wasn't crazy after all.

I gave her a fancy title, National Sales Manager, invested in some business cards, and offered to pay her 10 percent commission on all sales. She wasn't interested in small retail accounts; she was going for the big guys. With a style that impressed me and that would later inspire me to new heights, she picked up the phone for two hours a day and just started knocking down doors, calling some of the biggest retailers in the country. Before I knew it, she had a vice president of Meijer, a regional discount chain comparable to Wal-Mart, on the line, asking not only, "What's a Wuvit?" but also, "How did you get through to me?"

Wow. My manager and I were excited. Suddenly a door opened to possibilities I hadn't seen before. Still, I had to take a step back and make a critical decision, which would inevitably shape the entire future of my company. Do I go straight to discount retail?

I can't believe how many people call me today about their products, some of which truly are the next big thing, invariably interested in finding out how to get into only two channels of distribution: Wal-Mart and QVC. Why people think Wal-Mart and QVC are the pinnacles of retailing I don't know. Maybe it's because Wal-Mart is so big and QVC is so prevalent, insinuating itself into every home in America. Wal-Mart is America's largest corporation, with revenues eight times those of Microsoft! It employs 1.4 million people, more than GM, Ford, GE, and IBM put together. And you still think only high-tech entrepreneurs get rich? Wrong! If this isn't a testament to the economic power of manufacturing or distributing simple, everyday consumer products, I don't know what is.

I couldn't believe it. My new rep had the VP of a major national discount retailer on the phone, and I had to tell her no. There's a hard-and-fast rule in marketing that even with my inexperience I could figure out. That is: Start at the top of the retail chain, like high-end luxury, and move down.

You can always sell to a Wal-Mart after you sell to Saks Incorporated, but you can never sell to a Saks after you sell to Wal-Mart.

There are a couple of reasons for this. Every product or service has a "life cycle."

The Product Life Cycle

There are four significant stages in the life cycle of every product. Not every product evolves through them all. Many products fail at Introduction.

1. **Introduction:** This is the infant stage of a product, when it is developed, branded, trademarked, and distributed through a minimal number of channels, with luck the ones at the top of the food chain, where most new product innovation starts. You are typically pushing the boulder up the mountain here, trying to get the word out on your product and your brand, using whatever success you obtain at small retailers to leverage your way into big nondiscount retailers. Your cost of goods is typically higher at this point because you don't have the quantities necessary to negotiate any savings on your manufacturing. Stay small; crawl before you walk. Don't invest in large runs of product overseas.
2. **Growth:** This is when your product gains momentum in the marketplace and the boulder starts to roll down the other side of the mountain without much effort on your part. You've leveraged your way into multiple national channels of distribution, and you are finally able to look into investing in larger production runs, perhaps overseas, thus cutting your costs and making your pricing more attractive to wider streams of distribution, perhaps including discount retailers.
3. **Maturity:** You have achieved market saturation, and the fast rate of sales growth starts to decrease and stabilize. At this point, you probably have discounted your product from its original introductory price to support mass distribution in national discount chains. You are probably feeling the heat from competitors, and if you haven't brought fresh innovation to your product regularly, you will likely see a drop-off in sales when the consumer public simply grows tired of it.
4. **Decline:** In the final stage, your sales start to be eclipsed by new products with more innovative features or better branding and marketing. Decline isn't inevitable, or at the very least you can put it off for a good long time. You just have to work at it.

Though what I knew was limited, I could figure out going straight to discount retail meant going right to low margins without the benefit of big production discounts on quantity. I would have basically skipped the first two steps of the product life cycle, including Introduction, where I would get my product out there, build a brand, and tweak it to perfection, all without the extreme pressures of having to deliver large quantities on low margins.

Brand building is more important to the value of your product and your company as a whole than you will ever know at start-up.

I didn't fully understand the value of brand building until three years later when I was in the process of raising capital from angel investors through the sale of stock in my company. (How'd I do that? Read chapter 14.) Since I had been so careful with my brand, keeping it out of discount retail, including Wal-Mart and QVC, for so long, even sacrificing revenues to do so, my brand and company were worth a lot more to investors. To them, the product itself wasn't as important as the brand equity and the channels of distribution through which I sold the product.

If you have good brand equity and good channels of distribution, you can eventually make any kind of product you want, based on the strength of your brand in the marketplace, and sell it through those valuable channels of distribution.

That, in a nutshell, is the true value of any company. If you circumvent the process and take your product direct to discount, you may be Today's Special Value, win that particular lottery, and become a millionaire, but you certainly won't be building brand equity in your flash-in-a-pan product cycle, and you absolutely won't be taking your product to higher-end retail. My friend the entrepreneur and part-time chief financial officer had one of the best sayings I ever heard in the business world, and he'd recite it to me weekly:

"You bought those channels of distribution with all that hard work, money, and sweat. Now you have an obligation to shove new products into them continuously!" Boy, was he right!

It's remarkable to me how so many intelligent and successful people ignored the Product Life Cycle, calling me up and insisting that I connect them with my QVC and Wal-Mart contacts. If you're lucky enough to have friends or acquaintances who have such contacts, let me tell you the right way and the wrong way to get this information from these people. I couldn't believe how some people whom I had never met, who happened to know somebody who knew somebody who knew me, would call me and demand that I give them this information as if they were entitled to it. I had to work for more than two years to get the name of the "gatekeeper" at QVC, spending tens of thousands of dollars (I'll tell you why later), but these people thought that with one phone call from a stranger I would turn over every e-mail address and phone number on my Rolodex to them. One fellow, a president of a company that manufactured auto parts, first had his secretary call me and screen me, then put the call through to him, so that he could demand I give him the contacts information he needed to take his product to Today's Special Value–dom. The right way to approach me would have been to call me up personally, introduce himself professionally, ask me politely if he could bother me with a few questions, maybe even offer an invitation to lunch, followed by a polished description of whatever his product was.

With this sort of information I had, think about everything I would risk giving up if I gave it away. This person would use my name, so my reputation would be at stake if indeed he should use the same superior attitude with the buyer as he did with me. Without evaluating his product, I could be sacrificing my reputation by sending an unqualified vendor to the buyer, who is too busy to take unsolicited calls from vendors who aren't quite ready.

This high-handed man who called me was not ready. I went to his Web site, and though I thought he had a great product, he was using a particular college's brand or logo, for which he wasn't licensed. *That's a lawsuit,* I thought. He didn't even know he had to be licensed. I didn't have the time to educate him on the entire licensing procedure. I was already spending a great amount of my own valuable time sorting through it. He wasn't interested, anyway. He just wanted that name and number.

I didn't know all of this instinctively. A friend, who had a child in my son's young-fives class, was the daughter of an owner of an international health and beauty company that did a lot of business with Wal-Mart. My husband very politely squeezed every bit of advice he could from him after he flew his private plane to his grandson's birthday party, where there were pony rides for the kids. He was very generous. Everything I know about doing business with Wal-Mart is anecdotal, but he laid it right out. In a nutshell, his advice was to not start at Wal-Mart. Our margins were still slim and Wal-Mart was tough as nails on pricing. In addition, he told us that we would need to have EDI in place, as well as be ready to ship large quantities on a moment's notice. You have to participate, he told us, in their complicated vendor information exchange program, and you have to be capable of handling that internally. Besides, they want you to make sure that they are not more than 40 percent of your total business. They don't want to be able to put you out of business if they decide to drop your product. My husband asked him what his typical margin was and he said it was approximately 40 percent, but he was selling products that cost a dollar individually, in a company over a hundred years old, passed down from his grandfather, with manufacturing so large that they were producing in Germany on the machines his grandfather had build generations ago. Now there's a long product cycle.

I turned down the discount retailer, but the truth is, I wouldn't have been able to do it anyway and still make money. The decision wasn't as hard as I like to make it out to be.

My escape from cold calling was short-lived. Still, with the help of my friend, neighbor, and rep, I saw that the big boys were penetrable with a little persistence. My friend had a knack for getting through to whomever she wanted, and I had to attribute it to the fact that she was perhaps the most polite, the friendliest, the most enthusiastic, and the kindest person I have ever met. I didn't have to be that archetypal pushy entrepreneur, who is always doing the fast-talking hard sell, to be successful. This is the new millennium. My number-one buyer at a premier national retailer is the sweetest, most beautiful, most polite, and most delightful person you might ever meet. She gets whatever she wants out of us, including bare-knuckle pricing, by being so incredibly nice. If you're going to do business in this arena, you had better learn from the beginning, niceness counts. Don't think for a minute that you can swagger, be short, pushy, or high-pressure. It's actually a pretty small world and your reputation is all you have. Once that's gone, you're done.

I went back to the phones with a new passion and actually started to see some results. What I invariably discovered was that the people on the other end always wanted to know what my Web site address was and would almost always navigate to it while I was on the phone with them, evaluating me and my product as we spoke. Boy, it was time to set up a decent Web site! I put all cold calling on hold and tried to figure out a way to do it with no budget.

How to Build a Killer Web Site with Almost No Money and No Knowledge of HTML

I was out of money, and I knew absolutely nothing about how to build a Web site. I had at this point just a home page with a photo and a contact number. I didn't know anything about HTML, or HyperText Markup Language—the computer code gibberish that tech savants use to create Web pages—which meant that I probably would have to pay somebody to do that work. I had at least registered my domain name successfully, and I hit the Web running, searching and Googling every kind of Web site building program I could.

Web Site Hosting Versus Web Site Building: What's the Difference?
The Web site host is defined as the server that hosts your Web site. Usually a Web site host won't help you do anything to build your Web site. A Web site builder is usually coupled with a hosting service that offers you some

kind of template or software program that enables you to build your Web site by yourself with or without knowledge of HTML.

ESSENTIAL CRITERIA FOR EVALUATING WEB SITE BUILDING AND HOSTING PACKAGES

- **Cost.**
- **Hosting Service:** What is the total space you're allocated?
- **Web Site Design:** How easy or hard is it for you personally to handle their program?
- **Communication Tools:** Does it provide you with an efficient e-mail option with multiple e-mail addresses utilizing your domain name? Can you integrate them through a POP3 server with your favorite e-mail program, like Outlook? Does it offer fancy extras like newsletters, a customer-tracking database, and surveys?
- **Marketing:** Does it have built in an essential tool for submitting your site to major search engines and optimizing your ranking in those sites? This is critical. People need to be able to find you. Does it provide you with customized marketing reports so you can learn and grow?
- **Customer Support:** Can you actually talk to a human being, or are you only able to communicate through e-mail or, worse yet, a trouble-shooting template? If you can't find a phone number under the Contact Us tab, you're probably on your own.
- **E-commerce:** Does it have an integrated secure shopping cart function? How many catalog items can you list at what cost? Does it offer credit card processing, PayPal, or both? What do those services cost?

About this time, my husband accepted a job offer. It was the beginning of the end of his illustrious career. We weren't willing to move from our small town—mostly because our school system had one of the best special education programs in the state—and so my husband's opportunities were limited. Still, he was lucky to get any kind of job in his industry because it had taken such a monstrous and devastating hit that almost all of his peers could not find work. My husband went back to work, at a job he hated, for a company almost as strapped as my start-up, while I juggled all the demands of starting a business and assuming 90 percent of the duties of raising our two little boys.

I started my search for a Web site builder that would enable me to create my Web site for almost nothing, with absolutely no knowledge of HTML. This was not difficult to do. This was a number of years ago, so the options

I settled on then probably have evolved since. There are a few criteria you need to evaluate to determine just how much of a Web site you need and which services you absolutely need to pay for.

POPULAR SMALL BUSINESS DO-IT-YOURSELF WEB SITE BUILDERS

- www.bigstep.com
- www.citymax.com
- www.homestead.com
- www.domaindirect.com

GREAT FREE RESOURCES FOR DEVELOPING YOUR WEB SITE

- **www.webmonkey.com:** Self-titled as "The Web Developer's Resource," a great site for learning the basics of HTML, along with tons of other stuff you may never need to know but is still a lot of fun.
- **www.reallybig.com:** Great resource for free clip art, counters, backgrounds, fonts, icons, and tips and tricks.
- **www.pageresource.com:** Lots and lots of resources, including a free HTML tutorial
- **www.websitetips.com:** Your one-stop shop for an invaluable list of links to everything you need to know and more about do-it-yourself Web design.

E-COMMERCE: SELLING PRODUCTS ON YOUR WEB SITE AND HOW TO RECEIVE PAYMENT

- PayPal: This is particularly popular on eBay, but don't expect to do any serious business elsewhere using this service. It allows anybody with an e-mail address to pay you for retail purchases with or without a major credit card. It offers an alternative to applying for a traditional merchant account.
- Most of the good Web site building sites will offer you both credit card processing and PayPal choices when setting up your Web site. The decision is yours as to which service you choose. Having an online merchant account will usually allow you to process not only your online orders but also your wholesale and trade-show orders by accessing their processing portal online without the added expense of purchasing or leasing a terminal.
- Make sure you select a Web site hosting package that offers a secure

shopping cart service, which provides extra security to your customers when using their credit cards online.

I settled on Bigstep and opted to pay for the support of one of their design specialists to walk me through the program. It was maddening at first, but with perseverance I developed a knack for handling all the complicated options. I became so confident that I went to Webmonkey, picked up some HTML tips, and was adding lots of colored, bold, and italicized fonts just for the fun of it. I bought a reasonably priced digital camera, took pictures of my products, and put them on the Web site, then carefully completed the process necessary to submit my site to major search engines like Google, Overture, and Yahoo!

Be sure to check out the proper procedure for submitting your Web site for inclusion in each directory. Most of the top search directories require you to hand-submit, or turn in an actual hard-copy application for inclusion on their search engine. Some web-building services, like Bigstep, will do this for you. Then put as much effort as possible in coming up with your meta tags, or key words that may be searched, directing customers to your site. When I first submitted my Web site, I left out the meta tag word "Wuvits." People went to the web and typed "Wuvits" into the search bar and I never came up! You just can't have too many meta tags.

TIPS FOR ADDING PHOTOGRAPHS TO YOUR WEB SITE

- Bigger files are not better. Just because you have a 6-megapixel camera doesn't mean that you should format every picture to the highest resolution possible. Big image files take a very long time to load when customers are looking at your Web site. If it takes too long, they'll lose interest and click off.
- When formatting your photos for the Web, save the image as a .tif file instead of a .jpeg, or an interchangeable file format, which means people can view them in different software photo applications. They load quicker.
- Having a professional photographer take your photos is great, but it can get very expensive very quickly, with a typical half-day shoot costing up to $800. Invest in a tripod for your camera, set up a place in your basement or garage, hang a white paper backdrop, and take your own photos using a consistent light setup for every photo, even if they're taken weeks apart.
- Sometimes you can get local portrait photographers to take your product photos inexpensively, for hundreds of dollars less than a

normal product photographer would charge. See what they can do for you, especially around prom or homecoming, when they are in the studio for weeks anyway.

- Nobody uses film anymore. There are a few professional holdouts who will insist they use this medium. Forget about it. The extra cost of digitizing a film image will erase any savings you may get from using a film photographer.
- Don't post a scanned image to the Internet. This is an image you have scanned into your computer from an original hard-copy photo on your scanner. These are just typically really big files that take impossibly long to load, with sub-par results.

When it comes to designing your Web site, stick to this advice: Keep It Simple! Especially if you don't have any products to sell. One to two pages max ought to do it when you're just starting out. If you just have one page, maybe you can afford to hire a professional to make it look as good as possible. Enough cannot be said about the importance of a good Web site. You are so lucky you don't have to invest tens of thousands of dollars in a brick-and-mortar store anymore to have a respectable presence in our business community.

Think of your Web site as your virtual storefront. It's the door your customers come into on their way to meet you. It's probably the single most important factor prospective customers and vendors alike will use to evaluate you.

If it's professional looking and exciting, they will want to work with you, even if it's just you and your computer, working out of the basement while your children watch *Teletubbies* episodes. Your customers won't even know your situation as they pull up your Web site while talking to you on the phone and say, "Great Web site!"

My first effort at building my own Web site was not great. I used too much information in it with too many unnecessary pages. Still, I managed to get some retailers I was cold-calling interested enough while looking at it to ask me to send them a catalog. I didn't have a catalog—I only had one product! I knew I needed to invest in at least one piece of professional marketing collateral that I could send to these retailers when I got lucky enough that they asked me for more information. In order to do that, I had to hire a graphic designer.

6

YOU'RE GONNA WUVIT

I had an acquaintance who was a first-rate graphic designer. She normally charged $2,500 to design a simple product brochure, but for me she would cut that in half and do it for $1,250. I couldn't imagine spending what was probably the last $1,250 I had from my original $20,000 budget on just the design fees of a brochure, not including the printing costs, but I saw her work and decided I had to do something to promote my brand in the marketplace professionally.

It was just one of the many, many money decisions that would eat me up inside, because money was so tight. Just years later, I would be writing Purchase Orders worth $50,000 without even batting an eye. Even the cheap things in business, I discovered, cost so much more than I was used to paying in my normal life. I was getting essentially a piece of paper for $1,250 when normally I would have gotten a new washer and dryer for that. That was equal to a full year tuition for my son's preschool. I could have bought two months' worth of groceries with that money. After two days of pure agony she showed me a design that was brilliant in design and simplicity, with the simple catchphrase that would eventually contribute to making my first million: "You're gonna Wuvit."

Graphic designers are highly creative people, who are sometimes sensitive and emotional to a fault. I learned the hard way that you need to treat creative people with kid gloves. Remember that the work they do for you is seen as a personal extension of themselves. If you're going to be critical of their work, they're going to take it as personal criticism. Now, as a matter of course, I always start with praise for the efforts of any work a designer does for me, before I make my reasonable and politely phrased requests for them to change it. Creative people are motivated by praise and approval, and I've found that a little bit of extra care in these departments will result in a superior finished product. But I didn't learn this for years. I was on a crash course to disaster with the first highly creative person I ever worked with, a clash that would threaten my brand and the future of my company.

Something they never teach you in business school, at least not adequately, I think, is the critical importance of people management skills in the success of any million-dollar venture. As a mommy, don't worry, you're already a natural at this. You're no doubt confronted daily with the genius manipulations of your two-year-old, who understands exactly how to use guilt, reward, temperamental outbursts, and defiance to his or her own benefit. Though people grow up, they never really change. In my experience, the height to which you climb the ladder of success in the world is completely dependent on your ability to become divorced from and impervious to emotional knee-jerk reactions. If you can't separate business decisions from personal emotions, you're never going to become a millionaire.

I know it's hard to do, but you will always need to retain the appearance of an emotionless, calm eye of the storm, in the middle of a chaotic and fluid maelstrom of people, challenges, deadlines, demands, and an acute lack of money, if you want to be successful. Did you notice I said *appearance*? Everybody's human, with all the feelings that go along with it, but the expression of feelings must be reserved only for that moment when any business dealing reaches critical mass, for example, when you've done all that you can and all that is left to do is to scream to get results or revenge.

The Real Value of Professional Design Work

I had a finished brochure in front of me, and I couldn't believe how the investment of $1,250 could so radically transform the image I had of myself, my company, and my product. I went from a trifold brochure I laid out and printed off my own computer to a first-rate piece of work. I took it to everyone I could, my neighbors, my manufacturer, my reps, and they all remarked with the same enthusiasm, "Wow! You are somebody!" My husband thought this was a totally frivolous and exorbitant expenditure, but I could see what it did to the people when they saw it. It was a formal declaration to the world: I had arrived!

The lesson is that this a necessary cost of start-up. When done right, a professional brochure will immediately establish your credibility and brand in the marketplace. Don't blow it by doing it halfway. Don't waste money overdoing it. Each piece of marketing collateral you develop will become obsolete faster than the technology du jour. You just want to make a statement; you don't need to tell the whole story.

One company I know invested way too much at start-up on marketing collateral. They had an extraordinary Web site, with music and lots of flash and splash. It was awesome. They were software developers, so their Web site had to be spectacular. They had hired a top-notch graphic designer and paid thousands just for the design of their logo. Then they had produced every kind of advertising collateral you can imagine, from glossy brochures to printed coffee cups and pens. We went to their open house and found all the stuff lying around free for the taking by nonpaying friends and family members in a lavishly furnished office with an elaborate buffet that must have cost hundreds. Guests looked at each other and commented secretly, "Wow! Look at the money." It's not such a long story. They were bankrupt in six months.

WORKING WITH GRAPHIC ARTISTS AND DESIGNERS—EVERYTHING YOU NEED TO KNOW

- Find a gifted designer, whatever it takes. It's probably truer here than anywhere, you get what you pay for.
- Review a designer's portfolio of work before commissioning them to do a job. They may be great, with wonderful references, but their style may just not be compatible with yours.
- Remember that you are paying a designer for their vision and skill, not their time. Don't be frustrated if the designer delivers something brilliant to you that took an hour to execute with a big bill. Just be grateful that the design is brilliant.
- If the work is not brilliant, tell the designer. Every reasonable designer should work with you at no extra charge to get to what you really want.
- Try to avoid this situation by sitting down with the designer before the job and talking in as much detail as possible about what you see the end product looking like or what you want to communicate. Make crude drawings, use broad adjectives like "happy," "green," "natural." This is a language designers are used to speaking in.
- Bear in mind that designers typically require you to pay half up front and half upon completion of any job. You are going to work hard at the beginning if you want to set up any terms of thirty days net with any designer—meaning you'll have thirty days to pay them for any work they do—and that will only be on the remaining half due upon completion. Don't count on this happening unless you have a good relationship with the designer.
- Remember: You own the trademarks and copyrights on any of the marketing materials that a designer creates for you. It is absolutely necessary for you to execute a contract prior to working with any designer that states this simple fact.

- Never pay a designer the remaining half due at completion until you get a disk containing the computer file of the work. Be scrupulous about this. If not, you could find yourself with nothing to show for expensive marketing collateral you invested in if your relationship should suddenly end, which is not unusual with creative people. Make sure you receive all the proper files of the work, including the programs in which they created it, as well as a PDF file for your viewing.
- Don't ever give a designer carte blanche or you could get a bill that will ruin you. Make sure you commission all work with a written Purchase Order that spells out specifically what you want done and what price you've agreed to pay for it. Always ask for an invoice from a designer, and file it as a record that you own that work.

Cost-Saving Benefits to Working with a Designer

Designers have established relationships with all kinds of vendors, who extend them special pricing in appreciation of their regular business. Ask your designer to pass these savings on to you. Make sure you take advantage of these discounts by asking to be billed directly for any services you contract through your designer. This would include 10 to 20 percent savings at:

- Printers
- Photographers
- Modeling agencies
- Paper stock suppliers

I knew I had a good brochure that I could proudly send to prospective customers from cold calls, that I could distribute to reps to hand out to retailers they visited, and that I could give to buyers I met face-to-face at trade shows. Instilled with a new confidence—Web site: check, brochure: check—I was ready to relaunch my sales campaign, dreading all over again the two hours or twenty calls, whichever came first, that I would reserve for cold calling. To my relief, I received two offers in the mail from people looking to represent me as freelance marketers.

Marketing Company Number 1 actually sent me a business card, with a trifold brochure—no letterhead—with a yellow sticky note stuck to the whole mess saying "so-and-so told me you were looking for a marketer, give me a call." He followed up the next day by calling me, but I couldn't bring myself to tell him the truth, that I would never employ someone to market me who marketed himself with a sticky note.

Marketing Company Number 2 had a slightly better approach. He had actually written and self-published a book on marketing, and he sent me a copy, complete with an invoice, along with his business card and a note on letterhead asking if he could offer his services to me. This was a novel way to get my business, if I could have actually afforded it at the time. I thought it would be informative to read his book about self-marketing, but I couldn't get past the cover design, which was an amateur attempt to create a concept better left in the hands of a professional graphic designer. I knew I was ahead of the game already. Even to this day, it's amazing to me how many marketing and branding firms I come across that can't do as good a job for me as I did for myself.

Fortunately, women often already have a talent for making things look attractive. Maybe it's all those design shows we've watched on TV, maybe it's a gene only women possess, but women can almost invariably put together an attractive trade-show booth or a product brochure with only some creative ideas and a tiny budget. Apply those same creative ideas you had when putting together your baby's nursery to a brochure and you'll no doubt find the same success at creating a warm and appealing look.

Marketing: The Process of Bringing Goods or Services to Market

As soon as your information goes out in Dun & Bradstreet, you'll start to get all kinds of offers and correspondence from people looking to sell you every kind of service under the sun. Maybe one of these will be a direct-marketing group. It was about this time that I got a call from one of them. The man who contacted me was very, very nice. He had the sharpest brochures and advertising collateral I've seen, including a videotape I never had time to watch. I knew something was wrong when he was unable to send me an e-mail, because my e-mail server identified all e-mail from his company, based in Kansas, as spam, rejecting it, which was not a good sign.

He wanted to sell my product through TV direct marketing. You know all those commercials you sit up watching in the middle of the night when you can't sleep, for those handy-dandy must-have items you can't live without? He thought mine could be one of them. How did he know? I asked. He'd been to my Web site, he answered. Wow. Somebody was looking at my Web site!

I was really tired of the cold calling going nowhere, so I seriously considered him and his case for taking my product direct to consumers through thirty-second commercial spots on cable TV stations across the country. I'm sure every direct-marketing company is different, with a different package deal to sell you, but this is what he was selling me:

- As long as my product could support a 400 percent markup, I was a candidate for direct TV marketing. Of course that meant that if it cost me five dollars to make and I could sell it for twenty-five dollars, I had a shot.
- I would pay his company a minimum of $7,000 to $10,000 to create the thirty-second spot to be aired.
- They would take possession of the product on consignment, which meant that I didn't get paid until they got paid. Of the product that they would sell, they would get a percentage, which, when figured out, left me with two-dollar profit on my five-dollar cost, before all the other incidental costs like airtime.
- In addition to the cost of producing the spot, I would have to foot the cost for all airtime from the cable stations. I've since learned this can be very cheap or very expensive, depending on the market you're in and the airtime you're buying.

I admit to being tempted for a brief moment to go down this path, mostly because he was so good at convincing me that I had the next big thing! You can't help being human and getting excited every time someone shows enthusiasm for your product. Putting all vanity and flattery aside, I could not see making money on this deal at that point, and I let him know it. That was officially the end of all the naive hopes I had of finding someone who would magically transform me from mommy to millionaire with a wave of a marketing wand. I knew then without a doubt:

Nobody could, or would, for that matter, sell my product better than me.

My Wuvits were ready to ship to all my Chicago trade-show buyers, and I had to find a way to ship them. Though the United States Postal Service is improving every day, almost all professional businesses use UPS (United Parcel Service), FedEx, or DHL. These services can often be cheaper than regular mail, and the convenience of having a commercial account that can provide you with tracking information for every package, free insurance, daily pickup, online processing, and even a free thermal printer to print all your labels cannot be undervalued. Everything is negotiable, and many of these rates can be negotiated right up front with a salesperson from whatever service you choose. With just a phone call, you can get sent to you a published catalog of all their shipping rates and tier discounts, and you can go to work from there. Having a UPS shipper number and a FedEx shipper number is non-negotiable. If you absolutely need an overnight delivery, even if it's going to China, don't ever send it anything but FedEx. On the one hand, using those popular pack-and-ship stores everywhere might be convenient, but you'll soon discover that you are paying a dear price for that convenience, anywhere from a couple of bucks to ten bucks or more to send one package. On the other hand, it costs you nothing to set up your own business account in your home.

EVERYTHING YOU NEED TO KNOW ABOUT SHIPPING

UPS: You can set up an account with UPS that will allow you to process shipments, print labels, and track packages right from their Web site at www.ups.com. You can find contact information on the Web site. A UPS salesperson will visit you and get you set up with an account, even providing you with a thermal printer for printing professional labels.

FedEx: In addition to a UPS account, you're going to need a FedEx account. Visit their Web site at www.fedex.com to learn how you can contact a sales rep to set you up. Nobody gets packages to their destination overnight throughout the world like FedEx. Write down your FedEx account number in your day planner, because you'll need to refer to it often.

DHL: This is another carrier choice that is aggressively pricing its services to bring competition to the marketplace. You might want to check them out at www.dhl.com.

Since my manufacturer was also a fulfillment house—or a business that handles the entire ordering process for products, including manufacturing, warehousing, packing, mailing, and record management—it was a natural for me to use them to handle my shipping and fulfilling. They could offer me discounts on shipping that I just couldn't secure myself, because of the volume of shipping they did each day. They charged me $2.50 to fill a box and ship it once I e-mailed an invoice, so I didn't even have to store product in my basement. Since they were still sewing, they didn't charge me any warehousing fees at the time, but that would come later. It was still much cheaper than what it would have cost for me to rent my own warehouse and pay for utilities, maintenance, and insurance.

I grew to like the office manager who had told me at our first meeting not to get too excited: "We see dozens of people like you every day who don't go anywhere." I can still remember the incredulous look on her face when I came back from Chicago with $3,000 worth of orders for Wuvits. I showed her the brochure that my graphic designer had just finished, and I could see by her wide eyes, look of surprise, and comments that "this is first-rate!" that I had arrived! She admitted to me then that she had taken one of my Wuvits home and had become "addicted." She was converted from skeptic to one of the most passionate Wuvit lovers on earth in the three minutes it took to heat it up and place it against her chest.

"You need to get some boxes for shipping," she told me.

"Where do I get those?"

"Look on the ThomasRegister. Or try Uline."

"What's Uline?"

"Just go to uline.com and you'll find out. You need to get boxes that hold a dozen Wuvits. You want to make sure they fit as snugly as possible in the box. If not, they'll move around during shipping and the box will split open. They have hundreds and hundreds of in-stock boxes. Measure your product and pick one out that will hold twelve Wuvits as tightly as possible."

. . . .

ULINE

You're going to need boxes for all those packages you'll be shipping. Uline is the one resource small business owners turn to before they start making their own custom boxes. You can set up an account with them, and they offer next-day delivery on almost everything, anywhere. Visit them at www.uline.com and request a catalog. You'll be amazed at the breadth of products you can get.

. . . .

"Okay," I said, as I proceeded to discover the wonders of Uline online. Uline is a great resource for a company just starting out. You typically, but not always, will pay a little more money to get their remarkable assortment of products shipped to you with small minimums the next day at a reasonable cost. When you need to order custom boxes, which will happen someday, going to a local packager is the best choice. It took me quite a while to get custom box manufacturers to even call me back. Eventually, you'll find a good salesperson who will work hard for your business and appreciate it.

I wasn't getting anywhere in the cold-calling department, and when I saw hundreds of the 2,000 Wuvits I was paying to have made go out the door of the fulfillment company, I thought, *I gotta get to another trade show!* It was spring, and I started surfing the Web looking for the next big trade show that I could find that I could actually drive to with the set I had used for my first show in Chicago. Boy, I was feeling glad then that we had sold the fancy luxury car a year ago in favor of keeping the big old SUV. Not only could my kids throw up on the dark green leather interior without my breaking into a cold sweat and having a nervous breakdown—which happened regularly when they smooshed and dripped neon blue superstaining Superman ice cream all over the light tan carpeting and seat backs of my Toyota Avalon—but I could load it up with all the cumbersome boxes and furniture necessary for me to pursue my new career in schlepping. Suddenly I looked at all my neighbors' assorted SUVs with a new longing and appreciation; I seemed to be the only person out of a neighborhood of two hundred families full of soccer moms and weekend gardeners who had a legitimate need to drive one of these big gas-guzzling status-mobiles.

I thought I hit gold when, during my random searches on the Internet between mopping the floor, doing uncountable loads of laundry, and basically trying to keep my two young boys from killing each other or themselves, I discovered AmericasMart in Atlanta. Wow, that looked like an impressive venue.

AMERICASMART—ATLANTA

It's the largest wholesale marketplace in the world, consisting of three buildings totaling more than 4.2 million square feet, featuring permanent and temporary showrooms. Twenty-three separate markets are represented, and they attract more than 303,000 attendees from every U.S. state and over seventy-two countries. There are gifts, home furnishings, rugs, apparel, baby goods, jewelry, accessories, food, et cetera. Its Buyer's Guide has a circulation of approximately 250,000 registered retail buyers in the U.S., including everyone from small, independent retailers to major department store buyers.

I called them up immediately and learned that there were two major markets in every trade-show venue across the U.S.: July, when buyers came to make holiday purchases, and January, when buyers came to spend holiday cash. I remembered master rep's advice, that I had a gift item perfectly suited for the holidays and that buyers would be looking for it in July. Could I afford to go to this? I did the math and found out. I had lost money in Chicago. I had spent at least $3,000 on the booth space and trade-show set, not even counting the travel expenses like gas, hotel, and food. I had done $3,000 in sales, but that was revenue—not profit. It didn't take much number crunching to see that I had to make at least $5,000 in profits alone just to cover the cost of going to a show—or to break even. That meant in a very crude formula that I had to do $10,000 at the show in Atlanta to make it worthwhile. Was that even possible? I didn't see how. I kicked it around for months, calling the sales rep and asking for an application to exhibit, but when I got it, I just stared at in fear, along with the dwindling amount of money in my bank account, left over from the initial investment of $20,000.

Now let me be clear—I'm being honest about this $20,000 figure as the minimum investment you really need to start the smallest business venture. I've seen all kinds of books and stories and magazine articles and late-night direct-marketing TV commercials telling me how these entrepreneurs started with a $50 investment and turned it into a multi-million real estate venture, or eBay store, or even mega-store craft and hobby chain. That is not the truth. I could do the same thing and say I started a million-dollar company on a free sewing machine. I'm not going to be dishonest with you in an effort to sell you anything that isn't reality, which would inevitably result in your failure. You can see from my own story how fast I went through $20,000, on an item that cost practically nothing, in an office in my basement, with almost no overhead. I was staring at the opportunity of attending one of the world's biggest trade shows, at the biggest trade-show gift-buying season, at the critical end of my $20,000. Remember those lovely little shiny credit cards I had applied for and gotten, hiding them away in a locked drawer in my office for a rainy day? It was time to break them out.

I didn't decide this immediately. I looked at these cards longingly, with all the fear and loathing of credit card debt I had been trained to exhibit from my husband. I didn't understand the difference between good debt and bad debt—and wouldn't in fact for more than a year—all debt was *BAD,* especially the credit card kind. Still, I had cards with 0 percent interest for purchases in the first year. Surely I could justify that. That was free money. I hemmed and hawed, called and quit, kicked it around and debated, until I found out that AmericasMart not only took credit cards for all the exhibiting costs, but almost every exhibitor there used credit to pay for their space. With no new sales happening and my money gone on the production run, I called them at the last minute, was given a booth in a really good location that somebody had backed out of at the last minute, and filled up my truck—to drive off to Atlanta.

I was only slightly less frightened of going to Atlanta than I had been about Chicago. I had to drive to Atlanta all by myself. I had family in Atlanta, so at least I wouldn't be totally alone, and I could stay with them, saving hotel costs.

Driving your product into a show is still the best bet for any start-up business.

Later I would ship my set and products freight and fly in instead of drive, but that was at least a year from this point. When driving your stuff in, the hardest part is waiting in the marshalling yards for your turn to be shouted at by a burly Teamster with a cigar in his mouth to "get your truck moving, lady!" You end up backing into tight loading docks, with loud shouting dockworkers hurting your ears and smelly car exhaust clogging your lungs, as you wait for someone to unload your stuff and take it up to your booth. Don't ever tip these people. They're probably making twice the amount of money you are.

I had paid my graphic designer another $300 to come up with a big sign, which I posted on an easel—right up in the front of the booth, where everybody could see it—capturing the essence of the brochure she had designed, telling people to "sell something every *body* wants!" I set myself up in a tiny half booth, which was only seven feet by eight feet, and proceeded to sell Wuvits like crazy. I couldn't believe it! I had left half my set at home. I had only brought the absolute bare minimum, and my booth looked like it. Buyers didn't care. They only wanted to sell something every *body* wanted. I showed them the money, and they showed me theirs. I was so busy, I was asking people to write their own orders. Some of my family members in Atlanta came to help me and couldn't believe it themselves.

I had no idea how good of a show I was having until other exhibitors came up to me and said, "Wow! You're killin' 'em!" I knew I was on to something when another kind of rep showed up and started giving me a whole new song and dance I'd never heard. He would be the third of a long line of hucksters who were selling me something that turned out to be too good to be true.

This man leased a permanent showroom in another one of the buildings that make up AmericasMart. Most trade shows are made up of both permanent and temporary exhibitors. Permanent exhibitors lease showroom space year round, much like retail stores that buyers come to to buy wholesale. The permanent exhibitors usually sell products well established in the marketplace. Temporary showrooms are the little booths you lease for the week, the length of the temporary show. He had been walking the temporaries looking for what was hot and new in the industry and was stopped at my booth by the crowd in front of it that impeded his ability to get through.

It's conventional wisdom that buyers look to the temporaries for what's hot and new and the permanents for what's old and established—so don't start out with a permanent.

Getting Your Product into a Permanent Showroom

I was on the second from the last day of the show, and I had already reached that magical sales number I had previously thought was unattainable: $10,000! This new rep couldn't believe that I had done those kinds of sales in this tiny booth, and he wanted to get a piece of the action. He spent the next day hanging around my booth watching me make sales and selling me on how I had to move my stuff up to their permanent showroom. He promised me he would turn me into a millionaire in months, if I would plunk down $1,500 a month to rent my tiny area in his showroom and pay him an additional 15 percent commission on any sales. I was a little skeptical, especially when I looked at his shoes beneath his nice Ralph Lauren button-down and neatly pressed tan khakis—they were old scuffed-up sneakers that had seen better days. I'm totally of the school of thought that tells you that everything you need to know about somebody you can learn instantly from their shoes. Even given the fact that comfortable shoes are acceptable at trade shows, these were not only comfortable; they were also old and dirty. I think I could have saved myself countless headaches and thousands of dollars if I had only stuck invariably to this rule: Don't do business with people with bad shoes.

At the end of business that day on the temporary floor, I went up to the permanent building where his showroom was. These showrooms are always open later, and all the buyers crowd into them at dinnertime for free appetizers and cocktails. His place was no exception. I strolled through the merchandise he displayed, asking myself, would I buy any of it? The answer was no, but I couldn't admit it then. I was just enthralled with the idea of this guy turning me into millionaire. I met his partner/mother, who told me she was a former VP with a very famous cosmetics company based in New York, and they filled my head with every kind of intoxicating story of how they had done $100,000 deals there today with major retailers and catalogs and that the lousy $10,000 I had made that week was "peanuts" compared to what they would do for me. Surely $1,500 a month lease rate for the top of a tiny table they showed me could be mine was worth it? I don't know if it was the wine or their expert salesmanship, but I found myself taking out my checkbook. In a moment of sobriety, I said to myself, *Stop—can't you even try to negotiate something better?*

"I don't know," I answered them. "Can't I get some kind of test first?"

"We don't do that," the rep answered me. "You don't know how many temporary exhibitors would kill for the opportunity we're giving you. I got them standing in line. You'd better take advantage of this offer now. It's no skin off my nose. I got people waiting behind you. I just think you have a great product with a lot of opportunity. In fact, we're getting ready to go to Los Angeles for the big show there immediately after this. I got five other exhibitors down there begging me to rep their product at that show. See that linen tablecloth there? We sell that to Barbara Bush!"

"Okay," I said, looking down at my open checkbook and getting a glimpse of his old, tired shoes. "How about you take my product out to the show in L.A.? I just had an awesome show here. If you have even half as good a show, I'll sign the lease for a year at fifteen hundred dollars a month." I thought for sure he would come back with the orders to pay for this lease, since I certainly didn't have the money left in my budget.

"Ha! Ten thousand dollars is peanuts. I'll sell that easily. At the end of this show, just pack up your whole set. I really want that big sign you got. And your microwave. You can ship it all to our L.A. showroom. I just did a deal worth two hundred thousand dollars with Neiman Marcus. You won't believe the amount of money you'll make with us. Just write me a check for fifteen hundred dollars and I'll do it."

I was just so excited and pumped up on the fantastic show I just had that I thought it was a sure thing. I wrote the check and then spent another $600 express shipping him all the stuff he needed, including the sign, samples, and the microwave. I got back to Michigan, all wound up thinking about the tens of thousands of dollars' worth of orders he was going to come back with and telling my husband how lucky I was to have somebody with these kinds of connections in the industry repping me. Did he understand that we were on the verge of richness? To reward myself for my accomplishment, I decided it was a day for hitting the beach with my kids. I hauled them down, cell phone in tow, with the truckload of stuff required when squiring little kids to a day of "careless" fun.

What happened next was another one of those watershed moments of my becoming a Mommy Millionaire, of which I'm not proud. My cell phone rang, and it was this rep in California. He was having a crisis. The only thing that stood in his way of making me into a millionaire in the next forty-eight hours was a microwave. Apparently, my microwave wasn't delivered to his showroom, the show started tomorrow, and he had appointments with the nation's biggest and best retailers. I had to get him a microwave immediately.

"But I'm in Michigan and you're there in L.A. Just how am I supposed to do that?"

"That's your problem," he answered. "Call Lowe's and ask them to deliver it."

I panicked, looking into my phone's caller ID to get the L.A. area code so that I could call directory assistance in search of a Lowe's, when I realized I had lost sight of one of my sons in the breaking waves of Lake Michigan. I threw down the phone and ran into the water, screaming my son's name. Other parents could tell I was distressed and started to help me. After a few seconds of looking, which felt like hours, I found him fifty yards down the beach, chest-high in the water and being impelled out farther by the riptide as he laughed, jumped, and splashed, completely oblivious to the danger. I swore at that moment again that no business distraction would ever be so urgent and critical that I would get so worked up over it that it would compromise my ability to look after my kids.

I was even angrier with myself when this rep returned from his big show on the West Coast with a total of $2,500 of orders for me. He never returned my microwave, my product samples, or my invaluable $300 sign, not to mention the $1,500 check I had given him. It was an inexplicably bad show, he explained, with poor traffic. Plus, he had just relocated his showroom, so his buyers obviously had a hard time finding him. Still, he insisted that if I only paid him the $1,500 for the showroom lease space, he would sell my product that week on his return to the big prestigious catalog buyers he had appointments with in Atlanta. I didn't fall for that.

If you learn nothing else in reading this book, learn this: Nothing is so important—no phone call, no appointment, no work crisis, no urgent e-mail received on your ubiquitous BlackBerry—that it should interfere with an hour of quality time spent with your kids.

I realized I had sold 1,300 of the 2,000 Wuvits I had contracted in only seven months. Almost all of the sales were from trade shows, though I expended about ten times the time and effort on cold calling. I determined that cold calling, at least at this point, was a losing proposition.

Going Direct to Retail

I needed to find an entirely new way to sell Wuvits. What if I took my product myself direct from manufacturing to retail? The idea came to me as I took my kids to the local mall on one of the hottest days in July for a playful romp on the center's magical treehouse play center in air-conditioned comfort. As I sat there in a narcotic daze of Starbucks cappuccino and contented children's laughter, I watched older women selling Tupperware off one of the mall's retail carts or kiosks and bells started to ring in my head.

I called the mall's leasing manager and asked him if I could arrange for a weekend test of my product at one of the unoccupied carts. There were plenty of these, being it was the middle of July, the dog days of the retailing season. He told me that they never did this, but he reluctantly agreed after I showed up in person with a free Wuvit, and after I wrote him a check for $350. He could probably tell I wasn't going to sell painted cockroaches with your child's name applied with laser technology. He asked for some kind of merchandising picture for approval, and I showed him a picture of my Chicago trade-show set. He agreed, but not without giving me his expert opinion. He told me that I would never be successful. Nobody would want to buy this at a mall, was his conclusion. According to him, my markup was not even near the markup necessary to sell at a kiosk. Apparently you needed some really cheap junk, straight from China, that you bought for a quarter and sold for twenty-five dollars to make it work in that business. He told me that a good day for sales in July at one of his carts was three sales. "Three sales!" I said. "How can anybody make enough money to justify it?" He assured me it was only because of outlandish margins that anybody survived in the business. Instead of selling these silly Wuvits, I should be looking at mini–remote cars, hermit crabs, hand lotions, or the oldies but goodies, grains of rice with your name written microscopically on them and the infamous "chop-chop" machines.

I leased the cart in the mall, spent an entire Friday night after the mall closed at 9:00 P.M. schlepping in all my boxes while my husband babysat the kids at home. I set up my kiosk nicely, filling it up with as much inventory as I could fit in my truck. Wuvits of five different fabric styles were piled in very neat stacks, like the Gap. The leasing manager stopped by with a sign he had had made for me, wished me luck, and told me I would be considered successful if I made seven sales in two days. "Don't get too excited," he added with a jab. "We see people like you come and go all the time." Where had I heard that before?

I arrived at the mall early the next morning. It was the last weekend in July, and we were experiencing record heat. In Michigan, everyone is just minutes away from the beach, so on a hot sunny day in July you can bet that's where you'll find everyone. Nobody was in the mall.

I sold twenty Wuvits at twenty dollars each in the first four hours I was there. One of the male buyers laughed when he bought two and said, "Jeez, if you can sell me two of these on the hottest day of the year, just think what you can do at the holidays!"

Of course! That's what I would do. I went from doing a random test marketing of my product to rewriting my business plan in four hours. Other people who stopped gave me great advice, like more patterns, more masculine, more feminine, more this or more that. It was the best $350 I ever spent in my life.

My two-day test was a resounding success. At the end of the second day I had a visit from the leasing manager. I told him about the number of Wuvits I sold, and he couldn't believe it. He was excited and suggested I look right away into franchising my concept. Franchising? I didn't know anything about it, but I would get a real lesson—the hard way—in just months.

I took the information I had learned about fabric offerings and decided I needed to offer more high-end selections to customers. I had the business card of that salesman from the nation's premier home fashions manufacturer I had met in Chicago and called him up. Before I knew it, I was meeting him at his very swanky showroom at the Merchandise Mart, being treated to an elegant lunch buffet they were putting on to attract buyers who were there attending the huge office furniture trade-show event NeoCon. I was in love with all the fabrics I could choose.

Quality Design: Distinguishing Yourself in the Marketplace

I understood what offering all these fabulous designs would do for my product's appeal in the marketplace, effectively merging home decorator accent with spa therapy. I used all my feminine assets to take the salesman to the mat and negotiated a price on the fabric that was so low that the VP of the company, whom I met in their really swanky New York showroom years later, told me it was lower than what anybody else paid.

I was so inspired by the designs that I started to see opportunity in an area that was becoming an important cultural trend and was still an underserved niche in the marketplace: pink ribbon design. My mother-in-law and all her sisters had battled breast cancer and I had seen the qualities it took to get through the heroic battle of their lives: faith, hope, and love. I came up with a sketch for a design and asked my salesman if he could do a custom run of a fabric using my exclusive design. He said yes but wondered why anybody would want to do something featuring a simple pink ribbon. I pushed him and his designers at their New York studio for months to execute the vision I had in my mind, while all the time they questioned why I was even doing it. I was fueled by the same inexplicable passion that pushed me to create my first Wuvit prototype, so much so that I decided to risk $10,000 on a custom run of fabric featuring my exclusive design—I just felt I was on to something. I was right.

As soon as I sent in the Purchase Order, my salesman called me to tell me that the president of his company had held their monthly sales meeting in New York. The first matter of business was my pink ribbon design. "Who was this woman in Grand Haven and how did she see this trend coming before us?" he demanded of the sales force. Before I knew it, I was talking to their PR people in New York, who were putting together a national press release about how they were so proud to be involved with the printing of the first pink ribbon–inspired fabric with its inspirational message of faith, hope, and love. My story and design were featured on their Web site, touting my design vision and the wonderful benefits of my product, the Wuvit.

"This fabric is so great," my salesman said when I had received my shipment, piled high on two pallets and shrink-wrapped, "you should make other things with it, like tote bags." I thought, *That sounds like a really good idea!* Within weeks, I hired a woman designer who helped me to make a prototype of a bag that was no less than an architectural statement, using pink canvas to create a pink ribbon handle that stood up and proclaimed, *I've been through the fight of my life and I survived* by any woman who carried it. I put it out in the marketplace at my next trade show, and it was instantly featured in an industry magazine as representing a hot new trend in retailing! I took $10,000 worth of orders on the line of Wuvits and Faith, Hope & Love Daisy Bag in my next two shows.

The fabric sales rep had his own opinion. "Now you can stop making those silly Wuvit things," he said, seeing how my new line of Daisy Bags was taking off in the marketplace like a shot. I only laughed at him and told him that his underestimation of my product was what "drove me on to greater successes every day."

I was so right with this fabric that it eventually became my bestselling pattern over all the other beautiful fabric designs I offered at every retailer across the nation. I called up my sales rep to tell him this. His observation: "It must feel good to outsell the number-one manufacturer of home decor fabrics in the U.S." Yes, it did!

Before I knew it, I was getting so much national attention for this simple fabric design that I was meeting celebrities in New York who were interested in attaching their name to it as a means to raise money for their breast cancer foundations. I called up a couple of the other foundations and discovered that giving them money was not easy: They had rules about how their foundation's name could or couldn't be attached to any charitable donation. Going ahead would cost me thousands of dollars in printing and legal expenses, which I couldn't afford. As I tried to decide whether to spend the precious dollars in legal fees to make a charitable donation toward breast cancer research, I was excited about a request from a celebrity to coordinate an appearance at a trade show I had coming up in New York. My sales rep,

sensing my level of anxiety, gave me some good advice. "Don't confuse excitement with stress," he told me. "These are all good problems to have! Step
back, take a minute, and enjoy your successes along the path of entrepreneurship. This is exciting."

My graphic designer was equally excited. She was between jobs and willing to work for me at discounted rates. She wanted to ride this Wuvit train
with me to a new career, and she had all kinds of fantastic ideas for everything she could do for me to transform my brand into a powerhouse in the
marketplace, which included designing my cart merchandising, signage,
P.O.P. displays, and even location shots of me and my product, scouted, secured, and art-directed by her and photographed by a friend of hers who was
producing catalog shots of some of the nation's premier brands. This graphic
designer's formulation and execution of a creative idea was inspired. I wanted
more and more of this expensive drug—seeing my little company transformed
by first-class branding strategies—while my husband kept saying stop. If you
ask my husband today if this was a good investment, he would scream, "No!"
I believe her work was a critical element in my securing premier, national accounts. So the answer is, yes, it was worth the thousands of dollars I spent.

Buoyed by the mall leasing manager's enthusiasm, I immediately got to
work looking at the idea of selling Wuvits to kiosk operators for the holidays. If the other operators at this particular mall were making three sales on
a good day and I made ten times that on a bad day, I had to be on to something. I went out and bought all the books on franchising I possibly could at
the suggestion of the leasing manager but soon discovered that this was a lot
more work than I thought it would be. I just didn't have the necessary legs
behind my product yet to sell it effectively to somebody else. *What would be
the easiest thing to do?* I thought to myself: *Hire a franchising attorney, pay
him thousands of dollars, sell my product at barely more than what it cost me to
make it, and have a whole other sales job in front of me—finding franchisees?
Or lease a kiosk myself?* I couldn't make that decision until I had all the information analyzed objectively. I called the leasing manager again to find
out what the kiosk monthly rate was.

"For this particular mall, twelve hundred dollars a month for every
month except November and December, when it's seventy-five hundred dollars a month, plus a percentage of gross."

"Seventy-five hundred dollars a month!" I almost shouted. "That's crazy
talk!"

"I have some people who gross seventy-five thousand dollars in sales at
my kiosks at the holidays," he answered.

How could that be possible? I thought. Just how many Wuvits did it take to
sell $75,000 worth of product? How many would I need to sell every day for

the months of November and December to hit that quantity? How many did that break down to each hour? How would the cost of my lease and operating expenses—including employees—affect my bottom line? Just what was my break-even point on this?

I didn't know it then, but I was forming in my mind the essential Excel spreadsheet document that every entrepreneur needs to create before launching their business: the Break-Even Analysis. Up until this point, I hadn't really done this in earnest because I had no fixed expenses.

The Break-Even Analysis Spreadsheet

This is a tool for determining the amount of sales you need to reach for your revenues to equal your expenses. It helps you understand all your expenses, both fixed and variable, so you can reach an objective assessment of whether a financial undertaking will bring reward. A fixed expense is anything that remains constant on a month-to-month basis, like rent and employee salaries. A variable expense is something that is incurred only occasionally, such as advertising or a new equipment purchase. To download a free Break-Even Analysis Spreadsheet, visit the SCORE Template Gallery at www.score .org/template_gallery.html and click on Break-Even Analysis, in the Excel format. Once you've built your Break-Even Analysis, you're halfway to completing your first Cash Flow Spreadsheet.

I didn't know much about Microsoft Excel then. At first sight, it can seem extremely overwhelming and intimidating, and it is! I signed up for an online course available at my local community college, which cost me around fifty dollars and which allowed me to study at my own pace on my own time, usually after I put the boys to bed at night. I gave up halfway through the course, after mastering the very basics. Now I can build a fifteen-page spreadsheet that would impress any CFO. I didn't learn it from the class, I learned it from necessity, and you will, too. Don't be so hard on yourself at the beginning. Besides, you've got your free counselor at the SBDC, who is guaranteed to be an expert at this kind of stuff, so go sit across the desk from them, and watch and learn. That's what I did.

The Cash Flow Spreadsheet: Your Best Friend or Worst Enemy

Free online templates are available for downloading. You can get these templates from the Michigan Small Business & Technology Development Center (www.misbtdc.org/businessplanningtools.asp) or from SCORE (www .score.org/template_gallery.html). You can even make an appointment with a SCORE counselor for free, who will help you create this analysis step by step. To find your local SCORE counselor, visit www.score.org/findscore and type in your zip code.

The best and only cashflow spreadsheet you'll ever need can be found at www.misbtdc.org/cashflowspreadsheets.asp. Another option is Microsoft Office Online Templates (office.microsoft.com/en-us/templates).

THE BASICS OF WORKING WITH MISBTDC EXCEL SPREADSHEET

Don't panic! Don't even look at any page except the first. Focus on the simple details. You can do this. Just fill in one line at a time and it will all come into focus. Use the same information you utilized when creating your Break-Even Analysis, but in greater detail:

1. Forecasted sales
2. Variable expenses
3. Fixed expenses
4. Miscellaneous expenses

Additional information needed: cash position at start-up—how much money are you starting with?

What It Will Tell You

Everything you need to know about running a business. This document alone might be the most important document you will ever use in making daily decisions as well as long-term financial decisions critical to your success or failure.

The Michigan SBTDC template is set up even to calculate your Contribution Margin as well as your Break-Even Sales Amount. The amount remaining from sales revenues after all variable expenses have been deducted is called your Contribution Margin.

In a nutshell, the Cash Flow Spreadsheet will tell you what revenues you need to generate on a monthly basis in order to meet all your operating expenses. It's set up like an elaborate spiderweb. All you need to do is change the first line of revenue to see how good, or possibly how bad, things can get.

Secrets About Working with a Cash Flow Spreadsheet That Nobody Else Will Tell You

Experienced entrepreneurs have more than one Cash Flow Spreadsheet for the same year. I had up to six spreadsheets running at the same time, taking into account every possible scenario of good and bad sales, or unexpected employee costs, that I could think of. Then I averaged them all together into one spreadsheet, which took into account every eventuality equally, whether it was good or bad.

At the very minimum, you should have three spreadsheets:

1. **Worst-Case Scenario:** Forecasting what if everything goes wrong.
2. **Real-Time Forecast:** What is really in the pipeline in the form of Purchase Orders and what that new printer cost you last week. This is a constant work in progress. You should be adding data into this every week.
3. **Best-Case Scenario:** Forecasting what if everything goes improbably right, every prospect connects, every employee works at the highest level of productivity, *and* you land that dream client. Don't lie—but don't be modest, either.

When looking for money, especially when it comes to bankers who are writing you loans guaranteed by the Small Business Administration, show them Spreadsheet Number 3. Never show them Number 1 or 2. Show them the money!

When it comes to savvy investors like venture capitalists and angels, beware! I was actually told by one of these seasoned investors that providing written forecasts in the form of even innocuous spreadsheets like this can come back and bite you later in a big way. How do you get around this? Read chapter 14 on venture capitalists and angel investors!

Upon building my Break-Even Analysis for operating a mall kiosk at the holidays, I discovered that in order to gross the magical number of $75,000 alluded to by the leasing manager, I would have to sell 3,000 Wuvits at $25 each in two months. That equaled 50 Wuvits a day for sixty days. Or 4.1 Wuvits an hour for every twelve-hour day for sixty days. Were those numbers even possible? I was about to find out!

Thus began my love affair with the Excel spreadsheet. I went home, integrated all this data into my Break-Even Analysis, popped in my fixed expenses, variable expenses, and forecasted sales in increments of $5,000—$30,000, $35,000, $40,000, and all the way up to that impossible mythical number $75,000—and stared in amazement at the practical appreciation of just how much money I could possibly make in one season of holiday retailing. There it was on paper, as plain as day, for me to see. Later this love affair would turn into an obsession, which almost drove me insane. But for now, I was still in love.

My weekend test at the mall resulted in me selling a total of around forty Wuvits in twenty hours total, for an average of two Wuvits per hour. This, I figured, had to be the worst-case scenario; besides it being 100 degrees outside, it was the dog days of retailing. With this in mind, was the $75,000 number a possibility? All I had to do to achieve that was raise my retail price to twenty-five dollars from twenty dollars and double my sales from two units an hour to four and a half units. That didn't seem too unreasonable an expectation for the holidays.

HOW I MADE
$225,000 IN EIGHT WEEKS

Looking at the numbers I had worked up, I rewrote my business plan from a wholesale model to a retail one. I went out and read everything I possibly could in one week about the kiosk business, particularly the industry's magazine, *Specialty Retail Report.* The phrase "specialty retail" means a lot of different things to a lot of different people. If you work in the mall retail industry, it means one thing: retailers who operate from carts, kiosks, and temporary inline stores.

Specialty Retail

Specialty retail is defined as that segment of retailers who operate from carts, kiosks, and inline stores.

Cart: A pushcart that can be moved about in various retail settings, including outdoor venues.

Kiosk: A more stationary retail outlet, located in public corridors in malls.

Inline Store: Any store located in the permanent real estate of any mall, though specialty retailers will often occupy these spaces, particularly if they're between permanent tenants, especially at the holidays. You will often see game stores or stores selling exclusively holiday decorations take up residence in these spaces on short-term holiday leases.

GREAT SPECIALTY RETAIL RESOURCES

- *Specialty Retail Report,* the industry's trade magazine, is available at www.specialtyretail.com.
- The International Council of Shopping Centers or ICSC (www.icsc.org) has as its main function promoting the role of shopping centers in the marketing of consumer goods and services.

- SPREE, or the Specialty Retail Entrepreneur Expo & Conference, is a trade show sponsored by *Specialty Retail Report* that offers a "showcase of exhibitors ranging from manufacturers, wholesalers and turnkey concept companies to property managers, mall developers and service providers."
- The annual convention of the ICSC also offers entrepreneurs the opportunity to learn the basic concepts of retailing, including merchandising, inventory control, technology, and deal making, from some of the retail industry's greatest minds. Contact the ICSC for details.

Is Specialty Retail Right for You?

In my experience, specialty retail is an industry in transition. But there are still a few hard-and-fast criteria that will help you determine if specialty retail is right for you.

KEY ELEMENTS TO A SUCCESSFUL SPECIALTY RETAIL PRODUCT

Impulse-Buy Price: This is typically the magical retail price point of twenty-five dollars. Consumers don't think too hard and long about spending twenty-five dollars at a kiosk. They won't make an expensive purchase from a temporary retailer in the middle of a mall's public area.

Wide Demographic Appeal: If you have a product that appeals to men and women, seniors and teens, athletes and pain sufferers, you'll have a good chance at success.

Easily Inventoried Product: This is any product you can store in quantity in the extremely limited retail space you have on a cart or in a kiosk. Typically, you don't want a huge product with a low price point. You just can't turn this fast enough, and consumers will be reluctant to buy something big they have to haul around through the mall.

High Margins: You can create your own Break-Even Analysis to determine how much money you need to make and what your expectation of a "high margin" is. It's all relative.

KEY ELEMENTS TO A SUCCESSFUL SPECIALTY RETAIL SERVICE

Relationship-Based Services: More and more realtors, insurance agents, and even cosmetic doctors and dentists are buying advertising space at kiosks or are manning the kiosk with rotating shifts of employees to offer information or to cultivate sales leads in the community.

Direct Sales Organizations: Avon, Mary Kay, Tupperware—you can see these direct sales organizations taking up spaces at kiosks across the country. Sales reps can do direct sales from the kiosk to their established customers for commissions. It also offers them the opportunity to make new customer contacts.

Major Corporations Interested in Brand Building or Test Marketing: This is the newest phenomenon in specialty retail, the migration of big established retailers into this arena of consumer sales. Almost every major cellular phone service now occupies a kiosk in just about every major mall in America. Now major computer manufacturers are moving in, effectively finding an outlet to demonstrate their new technology and build brand awareness with the millions of consumers who visit malls every year. You may even see major consumer corporations launching new products, giving away free samples to curious shoppers. It could be one of the most cost-effective advertising strategies there is.

Ask Questions

In my journey to educate myself as hard and fast as I could on this opportunity, I contacted *Specialty Retail Report,* got one of the editors on the line, and just started asking her as many questions as I possibly could. She was kind enough to answer them. I referred her to my Web site, which she visited while I was on the phone with her. After our conversation, I sent a complimentary Wuvit along with my brochure, a nice personal letter on letterhead, and a business card, thanking her for her time. She got the Wuvit, tried it and *wuved* it, and called me personally to tell me so. She thought I had a perfect product for the kiosk business: It had a great impulse-buy price at twenty-five dollars, it had wide demographic appeal, and it was easy enough to stock in large quantities in the limited space each kiosk offered. Buoyed by her enthusiasm in my prospects, I took a risk and proposed to my husband the idea of operating four kiosks for the upcoming holiday season. I thought this would be a manageable amount while still delivering sufficient reward.

I plugged the mythical $75,000 figure into my Break-Even Analysis Spreadsheet for four kiosks and showed it to him, with my explanation that it was a manageable number to start with, while still possibly delivering significant reward. He reluctantly said, "Okay." Let me make it clear right now, my husband was not a willing party in all of this. Though he had always dreamed about starting his own business, he simply didn't have an entrepreneurial nature. He was cautious to a fault, methodical, and very, very skeptical. However, I was the eternal optimist, enthusiastic and willing to do whatever it took to execute a plan. We were completely opposite. A year later, my part-time chief financial officer would laugh about it as he watched my husband and me bicker about every little point. "You guys are perfect for each other!" he used to laugh. "You're so optimistic, and he's so pessimistic, you're so sales oriented and he's so numbers oriented, you cancel each other out! Somewhere in there between the two of you is the truth! You guys were meant to be together." I can laugh about this now, but I certainly didn't feel like that then.

I resurrected my old business plan template I had downloaded from the Internet and began rewriting it. I called up three malls within two hours' driving distance of me, made appointments with the leasing managers, and gasped when they told me what their lease rates were for the months of November and December. The first was the mall at which I had done my test. This was an almost brand-new mall, with over a million square feet of leaseable space and average sales per square foot of approximately $350; he wanted $7,500 a month for November and December, for a total of $15,000.

The next mall was a medium-sized mall with about half the square footage, with sales averaging the same $350 per square foot as the first mall, according to the leasing manager. I found this hard to believe as I walked the mall and saw discount dollar stores, with no premier retailers like Banana Republic or Pottery Barn as the first mall had. She wanted the same lease rates as the first mall. I eventually signed the lease, but I really should have listened to my common sense screaming at me, *Something is wrong with this picture!*

The third was a small but nice, almost brand-new mall, with an average of $270 sales per square foot, and a kiosk in a really great location, right at the crossroads of two entrances, a major retail anchor store, and the food court. He wanted only $4,500 a month for the two months for a total of $9,000. I sat down at the desk of this particular manager to show him my product. Don't assume you're going to walk into a mall and get a lease just because you've got the money. Most malls have more applicants for lease space at the holidays than they have kiosks, so you have to go in there and sell yourself to them. If you have something new, that is high-quality, and that merchandises well on a cart, with a high perceived value to the consumer, you can count on getting space. If you're selling ten-dollar sunglasses, lotion, or cell phone accessories, you might have a tougher time.

This was my third visit to a leasing manager's office in a week, and I came prepared with a warmed Wuvit in a thermal carrier for him to try. It only took one feel. He was so enthusiastic about my product and its prospects he could barely contain himself. I later learned that this could be a tough and unscrupulous business, but this leasing manager remains in my memory as one of the shining examples of professionalism and integrity during my entire entrepreneurial journey. He thought I had the next big thing, and he strongly urged me to "make as much money as you possibly can this year on it and franchise the concept to other independent cart operators next year in a big way. You don't even know what you have here; you can't see that far ahead." This advice would come back in a huge way in just months. But for now, he was just excited to give me his best location, and he insisted I pick another really great location at a mall outside of Michigan to test-launch my product.

Essential Criteria for Evaluating a Mall for Specialty Retail Leasing

You can find all the following information either by visiting a mall's Web site and clicking on their Leasing Information link or by calling the leasing manager and asking them specifically:

Square Footage: How big is the mall? What is the leaseable square footage? A prime mall would have a minimum of 1 million square feet of leased space. A medium-sized mall would have at least half that.

Sales per Square Foot: Every mall leasing manager knows this and can tell you it immediately without "getting back to you" on it. The highest sales per square foot figure you'll typically find is $400, and any mall that has these kinds of sales would be a very desirable place for you to start a specialty retail business. The bad news is that the lease rates will be high. The good news is you get what you pay for.

Area Demographics: Do the locals have a lot of expendable income? You can find this out by researching demographics to find out what the average per capita income is per household. It all depends on what you're selling and who your consumer is, but a $75,000 average household income is certainly better than a $35,000 average household income.

Anchor Tenants: These are the big-name retailers that hold down the mall and bring in most of the customers, like Macy's, Bloomingdale's, Saks, Parisian, Gottschalks, JCPenney, and Sears. The better quality the anchor, the better quality of shopper you'll have a chance of selling to. However, sometimes luxury shoppers will not buy anything from a kiosk. The more anchors, the more people will probably be in the mall.

Kiosk Location: The three most important things you need to know about leasing are location, location, location. Generally, first floor near an entrance or a major anchor is the best. Sometimes near the food court is also good, depending on what you're selling.

I added up the lease rates I had negotiated already: $15,000 for Mall Number 1, another $15,000 for Mall Number 2, and $9,000 for Mall Number 3, for a total of—gulp—$39,000! How could I possibly afford another mall? Another mall out-of-state? That was terrifying! Still, I thought I owed it to myself to find out what going to a really big metropolitan area, in a place where people had a lot of cash, would do for my sales. I thought of the family I had living in Atlanta again and remembered that mega-mall I had shopped at during my recent trade show: the Mall of Georgia.

I called the leasing manager, and told her about my great product as she visited my Web site while on the phone. She told me that I could have one of the best kiosks in the place for the same lease rate I was paying at Malls Number 1 and 2 ($7,500 a month), for a total of another $15,000. My hand was shaking as I added up the lease rates on a piece of paper: $54,000! How was I going to explain that to my husband?

By creating a Cash Flow Spreadsheet, that's how. Just because the total lease costs were $54,000, that didn't mean I had to come up with $54,000 cash. All I really had to come up with was the first month's lease payment, I figured, and the sales generated in November would pay for the lease payment due in December. So I only really needed $27,000.

That was still an obscene amount of money! Was I really going to risk that amount of money based on the results on one weekend test in July?

I reflected on the advice of Leasing Manager Number 1, who thought my results were so promising that I should look at franchising the concept right away. Then I reflected on the comments of the editor at *Specialty Retail Report*, who told me that my product was not only great, it was perfect for the kiosk sales model. Last I recalled the excitement that Leasing Manager Number 3 had, telling me that I was really going to go places that I couldn't even see yet with this product. "Make as much money you possibly can this year on it," he urged.

Most reasonable people would not have done what I did next. I signed leases for all four locations, putting down anywhere from $1,000 to $1,500 for each location as a security deposit. Most people would have been more cautious, more frugal, more intimidated by the costs, the logistics, the hard work. Most people would have sacrificed the opportunity for fear of the risk. But I had a husband in a job he hated, with no prospects of ever making the kind of money we were used to, in a profession he would never enjoy again, so we had nothing to lose. We were looking at the downside of a mountain we had been at the top of, and the only way to go was down. I wasn't going without a fight, for my kids' sake if for no other reason.

Becoming a millionaire means learning to recognize that fear can be conquered through information, where others allow a lack of information to create fear.

It was August, so I still had time to figure out how I was going to pull this off, including where the money was going to come from! What followed were some of the most intense five months of my life. I lost ten pounds, and handfuls of my hair started falling out of my head from stress. I actually started to collect it in a plastic bag, looking at it with fear at first and awe later, as a testimony to my supreme ability to just do what had to be done, regardless of how uncomfortable it made me feel. Looking back at it now, I realize it was one of the best, most successful and exciting times of my life.

By this time, I had become an expert at Excel. I had mastered the Break-Even Analysis and the Cash Flow Spreadsheet. I had plugged in my numbers in as much detail as I could possibly forecast, including employee salaries, miscellaneous expenses like utilities and freight, and, last but not least, the cost for the product that I had to manufacture to sell at all these kiosks! The magical number that kept coming up in my formula, where it said "Pre-Start-Up Position Cash on Hand," was $75,000; only when I plugged in that figure did all the other columns remain in positive cash flow for the four months of my operation from hiring employees to closing the kiosks down on December 31 where it showed a significant return on my investment in the final December column on "Cash Position at the End of the Month." My husband was sold, but I had to find $75,000. So I brushed up my business plan one more time and went looking for it where most people start out—a bank.

I started with phone calls and was told to make an appointment to speak to loan officers; I got them on the phone and they instructed me to bring along my business plan, a Personal Financial Statement; a Start-up Expenses Spreadsheet; the twelve-month Cash Flow Analysis; a four-year Income Flow Projection; an Opening Day Balance Sheet; and a Break-Even Analysis. Don't be alarmed. This sounds like a lot, but most of this information is redundant, so you can just transfer it from one downloaded template to another. You should have a Personal Financial Statement for your own purposes anyway, and an Opening Day Balance Sheet is pretty easy for a company just starting out.

Essential Financial Documents Necessary for Applying for Bank Loans

All of these templates are available for free download from the resources listed earlier:

Personal Financial Statement: This is a detailed listing of all your personal assets, including real estate, securities, retirement funds, and cash, minus any liabilities you may have, such as credit card debt, mortgages, car loans, etc. Banks are primarily interested in seeing a picture of your financial health and whether there are sufficient assets to leverage for loan purposes.

Start-up Expenses Spreadsheet: How much money are you asking for, how are you going to use it, and what assets do you have for collateral?

Twelve-Month Cash Flow Analysis: Probably the document that is going to receive the most careful scrutiny, so do it right.

Four-Year Income Flow Projection: Sometimes optional, this is just your "best guess" document.

Opening Day Balance Sheet: Just like your Personal Financial Statement, except this is a record of any assets and liabilities linked to your business. If you're just starting out, this shouldn't be very detailed.

Break-Even Analysis: You'd better be an expert at this by now, for your own good.

Whew! Can you believe many people go to the bank without even a business plan? Can you see now why I don't waste time talking to anybody who hasn't taken time to write a business plan? I'm talking about smart people, like doctors, who ask me for advice and can't even organize their thoughts, analyze their risk or reward, or can't be bothered to take a half hour and go meet with a SCORE counselor or, best yet, an SBDC counselor. In fact, don't even go to the bank until you meet with your SBDC counselor, who will help you craft all these documents and may even get you a graduate business student to work on your business plan for college credit, at no cost to you.

Here are two examples of people who failed at this critical step for two different reasons. Entrepreneur Number 1 capably put together all the required documents as well as an outstanding business plan. He secured the interest of savvy venture capitalists and was able to get cash for start-up from his bank, guaranteed by the SBA. His business opened with an abundance of resources, including offices, computers, expensive furniture, employees, and invaluable intellectual property in the software field. They were out of business in less than six months—every penny gone, with $12,000 a month in operating expenses alone, not including employee salaries! When he called me up for advice, I asked him where the revenues were. Where had he expected the money to come from to support his $12,000 a month in fixed and variable expenses on his twelve-month Cash Flow Analysis? The answer: They had optimistically built in revenue as "Consulting Fees" to make them more attractive to the banks that never materialized.

When it comes to financial projections, you can lie to a bank, but you can't lie to yourself. The sad thing is that if they hadn't had all the expensive overhead, they probably would have survived. They made the mistake of thinking they could go from sitting around at desks at their forty-hour-a-week jobs in a company that had been around for twenty years with a national client base to having the same "standard of living" in their start-up where they didn't even have one customer. Unfortunately, this occurs a lot more than you would think. Remember those three cash flow spreadsheets I kept simultaneously? One of them would have foretold this cash crisis and saved them a lot of time, money, and pain.

Entrepreneur Number 2 was a doctor who invested in real estate. An enterprising immigrant, who had key international sourcing connections throughout the world, had presented him with an incredible opportunity to get in on the ground floor of a new technology in his field. This doctor was guilty of a number of things. First, he gave away too much proprietary information for free without first protecting himself with an NDA. Then he didn't adequately evaluate the financial opportunity by creating a Break-Even Analysis or four-year projection or even writing a business plan. He didn't act fast enough; he sat on the opportunity until the foreign guy lost his patience and went looking for big money in big cities from VC firms. By that time the doctor was mad, letting personal feelings come before business, and he did something else that made me cringe. He hired a family law attorney, a friend of a friend, who didn't know anything about business and counseled him by saying, "Don't worry, I see people like him come and go all the time." Sound familiar?

I was still a babe in the woods myself, but I saw opportunity, on a Cash Flow Analysis Spreadsheet, while other people were still telling me I was crazy. The first of these was a banker. She wasn't my normal banker, but I had heard that this bank, which had just opened new offices in my town, was hungry to fund new businesses. I paid her a visit with my business plan and all its financials. She didn't even look at it. She just picked up our Personal Financial Statement, gave it a cursory look, then turned up her nose at my Wuvit idea, saying, "I buy stuff like this at craft fairs. Why would I give you seventy-five thousand dollars to sell it?" *If you read my business plan, maybe you'd know,* I wanted to counter. Then she dealt us a personal insult that struck me to the core: "Is that all your husband makes?" It already hurt us more than I can say that my husband was forced to take a job literally paying half of the salary he had made his best year, right before his industry self-destructed. I decided to cut my losses and get out of there before she dealt me any more personal humiliation. She was mean. When I see her now at the supermarket, I have to confess, I just want to walk right up to her and ask her in front of everyone, "How do you like me now?" But what kind of example would that be to my kids?

I ran to my next meeting with the other banker I had vetted, sitting down across the desk from her and pushing my two-inch pile of documents toward her, hoping for a different reaction. I started talking, giving her my narrative. She instantly picked up my business plan, read the Executive Summary, all the while "uh-huhing" to my narrative, turning immediately to the financial documents at the end of the plan as appendices, focusing like a laser on the twelve-month Cash Flow Analysis Spreadsheet, particularly the last line on the last column of December, "Cash Position at the End of the Month."

"You mean to tell me you can make this kind of money in just months of retailing at these kiosks?" she almost screamed.

"It's a distinct possibility," I answered.

"Who's doing your merchant accounts?" she asked, referring to the credit card processing service that every retailer needed in order to accept credit cards from customers. I was about to find out how lucrative this could be for banks—after she spent the next twenty minutes explaining to me all the uncountable fees—and she called her merchant rep and had her in her office in fifteen minutes to sign me up for four new merchant accounts.

Now this was a banker! She saw my opportunity and her opportunity at the same time. It didn't hurt, I would later find out, that her bank was one of the biggest underwriters of SBA loans in my state. If you learn anything from this, make sure you go straight to a bank that specializes in SBA lending. Otherwise, you're wasting your time.

. . . .

SBA FINANCING: WHAT IS IT AND WHERE DO YOU GET IT?

The U.S. Small Business Administration (SBA) is a branch of the federal government. One of its chief responsibilities is providing financial assistance to American businesses. The SBA does not actually loan money to businesses. It sets the guidelines for the loans while its partners, lending institutions like banks and community development organizations, make the loans. The SBA backs these loans with a guaranty that eliminates some of the risk to the banks. SBA loans can sometimes be easier to get because of that guaranty than traditional bank financing. To learn more about all the financing resources and programs available to you through the SBA, visit their Web site at www.sba.gov/starting_business/financing/basics.html.

. . . .

Sources of Capital for Start-up

Getting money to start your business usually involves the following resources in the following order:

- **Personal Savings:** You have to be willing to invest in your business before asking other people to do so, including banks.
- **Friends and Relatives:** Believe it or not, almost every entrepreneur I know has gotten money this way, either at start-up or later at a time of cash crisis.
- **Banks:** These are great places to obtain SBA-guaranteed financing.
- **Angel Investors and Venture Capitalists:** This is usually a mid-tier financing option for businesses. Start-ups can find this a hard nut to crack but not impossible. Keep reading to hear how one start-up raised almost a million dollars!

Criteria Banks Use to Evaluate Your Creditworthiness, or the Five C's of Credit

A bank wants to make sure you can pay the loan back. Besides your personal credit score, they're going to base their evaluation of you on the following criteria:

Capacity to repay: Is there sufficient cash flow to make the monthly payment?

Capital: How much of your own money have you put into the business? They want to make sure nobody has more to lose from your business failing than you. Banks typically want to see a minimum of 25 percent of the capital needed coming from personal assets.

Collateral: What assets do you have that can secure the loan, from your home to your commercial building?

Conditions: Are economic conditions favorable for your kind of business undertaking?

Character: What kind of person are you? Have you thought this out, provided a written business plan, arrived on time wearing a suit, acted with professionalism? These things are very important. When you've exhausted your capital and collateral, character alone can get you a long way. I'll tell you how it did for me.

The bank gave me the $75,000 necessary to fund my next phase of growth. It was secured by personal collateral, primarily equity in our home,

and guaranteed by the SBA. From application to check in hand took an astonishing two weeks. Your results may vary. We had an excellent credit
score, a well-thought-out and -presented business plan with all the required
financial documents, and plenty of collateral to secure the loan. We were
fast-tracked.

I remember sitting at the bank manager's desk at the closing, signing the
hundreds of documents, and being presented with one submitted by the
SBA, asking me how many employees I would hire, what I expected to pay
in salaries, how this revenue would impact the community I lived in, and basically how many tables my investment would put food on, directly and indirectly, in the next twelve months. I was beaming with this revelation. The
SBA was basically thanking me for having the guts to start a business under
every kind of personal risk known to man in order to fuel jobs and growth
in my community.

By signing one document, I stepped over into the ranks of those entrepreneurs who were responsible for creating the rich opportunities every
American had for employment. I would never drive by a small business
again without looking at it in a different light. We had gone from being unemployed to employers, and I felt a whole new sense of freedom, independence, and power from it. I had officially become Boss Mom, and I would
never be the same again.

Pay Yourself First

My banker thought my financials were first-rate, except for one minor detail: I didn't plan for my own salary in the Cash Flow Spreadsheet. "You
mean I get paid?" I marveled out loud, wondering at the joy of getting
money from a bank with which to pay myself. For now, as long as my cash
flow supported it, my banker thought it was irresponsible not to add in a decent salary. And so I hired myself, and did that ever feel good.

I had the money, the plan, and the determination to get it done. I needed
someone to help me. I had developed a great working relationship with the
office manager at my manufacturer. She would make a perfect part-time employee, because she could oversee the manufacturing of my product while
also helping me with key administrative functions. I didn't find out until I
hired her that her father owned the place. I would discover later an extremely expensive lesson about loyalty.

Hiring staff to work at mall kiosks was more difficult than I had expected. I put an ad in the paper and waited with my new employee for the
candidates to show up. Of six scheduled interviews, only two applicants ap-

peared. Employees proved to be the most difficult part of operating my business. I figured out quickly that paying a commission on sales was the best way to attract quality candidates in a retail environment that usually paid little more than minimum wage. Some of my more motivated employees ended up making more in weekly salary than I did.

I figured I needed a minimum of four employees at each location. That was a total of sixteen employees who had to have payroll done each week, including figuring deductions like state income tax, federal income tax, and FICA. Just keeping track of commissions would prove to be difficult. I needed help. I remembered the advice my millionaire mentors gave me: "Pay yourself first; then pay somebody to pay your employees." In hindsight, that was some of the best advice I've gotten. The paperwork alone for filing employment taxes is staggering. Most small businesses just can't do it. The best investment you can possibly make right at the beginning is to hire a payroll service.

How to Hire a Payroll Service to Pay Your Employees

There are many payroll services out there for you to choose from. In my opinion, the best one is Automatic Data Processing, Inc., or ADP. (www.adp.com). Their Employer Resource Center offers a wealth of information on everything you need to know. When you use their service, you can pick up a phone anytime and talk for free to a counselor one-on-one about important employment issues like how to legally hire and terminate an employee, retirement savings, and taxes. You can even do most of the work necessary to prepare your weekly payroll online. Other popular payroll services include:

- Paychex Inc. (www.paychex.com)
- Advantage Payroll Services (www.advantagepayroll.com)
- QuickBooks Payroll Services (www.payroll.com)

We decided that launching one of the locations a month early would give us critical experience necessary to open the other three simultaneously. This proved to be a smart decision. We opened the first kiosk at the same mall at which I had done my test, and it took off like a shot. I couldn't believe the sales we were doing in October, two months before the official start of the holiday retailing season.

I didn't have too much time to reflect on this, since I was literally working my ass off. I mean it. I looked in the mirror and saw that I had lost ten pounds! I had just weeks to hire twelve more employees, four of them in distant Atlanta, not to mention schlepping boxes of Wuvits everywhere, running around to buy office supplies, running my kids to school and soccer games. Finally, I filled up my truck with everything I needed to open my kiosk at the Mall of Georgia and drove down there alone to meet the three employees I had hired to work it. We were to meet at 9:00 P.M. on Halloween to set up the cart.

I parked my truck outside the mega-mall, just having driven the fifteen hours down from Michigan by myself, pumped with adrenaline to do what needed to be done. I had to go in and meet with my three new employees, who were looking to me to be their leader.

I have to say for the most part, I had hired really good people. Maybe it's cliché, but women are all about relationships. We became like a family very quickly, mostly because we worked hard at creating a community among our four locations, faxing everyone a daily newsletter with personal news about each employee and, more important, listing results of the other locations' sales figures the day before, indicating who was the top commission earner. I learned right away that money wasn't as much of a motivator as the competitive instinct, and that didn't cost me anything. Most people really just want to be the best they can be and to be recognized for it.

The three women in Atlanta were among the most competitive women I ever met. It was all I could do to keep them from killing each other to work the best hours in order to make the best sales. On the first night, they were nothing but kind. They were all older than I and more experienced, and they instantly commiserated with me that I had left two little boys alone on Halloween to go trick-or-treating with their dad, with nobody home to take their pictures or hand out candy at the house as they went on their rounds. I had pushed myself to the limit just to make their costumes by hand. That was something I would not sacrifice in the years to come in my demanding workweek.

The kiosk in Atlanta was different from those with which I was familiar, and I just couldn't figure out how to make it look good. The women tried to help me, but they couldn't. I sent them home with looks of doubt in their eyes about me, my product, and this whole concept. I worked until one in the morning, transforming the kiosk from boring to fabulous, just by trial and error. They arrived the next morning for training, amazed that I had pulled it off.

I trained three shifts one day for fourteen hours straight, then got in my truck and turned around, driving right back home to Michigan, exhausted but with a feeling of unbelievable accomplishment at having pulled this off. I got reports on my cell phone all the way up from my one management employee that the other two locations had opened successfully—I had already trained these people. Sales were already on track for our best expectations. I got home, slept as much as my four-year-old would allow me to in one day—which was just barely—and wondered anxiously what the next eight weeks of retailing would bring us. I remember telling my husband and family, "If only I could go to sleep right now, and not wake up till December 31!" That's how nervous I was.

I had too much at stake financially and emotionally to be anything but anxious. I filled in for kiosk employees, drove product here and there, worked on the books at night, and wrote the daily newsletter, while my management employee dealt with the inevitable employee gripes and handled all the shipping and delivery issues, keeping a strict control of inventory. We brainstormed and came up with great sales promotions, including our best idea: selling one Wuvit for $25, or two for $40, then two for $45 as the holidays neared, when desperate holiday shoppers provided a captive audience. She was excited to get each daily sales report and would text the numbers to me on my cell phone or send them by e-mail at the end of every day. I would hold my breath and look at them. They were awesome. They were unbelievable. They were a train that gained more momentum every day. At the end of eight weeks, we had grossed—on one little $25 product, at only four little kiosk locations—an unbelievable $225,000 of revenues!

8

THE SCAM ARTISTS
WHO STUNG ME AND
WHAT I LEARNED

It was a heady couple of weeks. I drove around on top of the world. I took a day off—my first in months—and took my family out to eat, thinking to myself, *I am a president of a company! I am in control of my own destiny. We'll never be unemployed again!*

This good feeling only lasted a couple of days. I came back to earth with a thud when I visited the manufacturer who was making my Wuvits to hear the following life-changing words from my part-time employee who also worked for the manufacturer.

"We've been continuing to manufacture Wuvits."

What? I thought. *They were keeping a secret from me?*

I couldn't believe it. I had just made a ton of money, but I was suddenly stuck with a ton of inventory I didn't want and didn't order. I had thought my part-time employee was loyal to me, but I was wrong. She was loyal to her father, who owned the manufacturing and fulfillment facilities. He saw I had a lot of cash to pay, whatever the bill.

My Mistake and How I Could Have Avoided It

You must set up a system to formally authorize every single purchase of raw materials, of designer's work, of manufacturing of product, with a Purchase Order. No Purchase Order? No payment! If I had an effective Purchase Order system in place, I could have told this scheming manufacturer to take a hike. I could have probably told him to take a hike anyway, but I didn't because I had a misplaced sense of loyalty to his daughter, my part-time employee. I allowed myself to be pushed around and taken advantage of without so much as one complaint. I figured, *Oh, well, I can sell this.*

Using Purchase Orders to Control Costs

A Purchase Order is a written authorization for goods or services, specifying the price and terms of payment, which becomes a legally binding contract once accepted by both parties. You should scrupulously write Purchase Orders for all goods and services your business uses, except for miscellaneous expenses that can be tracked with a credit card. I advise you to use Quick-Books to generate your Purchase Orders, which will automatically record all data related to this purchase and eventually generate a check for payment as well as track the inventory.

It's Not Personal—It's Business

I was too naive. I let personal relationships cloud my business judgment, and I was too inexperienced to think that people would deliberately lie to me just to get money out of me. I tended to misplace my trust in anybody who acted like a friend, and I was willing to overlook business considerations because of those friendships. I wasn't used to being the boss, and I just didn't know where to draw the line. Since then, I've learned that no matter how great my relationship is with an employee or a vendor, I always have to be the boss first. As long as I bring the hammer down whenever it becomes necessary, because too much conviviality has resulted in an atmosphere that is not optimally productive, it is all I need to do to get the relationship on track again.

We were obviously on to something. I felt like the hamster on the wheel all over again, being forced to find a way to sell the inventory my manager's opportunistic dad had made. He justified it with every kind of excuse known to man: "We just cut all the material you ordered; we can't be expected to count units when we're cutting." Of course he was expected to count the units he was cutting.

The holiday retailing season was over and wouldn't be back again for another year. I had already let all my employees go, and I didn't have any more leases. It was January, the major market month for wholesale trade shows, so the two of us packed up our trade show and went to Atlanta and Americas-Mart again.

We stayed at a fine hotel right on Centennial Park downtown and made reservations at one of the best restaurants in the city, determined to reward ourselves for our hard work. The manager from my Mall of Georgia kiosk came to dinner with us and pitched me with her idea of turning me into a millionaire! She was even more excited about our success than I was. "We have to find a way to take this nationally next year!" she urged me. "And I want to be part of it!"

I thought back to that leasing manager who said, "Make as much money as you possibly can this year on it and franchise the concept to other independent cart operators next year in a big way." But we weren't done making all the money we could yet. From what I knew about franchising, there wasn't a lot of money in it for me at this early phase. We had something hot, and we had to capitalize on it before we turned it over to others. We thought if four kiosks were good, twelve would be better. We agreed over dinner that night it would be twelve kiosks in 2003.

Meanwhile, my designer saw money—lots of money—and decided she wanted a share of her own. Money didn't change me, because I was working so hard to pay all the bills while using what capital I had to fund my growth, but it sure changed everyone around me. She wanted to be a part of my forward movement. She had started to show up at my kiosks, taking unauthorized pictures of them and my employees. I had asked her to help me redesign my Web site, giving her a nice down payment, and she delivered her first sub-par work, demanding full payment on the balance outstanding—$10,000—without even working with me to fix what was wrong. She started on work I hadn't authorized, and I asked her to stop. She started calling me twenty times a day, demanding that I pay her in full for the Web design she hadn't even done.

How to Protect Your Intellectual Property (IP) Rights When Using an Independent Contractor

I called the first attorney I had ever met with, because I didn't know anybody else at this time who did general law. He was what I call a bulldog, gruff and aggressive. If anybody could stop the harassment with one phone call, he could. The designer now claimed that she owned every bit of collateral she had ever made for me, including my trademark Wuvit, because she had copyrighted everything in her name when she made it. This is an excellent illustration of why, prior to working with any designer, you need to execute a written "work for hire" agreement stating that all materials they produce for you are your property exclusively. Even though I had such an agreement with her, she threatened to steal all my intellectual property and end my ability to do business. I had just made a lot of money and this designer was telling me I would never be able to make it again, because she owned everything. My attorney attempted to contact her, then she proceeded to e-mail my attorney twenty times a day, and my attorney was billing me for this. I asked my attorney to stop talking to her, to talk directly instead to the designer's attorney, but he refused. Finally the attorney quit, accusing me of micro-managing him, then sent me an astronomical bill wrapped in a thirty-six-page e-mail sent by the designer. The whole fiasco eventually ended up in small claims court, where the case brought against me was dismissed as baseless. Even the prosecuting attorney called me up to apologize for the actions of his colleague. Nothing can stop people from bothering you with nuisance lawsuits. Still, you need to do everything you can to protect yourself legally right at the beginning of a professional relationship.

If you hire an independent contractor, like a graphic designer, to do creative work for you like designing advertising collateral, logos, or even your Web site, don't assume that you automatically own the IP rights to it! Unless your designer is employed full-time by you, designers you contract on a job-by-job basis can claim ownership of the intellectual property they create unless you take these steps to protect yourself right up front:

1. Visit www.nolo.com or www.findlaw.com to read up for free on your rights. You can also find free document templates to download to create your own Independent Contractor Agreement Contract.
2. Execute a written "work for hire" agreement right up front that states that all the material they produce for you is the copyright property of your company. Search Google for "work for hire" to find information about creating this contract, or contact your attorney.
3. File a copyright on the work you contract. Visit www.copyright.gov to find out how.
4. Specify right in the contract that the finished work must meet normal professional standards before full payment will be issued. This will ensure that the designer will work with you to get the work right, rather than stick you with sub-par work and a big bill. Most designers are ethical and won't even think of doing this to you.
5. State in the contract that all work contracted will be supplied to you on disk prior to your issuing full payment.
6. When commissioning work from a designer, issue a Purchase Order with the agreed-upon price stated on it and the name and nature of the work they'll be doing. This is a good way to document that you exchanged valuable consideration with them—money—in return for their work, in the event that there is ever a dispute of ownership.

You can make these agreements as complex or simple as you choose. I personally prefer the simple. Just getting all the important issues out on the table right up front—you own the intellectual property, the work has to be completed in a satisfactory manner, you expect to get copies on disk of all the work created, as well as protecting the confidentiality of any trade secrets they may be exposed to in their work—will take a load off your mind and start the relationship off on a professional footing.

Money Changes Everyone but the Person Making It

I had just had a successful sales season. As a reward for my success, three people had stuck me with huge bills, for no reason other than that they saw the money. But the worst was yet to come.

I did my fourth trade show—my second in Atlanta—with a definite lack of enthusiasm. It was tough to get excited about a $20,000 show on wholesale margins when I had just sold $225,000 worth in eight weeks on retail margins. I was done with trade shows, I thought; I was on to something much bigger.

We went back to Michigan, all excited about our plan to launch our massive kiosk program in 2003. If we made practically a quarter million in eight weeks in 2002 at four locations, just think of what we could make with twelve! I had the team who believed it could be done and who wanted to make it happen. All I needed was the money.

I went back to rewriting my business plan, the third time in less than two years! I put together the financial spreadsheets necessary for my banker again. I was definitely going to need more money. She didn't even read my business plan this time; all she did was listen to me for five minutes, turn to look at the financials again, then fast-track me for another loan of just $75,000. I had total lease payments of more than $250,000 in just three months, not including my employees' wages and the production costs of my Wuvits, but still, $75,000 was all I needed to get this big machine operating.

Except for the Mall of Georgia, most of the malls we were in were small potatoes. We wanted to change that this year. We created criteria for our next malls—minimum million square feet of leasable space, target sales of $400 a square foot, major metropolitan areas—and started to research the best malls that fit those criteria and called their leasing managers. We were connected with a national leasing manager for one of the nation's premier mall chains, and she made our job easy. She put together a portfolio of her top malls across the country, including Denver, San Antonio, Philadelphia, Minneapolis, Chicago, and Bridgewater, New Jersey. Atlanta had been very good to us in 2002, so we decided to go back to our Mall of Georgia location and add another mall in the metropolitan Atlanta area as well. I had more family in Raleigh, North Carolina, and I knew that economy was hot. Two new malls were opening up with lease space available to me at bargain rates. Add in an Ohio location and one in suburban Detroit, and we had our top twelve picked out. But October was a long time away. I had to find a way to sell Wuvits in the nine months that were in between.

Franchising Your Concept

I knew opening twelve kiosks was going to be a lot of work. I wasn't 100 percent behind it until I evaluated the possible returns on franchising my program that year. I created a Break-Even Analysis to evaluate the risks and rewards. There certainly wasn't as much money in franchising, but it also didn't require the immense cash needs of twelve leases, nor would I have to go through the effort of hiring staff and managing operations for all those retail locations. Realistically, were we even capable of successfully opening all these kiosks simultaneously? We asked ourselves this a lot in these months. I had two capable and experienced employees who said, "You did four easily last year; we know what we're doing now; adding eight more shouldn't be that much more difficult." Still, I had a sinking feeling in my stomach. I started to consider the logistics alone and began to wake up in the middle of the night in a cold sweat. I began to get really nervous, aware of a distant storm brewing on the horizon.

Knowing that fear sometimes resulted from a lack of information, I called up my editor contact at *Specialty Retail Report* again to ask her advice. "Should I franchise right away, or should I open my own kiosks? I would make at least four times the money operating my own kiosks that I would selling product to independent operators."

"It seems to me," she responded, "that you already have your answer. Besides," she answered, "you are not really franchising. Franchising requires a license, secured by an up-front fee paid by the franchisor. You're not charging that. What you're offering is much simpler than that. Once you sell them your stuff, you won't have any control at all in how they market it, how much they charge, or even how they merchandise it. They could make any guarantees they want about your product, with or without your permission." This was cause for pause and concern.

According to her, opening this many retail outlets on my own was not an unheard-of phenomenon in the specialty leasing business. Owners of other successful products like mine did the same thing each year. Still, she advised, it wouldn't hurt to invest $350 in an ad in her magazine's annual holiday retailing edition, inviting independent kiosk operators to consider selling my product this holiday season. Although the deadline for ads had already passed, she could squeeze me in under the wire. I resurrected an old ad my former graphic designer had done for me, tweaked it to fit the circumstances, and put it in the forthcoming issue.

Just three weeks later, I received my first calls from independent kiosk operators looking for the next big thing to sell for the upcoming holiday retail season. The calls were coming in from the segment of the retail industry dominated by superhardworking immigrant entrepreneurs, who came from countries like India, Pakistan, and parts of the Pacific Rim to sell products they imported directly for high margins. I was taking a real hit financially to offer them the high margins they demanded, but even 400 percent markup didn't seem to be enough of an incentive to them. I couldn't do any better than that. I started fielding so many calls with so few results that I decided to create a separate Web site outlining this opportunity and its costs to them, allowing them to get all the facts with which to evaluate the deal without my sending off expensive samples and product brochures they requested over the phone. I began to understand that working with these people was not going to be any easier than running my own kiosks for four times the profits and I was more convinced than ever to go down this path.

How Not to Be Vulnerable

An entrepreneur and inventor are never more vulnerable to scam artists than when they're looking for ways to take their product into channels of distribution.

Confronted by the challenge of taking their product into channels of distribution, entrepreneurs and inventors become afraid and frustrated.

There are many people out there to take advantage of your fear and frustration in every way that it manifests by selling you something—including themselves and their channels of distribution—that is invariably too good to be true. Greed can cloud your judgment just as effectively as fear and frustration.

Fear and frustration are just a temporary state of mind. The only way to conquer them is through information, research, and hard work. The information necessary to evaluate risk and reward in deciding whether to license or assign your invention is not readily available to most start-up entrepreneurs and inventors. Vulnerable entrepreneurs and inventors will often trade their substantial long-term gross revenues for a small up-front percentage on net sales out of fear and frustration.

Start-up entrepreneurs and inventors assume that selling a product that they licensed for a small percentage on net revenues is less work than selling the same product on their own for a large percentage on gross revenues when this is not always the case. There are no easy answers to difficult problems, only hard work. Some people will make a career out of selling you their "easy answers." The more frustrated you are—desperate to find easy answers to your problems when there are no easy answers, only hard work—the more susceptible you are to anything these confidence men are selling.

There are no easy answers to difficult problems, only hard work.

I was feeling a certain uncomfortable level of frustration again, and one thing I've learned that they don't teach you in business school—not that I even went—was that there exists somebody to take advantage of your fear and frustration in every way that it manifests by selling you something that is invariably too good to be true.

I constructed my B.S. Detection Machine to help me sort through those pesky negative feelings that clouded my judgment occasionally and left me looking naively to someone who promised they could magically solve all my problems in exchange for significant sums of my money, whether it was a rep, a marketer, or a distributor.

The more frustrated you are—desperate to find easy answers to your problems when there are no easy answers, only hard work—the more susceptible you are to anything the confidence men are selling. Maybe you're not desperate at all; maybe they call you up and fill your head with all kinds of promises of making you a million dollars. It's human nature to take shortcuts through our reason and experience to arrive at dumb blind faith in anybody who raves about our product or service and claims to be able to make us rich. That's why I recommend passing everything through the B.S. Detection Machine before making any decisions regarding the transfer of revenues or especially rights to your idea.

The more somebody promises to make you rich, the more suspicious you should be.

The B.S. Detection Machine

Laugh about this if you will, but you can basically evaluate the wisdom of any decision by asking yourself a few key things, designed to remove emotion and fear from the decision process and replace it with facts and reality:

Ask what's in it for them. Nobody does anything without a financial motive, though they might pretend otherwise. Get out a pen and paper and look objectively at what kinds of financial rewards are in the deal for them. Make sure you understand in specific detail every cost associated with working with them. Are they hiding any? Be very careful of anyone who offers to pay you a percentage on net revenues instead of gross; this is not accepted as the best practice. If you still are willing to accept a percentage of net revenues, make sure you understand in detail and in writing what each cost is that will be deducted from gross revenues to come up with net. Anybody who cannot give you a specific, non-negotiable list of costs that come out of gross receipts is not reputable. Remember that everything is negotiable, so try to get rid of as many of those specific costs as possible.

Ask what's in it for you. Commit pen to paper again and figure out just how many units of your product they're going to have to sell at your negotiated percentage on net or gross to make the money they're promising you. How many units do they have to sell to make the $50,000 figure they're throwing around? Is it achievable? What would your returns look like if you tried to take it to market yourself? Call your local SBDC and ask your counselor what the typical margins are for a product like yours. They actually have a huge reference book that can tell you exactly what percent of a return a business can expect to make in net revenues—whether you're making kids' toys or auto parts. Margins of 20 percent to 40 percent are considered standard. If you don't want to take it to market yourself because you want to spend all your time with your kids, that's a valuable consideration. Just make sure you understand from the beginning what is required of you in making the product a sales success.

Ask them to prove it! Make sure this person can verify successes with other products or services. Ask for references for other people with whom they've worked and call them; when you speak to their references, have a list of questions ready to ask, like what the annual gross sales figure on their particular product was and how much money they got out of it. Ask your potential rep what kind of accounting system they use and how often you'll receive sales reports.

Ask them to put it in writing. Make sure you get a written contract specifying the exact terms of your agreement. Have it reviewed by an attorney who specializes in contract law. Always make sure you have an escape hatch that allows you to terminate the contract no longer than thirty days from when you provide them written notice of termination.

Do your homework. Trust but verify. Do whatever it takes to replace fear and frustration with research and information. Only then will you be in the position to make the best decision, one you won't regret.

Bad Things That Only Happen to Women

One huckster had seen my ad in *Specialty Retail Report,* which mentioned somewhere in the copy that we had sold $225,000 worth of Wuvits at only four kiosks in just over eight weeks, and called me up to pitch me his idea of how he was going to turn me into a millionaire. That was a wonderful thought to ponder! He was smart and smooth, the classic fast-talker. He prefaced everything he said with, "Now this is really high-level thinking," which seemed to be a patronizing way of saying to me, a woman, "You probably won't understand this, and you probably don't have the vision to see the big picture I do." As further evidence of this attitude, he went into this computer geek gibberish, telling me how he created this "platform" and "portal" with his esoteric knowledge of software code, dropping the name Microsoft as often into his rambling monologue as would reasonably allow. I didn't get it. What was he selling? Software? A retail portal built on his scalable, integrated software platform? Microsoft? I didn't care. He had me at "millionaire."

But he wasn't done selling himself. The next code words he uttered were maybe just as powerful as the *M* word. I still had said maybe five sentences before he launched into his next assault, mentioning that he had connections with angel investors and a major national retailer and that he could get me in touch with both. That was impressive. I had heard of angels but didn't know much about them besides thinking they were the Holy Grail of free money. I was using Google to search for every name he dropped during our phone conversation to see if I could get a clue about where he was going with all this.

I still didn't know what he was selling. It was obviously himself—a very elaborate pitch of himself, the purpose of which I still didn't know. He asked me to put together my business plan for the kiosks I was planning to open and FedEx it to him immediately. He would review the plan, possibly getting his angel contacts interested as well as the VP at a major retailer, who would probably want my product in his stores in a big way right away. This all sounded too good to be true, but I did exactly what he asked. I ran to FedEx to put my confidential business plan in an overnight envelope, paying thirty dollars for the privilege of doing so, and naively told the clerk behind the mail counter that this package could be worth a million dollars!

DANGER! YOUR BUSINESS PLAN IS CONFIDENTIAL:
HOW TO PROTECT IT FROM CON MEN!

Your business plan could be a golden cash register. You've worked hard at it to develop proprietary ideas and have no doubt outlined a strategy to take your ideas into distribution. Do not give your business plan away casually to anybody.

Remember that the only people who should be looking at your business plan are bankers, small business counselors, investors, and maybe close friends and family. If you do have the good fortune of meeting an individual investor interested in reviewing your business plan for the purpose of investing, ask that person to sign an NDA first. If they have money, and that's a big if, what's to stop them from taking your idea and running with it?

Don't ever think about asking an angel investor group to sign a Confidentiality Agreement before showing them your business plan unless you have the cure for cancer under your hat. They represent professional investors accredited by the Security and Exchange Commission (SEC), who are liable for any unethical behavior. (Though that didn't stop the one I met! Keep reading for that story!)

I dutifully waited for the fast-talker to call the next day. When he did, he was just slightly more specific about his plans than he had been the day before. He revealed to me that he had a Web site—guess that's where all his *platform* and *portal* expertise came in—through which he sold largely seasonal items. I got online and looked at it as we spoke. It seemed to be like one of those seasonal retail operations that come into vacant inline storefronts in malls just to sell Halloween costumes, or Christmas decorations, or board games, on a month or two-month temporary lease. It was like specialty retail, only online. I still didn't understand where I fit into this picture.

After praising Wuvits and selling himself, he finally laid his cards out on the table. He wanted to turn me into a millionaire by turning over my kiosk sales program as an exclusive U.S. distributorship to him. His plan was for me to extend the product to him on credit on the almost impossibly tight margins I was already offering the independent operators who had to pay me cash or by credit card, and he would distribute it for a substantial percentage per unit. Common sense already told me this wouldn't work, since the operators I talked to wanted bigger markups than 400 percent. How could we tack on his percentage to each unit and still sell it? If he was going to make a million dollars' worth of sales, and wanted the product on credit, that meant I had to carry a million dollars' worth of credit.

I knew it wasn't going to work, but still I plugged his scenario into my Cash Flow Analysis just to prove it to myself. In a perfect world, if he did everything he said, I would make the same amount of money selling wholesale to twenty kiosk operators as I would selling retail at one of mine, even considering lease rates and employee costs. Plus, he wasn't willing to pay me any money for the right to distribute, which wasn't kosher, even though he wanted exclusive right to distribute. Everything about this was a bad deal.

Three phone calls later from him, I finally convinced him that I wasn't going for this deal. Then he had another deal he wanted to sell me, couched all over again in this "this is very high-level thinking; I'm going to make you a millionaire" kind of parlance. Now he was selling me his Web site and warehouse and distribution facilities. He was creating a "cyber-mall" of all kinds of "phenomenal" products, to which his Web site was the portal. He filled my head with all kinds of facts and figures about the number of hits he got each day, the size of his server, the technical details of his platform, how scalable and integrated it was, the square footage of his warehouse, even the state-of-the-art conveyor belts he used to supposedly push out hundreds of thousands of dollars of product a week.

Again, he wanted exclusive right to distribute, though he wasn't willing to pay for it, and all the product on credit at just above my cost. He planned to sell it for full retail on his Web site, or rather my Web site, which had to pass through his portal, of which I got nothing but the wholesale cost of selling it to him on credit. Maybe if extremely large volumes of product were delivered through his supposedly established and diverse channels of distribution, there might have been a lot of money in it for me. But when I tried to negotiate a better deal, he wasn't willing to even give me a token percentage of the profits between cost on the product that I was giving to him on credit and retail price. We were done talking.

If he was confident he could effectively deliver a million Wuvits, then there had to be a way for me to do it, too.

Channels of Distribution: The Keys to the Millionaire Kingdom

The only way to make a million dollars is to sell products. The only way to sell products is to create a strategy to target, access, and sell through more and more channels of distribution. How do you penetrate more channels of distribution? I'll teach you everything you need to know to maximize your presence in the marketplace in chapter 13.

You are going to be confronted by all kinds of experienced people who know how to exploit your frustration for their gain. You owe it to yourself not to take a deal you're going to regret just a year or two later without at least trying to take your product to market yourself first.

I had investigated, tested, and evaluated all the available options, and the path forward was clear. I planned to open twelve kiosks for Holiday 2003. I had started to relax a little, looking forward to what I thought was going to be a relatively quiet spring with my kids, when I got a phone call from a friend: "QVC is having a New Product Search! You have to go!"

BEHIND THE SCENES
AT QVC

I wanted to be on QVC, like everyone else. QVC's channel of distribution was so prolific. Being on QVC was like having an advertising campaign reaching out into 87 million homes—that you didn't have to pay for. The opportunity to raise consumer awareness about your product while building brand equity was almost worth more than the revenue you got from selling your product. But making money or building your brand was not necessarily guaranteed to happen with an appearance on QVC.

There are a number of ways to get on QVC. None of them were more fun and more informative than participating in a New Product Search. I've been to two. I went to their headquarters outside of Philadelphia the first time. They came to Orlando, Florida, the second. The first one, when we went to their corporate headquarters, was an experience unparalleled since.

I went to my computer and typed "QVC New Product Search" into my Google search bar. I was delighted to see the usual austere "Thank you for your interest, but we're not having a Product Search at this time" page transformed into an opened window of opportunity that proclaimed, "We are having a New Product Search!" Hallelujah! I had just sold a quarter of a million dollars on a hot and new gift item that every*body* wanted. This had to be my shot at those million-dollar channels of distribution.

I registered online for my opportunity to win the Today's Special Value lottery that every entrepreneur dreamed about. I could pick which day of the three-day event I wanted to attend and rate the best time for me in two-hour blocks in order of priority. Within an hour I was e-mailed a confirmation of my appointment to meet face-to-face with a QVC buyer to demonstrate and sell my product.

Not only was I going to meet with a buyer, but for this particular product search they were conducting free seminars, everything from Building a Successful Business Out of a Single Great Idea to Thinking Big: How to Position Your Brand for Maximum Growth. This was just too good to be true!

I flew down with my one part-time employee, and we got a couple of

QVC NEW PRODUCT SEARCH: EVERYTHING YOU NEED TO KNOW!

For information on QVC's New Product Search, visit their Web site at www
.qvcproductsearch.com, but don't expect to find too much information there,
unless they are in fact having a New Product Search Event. New Product Search
Events can be held once or twice a year, sometimes at QVC's corporate headquarters at West Chester, Pennsylvania, just outside of Philadelphia, when you
go to them, or at various cities across the U.S. in a two-week span, when they
come to you on a road trip.

Check the QVC Web site frequently for news of a New Product Search
Event. The events are not regularly scheduled. I'm always caught off guard when
I hear they're having one. It's almost as if they deliberately plan these as stealth
attacks on American entrepreneurs. Once at www.qvcproductsearch.com, click
on the navigation link on the left titled QVC Product Search Event. If they
don't currently have one scheduled, it will say so, but you could click back there
a week later and find one, with all kinds of wonderful information to help you
prepare and register for the event.

rooms at the Sheraton in West Chester, Pennsylvania. I had forgiven her for
her father's transgressions, listening to her explain it away as an honest mistake while telling me that I needed the inventory anyway to sell. I needed
help, and she had done a good job. The hotel was offering a special discount
to Product Search participants, and the lobby was thick with every kind of
inventor/entrepreneur you could possibly imagine, from sophisticated and
professional teams who wore custom-monogrammed shirts with their product or company's name on it to the poorest dreamers who wore old jeans and
had nothing but a rolled-up drawing under their arm. One of the latter
types was checking in right before me. He was having a problem, because
the credit card he was using wasn't his; it was his parents'. The man must
have been at least forty. "I don't have a credit card," he argued with the hotel clerk. "Just call my mom. She'll tell you it's okay."

"This is my second Product Search," he was saying, "and I know this is
the one. I got a plan here," he said, referring to his rolled-up piece of paper,
"that is going to make me millions." I listened, absolutely stunned that a
person would bother to come down with nothing but an idea or drawing on
paper, in hopes of getting his idea on QVC. I was obviously, I thought, way
ahead of the game.

My employee and I sat down awhile for a drink at the hotel bar and heard
a buzz of conversation that all had the same common threads: "I can't show

you my idea—it's top secret." "All I need is twenty thousand dollars to turn this idea into a million dollars." "I've been sitting on this idea for four years now." We watched as people rolled in boxes, huge suitcases, and custom crates, all discreetly covering up their precious cargo, wrapping tarps around their oversize products or concepts, secreting them away from the prying eyes of other ambitious entrepreneurs. I began to worry, with my one little suitcase and basket of Wuvits, if I was disastrously unprepared for what was about to happen tomorrow.

My worst fears were confirmed the next day as I arrived at QVC's Studio Park and saw the carnival of people, products, and promotion that unfurled before me. Just driving into the grounds was an exciting experience. It was like a college campus with warehouses, customer service centers, and outdoor sets made up of house facades used for demonstrating rakes, hoses, and backyard grills. The Product Search was being held in the main studio building, which was also home to their executive offices and retail store.

There were at least three hundred of us, and we were ushered into a colossal room for registration, which was hung with a hundred different lighting rigs high above, with banks of curtains grouped here and there for whatever stage configuration they could possibly conceive. Today the multi-purpose room was being utilized as one big auditorium, three-quarters of which was jammed with inventors and entrepreneurs waiting in a long line to present their products to buyers who walked the ten long banks of tables that were set out for that purpose, each bank at least sixty feet long. My appointment wasn't till the next day, so I took my time checking in for the free seminars I was going to spend all day attending. The large table area was roped off, and we stood like spectators at a sporting event along with hundreds of others who watched as buyers evaluated the products before them. One man was getting a lot of attention. He had wheeled in a full-size mock-up of a back of a car, complete with bumper, and was demonstrating his "tailgate table," fastening it on to the bumper, extending a patio-sized umbrella from it, then setting up two collapsible chairs and a cooler as if he were in the parking lot on college game day. All the spectators stared in amazement as the QVC film crew pointed intense lights on him, filming his pitch to the buyer while our hearts collectively sank, thinking, *Oh no. I can't compete with that!*

Oh, well, I thought. *I'll give it my best shot. I did, after all, just sell over two hundred thousand dollars' worth of my humble product in eight weeks. Wonder if he did that.* Still, I considered my presentation next to his, baskets of Wuvits with some sell sheets I had hired another graphic designer to create, which were uninspired.

It was time for our first seminar and so we were led to a whole new auditorium upstairs, this one more like a theater setting with a proper stage and plush seating. The first presentation was a QVC Product Search Orientation. The intent was ostensibly to teach us itinerant millionaire entrepreneurs how to put our best foot forward in our upcoming sales presentations to the buyers. It turned out that it was more accurately QVC's own masterful sales pitch to us!

First up was the Vice President of Corporate Quality Assurance, who gave us a straightforward explanation of the QVC quality testing procedure. He explained how every product that passed through their doors had to be subjected to intense testing, which would include dropping it from a six-foot-high ladder. Everybody applauded politely at the end of his speech, after which we were introduced to the Director of Vendor Relations, who was going to tell us everything we needed to know about what specifically it was that QVC was looking for in a product, which they would be willing to drop six feet off a ladder. It all boiled down to a simple formula. If your product fits any of these criteria, you have a chance at getting on QVC!

Next up was the Vice President of Brand Merchandising, who would soon regale us with a sophisticated, multi-media presentation that left us all salivating for the opportunity that they were dangling before us. He was the epitome of classic East Coast, dark-suited business suave. He wove a perfect mixture of wit, humor, and information into his mesmerizing PowerPoint slide show, making us all laugh one minute and gasp the next.

He first explained the core concept of QVC's selling strategy: namely, Single Item Marketing. Single Item Marketing is exactly what it says it is, he explained. Instead of going into your normal retail environment, like a department store, where you are bombarded with thousands of different products all competing for your attention, you are introduced to one single item for a total of three minutes of your undivided attention. This is an entrepreneur's dream come true. Having millions of Americans, he explained, focused simultaneously on your product and all its features and benefits is something no other form of retailing could deliver. I was hooked. I was already successful at Single Item Marketing, which was what I had been doing at all those kiosks for eight weeks, just selling one thing—Wuvits.

SINGLE ITEM MARKETING

- The core concept of QVC's selling strategy
- Different from any other retail model
- Focuses consumers onto one item at a time, explaining its features and benefits

THE FOUR CARDINAL CRITERIA FOR A SUCCESSFUL QVC PRODUCT

1. **Is the product unique?** Everyone is looking for the next big thing to tempt consumers with, something new and unique that they haven't seen before and never even thought they needed until they saw it. Identify what the unique features of your product are and sell them! If you have something new to the marketplace and you're looking for an exclusive way to launch it, you might have a shot.

2. **Does it demonstrate well?** This is especially important on the visual medium of TV. They want a product that can magically produce a dramatic result right before the viewer's eyes, whether that's taking wrinkles out of a garment or stains out of a rug or picking up leaves in your yard. If your product is one of these, come up with a two-minute pitch that you use while demonstrating it, practicing in front of a mirror until you have it down. If you get in front of a buyer and give them a polished "made for TV" pitch, with a product that produces dramatic results, you're going to get fast-tracked to callback status.

3. **Does it solve a problem?** This is a niche that QVC loves. If you're a mom who has been plagued by a recurring problem, like where to put your water bottle when pushing your twins in their stroller during your daily walk, and you come up with a great problem-solving idea, like a holder that clamps on to the stroller handlebar, *and* you recognize that ten million other moms are looking for the solution to this problem and can effectively communicate that, you, too, could be fast-tracked to callback status. There are a million problems yet to be solved. Just wrap your head around this concept, start asking questions, and you'll be amazed at the ideas that will come to you.

4. **Is it timely or topical?** Did NBC News just do a story on your amazing stroller handlebar bottle-holding clip? Then you're hot and QVC will want to talk to you. Don't be afraid; call them up and ask to speak to a buyer. Or maybe Oprah just did a show about the crisis American women are facing with poorly fitting undergarments and you have the topical and timely product that can solve the problem in a new and unique way and produce dramatic demonstrable results on air while millions of Americans watch—you're golden!

The subject of his discussion was brands: how to build one successfully and how to achieve maximum equity in it. He began by showing us what he considered to be the best brands in the marketplace and then the worst, using the difference to illustrate what worked and what didn't. Target made his list of top brands because the logo alone evoked the name of the company and all the associations that went along with it and because it was so simple, uncomplicated, and graphically pure. You could see it once, then close your eyes and conjure it up in your mind effortlessly; the same could not be said for most logos out there. Another distinguishing characteristic of the top brands was their ability to make an indelible impression on the consumer. There was no confusing the Target logo in the marketplace. I compared the Target logo to my own Green Daisy logo in my mind and congratulated myself on intuitively creating a bold, graphic image that wordlessly evoked my company's name and all the fun, happy associations that went along with it. Other successful famous logos included Ralph Lauren's polo pony, which on its own had come to symbolize the essence of style, casual sophistication, and class, and the iconic IBM logo, the importance of which cannot be underestimated in the creation of a billion-dollar company.

Some of the biggest corporations in America were singled out for the worst branding strategies, which just goes to show you that even with unlimited cash and resources you can still get things terribly wrong. I won't name names here, but an example of bad branding to him was incorporating as a product's name any seemingly random series of letters and numbers, like "XL589." The worst offenders were those who had a dozen products identified by a series of numbers on the same theme, making it almost impossible for the average consumer to remember them easily and any differentiation there was between them in the marketplace. *That makes complete sense,* I said to myself. I was personally frustrated with anything too technical or that required too much of an exact memory when talking to a salesperson in a store after a Saturday morning soccer game with my kids as they jumped around whining that they wanted a Mrs. Fields cookie (another great brand).

According to this Vice President of Brand Merchandising, it was better to come up with a completely novel, nonsensical brand name that explained nothing about the product but stuck in the consumer's head like a catchy melody—*like Wuvit!* I thought—than to string together arbitrary letters and numbers or, worse yet, name it something completely boring that explained everything and left nothing to the imagination or to memory. Other brands singled out as being weak were those of companies that did not have a logo outside of their name. Branding was the pot of gold at the end of the rainbow for every entrepreneur, and creating an effective branding strategy right at the beginning would enable you to put it eventually on every consumer product under the sun, from underwear to lawn mowers, whether your company made it or not! Cha-ching!

Strategies for Effective Branding:
What Works in the Marketplace and What Doesn't

Company Name: Every company has a name, but you also need a logo to further identify and brand your company in the marketplace. A company name and its logo should be well thought out at the very beginning to launch a branding juggernaut.

Logo: Keep it simple and graphic. If you can see it once, close your eyes, and remember it, it's probably a good logo. Also, if your logo can graphically communicate the name of your company, like Green Daisy, you've created a successful logo. Examples of companies with good logos: Target, Polo Ralph Lauren, IBM.

Product Name: Focus on creating a memorable name that will get stuck in the consumer's mind like a catchy melody, like Wuvit, instead of being too descriptive in a literal sense, like Natural Heating Pad. Classic mistakes made by even the biggest companies include assigning a product a name that is a seemingly random grouping of numbers or letters, like XL589.

Next he did a brief analysis of the entrepreneurs who had come to QVC at a New Product Search and won the Today's Special Value lottery. What did they have that distinguished them from the rest? A great product was a given, but having a great product alone wasn't enough to guarantee success on QVC. I couldn't believe it when he said that the one characteristic unique to every Today's Special Value millionaire was a great personality. What? That's right, a great personality, whether it was real or one created specially for public consumption. Having a great story to tell the consumer was an essential criterion for success, one that could make them laugh, cry, or just generally like you enough to want to buy your product. He discussed some of their current top sellers, starting with the owners of the Chesapeake Bay Gourmet company, who regularly sold out of their jumbo lump crab cakes, because they "are just two of the nicest, most genuine and sincere people ever put on TV." Then there was the owner of the Quacker Factory, whose embellished sweaters had become a Today's Special Value staple, because its colorful and charismatic founder was so funny, warm, and endearing to the millions of QVC viewers who sat in their underwear in homes across America watching. In other words, you had to make for good TV! Don't ever underestimate the power of a good story, effectively communicated through branding. Everybody loves a good story, whether it's told on TV or not. It creates emotional resonance with the consumer, which is important in distinguishing your product from the millions of other products that are out there. Remember: The easiest way to consumers' wallets is through hearts, not heads.

Today's Special Value Lottery Winners: What Do They Have in Common?

A great product is a given, but that isn't enough to go onto to millionaire success at QVC. In order to take your product into the stratosphere, you need a few other elements:

- **A Likable On-air Personality**: Whether you're really enthusiastic or really laid-back, it doesn't matter; both types of personalities have been successful on QVC. Be yourself and it will be communicated to the viewer.
- **A Good Story**: If you had to go through hard times to get where you are, that's interesting and will endear you to the consumer. Or maybe you just had a baby, lost fifty pounds, and came up with the perfect diet, book, or nutritional supplement to get it done; people want to hear about this.
- **A Perfected and Practiced TV Pitch**: Before you ever meet with a QVC buyer, make sure you have your two-minute TV pitch down perfectly. The only way to do this is to practice, practice, practice, either in front of a mirror or on videotape.
- **Anything That Makes for "Good TV"**: Some QVC regulars are known to dress up in fairy costumes with a whole entourage of fairies in tow to create a delightful experience the viewer enjoys watching long enough to order.
- **Enthusiasm for the Product**: If you don't honestly believe that your product is something the consumer needs, you aren't going to go far. This is why I believe reps can't be as effective at selling your product as you can. They don't have the same enthusiasm you do.

He had me at "hello," but the brand and merchandising expert went on to end his presentation in such a dazzling manner that members of the audience were left breathless, ready to rush the buyers who waited to evaluate their products with a fervor that might actually have been dangerous. He started talking about the sheer demographic power of QVC and its ability to deliver products, or at least an awareness of products, to just about every home in America. A map of the U.S. flashed onto the screen. "QVC is watched in eighty-seven million homes across the U.S.," he said. "To get an idea of how many homes that is, and how effectively we track our customers, watch this." He pushed the button on the handheld remote control from his computer, which was flashing the PowerPoint slides across the screen, showing another slide of a town in California, with a cluster of yellow dots blanketing the map of streets. "Every dot represents a household in this town that has ordered from QVC at one time." To me, it looked like one giant dot; there were so many individual dots it was hard to see the trees for the forest. With a technology second surely only to that of the U.S. military, he pushed his button again, and the slide zoomed into a square mile of the town, with each yellow dot now plainly distinguishable from the other. "Here's a picture of how many homes in any average square mile, in any average town across America that we have sold to." You could hear an audible gasp from the audience as the square mile revealed three-quarters of the homes with yellow dots. He pushed his button again, zooming into one square city block. "And here's a view of how many homes in a single block in any average town in America that we have shipped packages to." There were approximately ten houses, seven of them with yellow dots on them. If you didn't really want it when you came, you really, really wanted it now. It was all I could do to not get up and run out the door, chasing down an unsuspecting buyer. It filled us all with an enthusiasm that, for me at least, might have been counterproductive in my presentation, and which I would regret later.

I was looking forward to the next presenter scheduled the most. He was a professor and lecturer at the prestigious Wharton School of Business at the University of Pennsylvania. In the business world, it didn't get any better than an MBA from Wharton, except perhaps a BA from Harvard. The presenter was quick to point out that he had a degree from both. The subject of his presentation was building a successful business out of a single great idea. This sounded like exactly what I needed: I had a single great product; how did I take that into a bigger, broader business model?

This presenter wanted to set us straight right away; he wasn't so much an academic as an entrepreneur himself. He had a little harder-edge, was a little less suave, with a little more honesty than the previous presenter. He didn't operate in a perfect corporate world, making six figures without ever risking his own cash, driving a Mercedes, with six weeks of vacation, as the brand expert before him probably had. He wasn't interested in discussing the academic qualities of branding strategies; he was more consumed, he admitted, with finding new ways to make his business survive one crisis after another. He had come to deliver us just one message, and it's a message I'll never forget. I've quoted it at least a hundred times myself since then, and I've heard it come out of only the smartest, most experienced, most war-ravaged entrepreneurs I've ever met.

"I have a business degree from Harvard," he began, "and an MBA from Wharton. My parents spent a minimum of $125,000 purchasing this education for me. Let me do you all a favor and save you that expense. I can put in a nutshell everything I learned from four years at Harvard and two at Wharton. Are you ready for this?"

We all nodded that we were, our pens drawn and ready to write down on paper before us the edifying words that were about to be transferred from him to us.

"Number one: Cash is King. Number two: Sell your mother for Cash if you can."

What?! I thought. That was very un-Wharton-like. That was it? That's all the knowledge and expertise he had to pass on to the hundreds of entrepreneurs who were gathered in this room just for the privilege of hearing what he had to say. I know I got in here for free, but I was hoping for more than that. Everybody looked around at each other as if they, too, were expecting more.

"WHAT I LEARNED FROM FOUR YEARS AT HARVARD BUSINESS SCHOOL AND A WHARTON MBA"

1. "Cash is King."
2. "Sell your mother for Cash if you can."

The wisdom of his advice was beyond me then. A few years later I would have understood completely, probably even laughed at his wry observation.

For an entrepreneur there is never a shortage of ideas, opportunities, work, or eventually even sales. The only thing that is in persistent critical shortage for the start-up entrepreneur is cash.

As I look back, it was the best advice he could have possibly given us; ideas and products are Jacks and Queens, but Cash is King. The message he was giving us was to go out and find cash. Find a lot of it. Find it wherever you can. Make it your job. Don't ever stop looking for cash; you'll never find enough. Constantly dealing with a cash shortage at the beginning is not, I learned, a personal reflection of your inability to run a business; it's just part of business! Everybody's got to face it and conquer it; even, apparently, Harvard and Wharton graduates!

WHAT THIS MEANS TO YOU

- There's no shortage of opportunities, ideas, work, or even sales at the beginning. The only thing that is in critical shortage is cash!
- Constantly dealing with a cash shortage at the beginning is not a personal reflection of your inability to run a business; it's just part of business.
- Looking for cash is a full-time job.
- You should *always* be looking for new sources of cash.
- When it comes right down to power and control of your company, the person holding cash holds the high card.

This presentation was very effective, especially comparing it to the presentation before him. There wasn't even one PowerPoint slide to be seen. It was just straight talk coming from somebody who had obviously been there, done that.

After that, the audience broke out into a spontaneous Q & A, which the panel was generous enough to answer.

QVC Q & A: ANSWERS TO YOUR SPECIFIC QUESTIONS

- **How soon after our meeting with the buyer will we know if you're interested?** Those who are selected will be contacted by a phone call about four days later. If you didn't get selected for a callback, you'll receive an e-mail.
- **What happens if I'm called back?** A product sample will be requested and evaluated against our tough quality standards. If it passes, a buyer will work with you to create a sales strategy. A Purchase Order will be issued, and you will need to ship your product to our warehouse.
- **How long does it take to get on the air after my product is approved?** It usually takes three months to go from Purchase Order to an on-air presentation.
- **What is your minimum Purchase Order?** Typically our minimum initial Purchase Order is $20,000 at wholesale cost.
- **Can I drop-ship your customers (ship directly from your warehouse instead of QVC's)?** No. Everything must ship out of our warehouse for quality control purposes.
- **How long do we get on air our first time out?** Your initial presentation usually lasts three minutes. After that, it all depends on the results of the first presentation.

- **What if I don't sell all my product in your first presentation?** You will be allowed to come back until your product sells out. [Though this was his explanation that day, I know many entrepreneurs who have been on QVC didn't sell out of their product and had it returned to them, sometimes only after one three-minute presentation.]
- **Will QVC help fund my idea to take it from paper to product?** No, QVC does not provide any kind of funding for product development.
- **What is the best time to be on the air?** It could be any time of day. Midnight on the East Coast, when we debut Today's Special Value, is only 9:00 P.M. on the West Coast, prime shopping time. What's more important is that your product gets presented with products that have a niche similar to yours, such as home improvement, appealing to the same demographic of buyers.
- **What are your customer demographics?** "Did you see our map with the yellow dots? Everybody." Depends mostly on the product segment. Certainly includes *Fortunate Retirees*, otherwise known as baby boomers who have retired with a lot of disposable income.
- **What's your target retail price point?** We don't typically do anything under fifteen dollars. We need to generate a certain amount of sales dollar for each minute we're on.
- **Do you discount our product?** QVC sells products at a price below Manufacturer's Suggested Retail Price (MSRP). We need to offset the costs to our customers of shipping. [If you're already selling your product to other major national retailers and you're going to undercut them on price on QVC, beware. Think this through.]

We got up the next morning, anxious to get it over with. It was our turn to get in a long line and wait for our big moment when we would come face-to-face with a buyer. It was chaotic. There was a QVC employee at the head of the line whose job it was to figure out what category you fit into and direct you to the appropriate bank of tables where that particular department was buying. She couldn't figure out where to put me with a product called a Wuvit, so after a half hour I spent watching other exhibitors walk by me in line, she stuck me in a row where they put everybody in the same boat. Don't make this mistake. Insist you go into the proper category for your product so you meet the right buyer.

PRODUCT CATEGORIES THAT QVC BUYS FOR

- Apparel
- Food

- Home decor
- Electronics
- Personal care
- Health, fitness, or sports
- Furniture
- Jewelry
- Dietary supplements
- Home textiles
- Collectibles
- Gifts
- Toys
- Hardware

PRODUCTS QVC DOES NOT BUY

- Guns
- Furs
- Tobacco products
- Service-related products

We were ushered to our table and I couldn't have felt more unprepared than I was. It was immediately apparent to me that some people had been to Product Searches before. Those were the ones who knew that they had exactly six feet of tabletop with which to display their product. Among other things, some of them had custom tablecloths, stand-up easel signage, boom boxes with music, press clippings, treats for the buyers, on and on. I had two baskets filled with Wuvits and my sell sheets.

The woman who decided where I should go put me in a food area so that I could use a microwave, which was covered with food inside from the hundreds of exhibitors who had used it already that day, and I tried my best to warm up my Wuvits without getting foodstuff all over them. I was too nervous to focus on anything else anybody else was selling, but I do remember seeing some really tan and thin, aging Russian women selling dietary supplements, a quiet professional man who was setting up his line of children's books, a really blond forty-something psychic who was espousing her philosophy on how to be happy, outlined in her books and tapes, and a luggage salesman who appeared to be from India.

There were all kinds of people from every corner of the U.S. and even China; they came in the place straight off the airplane wheeling in the biggest suitcases I've ever seen in my life, laying their stuff out, showing it, then turning around to head right back to the airport for the flight home.

Then there was the food. There was everything you could imagine: cookies, candy, fudge, drink mixes, dips, appetizers, cheesecakes, and caramel apples. A lot of the people there to sell foods were wearing really kooky costumes, with wild hats with things sticking out of them, or bright feathered boas, or hot pink custom silk-screened T-shirts, or really colorful aprons. They all looked like they were having the most fun, and it looked like the endgame in that category was to get the most attention.

What Not to Do

I warmed up my Wuvit, my employee at my side, and waited. There must have been at least ten exhibitors at each bank of tables, with each one being allotted one six-foot-long segment. We stood on one side, and the buyers walked up and down the other, perusing the products, trying not to make eye contact with you, deciding if they wanted to stop and ask you questions. There were a lot of buyers looking and not a lot buying. After fifteen minutes of this I jumped on the next buyer who happened to walk by and just glance at my product. I was so tanked up on adrenaline from the previous day's presentations, I practically leaped over the table to get to him. "Would you like to try a Wuvit?" I asked him, launching into my spiel while pressing a Wuvit first onto his shoulder, then his back, telling him how I had created this *unique* product with really *timely* appeal that *solved a problem* for a really *broad demographic* of people, which would *demonstrate well* on TV. I was so nervous, I don't think I stopped talking once in fifteen minutes to even take a breath, telling him I don't how many times that I had just sold $225,000 worth of product in eight weeks. This man listened to me, then finally got out: "This is great. But I don't buy this stuff. I'm in a different category. Sorry."

And just like that, my first Product Search Event was over. I was told it was time for me to go, because I had had my fifteen minutes of time with a buyer. It didn't matter that it was a buyer who didn't purchase my category. He didn't even explain this to me as he listened to my pitch with nothing but a few comments. That was it and I was told to pack up my stuff, watching as the two men next to me got a buyer to buy their ill-conceived airbrush self-tanning system practically without even showing the least bit of enthusiasm to her inquiry. Later, when I got back home, I would reflect with a ton of regret that I had simply blown my shot by being too nervous, too enthusiastic, and too much of a hard sell. Lesson: *Just be yourself.*

I would have numerous other shots at landing QVC, including reps, personal contacts, direct solicitation, even another Product Search, all with their own unique learning curves. The lesson is, don't give up. Keep learning from each failed attempt and go back and get right the next time what you got wrong the last. It was easy to tell who had been to a Product Search before and who hadn't, and it really seemed to make a difference in their odds at getting selected. I wish I knew then what I know now; maybe I would have had a different result. Now you know, so you have a better shot than ever.

Using a Rep to Get on QVC

I came back to Michigan with my tail between my legs. I really thought I had QVC in the bag when I went down there, and I told everybody so. I had a lot of work before me to launch my kiosk program, but I had been bitten by the QVC bug and I couldn't get it out of my system. The mother of one of my son's classmates turned out to be a marketing rep, who had connections with major catalogs as well as with a woman out of Philadelphia who was a regular on QVC, not with her products but with the products of people like me. I signed a rep contract with the local woman, who then called the woman in Philadelphia to see about getting my product on QVC. So now I was up to my fifth rep, with no significant sales to show from any of them. I liked this local woman and believed she could get done what nobody else could. Besides, I now had some leverage behind me; who could turn down a product that had the kind of success I just had?

It wasn't more than a day later that we heard from the woman from Philadelphia, in response to my rep's inquiry. She heard about my sales numbers from last holiday season and put us on speed dial. She was really hard and brassy and didn't mince words. This was her deal: She would get me on QVC for 20 percent commission. That didn't include the 10 percent commission contract I had with my local rep. This was going to hurt; my product costs were still high, because I was manufacturing in the U.S. In addition to that, she wanted an exclusive right to distribute to QVC, for which she wasn't going to pay me anything. She wasn't done there. She insisted that she had to bank the money, which meant that I would send her the product on credit, she would ship it to QVC and invoice them, then when they paid her, she would give me my percentage, which I had to trust her to give me without taking in excess to all the other miscellaneous expenses she told she would bill me for, including travel and lodging, meals and mileage. QVC's first rule is that they have to sell the product below suggested retail cost, which meant that they would beat me up on the price for sure. Once I did my Cash Flow Analysis and figured out there was almost no money in the deal for me, I called up my local rep and said I couldn't do it. "Let's try and negotiate this deal," I told her. My rep told me she'd cut her commission in half if the other woman did the same; that way we'd all end up making money. We flew this past her in Philly, and she just laughed at us and said no, "take it or leave it!" We couldn't believe it, being the nice midwestern girls that we are, that she was handing us an ultimatum, her way or the highway. I wanted QVC so bad I could taste it, but there was just too much risk—carrying the cost of the product on credit for months, trusting that she would pay me anything, giving up my own right to sell to QVC, wondering if her brash personality would poison my product on air—to justify the slim rewards, if there were even any to be had. I thought about it for five minutes and told my friend to call her back and say no deal. My friend reported to me that the woman laughed out loud and screamed into the phone before hanging up, "She'll never get on QVC without me! You'll see!"

Nothing motivated me more than to have somebody tell me I couldn't do something. My rep resolved that we'd find another way to sell Wuvits.

Breaking Down the Doors of QVC

My next shot at QVC would come only two months later, right after I launched my kiosk program for Holiday 2003. One of the malls I leased space in was the King of Prussia, just outside Philadelphia and right in QVC's backyard. I knew one of the buyers was bound to discover my great product on a shopping trip. I was almost right. One of the employees I ended up hiring was a former buyer's assistant at QVC, and she loved my product so much, and thought it was so perfect for them, that she gave me the name, e-mail address, and direct dial phone number for the "gatekeeper" of their buying offices. Don't bother trying to call me up to get this information. Many have tried and nobody has succeeded. You don't really need that number to get through to a buyer. I already showed you how to knock down the doors of any customer with just a phone book and a few clicks on their vendor Web site.

Even more important was the employee's willingness to let me use her name when calling. "They all know me there. Go ahead, and tell them I love this product and gave you their phone number." I didn't waste any time. I put together an expert e-mail introducing myself, flaunting my reference, and giving a link to my Web site, reading and rereading to make sure it was perfect. I took a deep breath and pushed send.

I was stunned to see a response in my e-mail in-box early the next day. I couldn't read it; I was too nervous. My husband was at work, so he couldn't read it, either. I couldn't even bring myself to click on it long enough to forward it to someone else to read to me. It sat in my in-box the whole day till my husband came home. I made him read it when I wasn't in the room, so that he could report the contents.

"Here, I printed it off for you to read it," he said, handing it to me.

"I can't read it!" I screamed.

"Well then, I'll read it to you."

"Don't read it to me!" I screamed. I thought my heart was going to stop.

"Well, what do you want me to do?"

"Just tell me what it says!" I screamed. My kids just sat there staring at me, wondering what all this screaming was about.

"They want you to send a sample. There! Are you happy? Did I do it right?"

"Who-hoo!" I screamed, this time jumping up and down. My kids were now worried.

Thus began what was the start of a beautiful relationship. I sent my product with my press kit, and they liked it. My contact, the gatekeeper, had one primary job: evaluate potential products and determine who the appropriate buyer was for them. After she made that determination, she would hand the ball off to them to take it in for the touchdown. After the two days I had spent at QVC just months ago, I thought I knew everything there was to know about the buying process. Was I wrong!

There was something about me or my product that this gatekeeper seemed to like. She shopped us around from buyer to buyer, looking hard for a fit into their particular buying program, working every possible angle to sneak it in that she could think of. She was kind to me, and I appreciated it very much. It got to the point that we were exchanging occasional casual e-mails just saying, "How's it going?" Every time an e-mail from QVC would pop up in my in-box, I'd have my usual heart attack. The suspense was killing me.

One day another e-mail popped up in my in-box from a different person with the QVC.com suffix on the address. I called her at her request, and she explained that she had been referred by the gatekeeper. She loved my product, particularly the Faith Hope & Love pink ribbon line including the Wuvit and the Daisy Bag. She was putting together a show in October to support breast cancer awareness. Much of the proceeds was going to be donated to breast cancer research charities. Would I be on the show? What?! "Of course I will," I answered.

"Good. I'll put together the Purchase Order. This is the date. Put it on your calendar. We'll order at least one thousand sets. I'll contact you soon with the details."

Wow! Was I just booked on QVC? "This is it! This is our big break," I told my husband, friends, and neighbors. We were going to be rich! I went to bed that night worrying about what I was going to look like on TV.

A week later, I got a call from my buyer. I picked up my pencil, ready to write down all the details for my upcoming appearance. "Hi," she started. "I hate to tell you this, but I'm not going to be able to move ahead with my program. Management decided they wanted to sell their own pink ribbon products instead of those of vendors. Sorry. I really tried. I'm disappointed, too."

What?! Did I just get unbooked from QVC? It never occurred to me until then that buyers had bosses, too, and that they had to do what they were told. I've since come to have a lot of sympathy and respect for buyers. They have one of the toughest jobs there is. They risk their futures and their reputations on every product they pick up. Be very, very nice to them.

I was down, but I wasn't out. I let my friend the gatekeeper know that I had been dumped, through no fault of my own. Within weeks, she found me another buyer to contact. This all started with a phone call and an e-mail! I didn't have to even pay the cost of a plane ticket and hotel room. The Product Search was fun, but this was producing results! Since then I've discovered that a phone book and a telephone are all I need to do to make million-dollar sales. No reps, no contracts, no tiny percentage on net revenues.

This next buyer was putting together a program of personal care and spa items. She didn't quite understand mine, but she was willing to consider it. I sent her all the information I could think of along with a great e-mail telling her why Americans were sure to *wuv* Wuvits. She got back to me a week later and told me it just didn't fit the product selection she was putting together.

I was just rejected by QVC for the third time. There was more to come! After going through another buyer vetted for me by my invaluable resource the gatekeeper, I began to understand how the whole buying process worked, or didn't work in my case. You can have all the elements that QVC is looking for, but if your product doesn't fit into a program theme they're building, it won't do you any good. Though it was Single Item Marketing they practiced, they just can't put on one item after another, with no regard to whether they fit together or not. If they did that, you might see jewelry, followed by a vacuum presentation, followed by tools. Instead, each buyer has to build a program varying in lengths of time that can segue from one product to the next every three to twelve minutes and keep the same demographic of buyer interested in buying. Since my product was so different from everything else they were selling, they could never quite figure out what to do with it, particularly what products it fit with. The pink ribbon theme was an obvious niche that I would later exploit successfully.

> ### QVC: NOT THE ONLY GAME IN TOWN
>
> QVC was not the only game in town, despite the perception that it was. There are many TV shopping channels to pitch your product to, including the Home Shopping Network (HSN).

QVC REPS: HOW TO FIND THEM AND
WHAT THEY KNOW THAT YOU DON'T

There exists a certain breed of sales rep that does nothing but look for new products with which to pitch TV marketers like QVC and HSN. Some of them are good, and some of them you need to pass through the B.S. Detection Machine. Here's what you need to know:

- The best place to find them is at trade shows or through personal references.
- The good ones have been on TV themselves selling products they rep.
- You benefit from their established relationships with buyers, who understand that they know how to qualify, package, and present products.
- Buyers prefer to work with reps because they can be brutally honest without considering the feelings or emotions of the entrepreneur or inventor, which can sometimes complicate a business decision.
- Reps understand that they need to integrate a product into a buyer's program or develop a package around a product in order to sell it.

People I Actually Know Who Have Been on QVC, and Their Stories

I've met at least a half-dozen entrepreneurs who have been on QVC. I'll tell you their stories. Everything they told me appeared to be confirmed by what I saw with my own eyes. I'm giving you these examples to help you realize that getting on QVC or any of the other home-shopping channels isn't necessarily the answer to all your distribution problems. You actually have much higher percentages of success with traditional channels of distribution, which I'll teach you how to penetrate. Go after this; I know you can't resist, just as I couldn't. Remember that getting on air doesn't necessarily mean you're going to make money or build your brand, so don't be disappointed if neither happens. Just keep going looking for the next sale.

Entrepreneur Number 1 is a relative of my husband. His father-in-law, my husband's uncle, owns a chemical company in upstate New York, where he formulates and bottles health and beauty products and cleaning solutions. One of his scientists formulated a new car wax that is superior to anything on the market. They took it to NASCAR and got it approved and were licensed to use the NASCAR brand to promote it. It was a major achievement, so impressive that they hired a rep and got themselves a spot on QVC. After months of preparation and a fortune spent on manufacturing inventory, the young man was ready to make his pitch on TV. He was professional and prepared, but they moved him at the last minute to a spot at eight on a Saturday morning in between products geared toward older women. He didn't have a chance selling NASCAR-approved car wax to women who were buying support hose and sleepwear. He had three minutes, and they never gave him another chance to come back to "sell out his inventory."

Entrepreneur Number 2 was an exhibitor I met at a trade show in New York who sold exquisite handmade bead jewelry he bought from poor women in third-world countries through a free-trade program. It was mostly purchased from women and their families living on subsistence farming in Vietnam and Cambodia, providing them with the money they needed to survive. He and his wife were a wonderful new age couple who were doing what they loved. They had, he told me, been on the air three times, selling about $40,000 of jewelry each appearance. They hadn't been asked back again despite this, and he thought that that was because QVC was going more in the direction of traditional jewelry.

Entrepreneur Number 3 was a woman I also met at a trade show who had come up with an ingenious purse organizer that got a lot of press attention from very big sources. She was excited about her upcoming presentation, but when I saw her the next time, she just told me it didn't work out, despite her on-air presentation.

Entrepreneur Number 4, whom I met at a trade show, had developed a unique, patented in-home paraffin wax treatment that was voted best new product in the show. This got the attention of a rep who specialized in pitching products to QVC. Within months, the entrepreneur had a deal to go on air. He had spent a lot of money hiring a professional spokesperson, recommended to him by his rep's contacts at QVC, who would do the on-air presentation. She was more experienced and certain to give a better performance than he could, and it's obvious how critical being good on air is to the success of a product. Last time I checked in with him, three months later, he was still waiting for his big on-air shot.

Entrepreneur Number 5 is the president of a large, established company with very good brand recognition specializing in a segment of collectibles with which QVC does very well. He's been on QVC more than a dozen times. Their company manufactures in China and imports into the U.S. for distribution. Their volume is so big that they will bring over multiple container loads at one time just for their appearance on QVC, shipping it straight to their loading docks. He made me aware that QVC does a lot of manufacturing of its own in China of some of the brands you see them selling, paying the spokesperson you see who represents them, and observes that it can be hard for a young business to break into the market when they have to compete with those kinds of margins. His business is more specialized than others; his products have more of a niche appeal, and the demographics of QVC buyers are optimum for his sales. QVC is very good for him.

10

FAILING IS EASY—
GETTING UP AGAIN
IS WHAT'S HARD

So I got QVC out of my system, as well as the idea of turning over my million-dollar product to somebody else to sell, and barreled full-steam-ahead with my kiosk program. My part-time employee and I started going over the logistics, including Wuvit production, leasing details, and employees. I saw the tasks in front of me clearly, and knew they could be done, but I couldn't believe I was going to have to do them. I recalled the comment of my millionaire mentors: "I remember how hard I worked when we were just starting out, and I never want to work that hard again." I thought then that they hadn't worked for two years. They had two beautiful homes, one on a lake with a boat, and both were paid for. How could that not be worth a year of really hard work? Just a year later, I would agree with their pronouncement wholeheartedly. A year after that, I would say, "I never want to do that again, but am I glad I did!" The further it gets behind me in my rearview mirror, the more I can look back and laugh and see that this was hard, but it was exciting and transforming in a good way, and it gave me opportunities I could never have dreamed about.

I took my family to visit my sister who lived in the heart of Palm Beach, Florida, where even her daughter's high school peers drove Mercedes and had valet parking for their birthday parties on their intercoastal estates—the right kind of estate, one side bordering the Atlantic, the other bordering the waterway, with deepwater drayage for their yachts. I knew these people must have taken a risk sometime in their life, to get rich. It was time to take a risk.

Short-term Pain Equals Long-term Gain

I looked at the work in front of me and almost couldn't breathe. I laid my head down at night and couldn't stop thinking long enough to drift off to sleep. I'd finally fall asleep, only to wake up with a start in a cold sweat. I was used to being sleep deprived, after just having two little boys, but this was something completely different.

The final, nerve-shattering moment came when my second employee—the former kiosk manager from Atlanta who proclaimed her desire to "make me a millionaire"—flaked out on me. I needed someone of her skill and experience by my side to pull off my expectations, but her life got crazy, she got divorced, took a trek in the Rockies for two weeks with her new boyfriend, moved into a waterfront estate on Lake Lanier, and started to flip houses. I made an employment offer to my second-choice employee, which she accepted. To her credit, she took a tough job and handled it.

The money logistics in this operation would be enough to scare the sleep out of most entrepreneurs. We were taking enormous risks, but they were risks that were evaluated in minute detail by the most conservative of risk takers—a bank—and my banker commited to giving me money to get it done, to sign me up for eight more merchant accounts, to get behind me and rally me on in a way that bankers never do. The facts were there and undisputable. I ran every single dollar I made through her bank, and she followed the astronomical deposits with the same kind of proprietary glee that I did. To put it as simply as possible, I had a minimum of $500,000 of expenses in the twelve weeks that transpired between October 1 and December 31. Still, my husband and I built a Cash Flow Spreadsheet—I actually built five, including best-case scenario, worst-case scenario, and everything in between, using the indisputable data of my own numbers last year—and determined that we only needed another loan of $75,000 guaranteed by the SBA, if we took a temporary loan out of our 401(k) of $100,000. The IRS will allow you to borrow money out of your 401(k) with no penalties for a maximum of sixty days; if you don't pay it back by then, they hit you with penalty of 10 percent on top of any tax bracket you're in.

I planned to open all my twelve locations October 1, when rents were as cheap as $1,500, giving me a whole additional month of revenues at twelve locations that I didn't have the previous year. Even according to my worst-case scenario spreadsheet, I would generate enough revenue in sales to pay my November rents—which were as much as $10,000 a location—for twelve kiosks. We would take the $100,000 out of our 401(k) on October 1, wire the lease payments to each leasing manager for each kiosk, and not have payroll due for three whole weeks. The revenues in sales would be rolling in then to cover that. Then we would redeposit our $100,000 back into our 401(k) exactly sixty days later on December 1, when we knew there would be serious money rolling in, just based on our own results last year. My bank was doing cartwheels that we actually had $100,000 cash to fund our business and that we were willing to risk it. They were green-lighting everything, congratulating me on a genius business model. "Get in there and get out! That's brilliant," they would say. "No yearly overhead. No yearly employee salaries. Only operate three months of a year, during the peak retail season—that's genius!" Even my insurance agent congratulated me on the plan, writing the mandatory $2 million in liability insurance I needed to carry during the duration of my leases as required by the malls. "Wow," he said. "I wish I could only work three months a year! Let me introduce you to my CPA. You know, our company provides wealth management services."

On paper, I was going to make a million dollars in revenue by the end of the year. This was better than QVC! Naively, with a million dollars in gross revenue, I thought my husband and I could do whatever we wanted. It wasn't a bad start.

I was interested in a quick exit strategy, selling the business outright as my millionaire mentors had done or finding a way to distribute or franchise. Then my husband and I would get a house on a lake somewhere, forgetting I ever did any of this. My husband was more about building a business, one that he could nurture and grow and pass along to our boys. I made all kinds of promises to my family members, particularly my mother-in-law. My own mother had passed away when I was only twenty-one, so my mother-in-law was the closest thing to a mother I would ever have. She had had a tough life

. . . .

HOW TO MAKE A MILLION DOLLARS

Depending on the kind of industry that you're in, you only have to have net revenues of as little as $200,000 to have a company valued at as much as a million dollars for sale purposes. The only way to figure out a company's worth is by utilizing the standard formula of EBITDA (Earnings Before Interest, Taxes, Depreciation, and Amortization).

A very general rule of thumb in finding the value of your business for sale purposes is to take the amount of cash left at the end of a fiscal year after all fixed, variable, and miscellaneous expenses are deducted and before interest, taxes, depreciation, and amortization. Multiplying this final cash number by anywhere from two to five, depending on the industry you're in, will tell you what the typical asking price for your company would be in the open market. Typically, you need to have a minimum of two years of similar EBITDA figures before you can get the serious interest of investors or buyers.

Don't get too excited about EBITDA. As my chief financial officer likes to say, "You can't put EBITDA in a bank." In other words, it isn't money until it's cash.

. . . .

and never really had a dime to her name, though she enjoyed a rich life filled with the love of family, friends, and food. I was going to take care of her, I promised. I wanted to buy her that nice new car she never had. I was going to send her on that beautiful Caribbean vacation that she never had. I was going to pay off her credit cards, which she ran up mostly just buying her grandkids gifts. I was scared, but not as scared as I was the year before.

The Power of a Positive Cash Flow

I had worked out another element of my system to do this with so little cash. I had talked my Wuvit manufacturer into giving me sixty-day payment terms, instead of the thirty-day I was used to getting. That way, I could manufacturer Wuvits to sell at my kiosks that I wouldn't have to pay for until I was halfway through the retailing season. This was certainly one of the advantages to manufacturing in the U.S., instead of China. I didn't have to come up with a large amount of money up front to fund production I wouldn't be selling for at least 120 days. The minimum production cycle in China is ninety days from the day you put half down with your Purchase Order: thirty to source it, thirty to make it, and thirty to ship it. You can add on another thirty days just to get it from your warehouse to your locations, get it set up, and get it sold. Sure, the margins weren't as good manufacturing in the U.S. as they were in China, but I was taking it right from manufacturing to retail, so I had a little room to play with. I had my hands full already. I just couldn't worry about manufacturing in China, too!

I was planning on selling—at the worst—an average of 3,000 Wuvits per kiosk, for a total of 36,000 or a possible $900,000 worth of revenue. The actual figure I was planning on was 45,000, for revenues as high as $1,125,000. That was a lot for my manufacturer to turn around. They had to get a running start on it, they told me. They could only manufacturer 6,000 units a month at full production capacity. If I needed 36,000, they would have to start in July. That would work better for me, because then I could tailor production in response to sales when we opened in October, cutting it back or ramping it up, whatever the situation called for. I even had the option of stopping production then. I ordered all the necessary raw materials to keep them in production from July through December, faxing in a series of Purchase Orders to my vendors that would keep materials coming in in a steady stream every month, just enough to keep them in maximum production mode. Anything that was manufactured in July wouldn't be billed till August, and payment wouldn't be due until October, when I would be selling product. My banker couldn't have been more pleased. Everybody was going to make money. All my risk was mitigated.

The Birth of Sleepy-head Fred

My pink ribbon–inspired Faith, Hope & Love fabric had been a runaway hit at my kiosks the year before, leading all sales, and I couldn't keep the Wuvits or the Daisy Bags in stock that were made with it. I wanted to come up with an idea for another hot item for 2003, and it came to me in the form of a phone call that very day. A complete stranger was calling me at ten o'clock at night to ask me if I could drop off a Wuvit for her three-year-old son who refused to go to sleep without one. "We've lost our Wuvit, and we don't know what to do," she practically cried into the phone. "Help me! We haven't slept for two days! He won't go to bed without it!"

I got in my car, driving to her house to drop off the Wuvit at 10:00 P.M. thinking to myself, *Hmmm, puts three-year-olds to sleep . . . could that possibly be worth something to somebody?* As the mother of young children myself, I knew the answer was a resounding, "Yes!" I and millions of other parents across the U.S. would pay any amount of money for a "magical sleeping pill for kids" that could put them out at will with gentle, soothing warmth. I got to work designing a whole new fabric, using a cute little-bear character face to appeal to both boys and girls. Again I was overcome with a passion to pursue this idea to fruition, spending thousands of dollars to do a custom run of fabric through the same national home decor design house so that I could have an exciting, groundbreaking product available at all my kiosks across the U.S. in time for the holidays. My instincts were right again, as it went on not only to huge sales but also to earn a distinctive honor granted by a major national publication.

Should Have Used the B.S. Detection Machine

Curiously, right out of the blue a month or two into this, the manufacturer— the father of my part-time employee, who had now become my full-time employee—let me know that he was selling his business. "Selling your business?" I asked. "Who is going to sew my Wuvits? Will I get the same sixty-day-payment terms? Will they do the same quality job? I have so much riding on this right now, what do you mean you're selling your business?!"

"Don't worry," he assured me. "Nothing will change, except ownership. I'm going to exit by December."

"What?" I argued. "For what I'm paying you, why don't I buy it?" I considered for all of five seconds the idea of running an ancient manufacturing and fulfillment house.

I met with the new owners the very next week. This deal was done. The former owner made a very big deal about trotting me in, telling them about my success last year and my imminent success this year and how much money I was going to be running through their new purchase in the next six months in the form of manufacturing, and how very wonderful it all was for me and them. He seemed more enthusiastic than my banker was and was even more of a cheerleader about my prospects for a really big future than I'd ever seen him. His enthusiasm left me with a big nagging question that should have been deposited in my B.S. Detection Machine: If you were so confident I was going to be driving huge amounts of revenues through your place in manufacturing in the years ahead, why were you selling it? I didn't ask it, because he had spent an equal amount of time telling the new owners about how smart I was to come up with this ingenious invention, which would make me and them millions of dollars in the next twenty years. With that, he had turned off my critical thinking faculties, because my head was so swollen with dreams of my own grandeur. The new owners made assurances that they didn't know enough about this business, manufacturing, and fulfillment to do anything different from what was being done now. One was a former salesman, and the other was a family practice lawyer. "We're not going to turn the *Titanic* around," they assured me.

I plowed ahead into the crushing workload I had before me, getting out of bed, consulting my calendar to find out what city I was supposed to be in that day, and doing whatever it was that had to be done. This included traveling to all of these cities where I was opening kiosks. Finding good employees to work at a kiosk wasn't an easy thing to do. Kiosks had become so stigmatized for having low-quality products sold by indifferent employees that paying top dollar with commission was the only way I could attract quality people. The hardest thing I've had to do in my entire entrepreneurial journey has been managing employees, and I really only had them in any significant number for a total of five months in all those years. This was a very difficult process, but with just a few exceptions I had the best employees working for me any employer could have wished for. I became an expert by the end in finding them, employing them, and motivating them, though my first attempt at it was a disaster.

STEP-BY-STEP HIRING PROCESS

Employment Packet: I would make a packet up and send it off in advance to any employee I was interested in interviewing, containing a letter in-

COST-EFFECTIVE WAYS TO FIND EMPLOYEES

Advertising in traditional newspapers can be very expensive, costing up to $500 for a three-to-five-day ad with limited word counts, producing varying results. If you're offering a good wage, put it right in the ad so that you can attract the best employees in a very competitive marketplace.

Many newspapers now offer a Web-based component to their newspaper classified sections, usually for free when you place an ad in their paper. Sometimes these offer unlimited word counts and access to savvier job hunters. Ask the newspaper if this is available and how you can best take advantage of it. They'll give you lots of tips.

National Internet job search Web sites like Monster.com and CareerBuilder.com offer economical plans that allow you to post ads with lots of copy in multiple cities nationwide for no extra cost.

Local colleges have a database of jobs perfect for the college student. You can usually post these for free as an employer.

Also check with your local government for any job databases they maintain for people receiving unemployment benefits. These people are usually skilled and motivated to find work.

troducing our company, a more detailed job description with pay, a confirmation of our interview date, time, and location, and a blank job application, which I asked them to complete in advance.

Completed Job Application: Even if your employee brings you a résumé, for your own legal protection you need to have a completed and signed job application with Social Security number on file, certifying that the information they give you is correct as well as authorizing you to check references. You can buy most blank forms at any office supply store.

Interview: You need to have at least one interview with a potential employee. See the list of standard questions that follows.

Reference/Background Check: You need to check a minimum of three references, at least two of which must be job related. Most companies now are reluctant to give out any personal information for fear of lawsuits. At the very least ask them to verify employment and tell you if the employee was fired. If you're hiring anyone for a position of responsibility, you really should do a criminal background check. You can get these online at a reasonable rate, provided you have a Social Security number for the applicant.

Offer of Employment: I extend a written offer of employment to each employee that states the title of the job, the responsibilities involved, the rate of pay, and whether it is a temporary or permanent position. This has saved me from paying unwarranted unemployment benefits more than once to temporary employees. Make sure the employee signs and dates it, then keep it in a personnel file with all the other materials listed here to protect yourself in any disputes.

IRS Form W-4 (Employee's Withholding Allowance Certificate): Completed and signed with number of deductions noted. You can print this form right off the Internet at www.irs.gov/formspubs.

Employee Handbook: This might seem like a lot of work at first, but it is worth every minute you put into it in the long run. It can protect you in any legal disputes that may arise. At the minimum, it should state information about your company, safety procedures, clearly written reasons for terminations, job descriptions and duties, attendance, dress, smoking, and contact information, emergency or otherwise. Have the employee sign a form that states they have received a copy and reviewed it, and keep it in their employee file.

• •

LEGAL EMPLOYMENT ISSUES

Job Discrimination: It is illegal to discriminate against potential employees based on race, color, religion, sex, or national origin. There are also certain legal protections guaranteed to people with disabilities, pregnant women, and people over forty years of age.

Terminating an Employee: Firing employees is hard. You should provide an employee with a written reprimand for specified improper conduct at least twice before firing them. Keep a copy in their employment file, in case they file a claim for unemployment benefits. My style was swift and certain. I'd ask for the keys first. Once they gave them to me, I'd say, "I'm sorry, I have to let you go. You know why. We've discussed it, and I've provided you with written warnings. I wish you the best of luck in your next job." Remember that each state has different laws about paying a fired employee. Some require that you issue the check immediately instead of waiting for the normal pay cycle. If that's the case, bring the last check with you when you fire your employee.

Workers' Compensation Insurance—What You Need to Know: Workers' compensation is insurance that you are required to carry that provides compensation for any employee who is injured on the job. Each state has different laws governing workers' comp. Speak to your insurance agent for information, or visit the U.S. Department of Labor's Web site at www.dol.gov.

• •

Training: You need to train your employees adequately, and they must be paid their hourly rate for training.

TYPICAL INTERVIEW QUESTIONS

- Tell me about yourself.
- What are you looking for in a job?
- What are your short-range objectives?
- Why did you leave your last employer?
- Why do you want to work for us?
- What interests you about the position?
- Why should we hire you?
- What do you know about our organization?
- What would your previous supervisor say are your greatest strengths and weaknesses?
- What do you feel are your strongest points?
- What do you feel are your weakest points?
- Tell me about your greatest accomplishment.
- Where do you see yourself in five years? In ten?
- Have you been interviewing with other companies?

Employees You Shouldn't Hire

Besides the obvious red flags, like criminal convictions, you also want to be careful about hiring employees who have filed expensive insurance claims against former employers. If a potential employee reveals to you that they have significant medical considerations that may be aggravated by working for you, you may want to compensate them with a 1099 form. By giving an employee a 1099 form, you employ them as an independent contractor, which may give you certain protections. Talk to your insurance agent.

My Own Employee Horror Story

I hired an employee to manage one of my kiosk locations in New Jersey. She was extremely polished, attractive, and friendly, a perfect employee, on paper and in person. She had just been downsized from a professional career job and was looking for temporary seasonal employment. I called all her references, and she checked out great. She was flawless, selling, stocking, managing other employees, filling in for them when they didn't show up, until the cops came and arrested her at work!

She had been writing down the credit card numbers of my customers and

WHAT'S A 1099 FORM AND WHEN SHOULD I USE IT?

A 1099 form is given out at the end of the year to any employee or subcontractor who provided you with more than $600 worth of services in the calendar year, which provides a record of their income while also reporting it to the IRS.

A 1099 form, unlike a W2 form, is for someone who is not a formal employee. You are not required to deduct federal or state income taxes or Social Security from the income you paid them. These employees are required to pay these taxes themselves at the end of each tax year.

A 1099 is a federal tax form, so its use is consistent in every state. Check with your tax advisor about the precise use of a 1099.

selling them on the black market. The cops had been observing her at my kiosk for weeks before they finally arrested her. They didn't tell me this, explaining later that they didn't want to jeopardize their investigation. This location was closed immediately for the remaining retailing season, costing me tens of thousands of dollars.

Learning from Our Success

Just as we had done the year before, we decided to open a kiosk in Denver a month earlier than the rest to "go to school on," ironing out the inevitable kinks before launching the remaining locations. On the flight out, I looked surreptitiously at the computer screen of the man sitting next to me, open to his own Cash Flow Excel Spreadsheet. He was obviously agitated and going over it again and again, trying to make the negative $450,000 number on the final row of the final column disappear. $450,000 of red ink! It hurt just to look at. He sighed deeply, shook his head, took out the expense for employee salaries, put it back in again, then sighed, covering his face with his hands. I could feel his pain. I compared my spreadsheet in my head to his and thought, *Thank God that will never happen to me.*

I had booked a room at the Embassy Suites and used their lobby for my interviews. We had come up with a very complex compensation package for our kiosk managers that consisted of a wage, a selling commission, and a managing commission, which would be paid at the end of the holiday retailing season based on total sales. The total commission package was worth thousands of dollars to the manager. This compensation was the only way I could talk anyone with any experience or skills to come to work for me in a temporary position at a glorified cart. I had six interviews lined up, and I put together my presentation, running over it in my hotel room right before they started. Reviewing the compensation schedule, I was aghast to find that my employee in Michigan had written the compensation formula wrong, using flawed figures and flawed math. I was five minutes away from meeting my first interviewee, and everything I had to show them was wrong. I had put an ad in the local newspaper that cost me $500, flown out to Denver, another $500, and had a room at a nice hotel for two nights, another $500 with all the expenses added in. I had spent $1,500 of my precious $75,000, and I was not prepared. I called my employee in Michigan, asking that she fax me something corrected ASAP. She had only recently revealed to me that she was pregnant, so every communication was now filtered through her extremely volatile mix of hormones and stress. I lived through the next four months of this high-stress business venture listening to her either cry or scream, and I would do my share of both, too. I thought this first blunder was an omen that things were going to spiral out of control. I was taking a risk with $100,000 of my and my husband's own money, wondering if it was too late to stop, too late to go forward, feeling doubt and mesmerizing, mind-numbing, all-powerful fear.

I proceeded to the lobby, pasted a smile on my face, and interviewed the two applicants who showed up of the six scheduled. I sold them on why they wanted to work for me more than they sold themselves on me. I came away with one qualified and willing applicant who agreed to be my manager and to interview and hire the other personnel I had to attract.

I did what I did in Denver eleven more times with the help of employees in all the other cities we were opening in. In each city I set up a business account with a new bank, having a proverbial red carpet rolled out for me. Invariably, I was invited to speak to the branch manager in their office, enjoying free coffee and doughnuts while they explained to me their line of credit quick-approval loans available to someone with my exceptional credit score, as well as all their wealth-management tools. We were able to cobble together a precarious team of employees for each location, doing "whatever it took" to solve their almost daily crises, the resolution of which would enable them to come to work that day, whether it was to send them a $100 advance on wages to buy groceries for their kids or just to talk them through an argument they had with another employee. We were on the phone practically 24-7 just handling personnel issues, soothing over tears, anger, jealousy, or disappointment, with precious little time to focus on sales. We all made more than one emergency trip to one location or another just to put the cart back on the rails when it went catastrophically awry. I remember one particularly brutal trip to Philadelphia during which I worked for two solid days all alone while I solved an unexpected employee crisis by calling on a temporary employment agency to deliver me two emergency employees, whatever it cost. Contrary to all reasonable doubts, it all worked.

TEMPORARY AGENCIES: THE PROS AND CONS OF USING THEM

- If you're going to have to pay $500 for a classified ad to find a temporary employee, you may want to consider a temporary agency instead and save yourself the cost of the ad. Some national agencies include Kelly Services, Manpower, and Adecco.
- Temporary agencies will take all the work out of finding a good employee for you, interviewing them, checking their references, sometimes even training them. Agencies can almost always deliver to you, sometimes with as little as a day's notice, a qualified first-rate employee who they already know is going to do good work. My QVC contact came from a temporary agency.
- When you hire a temporary employee through an agency, you can expect to pay at least 50 percent more in wages than you would a normal employee you hire. The trade-off is that you don't pay any employment taxes or insurance, so this is not as bad as it sounds. The employment agency will pay the employee a wage you negotiate—"negotiate" is the key word here—and bill you for that employee's wages, which may give you a two to three-week cash flow buffer zone. You may even be able to pay for the employee's wages with a credit card.

Your Best Friend and Your Worst Nightmare—
Plotting the Course with a Moving Target:
The Monthly Cash Flow Spreadsheet

Since we had done the kiosks the previous year, I had reasonable expectations of what sales should be. I had built my five Cash Flow Spreadsheets using the cold, hard numbers we already had. If malls could be rated on a scale of 1–4, with 4 being the best, all the malls we had this year were 4s, while we only had one 4 last year, the rest being 2s and one 3. I even had one "control" mall, the Mall of Georgia, at which we had done record sales for eight weeks the year before. That would be the yardstick for determining whether we were on track with last year's sales, telling us when we had to tweak them by motivating employees or even making more Wuvits! I took the data from the four locations last year and made my five spreadsheets: Number 1 was titled "Worst-Case Scenario": This used data from my lowest-producing mall last year, where I made $42,000 in eight weeks, a 2 on a scale of 1–4, assuming that all my rated-4 locations this year unbelievably did this badly. Even in this scenario, I ended up making a profit of $125,000. Number 3 was titled "Average Scenario": This one averaged all the revenues I made last year, adding in the month of October for all the twelve locations, and used it as a forecast for best average revenues for each mall. I calculated that the average gross at these locations would be $70,000. These numbers are what I really considered to be representative of my worst-case expectations. Number 5 was titled "Best-Case Scenario": This took last year's averaged numbers and added in $25,000 for each location. This was my goal and I actually believed it was doable. The other two spreadsheets fell in between, factoring in other variables like unanticipated employee expenses, including travel and commissions. Like last year, I returned exhausted from the hiring and opening road and turned the day-to-day operations over to my management team and hunkered down in my basement, watching the daily sales reports come in and plugging the numbers into one of my five spreadsheets—obsessed.

The Real Benefits of a Business Plan—Now You Know! When You Lose Sight of the Horizon in an Ocean of Detail and Crisis, Just Remember the Mantra "Work the Plan"

My husband and I had taken our $100,000 out of our 401(k) on October 1; we had until December 1 to return it. That was the plan, and I had no doubt that it was going to work. We waited for the money to start rolling in as it had done last year. I was already looking at big new SUVs to buy with the cash before the end of the year when the big tax deduction on them expired. My banker was calling me weekly for updates, as excited as I was. My financial planner, who was visibly shaken that we had taken the $100,000 he managed out of our 401(k), couldn't hide his skepticism that we would ever put it back.

Half of October passed. We started out with an incredible bang, showing record sales at several locations, which charged up our employees with a shot of enthusiasm for all the money they were soon going to be making. Then things went south quick. October passed with the leases for November due, without the revenues to pay them! Where were they? They just didn't materialize? How did that happen? "It's a late holiday buying season," all the pundits were screaming, in an incredibly nervous retail marketplace! My husband began to get really nervous, too.

"Close up some of the kiosks," he screamed.

"It's only October!" I screamed back.

"I don't care," he said. "Can't you see the writing is on the wall? I don't want to pay rents of ten thousand dollars at each location if we're not making money!"

"We haven't had a chance to make money!" I answered. "We've invested so much money to get to this point! It's a slow start to the holiday buying season, that's all. We can't walk out now right before the money rolls in!"

At least we could still control our inventory, I assured him. That's the beauty of manufacturing in the U.S., just-in-time manufacturing. We can stop the manufacturing now, plan for our worst-case scenario—Spreadsheet Number 1—coming true, and still make $125,000.

"Stop it," he demanded.

I immediately called my employee whose father had just sold the manufacturing and fulfillment facility that made and warehoused my Wuvits. "Stop the manufacturing," I told her.

"We can't stop it," she responded. "You gave us Purchase Orders, and now we're going to make it."

"What?" I answered? "Are you kidding? You see these sales numbers! How am I going to pay for it if I don't have the money? Besides, this was always Plan B, adjusting the inventory to suit the circumstances as we went along. You knew that. That's why the Purchase Orders were given in stages with dates for manufacturing, complete with cancel dates. That's why the raw materials were coming in in stages, to keep you in production at your maximum level while allowing me to adjust production in response to sales. Stop the manufacturing!"

"We can't stop the manufacturing because we're already done!"

What? I thought to myself. *Already done?* "I thought you could only manufacture at the most six thousand Wuvits a month?" I reminded her. "That would put you at twenty-four thousand maximum right now."

"We opened another sewing facility in July. We've been making four thousand a week for a total of forty-eight thousand."

"What? And you didn't tell me?" I stuttered out. How could my employee have misled me on the production of $200,000 worth of inventory? She was my support system in this daily war we waged; she had been through last year's battle with me, and we shared that immutable bond. She wouldn't do what she had done to me last year, only this time on an even more colossal scale? I thought we had fixed all those problems, manufacturing with Purchase Orders while communicating clearly how it was going to work this year. After all, there were new owners. It all looked so good on paper, but again there was that unpredictable human element that you could never totally figure out, manage, or trust.

There was no time to think; it was a time of action. Now I really had to find a way to sell inventory. The very next day one of the leasing managers from one of my malls called me.

"Your product's not doing well. You're not going to make it here. I have someone who wants to buy out your lease, effective immediately."

I couldn't believe my ears. We had been there for just a month. The holiday retailing season hadn't even started yet. How did she know I wasn't going to make it? I was instantly suspicious of her motives. I had one of the best locations there; did she want to get rid of me in favor of the "friend" of hers?

My husband screamed, "Take the deal and run!"

My employee, for what it was worth at this point, screamed, "You can't run now; the Christmas buying season is about to begin!"

I was looking at the numbers. *They don't lie,* I told myself, pulling out my worst-case-scenario spreadsheet and seeing that our sales were down 20 percent from that worst forecast! I called my banker for advice; she knew better than anybody what was real and what was fear.

"Work the Plan," she said.

"What?"

"Work the Plan," she repeated, like a hypnotic mantra, which I would repeat to myself a thousand times in the weeks to come. "You had really good information," she explained. "Numbers don't lie. You've written a good plan using your good information. Let's face it, we gave you the money! When you can't see what's happening anymore, because you're caught up in crisis, just remember, Work the Plan."

Worse Than Worst-Case!

I couldn't afford to cut and run when we were just about to start the Christmas buying season. I had to stay and make the money I needed at least to break even. I began to realize that it was way worse than worst-case and I needed to win in a big way just to break even, forget about making money. Especially now that I was stuck with all this inventory all over again. November 1 came. We needed to find a way to make lease payments, even though the revenues weren't there to pay for them. My husband got on the phone to do what he is so incomparably talented at: schmoozing. He's just so genuinely nice, you can feel it coming out of the phone. He got them all to take half the lease payment instead on the first, with the other half to be paid on the fifteenth. We had just enough left of our $100k to get this done. We had thirty days to pay it all back to our 401(k) and our financial planner was calling. I could feel his disappointment and skepticism in me coming through the phone.

We plowed into November, assuring everyone in our daily newsletters that the holiday retailing season was about to blow up in a big way. "Watch out!" we encouraged them. "All those late shoppers are going to show up at the last minute. Then you're going to be swamped." We all waited, but still nothing happened. We were halfway into November and revenues were flat. Even my managers who had done this before were saying they had never seen anything like it. Every day one of them would call me and say, "KB Toys is closing stores, did you hear?" A toy store closing stores during the Christmas buying season? Then another one would call me from a mall halfway across the country. "Bombay Company has closed their doors, a week before Thanksgiving!" What? Another retailer closed their doors during the biggest retail buying season of the year? Even the Mall of Georgia was struck. My manager there called me up to announce: "FAO Schwarz is closing—bankrupt!"

I couldn't believe this. I was glued to the news, every news source there was, from my daily retail industry newsletters from PlainVanillaShell (www.plainvanillashell.com) to the weekly facts and figures coming out of Washington; both painted radically different pictures. For every story I found lamenting the fate of the marketplace at this critical shopping season in retail trade news sources, I found a totally different story from Washington. "The Commerce Department reports that consumer spending is up 20 percent over last year!" the news reports declared. "Consumers are planning on making more expensive purchases this holiday season than ever before." What? Businesses were going bankrupt! "Consumer confidence is up to new highs!" What? All the trade publications I was reading geared to the retail market were contradicting every single one of these reports coming from the Commerce Department with equal and opposite reports. Where was the truth? I had kiosk locations across the U.S., from Denver to New York, San Antonio to Minneapolis, and all of them were tanking. This was not just my problem. My frustration hit a head when I heard NPR's *Talk of the Nation* radio show, featuring one of these Washington bureaucrats quoting all this hyper-positive propaganda, and I called in to tell him what was really happening in America, with the host putting me right through to the air! Still, many people would insist that was indeed just my problem.

At least I had Atlanta as a beacon of truth. My revenues, in a great location, with an even better staff than the year before, were off 45 percent. All my revenues were off 45 percent across the board. The results from the giant experiment were in. Still we needed to come up with the money we needed for December rents. "Work the Plan," I kept repeating to myself. "Holiday shopping season latest ever on record," the news reported. "Consumers will make one mad dash at Thanksgiving." My husband and I pulled out every single one of these beautiful platinum credit cards we had stored away for a rainy day and took every cash advance we could on them—a whole hell of a lot! We missed the December 1 deadline for the redeposit of the $100k into our 401(k).

I was going to bed terrified and waking up even more anxious every day. Still, there were times I would stand in the shower, the kids mercifully addicted to their new GameCube, feeling an incredible wave of peace wash over me with a feeling that "everything is going to be okay." We were too busy to do anything but eat Chinese daily, and every fortune cookie every day for weeks coincidentally had the exact same message: "You will be successful in your business." I collected six of them, put them in a little frame, and each morning while my kids ate breakfast I stared at it, wondering just what the hell I was going to do.

11

SEND LAWYERS, GUNS, AND MONEY! WHAT TO DO WHEN EVERYTHING GOES WRONG

By the middle of December, my husband and I realized this was a full-scale disaster. He immediately went into damage-control mode, shutting down the kiosks that had dropped off the sales chart. We had to stop the bleeding first. My bank had given me a $75,000 loan for this operation, but they expected payment of it by January 1, only six months after they had given it to me. Besides that, we had bills from our other creditors that were due immediately! I called a friend, a VP in banking in Florida. I had $95,000 left in my bank account and didn't know what to do.

How to Protect Cash Assets in an Emergency

"Get it out of there right now!" she told me. "You have to scramble to protect your cash assets! You're going to need that cash to hold off as many creditors as you can for as long as you can. Banks won't tell you this, but if you owe them seventy-five thousand dollars and the money is sitting in your bank account, they can take it without your permission. Just like that! I'll set up an account for you at my bank; wire me the ninety-five thousand dollars today! Don't go to your branch to do it. Drive to another town, go to a bank where nobody knows you, and fill out the wire transfer paperwork. By the time they figure it out, it will be too late!"

"But I owe them that money! How am I going to pay them that loan?"

"Don't worry about it. Once they realize the money isn't there, they'll term it out with you over five years or something like that. But they will want the cash first. If you go in there and talk to them about terming it out and they see you've got the money sitting in the bank, they'll take it out while you're sitting in the office, waiting for them to decide. What, are you kidding? This is a bank we're talking about!"

There would come a time to assess the full damage later. For now there was nothing but disappointment, fear, and regret, with plenty of blame to go around. I blamed my husband; he blamed me; we blamed our manufacturer, who blamed us. Even our banker had forsaken us. Our financial planner had not sent us a holiday card for the first time in five years. I know he blamed me.

It's Only Money

I blamed myself, too. My husband and I were fighting bitterly under all the incredible stress, but I woke up one morning after it was all over, did a quick reality check, and realized I owed him the biggest apology of my life.

"Honey—I'm so sorry," I said.

"For what?" he answered me.

"For what? I've ruined everything! I just put you through hell! I took every dollar we ever saved alone and together and flushed it down the toilet! I exposed our family to unacceptable risk, and what do we have to show for it? Nothing but disappointment and debt!"

"It's only money," he said.

"What? I just ruined us!"

"Ruined us? What are you talking about? It's only money. Forget about it. We still have each other. We still have those two beautiful boys down-stairs. Do you think we lost any of that? We still have our love. What's money? Money is money. Money is a tool to get what we want. We took a risk, and we lost. Big deal. We'll get more money. You can always get more money. You can't replace people you love. We still have each other."

"But we have nothing! We lost it all! It's all my fault!"

"What are you talking about? Look at those two beautiful boys down there and tell me we have nothing! What happened to us is nothing. Losing one of those boys to a terminal disease, now that's something. Count your blessings and thank God that we're not going through that instead! Money is nothing. We'll get through this. As long as we have each other, we have everything. Now stop talking like that. We'll figure out what to do."

My Husband, My Hero

My husband is the hero of this story. I can't imagine going through what we went through and not having each other to hold on to. Business failures like ours were a dime a dozen. Let's face it, more businesses fail in first five years than succeed. That's not a crime. What is a crime is when these failures end in divorce, too. That's when everything truly is lost. I suppose our marriage could have ended, too, if one of us didn't summon the emotional courage to face our problems and do what was simply right.

My husband soon learned that the company for which he worked was all but going out of business. He would be without a job again in just months.

We had no safety net to catch us this time. I looked at my beautiful house with a whole new appreciation. I can't believe I had thought it wasn't good enough. I can't believe it made one bit of difference whether I had hardwood floors in my kitchen or vinyl. I would never care again what kind of car I would drive. Money would never mean money to me again. Money had just one value to me: freedom. As long as there was enough money to put food on the table to feed my beautiful children, nothing else mattered. As long as I could look into the bright laughing eyes of my children and depend on a husband to support me no matter what mistakes I made in life, I could work at Wal-Mart and live in a tarpaper shack and still be happy. I remembered a favorite saying of my mother's: "Just because people have more money than you doesn't mean they're any happier."

Confronting Bankruptcy: Doing What's Right, Not What's Easy

As my husband and I sorted through the wreckage, we both confronted the possibility of declaring bankruptcy. We saw an attorney who told us our only choice was to go bankrupt. He advised us that we had better do it soon, because it was going to cost us $10,000 to get it done.

This was the lowest point of my life, in a life with a lot of low points already. Can you believe I was about to discover in this mess of problems that God's providence was around me every day? Another saying I've heard quoted by successful entrepreneurs: "There are no atheists in foxholes."

I finally made my first appointment with my husband to see a counselor at the SBDC. I had not followed the advice I am now able to give you. Learn from my mistakes.

We gathered up our sorry financial documents and laid it all out on the table for our SBDC advisor to consider, giving him a fifteen-minute narrative about what happened. I tried to explain away the terrible mistakes I had made.

"You didn't make any mistakes," he said, leaning back in his chair with his hands folded behind his head, thinking in silence for an excruciating five minutes before he said it. "Given all the information you've given me today, if I had it to do over again, I would do it. Your business plan didn't fail. It was a good business plan. You had a lot of good, reliable data. Sometimes there are just circumstances beyond your control. That's just the way it is, plain and simple. That's business. Yup," he commented matter-of-factly.

"But now we're going to have to go bankrupt!" I answered him, railing at the unfairness of the universe more than anything.

"Who says you're going to have to go bankrupt?"

"The bankruptcy attorney, that's who!"

"Of course he's going to say that! What's he charging you to go bankrupt? Ten thousand dollars? That's a classic 'What's in it for him?' question!"

This man was speaking my language. He was definitely different from any counselor I had met before. Half academic, half blood-and-guts business veteran, he would assume the role of General in my life, commanding me to do things I never thought I could do, leading me through the battle for my business. You can't always trust attorneys to give you objective, impartial decisions. You go to them, usually in crisis, thinking they're going to be your savior and help you figure out smart strategies for business survival, but many are primarily motivated by personal gain. They're not necessarily looking out for your best interests. Most of them don't know anything about business. Go to your priest if you're looking for a savior. Go to your SBDC advisor for business advice. Go to your attorney for legal advice only, then run it through your B.S. Detection Machine, asking the classic first question, "What's in it for him?"

"Whatta ya gonna do with all this inventory?" the General asked me next.

"I don't know!" I responded. "Let's just go bankrupt," I said to my husband.

"You're not going bankrupt!" the General stormed. "What's wrong with you? You just sold over a half a million dollars on this product in twelve months! Go out there and sell more! We gotta figure out a way to get cash flow. Got any opportunities to sell it?"

"There's a trade show coming up in Atlanta in a couple of weeks. I could try and go down there," I offered. "I'm not going back to any kiosks!"

"No. You're going to go wholesale."

"Okay," I said.

"You're going to push out this product, get some cash flow, start to service this debt, then regroup."

"But there's so much debt!" I said, feeling the pain of the incredible debt that was about to suffocate me and my husband.

Debt Is a Tool: The Difference Between Good Debt and Bad Debt

"Screw debt! Debt's a tool. As long as you have cash flow to service your debt, don't even worry about it!" the General proclaimed, bringing a fist down on the table for emphasis. "Most of this debt is inventory that you can sell. That's an asset—most of your debt is secured by assets. You think there's a business out there that isn't carrying debt?! This is good debt—the start of a business. Everybody's balance sheet looks this bad!" I thought back to that guy's spreadsheet I had seen on the plane with $450,000 of red ink, thinking he was right. "There's good debt and bad debt, and this is definitely good debt. Bad debt would be anything not secured by assets, and you've got lots of assets in the form of inventory."

As you'll remember, "debt" was a four-letter word to my husband and me. The absence of any debt had been our goal, as well as our measurement of the success of others. He wanted us to view our debt differently than we were used to. I would soon see that some of the richest people I met had astronomical debt, like investments in twenty-five-story buildings. One of the richest could barely cut me a check for $12,000 without seriously carving into his cash flow—even his grocery money that week. For the really rich, life is like a game of Monopoly, when the person with the most investments and the least cash wins.

"This is what you're gonna do," the General began. "You need to get cash to make these debt payments. I've got a couple of ideas. What do you charge wholesale for these Wuvits?"

"Well, there's the wholesale cost, plus an additional fifteen percent on top of that which goes to rep commissions."

"Good. You got reps making sales. How much are they bringing in monthly?"

"None," I admitted with chagrin. "I've been too busy with retail to worry about this. None of my reps are really making sales."

"Then you are going to go to Atlanta and slash the wholesale cost by fifteen percent and get rid of these rep commissions that you're not paying. Next you're going to develop a strategy of Advance Pricing."

Advance Pricing: What It Is and How It Changed My Business Overnight

"What's Advance Pricing?"

"Have you looked into manufacturing in China yet?"

"Yes, I have. I can lower my costs by forty percent. I just need a lot of cash to float the production for 120 days. I can't do that now!"

"Okay. Say for example we are selling widgets at ten dollars wholesale cost. Now we take half of the forty percent savings you would get from manufacturing in China—you gotta keep some higher margins for yourself—bringing the wholesale cost on widgets down twenty percent to eight dollars. That's Advance Pricing: pricing your product at the costs of your Chinese manufacturing. Doesn't matter that you're not doing it there now. You need to attract the customer, probably some really big retailer, who is going to buy in quantities big enough to merit you taking your production overseas. The only way to attract that big customer is to give them a really good price reflecting your quantity discount costs in China. In other words, you gotta take a hit on the front end, so you can make it back on the long. Think of all that inventory you got sitting over in that warehouse as money in the bank. You just gotta convert it into cash. You gotta go to Atlanta," the General commanded, "and sell a big retailer thousands and thousands of Wuvits at your Advance Pricing costs."

Sell a big retailer thousands and thousands of Wuvits? No pressure!

"Next," he went on, undeterred, "you gotta find someone to help you sell this inventory besides these reps, who aren't selling. Can you hook up with any showrooms down there?"

I thought about the one showroom I had already worked with, shaking my head at the hopelessness of that prospect. "I have someone I've worked with before. But I already know that's not going to work."

"Make it work," he boomed, handing me another command: "Do whatever it takes, including selling your product at cost for cash."

The Importance of Cash Flow: How Selling My Product at Cost for a Limited Time Saved My Business

"Selling our product at cost?!" My husband finally spoke. He was practically hyperventilating.

"You need to get rid of it," the General answered. "And you need cash flow. You can't lower your price that low direct to customers without them expecting that price all the time, but if you find a showroom that will sell your product to another big customer they might know at your Advance Pricing costs, it's all good. They'll be really motivated to make a big sale, and you'll move inventory and raise cash."

If selling my product at cost would bring cash through the door, why not? To have it sit in the warehouse could result in my bankruptcy. However, if I sold it at cost I'd at least pay for it, sloughing off part of the cash to make my monthly minimum credit card payments.

"Here's the name and number of somebody I want you to call. You're going to need him. He's been in the same spot you are once before himself. He just sold his company and retired, but he's willing to help people like you, out of the goodness of his heart. He's a part-time chief financial officer. You're going to need someone with his skills to make sense of all of this."

I looked at the card the General gave me. It had a name, followed by all kinds of expensive-sounding acronyms, including "CPA," "MBA," "CFO." "A CFO? What's that going to cost?!"

"I told you, he sold his company and retired. He's not much older than you. He'd be helping you out. He's been in your position and knows what to do."

CHIEF FINANCIAL OFFICERS—WHAT THEY CAN DO FOR YOU THAT A CPA CAN'T

Don't expect a freelance CFO to do your taxes or even to do basic bookkeeping. A CFO will organize a company's financial statements to provide the best and most accurate economic snapshot for owners and possible investors. This is much more complicated than you would think.

Everybody I know who has used the services of a CFO needed them when in crisis, usually as a result of rapid, undisciplined growth, or when they were in search of capital from investors, also often a result of rapid, undisciplined growth.

CFOs are more than CPAs. The best ones are tough, real-world business-people who know how to take creditors and bankers to the mat to protect your business's economic viability.

A CFO will help you analyze costs more closely, so you can adopt more prof-itable long-term financial strategies.

There is a whole industry of freelance CFOs out there. I've had three of them. Call up your SBDC office for references.

The best CFOs charge up to $200 an hour. This is a bargain when you con-sider many CPAs charge the same and give you half as much.

There's no end to what a CFO can do for you. My CFOs have done every-thing for me or their other clients from terming out debt between two parties to hedging euros and natural gas futures for their international customers.

The next day our new part-time CFO was sitting in our living room. I wanted to find out how somebody could have once been as bad off as we were, then turned it around and sold his company, enabling him to retire. He didn't look to be more than five years older than us.

"I didn't make enough to buy my own Caribbean island," he explained, "but I don't have to worry about money for the rest of my life, either."

"What are you going to charge us?" I asked him after going through our narrative and showing him our pathetic balance sheet. "Look at our balance sheet. Have you ever seen a worse one? We don't have any money."

"Everybody's balance sheet looks that bad!" he assured us with a wave of his hand. Apparently, we were joining a secret society of entrepreneurs, in which everybody shared a common language and the same abysmal problems without ever discussing them with the public.

"What about going bankrupt?" I asked, looking for the tie-breaking vote on the conflicting advice I had gotten from my attorney and the General.

Finding the Courage and Determination to Fight for My Business

"Because it's not right! It's like the nail in the coffin of your business. You can get out of this! This is nothing. Everybody's been through times like these! Fight for your business! Fight! You just have to go make sales. Bring in money; that's all you should worry about right now. Find a way to drive cash through the business."

"What about all that inventory?"

"We're going to straighten that out right away. I'm going to go in there and negotiate a new number on what you owe; then we're going to term out the debt in a personal guarantee loan with seven percent interest, payable over five years. Get that monkey off your back right now. That will give you some breathing room and let you sell that inventory to make the cash you need to make this business run!

"I'm going to knock at least thirty percent off of the cost of the stuff. If anybody asks, I didn't say this, but what they did to you was a crime. That's the oldest trick in the book. An owner inflates his manufacturing receivables so that he can drive up the price on his business. The new owners were left with a ton of costs, and no money to pay them off. They're going to take whatever deal I give them, because if they don't, you won't pay them a dime. I'll tell them that you're going to go bankrupt. Let's face it, you won't have a choice. That will scare them! They don't know how to sell that stuff. They'll be caught holding all the costs!"

This guy was the real thing. He knew exactly what to do. His disclaimer, "If anyone asks, I didn't say this," impressed me. He seemed to understand that two parallel universes operated at the same time in business: In one lawyers, CPAs, and accountants functioned in an antiseptic environment in cushy offices and every decision was made strictly by the books and numbers; the other was the real world, in which people were getting dirty all the time. This guy understood that the secret language of this society of entrepreneurs was leverage, and he really knew how to speak it.

Leverage means using any tool you can find to gain advantage over another, whether it's money, the promise of success, or even a threat.

Terming Out Debt Between Two Private Parties

If you find yourself in a difficult situation and you owe a vendor a lot of money, hire a CFO to draw up a legally binding agreement to term out the debt for a prescribed amount of time at a reasonable annual interest rate. This will enable you to negotiate payment terms that your cash flow can support, with the possibility of repairing your relationship with the vendor to allow you to continue doing business.

In Search of a Miracle

I packed up my trade-show set, put it in my truck, kissed my babies goodbye, and drove off to Atlanta. At least I didn't have to worry about who was going to take care of my kids when I was gone, since my husband's job had come to an abrupt end, meaning we'd have unemployment benefits for a while to put food on the table. I was on the road for six hours when inexplicably my truck went dead, right in the middle of a hundred miles of southern Indiana cornfields. It was getting dark, my battery was dead, and my cell phone was on its last bar of power. I had planned to drive through most of the night in order to get to Atlanta in time for the show setup the next day. If I missed the setup window, I wouldn't be able to participate in the show, and the General had commanded me to pull off the impossible if my business was to survive. But just getting myself there in time wasn't my biggest concern; my entire trade-show set was in the back of my big truck, which means I needed to get it there, too. I knew it was going to be just about impossible to get my truck fixed before I needed to be in Atlanta, in less than eighteen hours. I also knew that finding a car to rent in the middle of nowhere that could hold all of my trade-show set was probably impossible. I was licked. It was five minutes to six when the tow truck driver pulled into the only car rental place in a town with a population of 6,000 people, an Enterprise franchise that had just opened only months before.

"Oh, we were just about to close!" they said as I walked in the door.

"Is there any way you can help me?" I asked. The tow truck driver waited outside for me. "I need a truck for a week rental."

"We just drove off the lot today a Chevy Yukon we bought to rent to customers!"

"You're kidding me, right?"

"No, I'm not! We've had it sitting out there for no more than two hours! We didn't know if buying it was a good decision. We didn't know if anybody would ever want to rent it. And here you are, wanting to rent it for a week!"

"Well, I guess you've made your first month's car payment on it with me," I said, grateful over my unbelievably good fortune.

The tow truck driver dropped my truck at a local garage, where I drove to transfer all my trade-show stuff into the rental. The second I transferred the last box and closed the tailgate it started to pour rain. I knew I was going to have a good show because someone or something was obviously pulling off miracles to get me there.

I had picked up a prime booth space at the trade show. I had asked my brother-in-law, who was between jobs himself, to help along with the manager of my kiosk at the Mall of Georgia. "We need a one-hundred-thousand-dollar show," I told my temporary employees. "We'll try," they answered.

"You have to go up to this showroom on the seventh floor with me," my Georgia employee said.

"Why?" I asked.

"It's the most popular showroom here! Everybody in Atlanta shops there for wholesale!"

We went to the showroom and I couldn't believe what I saw. It was crammed with every kind of merchandise possible, all jumbled and practically piled up, as wholesale shoppers tore through the goods, picking up armfuls and pushing others out of the way. It was nothing like the wine and cheese showroom that I had worked with before.

"This woman wants to sell you some merchandise," my manager said to the owner, a man of Arab descent who spoke with a thick accent.

"What does she sell?" he asked.

"Wuvits and Daisy Bags," she answered.

"I know those. You have the ad in the *The Market*!" he said, holding up the show directory where I had placed an ad six months ago when I was still flush with cash. "I take some. What price?"

What? He was going to buy my stuff? Did I want it in this crazy showroom? I looked around at the dozens of people making purchases, while others waited outside to get in, and thought, *Sure, why not?*

"Here's my card," he said. "You come and see me after the show. We talk. I buy."

What happened next was inexplicable. My employee and I went down to our booth and started to write orders like crazy. It was just wave, after wave, after wave of people. I was telling people the truth, that we had sold over $500,000 worth of Wuvits in the last twelve months. We were selling so much our throats were dry from talking, unable to get away for even a minute to get something to eat or drink. We had cut our prices 15 percent—effectively eliminating the concept of ever working with any kind of reps or distributor. In response, we were writing so many orders, we actually were handing the forms to the customers to write their own. We continued to sell to our individual audiences of two, sometimes three buyers, all of them anxious to see what was so hot that it had people lined up in the aisles to buy. I looked up at one point to see the Arab man who owned the showroom on the seventh floor staring at us in amazement, giving me a big smile, a thumbs-up, and a "call me" sign with his hand up to his ear. I started to go up to him when I was interrupted by two women, one of them carrying a big professional camera.

"Hi, we're from *The Atlanta Journal-Constitution*," one of them said, handing me her card. "We love this little Sleepy-head Fred character of yours," she explained, referring to the special bear-faced Wuvit I had designed for kids, after getting that late-night call from a stranger who had asked me to make a special Wuvit delivery to her sleepless child. "We've walked the entire show, all three buildings and four million square feet of it, and we think this is one of the top things here. Can we photograph it? We're doing an article of our Top Five Picks of the show. It will be in the paper tomorrow."

Never Quit—Things Can and Will Change Dramatically Overnight!

"Can you photograph it? Of course!" I couldn't believe that this little Sleepy-head Fred I had designed in response to the pleas of a stranger turned out to be one of the Top Five Picks of the show! There were millions of products here, and this irresistible little kids' Wuvit stole the show! I thought about how close I came to quitting. I went back to my hotel that night, having a complimentary drink in the lobby with my employees. We struck up a conversation with another couple, celebrating their tenth anniversary with a romantic escape to this hotel. "Our kids have Freds!" they proclaimed with glee. "We wouldn't be here without them. They really work. They won't go to sleep without them. You make those? We *love* you!" It was so exciting to realize that my product was out in the national retail marketplace, being purchased by people who lived five hundred miles away from me, and loved by their children. And I had thought of quitting?

We continued to sell at the same fervent pace, and we actually ran out of order forms. We were in the middle of the second from last day of the show, we had written $60,000 worth of orders, and I had to make a run to the copy center a block away to get more order forms! I came back to my booth as fast as I could, and my employee, all excited, handed me a business card and said, "Look who was just in your booth while you were gone! They want you to call them!" The business card said "Saks Incorporated."

12

HOW THE WORST THING THAT EVER HAPPENED TO ME TURNED OUT TO BE THE BEST THING THAT EVER HAPPENED TO ME

I got back to Michigan and started to make my way through the hundreds and hundreds of orders I had taken, taking the stack of business cards I had from the big contacts I made at the show and piling them up on top of an already huge pile of work. The good news was that there was definitely some cash to be flowed out of that stack! The bad news was that it was just my husband and I who had to do all the work. If there was ever a time for Mommy Millionaire Rules, it was now! My brother-in-law, who was between jobs after the major telecommunications company he worked for more than fifteen years went into free fall, was out of unemployment benefits and in need of a job himself. Even though I was in perilous financial straits and he lived in Atlanta, I gave him a job, paying him to answer my toll-free number and provide customer service to all these hundreds of new customers we now had. The next six months of work would be punctuated by the interruptions of children who wanted chocolate milk, cookies, or help wiping their butts—only when we were on the phone with a business call. We tried to juggle it all. It wasn't easy and we didn't always succeed, but at least we were there when our children went away to school and when they got back. We never went anywhere else—movies, friends' houses, dinners out—because there was always work to be done. I would break into a big smile and thank God—I was still counting every blessing I had with gratitude—every time I heard the sound of my kids' boisterous laughter above me as I worked out of my basement into the middle of each night. I felt such a sense of relief as they played board games or GameCube with their dad, who for once wasn't traveling three to five days a week for a job and hating every minute he was away from them. My husband and I had the pleasure of seeing, touching, and kissing our children whenever we wanted throughout the day. Even though things were tough, exciting, precarious, and interesting, we were experiencing financial freedom for the first time in our lives and spending every dollar of it on our kids. My husband strutted around with pride, explaining to everybody that he was now Mr. Mom and admitting that it was a role he reveled in and had desperately missed before.

The Power of Schmooze:
How to Handle Creditors at a Time of Cash Crisis

I had been to Atlanta and delivered to my SBDC counselor the major retail prospect as well as a cash buyer that he had demanded. My first call was to the Arab man who owned the showroom. In one conversation, I arranged to sell him approximately $10,000 worth of product at an unbelievable price, if he paid me cash. "Sure," he said. "No problem. You send it Cash On Delivery [C.O.D.]. I give you a check." Ten thousand dollars' worth of product C.O.D.? I'd have to trust him to pay me after he got the merchandise. I didn't have much choice. I asked him to fill out a credit application, which he did, not without letting me know he was insulted that I would ask. The report came back from his bank: His average balance was high six figures! I shipped him, he paid me, and I made three more shipments to him in the months ahead. I was making almost no money, but I was running cash through the business to make small, regular payments to my creditors with, just barely keeping the wolf away from the door. My husband and I were making the absolute minimum payments necessary to get by. He applied his unparalleled talent for schmooze, sweet-talking everyone with a story that we were experiencing a "temporary setback." We discovered that as long as we took the creditors' calls and promised to send them even a nominal check—which we did the minute we hung up—we could keep them at bay long enough to recover. My new part-time CFO, who was working for me gratis out of the goodness of his heart, was busy doing forensic accounting, trying to figure out just how bad the damage was, and finally setting up my QuickBooks, while urging me every day to "get sales, get sales!"

Next I looked at this Saks Incorporated business card. This was my big chance. I put together some samples of Wuvits, along with my ingenious "You're gonna Wuvit" press kit and a line sheet, printing one off that showed the higher prices I was selling them at before my "Atlanta Show Special Price." I knew they were going to beat me up on price, so I wanted to leave lots of room for negotiation. I overnighted the package, because that's what all the buyers expect when looking at new product, then followed up with a phone call and e-mail the next day asking, "Do you Wuvit?"

She did! She did wuvit! She called me immediately and told me she was doing a style out, when they bring new products and merchandise onto the floor in January and July, and wanted to know if I could send her overnight ten of my "beautiful press kits" with ten Wuvits for the ten male executives who made up the top brass in the executive suite at Saks Incorporated, based in Birmingham, Alabama. "Absolutely," I answered, working till five in the morning to get them all printed and put together in time for her big presentation. What happened next might qualify as one of those rare inexplicable moments in life when unseen forces in the universe were at work.

The president of Saks Incorporated was George Jones at the time. Saks Inc. then had three retail divisions east of the Mississippi, Parisian, Proffit's, and Carson Pirie Scott, with a total of approximately 250 stores. I was working with a buyer for Parisian. In her presence, people would become spellbound by her stunning beauty. It was more disconcerting when you discovered that she was even more beautiful inside than she was out. Nobody could resist giving her whatever she asked for. Her plan was to warm up ten of my Wuvits and place them on the stressed-out executive shoulders of the ten men who ran Saks Inc., pitching them simultaneously to bring this hot and new product to their stores. She told me that she marched into the room with her assistants, a "You're gonna Wuvit" press kit before each man. They proceeded to place a warmed Wuvit on the shoulders of each man, including the number-one man, George Jones.

Mr. Jones—this is where I get really lucky—had just come back from safari in Africa with his sons and was describing the unexpected luxuries of the safari. "We were out in the bush," my buyer recalled him saying, "in the middle of wilderness, with only cots to sleep on in tents, set up in a different location every night. Still, they managed to spoil us by slipping hot water bottles into our cots just before we retired, making them all warm and welcoming. It was—" My buyer placed the warmed Wuvit on his shoulders right as he was finishing this thought. "It was just like this!" he announced, oohing and aahing along with nine other men dressed in dark business suits who were suddenly feeling the *wuv*! She told me later that you could go up to the executive suite at Saks Inc. on any given day and find these same men working at their desks with Wuvits on their necks.

The presentation was a success. All the men *wuved* it, especially Mr. Jones, who was reminded of his luxurious safari in Africa. My buyer asked me for my best price, in case she could talk management into rolling it out in a big way. I needed cash and could have given it away at a song but took a deep breath, shot back my Advance Pricing price by e-mail, one that was easy for me to live with, then spent an excruciating two days waiting to see what she thought. Did I charge too much? Did I not charge enough? On the one hand, if I charged too much and blew the deal, things would definitely get more difficult. On the other hand, maybe I didn't charge enough. I had been polluted by the nightmare stories others had told me about working with big retailers, by hearing that they had a "license to steal," that "charge-backs and EDI will rob every bit of profit you do make." I had no idea at the time what an acceptable margin was for a retailer. I didn't have a clue what EDI or charge-backs were and what extra costs they would add to my own bottom line. I called my SBDC counselor, the General, and asked him if I made the right decision; he told me it was a good price and that I should just hang in there and hold my ground.

EDI the PO to the DC ASAP!

What happened next can only be compared to war, because I was bombed shortly after with a Purchase Order. It gave me an almost impossible dead-line of two weeks to fill an order for thousands and thousands of Wuvits, to be shipped using the Electronic Data Interchange (EDI) system to their DC, or Distribution Center, complete with Universal Product Codes (those bar labels on everything that computers scan at the checkout) and P.O.P. signs, designed and approved by their merchandising department. I learned we were going to all forty of the Parisian stores for which my buyer bought. I wouldn't know how big an accomplishment this was until we were almost two weeks into the process, when shipping and logistics people working at their DCs asked us, "What is a Wuvit, and why are you going to all our stores without a test? We've never seen this before!"

We received our Excel spreadsheet Purchase Order by e-mail and mar-veled at the numbers: 550 Pink Ribbon Wuvits (we had 561 in stock), 750 Black Toile Wuvits (we had 783 in stock), 750 Burgundy Toile Wuvits (we had 802 in stock), and on and on down the sheet with similar results. It was beyond coincidence.

We had to get to work to understand this EDI system, which came with a huge learning curve on every level, from technical to where you put a label on a box. Not only that, but we also had to secure UPC numbers for all our products and send them with the item numbers to the buyer as soon as pos-sible so they could EDI the Purchase Order. They were talking another lan-guage and we didn't understand any of it. To help us with all this, the buyer e-mailed us a link to a vendor portal, where we could download and print an ominous tome called the SDFG manual, 350 pages of technical gobbledy-gook telling us how to get set up as a vendor, whom to contact for approval of our label size, what the precise tolerance was for our box labels to an eighth of an inch, what the payment terms where, when we got the check, and how to avoid charge-backs!

WHAT IS EDI AND WHERE DO I GET IT?

EDI stands for "Electronic Data Interchange," or the exchange of data from one computer system to another. EDI is a standardized system that allows trading partners to exchange data through the Internet, particularly Purchase Orders, invoicing, charge-backs, and payments. Most·retailers nowadays require you to be EDI compliant, though some may grant you an exemption your first time out of the gate.

Almost nobody does all their EDI functions in-house unless they are a large company. There are hundreds of third-party EDI providers available for you to use with varying levels of service at varying costs. The best way to find a good EDI provider is to check your particular retailer's vendor manual, where they usually list resources across the U.S. You can use the same EDI provider with multiple retail accounts.

EDI is a precise system that tracks inventory and its movement through the supply chain. Every little detail matters, from the placement of a shipping label on a box, to the processing of an ASN, or Advance Shipping Notice. You must be detail oriented and meticulous in your execution of EDI requirements if you want to avoid very costly charge-backs.

WHAT IS A CHARGE-BACK AND WHY AM I SO AFRAID OF IT?

A charge-back in the relationship between trading partners refers to a fine or a fee passed on to the vendor by the retailer. Common charge-backs can come from attaching the wrong UPC code to a product, shipping a freight shipment after the deadline stated on a Purchase Order, or even placing the tags in a spot not accepted as standard on boxes or even product tags.

Since so much inventory is traveling to so many stores through so many DCs from so many different vendors, information provided to retailers through their EDI systems is critical. If it's wrong due to your inattention to detail or your carelessness, it can result in extremely costly human hours to sort out the mess on their end. Somebody has to pay for this, and it's going to be you through a charge-back.

Everybody has their own nightmare story about charge-backs. The truth is that you can avoid most charge-backs by knowing their system in detail and paying very close attention to doing things right. Pick the most anal-retentive person who works for you to do this job and you should be okay.

UPCS: WHAT ARE THEY, WHERE DO I GET THEM, AND WHAT DO THEY COST?

A UPC, or Universal Product Code, is the standard bar code symbol you see on almost all packaging. The Uniform Code Council, or the UCC, has recently been renamed GS1 US. You can access their Web site at www.uc-council.org, where you can read all about them and the services that they offer. The UCC is where you go to buy UPC bar codes.

The purpose of the UCC is to create a standardized supply chain solution between trading partners in the U.S. and across the world, by coming up with codes and numbers that are universally recognized by everyone's computer system. You need to join the UCC, then request a UPC prefix, which is made up of a series of numbers on your UPC that identify you. The last few digits of the UPC can be assigned by your company for identification of your particular products.

The UCC does not print your bar codes. Once you get your prefix assigned, you can go to many different printers in your town who have bar-code-printing capabilities, or you can purchase software that will allow you to print them yourself. The UCC will have a free list of resources for you.

The cost of joining the UCC is determined upon application and is directly related to your company's gross sales and the number of individual products for which you need UPC codes. The minimum you should budget for membership is $500.

How to Become a Vendor: Using the Vendor Manual

I dropped the manual on my husband's lap; it turned out that his being unemployed was a good thing, because he ended up reading it cover to cover with a highlighter and he ended up using information from every page. I drove to the warehouse of our manufacturer, knowing that my CFO had them on the ropes and was beating them up to term out the money we owed them in a loan. Would they shut me down and refuse to allow me to ship this order when I didn't have any money to pay them? I sneaked around, trying to avoid their notice, and started to do a hard-count inventory of the product they had. I stood looking at the mountains of boxes that needed to be shipped in just days—or the Purchase Order would be canceled. I broke them open to inspect them and discovered with exhaustion that almost all of the product was put together incorrectly.

Using Your Backbone to Stand Up for Yourself

Though sewn correctly, the Wuvits were almost all packaged wrong. Parisian wanted the same simple packaging I had used of raffia tied in a bow with a tag. Making money in retail is all about maximizing the sales dollars per square foot. You could put 150 Wuvits on a four-shelf étagère in a two-foot-square footprint of space on the retail floor, netting up to $3,750 in sales revenues. Big retailers calculate sales per square foot of floor space, and not every product can accomplish those kinds of sales in a footprint of two square feet. This was a classic case of less is more, and *less* had to be exactly right.

When I opened the cartons, I found that the raffia had been tied sloppily and the tags were falling off most of the Wuvits. I channeled the spirit of Martha Stewart and just started breaking open boxes, retying by hand eight of ten Wuvits in each box that were done sloppily. After two hours, I was only into five boxes. I realized I had hundreds and hundreds more to go, stacked up four feet high on dozens of pallets before me, when the new owners came by to tell me it was time for me to go.

I stood up, inserting an imaginary steel rod in my backbone, and told them, without one sign of a tear, that the product was tied wrong and that I needed to get the order out if they wanted to be paid. They agreed they wanted to get paid. The next day I came in at dawn and found a team of eight employees to help me. I worked side by side with them retying Wuvits for three days straight, listening to them laughing, joking, and no doubt talking about me and my silly product in Spanish.

We pulled it off. In two short weeks we designed posters, retied Wuvits, applied UPC stickers, made P.O.P. displays, as well as created informational literature for the sales associates to answer the inevitable question, "What's a Wuvit?"

Getting set up as a vendor can take up to two weeks of full-time effort, but don't feel confident after you have done one—each is different! With an immense sense of relief, I watched my husband slap the last EDI-coded label on the last box, shrink-wrapping the last pallet to be put on the truck. I didn't know it then, but I was about to boldly go where few women have gone before.

Sales Success: It's All Relative

My product was out on the shelves at forty Parisian stores, even though there wasn't a Parisian store within 150 miles of my home and I never saw

WHAT IS P.O.P.?

Anything that advertises a product at its Point of Purchase, such as a retail store, including:

1. Product tags
2. Signage or shelf talkers
3. Handout cards
4. Custom display racks, from shelves to poles
5. Any signage attached to custom displays, including pole toppers

them there. I was excited for all of seven days, before I got the first weekly sales report from them. We had sold 500 units at forty stores in the first weeks of launch. I had sold that many on a weekend at one kiosk! Selling that number at forty stores had to be an omen of doom.

I asked my brother-in-law in Atlanta to go to the nearest store carrying Wuvits to take pictures of the merchandising display and to e-mail them to me. While there, he talked up the store manager, pumping him for what he thought about this new Wuvit thing. "We love it," the manager reported to him. "We've even created this whole new merchandising plan called Girlfriend Gifts for it." My brother-in-law was psyched. He called me and said, "Don't worry. It's all good. They love it. Look at the pictures." They were great. Still I thought, *These sales are terrible.*

I called up the General, to let him know that I had crashed and burned again.

"How do you know those sales are bad?" he asked.

"I know what I did at my kiosks! I have two years of historical sales data. I've never done sales that bad before."

"Seems to me," he observed, "this is a whole different shooting match. They sell thousands and thousands of products. I don't think you can expect to see the same numbers in their stores as you did at kiosks in malls. What are they doing different from you?"

"They're not demonstrating the product," I answered. "If you demo it, you can sell it."

"Then go out there and demo it."

I knew in my heart that he was right. I called up my buyer and asked her if she would allow me to go to the Parisian outside of Detroit to do what I billed as a "Demo Event." "Just let me have a couple of hours in a store with

Wuvits and a microwave," I proposed. "Let me show you what I can do. You won't be disappointed."

She agreed and I got in my truck and drove three hours to Detroit at the crack of dawn to be there when the store opened at 8:00 A.M. The store was having a Charity Day, at which community shoppers came out early to take advantage of big discounts bought with a special ticket, the proceeds of which went to their local school. When I walked in the door to the store, nobody who worked there knew or cared what a Wuvit even was. I knew the Wuvits were in the intimate apparel department, so I found them, carried them all down to a shelf that had been set up for me on the main floor, and dragged in a microwave I had brought along just for this purpose. I asked passing shoppers, "Would you like to try a Wuvit?" People loved them. Soon I had them standing two to three shoppers deep to figure out what I was doing. My entire display rack was empty in two hours. I had sold, at my count, twenty-nine Wuvits in that time, surprising even myself. If they had done that at all forty of their stores simultaneously, that would have equaled 1,160 Wuvits in one day. Now those were the numbers I wanted to see in a sales report! I went home to Grand Haven and called my buyer in Birmingham, Alabama. "What could I possibly do to make that happen?" I naively asked her.

She hadn't thought my little experiment would produce such incredible results. As an added benefit, non-demo sales had increased 500 percent at the store after my visit. When I walked in, nobody knew what a Wuvit was—by the time I left everybody was talking about the *Wuvit Wady* who had sold twenty-nine of those things in two hours! If one Demo Event was good, surely more was better. I asked her if I could embark on a cross-country tour of her stores on a Wuvit-launching odyssey. I don't think she really knew what to expect when she said yes.

I certainly didn't know what to expect, either. I drove five hours to Indianapolis, where I did two Demo Events at two different stores, one right after the other, then turned around and drove home. My results continued to be remarkable. Soon I was greeted by excited store managers who were anxious to do whatever it took to make sure my sales that day were better than they were at the last store. I didn't know it then, but they were competing with each other to see who could sell the most of this largely insignificant little product. The effects of my nonstop tour had driven a company-wide awareness of my product, which otherwise would have no doubt been lost on the shelves in anonymity. Not only was competition among the managers generated, but I earned a place in their nationwide sales circular for Father's Day with distribution to more than 7 million households. Wuvits were featured on the inside cover next to Tommy Bahama, Ralph Lauren, and Kenneth Cole, with a record 25 percent sell-through in one week to boot!

· ·

WHAT IS A SELL-THROUGH?

A sell-through is the number of units sold in a week relative to inventory, expressed in a percentage. Retailers typically look for a minimum 4 percent sell-through each week on a product to be successful, but it's all relative to the amount of inventory on the shelves.

· ·

I was making marathon cross-country trips of thousands of miles a week, lugging around my microwave and Wuvits, and doing as many as three store Demo Events in one day, with an hour-and-a-half drive between each, exhausted. I remember calling my kids, then listening to my husband tell me, "What are you doing this for? You're not making any more money doing this! We've already made the sale. You're eating up what little margins we have in all these travel expenses!"

I couldn't answer him. I didn't know why I was doing this. He was right. I wasn't making any more money on the sale, and it was eating up my very slim margins. I didn't know what to do. I was only one person, after all. I called the General for advice.

"Why am I doing this?" I pleaded, grateful that he answered his phone and I didn't get the usual voice mail.

"Because you have to," he answered. "You're selling a lot of Wuvits, right?"

"Right."

"And sales increase significantly after you've been there, right?"

"Right."

"Seems to me you gotta go to all forty stores. Get your sales up first, then work on your margins. By the end of this year, if you can make sales happen in a big way, you should have an EBITDA of $150,000, which means your company is worth as much as $750,000."

"What?!" I gulped. I wasn't trained to look at the big picture like this, nor did I have a clue how to evaluate this scenario. "But I have so much debt! Nobody is going to buy my company with that debt!"

"Nobody gives a damn about your debt! They're not buying your debt, they're buying your revenues. That debt goes away the minute they pay you your $750,000. It's your responsibility to pay it off, not theirs."

"I never thought about it that way," I admitted. I had been at this just over two years, and I had a company valued at three-quarters of a million dollars. I had been so busy, I didn't even stop to think of an exit strategy or what the value was of what I was building. Hard work does have its rewards—big ones at that. You just have to change your perspective to get a visual on the big carrot at the end of the stick. Having an asset that could conceivably be valued at three-quarters of a million dollars after two years was exceptional. I didn't know of any other investments that were producing those kinds of returns for anybody!

"Just go out there and sell! Don't even think about it. Just do it!"

I had my moment of doubt, and he was there to give me the big picture. He wasn't going to put up with no sissies, no cowards, no complainers, no criers, and no quitters. Especially no quitters.

I drove all the way home, feeling relief and joy at seeing my kids after a very long week as I drove up to the house to find them out on the lawn waiting for me, waving me in like an approaching plane to the tarmac with flashlights in the darkness, screaming, "Mommy!" loud enough for every neighbor to hear.

QVC Again!

I heard on the news that QVC was having another Product Search. If I got on a plane tomorrow, I figured, I could catch the one they were having in Orlando. I didn't get on QVC, but what happened there was life changing. That is when I heard that anonymous woman's plea for this book. The next words were from the exhibitors with whom I waited in line. One of them was there with his business partner; both their wives were there, too, each pushing a toddler in a stroller. They had created and patented a unique tool, with which they were getting a test in a major home improvement store chain. I told them how I had just launched at Saks Inc. and how I supported the launch by crisscrossing the country to visit individual stores. He told me about how he couldn't even count on his retailer to correctly display the P.O.P. product illustration he had spent money to create. "Go there and do it yourself," I told him.

"I'm not going there!" he complained. "That's forty-five minutes from my house! I'm not going to waste an afternoon going up there, fixing the display, then driving home! I spent a lot of money creating that display for them. I'm not going to waste more money or my time babysitting it!"

He thought what I was doing was sheer stupidity and didn't mind telling me so. I wanted to paraphrase Dr. Phil and say, "How's that working for you?" but as of then, all the information was not in on whether all this traveling was indeed a good investment of my time. I was about to find out, though. But not before I had real crisis to deal with.

I returned home to find my husband sitting silently with tears in his eyes, his ear anchored to the receiver of the telephone. "What's wrong?" I asked, immediately sensing doom.

"My mom is in the hospital," he replied. "It doesn't look good. She had a heart attack, and they found out her breast cancer is back. It's in her spine."

She was the closest thing to a mother I had and the only grandparent my kids knew. The writing seemed to be on the wall, I could read it in everybody's voice. This was her third relapse with breast cancer and now it seemed to have taken an even more ominous hold. She was admitted into the hospital in Raleigh, North Carolina, where she lived, and went directly to intensive care. We received daily phone calls that were more and more dire in her prognosis. I hadn't even had a chance to buy her her new car or pay off those credit cards she had run up buying gifts for all her grandkids.

My husband flew down. I was doing all I could to keep our ship from sinking single-handedly, answering phones, shipping orders, talking to creditors, paying bills, while also trying to care for two little boys, who were now off of school on summer vacation and in need of constant supervision. I was talking to my mother-in-law, who could only listen on the phone, too weak to speak. Parisian was ordering Wuvits monthly and I had to oversee the order and shipping process by myself. Unable to get away, I was stuck waiting, working from dawn to dusk, alone with my kids while my husband spent weeks in Raleigh, waiting for the end.

How One Phone Call Saved My Business: Staving Off Financial Collapse with the Power of Personality and Passion

One of my vendors, from whom I bought large amounts of fabric, called. It wasn't my normal salesman calling. It was their Vice President of Finance, calling to inform me that they were officially cutting off all my credit, effectively immediately. I couldn't believe it. We had managed to bounce back from serious arrears in payments to being almost current, using the money we were making with Parisian to pay off our creditors. Why would they cut me off now?

"Because we don't want to get in the same position," he answered.

I had nothing else to lose. If they cut me off, it would mean the end of my business, because nobody else would give me fabric on credit until I repaired my credit rating again, and I didn't have cash to pay for it. I didn't work this hard to get a national account like Parisian to let that happen.

"You can't do this," I said, in my friendliest, most polite voice, interrupted by the sounds of my kids in the background, who were screaming for me to push them on the swings. "Do you know that I just rolled out to forty Saks Inc. stores—no test—and that my product is one of the favorites of Saks president George Jones?" My vendor admitted he didn't even know what a Wuvit was. "Do you know that we were just in a Parisian ad circular going to seven million homes, featuring our product on the inside front cover next to Tommy Bahama, Kenneth Cole, and Ralph Lauren?" No, he didn't know that, either. "Do you know that our new product, Sleepy-head Fred, was recently chosen by *The Atlanta Journal-Constitution* as one of the Hot Five Gift Picks in the U.S.?" No, he couldn't say that he did. "Did you know that not only did we ship forty stores, but we have filled and shipped Purchase Orders every month since our rollout, recording record sell-throughs for Father's Day? This is just the start for us. I'm talking to every major retailer in the U.S. right now!"

"Wow," he responded. "You don't need a five-thousand-dollar credit line; you need a fifteen-thousand-dollar credit line!" he exclaimed with as much enthusiasm as me. "How about I set that up? You need more than just a vendor; you need a vendor partner." I didn't know what that meant exactly, but I liked the way it sounded. He gave me the impression that instead of cutting me off, he was now invested in my success and the success it could bring his company indirectly. Without the quality cachet of his brand attached to my product I would have lost just about everything. I had literally come a hair's breadth away from the collapse of my company. Instead of accepting the pronouncement of a man who was just going by the numbers, I had summoned the courage through personality and conviction to turn it around.

Cold-Calling Macy's

I was embellishing the part about "talking to every major retailer," but when I hung up, I thought, *Why aren't I?* It made me feel good to hear my litany of successes out loud and to see the exciting effect it had on the person on the other end of the line. I considered what other retailer I wanted to see my product in. The name came to me immediately—Macy's.

After a half day searching on the Web, I discovered that Macy's did business as Federated Department Stores, with their corporate headquarters located in Cincinnati, Ohio. I couldn't find a phone number on the Contact Us tab of their Web site, so I looked up Federated Department Stores in Cincinnati on Switchboard.com, and a number came up.

I began with my classic elevator pitch: "Hello, I'm Kim Lavine, president of Green Daisy, Inc., manufacturer of the newest retailing phenomenon, the Wuvit, one million dollars in retail sales in just over two years on a product I made as Christmas presents for my kids' teachers!"

"Green Daisy? What a great name!" said the woman's voice on the other end warmly. "What did you say you make, honey?"

"The Wuvit." Sometimes it's better to say less than more. It gets their attention, and you can actually hear the wheels in their heads turn as they think about the crazy thing they think they just heard you say.

"The what—?"

"The Wuvit! I'm otherwise known as the Wuvit *Wady*." I laughed, acknowledging that I had a crazy-named product that was intended to elicit the exact response I was getting at the moment. "It's your own personal designer spa therapy pillow. You heat it in the microwave for two to three minutes and it stays hot for up to hours! Or you can freeze it overnight for long-lasting, no-drip icy cold!"

"You don't say! I've never heard of anything like that before."

"It's so unique, it's patented," I responded, on automatic pitch pilot. "Could you please give me the contact information for the appropriate buyer for it?" I asked, remembering to always ask for the sale.

"Green Daisy! What a cute name! Wuvit! I *wuvit!*" the kind woman mused on the other end of the phone, no doubt taking a break from her monotonous and ceaseless task of answering a very busy switchboard just to transfer calls all day. "Honey, I'm not sure just who to tell you would handle that, but I'll give you the number to Lorraine in New York. She'll know for sure who would handle that. Wuvit! Here's her phone number. It's just Lorraine in New York. Just call her, and she'll help you. Good luck! I hope they *wuvit!*" She was amused by her own play on words and gave me the direct dial number for Lorraine.

The minute I hung up I called Lorraine in New York. I got voice mail, of course, and so I left my voice-mail pitch, telling her that I was instructed to contact her by Macy's Corporate, thanking her for her time, and asking her to please contact me at her earliest convenience. Just an hour or so later I got another call, this one utterly devastating. My mother-in-law, Lorraine, had tragically succumbed to her third and final battle with breast cancer.

What's Really Important

My husband and I pulled ourselves together, put our two little boys in the truck, and headed to New York State, where his mother would be buried next to his father, who had preceded her twenty years before. Even though she was what most people would call broke most of her life, I have never known a happier person than her. She taught me that love of family is what really mattered and it didn't cost anything to love. When she looked at my children with her incomparable kindness and patience, playing endless games of Sorry! with them, brushing their hair, and holding their precious faces in her hands like they were the greatest treasures on earth, I was more grateful than anyone ever was. Though she was gone in body, her spirit indisputably remained, playfully reminding us in the most Lorraine-like ways that her love still surrounded us and that her reward in heaven was to look down at her grandchildren nightly sleeping in their beds. I would continue to sense the imminent nearness of her angel.

We arrived back at home five days later. Among the dozens of voice mails left on our machine was a message from Lorraine in New York. She had gotten my voice mails. She reported that the management at Macy's was very intrigued by my messages and had visited my Web site, and she invited me to send a sample of my product to the following four vice presidents, for whom she listed all the contact info, from addresses and phone numbers right down to their direct e-mail addresses. I spoke to each one of them the next day. They all took my call when I said that Lorraine had asked me to contact them. Besides being moved by my story and my persistence, they all wanted to know how I had pulled this off.

"Do you know who Lorraine is?" they asked me in amazement.

"No. I don't," I admitted. "I was just told to call Lorraine in New York."

"She's the executive assistant to Janet Grove, one of the *top* executive officers at Federated! How did you ever get her direct number? Somebody up there must like you!"

13

BREAKING DOWN THE DOORS
OF BIG RETAILERS

Days later I received a phone call that would change my life forever. It was my buyer from Parisian, inviting me to Saks Incorporated's corporate headquarters, in Birmingham, Alabama. I was getting ready for my trade show at AmericasMart in Atlanta, and she wanted to know if I could meet with her and her manager after the show to discuss putting together a special program for Wuvit sales for Holiday 2004. I put together an agenda of things I wanted to talk to them about. I worked at the show every day with my team, then went back to my room at night to create a fifteen-page PowerPoint presentation. Using my own sales data from my two years of holiday retailing on Wuvits, I mixed in the early results of my demoing in their stores, to illustrate just what kinds of phenomenal revenues they could make selling a great gift that every*body* loved at the holidays, all at the magical retail price point of twenty-five dollars!

I had another great show in Atlanta. The same exhibitors who were next to us in January were becoming used to seeing us busy and started saying, "You can tell how good the show is by how well Green Daisy is doing." Still, I wasn't even "making money" at these shows. I was going further and further into red ink, as just about every other exhibitor around me was, hoping to achieve enough momentum in the marketplace that the idea of attending a trade show became superfluous.

I had a Gold American Express credit card, which I had protected at all costs; since it had no limit, I could put the whole cost of the show on it and pay it off thirty days later on the receivables of the orders I wrote. Everybody was doing this. We were all in this mad race against time and money, together.

The cycle of exhibitors was beginning to become apparent to me. Many came to two, maybe three shows until either they ran out of money or they got wings and flew. More people were running out of money than flying.

The Sucking Noise of Business
Leaving America for China

I was still selling my product on the narrow margins I could eke out, manufacturing in the U.S. It was great when I was going from manufacturing straight to retail, but for wholesale it wasn't getting the job done. Still, I didn't have the money necessary to front a run of product out of China, carrying the cost of a lot of inventory for 120 days. Besides, manufacturing on speculation was what sending your production over to China required, and my new CFO would not budge. No manufacturing without a Purchase Order from a big retailer, he demanded. At this time, everybody was making a mad dash to manufacture in China. I could actually hear the sucking noise of business leaving America if I listened hard enough. People were doing everything they possibly could to find a way to cut their costs in half and pay these extraordinary high trade-show costs. I was in Atlanta again and decided to walk the show to look at goods. I noticed products with twice the man-hours and materials into them than mine that were selling for half my wholesale cost. How could I ever compete? I was caught between a rock and a hard place: I would never have the money to fund overseas production unless I lowered my costs, and I couldn't lower my costs until I took my production overseas.

Taking Your Manufacturing to China:
The Winners and the Losers

Still, I needed to try. One of my fellow exhibitors at the Atlanta show told me her story, and I listened with shock and amazement. She got up one day, got on a plane to Hong Kong, got out of the plane, and started to walk the streets of Hong Kong, not knowing one person or one word of Chinese. She sold inexpensive jewelry trinkets and watches, so finding the goods wasn't as hard as you would think. Apparently all similar products are grouped in one location in Hong Kong, so once you find them, you are there. After one visit, she was successfully importing her inexpensive beads and jewelry trinkets, coming up with unique and attractive combinations and selling whole racks of them to the tourist retailer. Next thing I knew, they were opening a mammoth retail center in Gatlinburg, Tennessee, selling all the other inexpensive goods that they could find to import for pennies for dollars.

I had failure stories, too. One of the companies I bought raw materials from, based in the textile belt of the South, called me up one day and told me they were closing down all their operations and moving to China. They had recently been acquired by one of the biggest commercial banking operations in the world based in New York. The new VP was apparently a real cowboy, and he was on a mission to buy up as many U.S. companies that supplied materials to the cut-and-sew industry in the states as possible, with the plan of taking it all to China and making the materials and the goods at a fraction of the cost, becoming one of the biggest cut-and-sew operations in China. It all looked great on paper. When they packed up their machines in the states to ship to China, they single-handedly put one entire city out of work in South Carolina.

I received a phone call a couple of months later. My salesman was in a state of crisis. He didn't have any goods to sell and didn't know for sure when he would. Nothing had gone according to plan. The experiment turned out to be a train wreck, colliding with Chinese customs, culture, and rumored graft. Their machines, he reported, were still idle months after arriving there. They didn't know when, or even if, production would start again. I was amazed that even the big boys were crashing and burning. If they couldn't pull it off successfully, just think of what a start-up business owner faces trying to run to China right away for production.

Manufacturing in China: Not a Question of "If" but "When"

If I was going to compete and survive, I had to take my manufacturing overseas as soon as possible. There was a lot of lip service being paid to buying goods made in the U.S., but the honest truth is that except for a very small percentage of trade protectionists, American consumers really don't care at all where the stuff they buy comes from as long as it's cheap. The same union employees making cars in factories all over Michigan who were criticizing people for buying imported cars were driving straight to Wal-Mart after work to buy from a store where almost everything is made in China. Wal-Mart is the single largest importer of goods from China into the U.S. One of the reasons, I've since learned, that Wal-Mart can sell stuff so inexpensively is that it manufactures in China up to 60 percent of the goods it carries, importing them directly. Wal-Mart isn't alone. Most of the big retailers are doing it nowadays. Even my SBDC counselor and my CFO both concluded, "It's not a matter of if you go to China; it's just a matter of when." Clearly I didn't have a choice.

In my attempt to find a way to get it done, I called up a Chinese-American man I had met in New Jersey while at one of my kiosks in 2003.

Though he grew up in China, he had immigrated to the U.S. and had an MBA from a prestigious East Coast university and worked for Fortune 500 companies in New York. He had approached me in the mall about his rug-importing business while I was opening my kiosk. It's amazing how casual encounters can become extraordinarily important potential business partnerships.

My Chinese MBA, as I'll call him, told me everything I needed to know about working with the Chinese that nobody else would. According to him, the Chinese are not creative people; they are industrious. They can take a concept and reproduce it a million times with reliable quality; just don't ask them to design anything. Sourcing raw materials involving design like fabrics in China can present a challenge. The Chinese care a lot about cash. Cash is the measure of all success in China. Stocks, strategic partnerships, equity ownership in American companies aren't worth the paper they're written on. The Chinese don't invest their money; they just like piling up huge amounts of American cash, with which they presumably stuff their mattresses, because they don't trust banks, either. Also, the Chinese aren't interested in anything but huge production runs. Don't come over there unless you want to produce a minimum run to fill a twenty-foot overseas shipping container.

So much is being produced in China that just getting someone interested in quoting you a run can be difficult. They have so much leverage, they can sometimes jerk you around almost immediately, raising prices once they start, delaying ship dates, putting bigger-paying customers on the production schedule before you. Even my friend who was the president of the major collectible company, who was importing container loads each month just for QVC, was kept on a very short leash. Once he had to pay $30,000 in late-shipment charge-backs because his containers were delayed out of China. One of his competitors had come in with a production run bigger than his, bumping him back. My new friend, the Chinese MBA, spent two weeks in China on my behalf and at my cost, filling me in on even more important unspoken rules for doing business there. Most important was, it wasn't what you knew, it was who you knew. China reveres ancient family kinships. Graft is a natural and accepted part of doing business there. You needed to understand this complex subculture to succeed there, and the only people who could do that were Chinese. The huge American commercial bank that had bought up my cut-and-sew vendors went to China like arrogant cowboys and ran full speed into disastrous failure. All the money in the world can't buy you success there unless you understand and master the subtleties of their culture. My Chinese MBA came back with a lot of good manufacturers and sourcing contacts, but I was still missing the essential component to make the big machine work: cash.

My First Clue That Money Wasn't All It Was Cracked Up to Be

In one of my darker moments, I called my millionaire mentors for advice. "Did you ever feel like just giving up?" I asked my friend.

"What, are you kidding?" she answered me. "There were years when we would get up every day and ask each other, 'Is this the day we close the doors?' "

I took some comfort in hearing that I wasn't alone.

I met them right before they sold their company. They had a one year earn-out package, so even though they officially didn't own the business anymore, they had to work for one year to hit revenue thresholds for which they could earn huge bonuses, worth up to a million dollars on top of the selling price of the company. I remember how hard they worked that year to hit those thresholds; they came to my holiday party, and I remembered looking at both of them, thinking they looked like soda cans that had been crushed by a foot, then pulled open again. Six months later they were free, netting their tremendous earn-out bonuses and buying with cash two homes together worth a million dollars, one on a prime vacation lake, with boats and cars to go along with it. The next time I saw them they were tanned, relaxed, and looking younger than their mid-forties.

The funny thing is that they both couldn't stand being "retired" for more than six months. He got a coaching job, his second career aspiration, and she asked if she could come to work for me! She said, "There are only so many school and charity functions I can volunteer for and lunches I can take with friends each week. I'm bored. I don't care if it's just answering phones or stuffing envelopes—give me something to do." This was my first clue that money wasn't everything it was cracked up to be.

Inside the Hallowed Halls of Retail

I drove from Atlanta to Birmingham, Alabama, for my meeting at Saks Incorporated's corporate headquarters. I got a hotel, went to dinner at a local hole-in-the-wall famous for beer and barbecue, and marveled at the shiny and beautiful women, impeccably dressed, with the very latest $300 Kate Spade bags on their shoulders. I've since derived a respect and awe for the southern woman, who would trade just about any household convenience for a full mani-pedi and the absolute newest accessories. They were always beautiful and put-together wherever you saw them, none more so than my stunning buyer.

As I walked to the main building of Saks Corporate, part of me wanted to jump up and down because this was a huge milestone on the road of hard knocks and the other part of me was too nervous to speak. I entered a stunning black marble atrium of consummate elegance and taste. As I checked in with the receptionist I noticed that all the black leather couches that surrounded her desk in a circle were occupied by dashing and darkly handsome European men speaking Italian on their BlackBerries. The omnipresent Chinese contingent was there, too, with their oversize wheeled suitcases, fresh off the plane as usual with their luggage tags still evident, as were East Indians, there to sell shoes and luggage. I was ushered to a "vendor appointment room," one of at least eight that formed around a circular hallway, containing shelves to display your product and glass doors from which you could spy on other vendors selling their wares. I set out my Wuvits, Daisy Bags, and Groovy Bags on the wall-mounted shelves. A vendor waiting to see a luggage buyer in a room next to mine came into my room. He took one look at a new, updated messenger bag I had designed and prototyped, which I had brought to show the accessory buyer, and said, "I like that. I'm going to go home and knock that off in China soon as I get back. You manufacturing in China yet? No? That's good. You won't be able to compete in price then."

I am not making this up. This conversation took place exactly as written. Then, more than ever, I knew I needed to take my manufacturing to China.

My stunningly beautiful buyer arrived shortly after, impeccably dressed in the highest possible heels, toting what looked like the complete unabridged *Oxford Dictionary* in black three-ringed binders, along with her assistant and her boss, all carrying similar tomes of paperwork. My buyer explained to me that this was the report data on just four months of retailing on my one little product alone, and I realized the extent of her workload. Today's retail buyers are harried and overworked, under extreme pressure to generate new profits as their careers rise and fall on the success of the products they take on. It was getting harder every day to make a dollar, and buyers, just like entrepreneurs, are under greater pressure every day to make one. Make their job easy and just show them the money.

"We're here to try to decide how to forecast our Wuvit sales for the holidays," my buyer began.

"Well, I put together this presentation to help you do just that," I responded, pushing the fifteen-page PowerPoint presentation before them that I had stayed up nights for a week to put together.

I could tell they were impressed. The DMM, or Divisional Merchandising Manager, who was my buyer's boss, looked through it and laughed. "Guess we'll have to take our numbers from four months of retailing on it and just throw in the shock factor! You know, this is the little product that could!"

"It is?"

"Oh yes! We love it!" she said, still laughing, while my buyer relayed the famous George Jones story. "You're on our company-wide bestseller list monthly!"

"What's that?"

"That's a weekly newsletter that goes out to all our divisions, including Carson Pirie Scott's hundred and fifty stores and Proffitt's sixty stores, listing what products have the highest sell-through. Your Wuvit has been on it almost every week!"

I was thrilled.

"As a matter of fact, you're going to be rolling out to all the chains—that's another two hundred and ten stores—for the holidays. Are you ready for that?"

I was so excited I could barely speak. I thought about the quantity of product that meant I had to produce and what it would cost me to make, tempering my excitement. Still, this meeting was a regular lovefest.

I congratulated myself for going out on the road to support the launch of my product. The early sales I racked up sold them on the power of demoing this little product, and they were about to give me a big green light to pursue it with a vengeance in the next critical five months of holiday retailing.

What happened next can only be described as a blur. I drove home to Michigan in a haze of elation. Adding another 210 stores to my existing 40 was going to present me with almost more challenges than rewards. Good thing that major fabric manufacturer had raised my credit limit to $15,000. I was going to need it. We ended up shipping 25,000 Wuvits in four months to the rest of the Saks Inc. chain. This was the kind of accomplishment that would stun other retailers on the other end of the phone line when I cold-called buyers. One of them was a buyer at Macy's.

Macy's was a little more reluctant to get on the Wuvit train. My buyer there was told he had to run my product by one of the VPs I had spoken to, and he let me know that he wasn't happy about that. I would soon learn a valuable lesson.

Your product's success is determined by your buyer's talents and commitment to its success.

This buyer was not committed. We were given a ten-store test, many of which happened to be on the East Coast, including Macy's flagship Herald Square store in New York. My family and friends in New York were excited to buy the product at this veritable institution of retailing. They called me with frustration to tell me that they had walked every floor and asked every sales associate and still couldn't find a Wuvit. I put the Macy's locations on my Web site, and soon buyers who had bought Wuvits the previous year at my mall kiosks were calling me to tell me that they tried to find the product at Macy's and couldn't.

I had my assistant call every one of the stores to ask if they were selling Wuvits. Eight out of the ten stores told her that they had no idea what Wuvits even were; one out of the ten told her, "We have them. They're in the stockroom. We were told not to put them out."

Clearly this buyer did not like my product and no amount of schmoozing could fix it. Wuvits were destined to fail the test, which meant there would be no rollout at Macy's. I called my buyer to confront him with my information. "They won't sell if you don't have them on the floor, and eight out of ten stores don't have them on the floor," I pleaded. He admitted he knew this and didn't care. He was planning to put them on the floor after the holidays and discount them, he told me, just to get rid of them. I was so frustrated that I had come this far only to be prevented from having a fair chance that I called the General, and asked him what to do.

There Is Nothing More Dangerous Than a Person with Nothing to Lose

"Seems to me," he contemplated, "he left you with nothing to lose. You should learn from this. There is nothing more dangerous than a person with nothing to lose. You got the names and numbers and e-mails of all those VPs?" he asked me.

"Yes," I admitted, the wheels turning in my head.

"You're gonna fail if you do nothing. You might as well fail fighting for yourself!"

Stand Up for Yourself

I took out a pair of brass balls someone had given me for a joke; these conveniently would come in handy a number of times in the next few years. I wrote an e-mail, copying in the four VPs, and sent it, pleading with my buyer to put the product out on the floor so that it could sell and I could have a fair test. I had no idea what catastrophe I might have unleashed. One of the VPs called just a few days later. He had spoken to the buyer and was fixing the situation right now. But it was too late; the holiday buying season was over.

I saw that VP in New York just a few months later, when he showed up at my booth at a trade show there. I was amazed that he remembered me and felt compelled to search me out of the hundreds of exhibitors at the huge Javits Center. "Keep pushing!" he told me, while I shook his hand. I was awed that he had come to visit me and amazed that he cared this much. "I want you to call every buyer in the Macy's chain till you find someone committed to this product's success. Tell them that I personally told you to push it through the stores! Don't give up until you do!"

I was shaking hands with one of the top VPs at Federated Department Stores, who was rallying me on with an inspired pep talk, and all this came out of one cold call. I couldn't believe it. I walked out into the aisle and blabbered like a baby to my fellow exhibitors, "There goes a senior VP with Macy's!" while they all oohed and ahhed and looked longingly at the back of his perfectly tailored suit disappearing into the hordes.

I spent almost the entire months of October, November, and December in 2004 on the road, traveling to every Parisian and Proffitt's store that would have me, doing Demo Events with increasingly phenomenal results. I missed both my kids' birthday parties and their school Christmas parties. I felt bad, but I made it up after the first of the year, when I organized the Valentine's Day parties for both their classes and volunteered at the end-of-the-year parties, too. The boys came to understand that their mom was not available in the last two months of the year because it was her busy time. Still, I managed to be home every Monday of every week, when I did back-pack books for both their classes, reading from 9:00 A.M. to noon with all the kids in the class individually. There were sacrifices, but there were definitely rewards, too, and all the rewards were linked directly to my kids.

I made a massive store blitz in the third week of December, hitting fifteen stores in five days and traveling thousands of miles to do it. I was amazed in Birmingham when I visited the flagship stores for Parisian and Proffitt's on the same day. It became apparent that each manager would not be outsold by his competitor. They pulled out all the stops, doing everything they could to make sales, making announcements on the P.A. system, stopping customers themselves to say, "Hey, have you tried this?" and even strongly suggesting that their employees buy Wuvits with their store discount for Christmas presents. The number-one manager at Parisian's flagship store actually stood there and counted how many I sold, knowing the record was forty-three in two hours. When I told him I had to go to my next store demo, he asked a sales associate to run a report to see what number I had sold: It was forty-two. He instantly bought two more himself, just to make sure he had the new record. I could not believe what this little product was driving people to do.

One of the managers in Cincinnati, whom I had visited earlier in the year and sold twenty-seven Wuvits in a couple of hours, decided to have his own Demo Event without me. He sent me an e-mail the next day—he had sold 107 in just hours! This was like a giant pep rally.

I was making money to pay off our debt, and I was still driving a six-year-old truck, with my second car the old Ford Tempo that used to be my mother-in-law's. I could barely get through the last day of my last marathon demo schedule. I arrived at one store in Alabama to find a big pile of untied, messy Wuvits and just wanted to cry. This was a lesson in how critical merchandising was to the success of a product.

Things Aren't Always What They Seem

I was thinking this was a prime example of a store where this product had failed when the department manager came up to me. She was the wife of a Southern Baptist minister, so I believe that God put her in my life that day for a reason. At first I could barely look at her, as I was tying Wuvits as fast as I could, my feet killing me after having spent eight hours on them.

"I'm sorry those look like that," she said. "We've been selling so many, they had to ship some over from another store just to get ready for your Demo Event."

I was shocked. I thought this was a clear illustration of the kind of failure that is inevitable when you are so critically underfunded and undermanned.

"Yes. Our store is the number-three seller of Wuvits," she said proudly. "I love this product. I sell it to everybody who comes here. You remind me of Karen Neuburger, in fact. I remember, she was out on the road like this ten years ago, doing the same thing you're doing now."

I was on the verge of a nervous breakdown just five minutes before that, feeling like Sisyphus pushing a boulder up a hill that would constantly roll down. And here was the manager comparing me to the creator of a $100 million brand! She lifted me up and showed me that things aren't always what they seem and that angels can reveal themselves to you in the darkest and most unexpected places.

14

FREE MONEY: WORKING WITH ANGEL INVESTORS AND VENTURE CAPITALISTS

I got home just in time to celebrate Christmas with my family. Christmas Eve was spent shopping for my kids' gifts from Santa and staying up all night to wrap them. For the first time ever, I didn't want anything for Christmas. Ironically, I found myself thinking I already had everything! My son, after opening all his presents on Christmas morning, looked at me with all the challenge a seven-year-old can muster: "Mom, if Santa's elves are making all the Christmas presents at the North Pole for all the kids in the world, how come there are UPC codes on the boxes?"

I had to think fast. Seven years old was just too young to let go of belief in Santa. "Santa needs to control his inventory too," I explained. "Do you know how many presents he has to make and deliver? This is a modern world, and even Santa and his elves have to use whatever technology they can to make sure every boy and girl in the world gets their presents on time."

He bought it and went to the school the next day to tell all the kids how Santa had his own EDI inventory control system.

My First Million Dollars

I was in a continuous state of panic that wouldn't go away for even a minute. My body was in a perpetual fight-or-flight, adrenaline-pumping state. There was always too much to be done with too little time to do it in, and our debt had started to catapult into critical mass as our credit card companies raised our interest rates to obscene heights. It was then I came to the revelation that in just over the last two years I had made my first million dollars!

My CFO had managed to cobble together some financial statements, including a balance sheet and a Profit & Loss for 2004, before he left right after the first of the year for an exciting new life in San Francisco.

"Look at this!" he announced to me before he left. "You made money last year!" He stuck out the P & L and a copy of my tax returns he had prepared for proof. "That's awesome!" he proclaimed in his enthusiastic way. "I want you to take this P & L and go to your banker and show it to her!" He highlighted the positive number on the statement for emphasis. "I mean, with what you guys had to recover from last year, it's just unbelievable. She's going to be really impressed!"

I was so excited. I couldn't believe it. Even though I was drowning in debt, I technically made money! Making money in just over two years of starting our business was an exceptional accomplishment. Conventional wisdom says that most businesses won't make money in the first three years.

"If only I just didn't have that bad year in 2003," I said, "just think where we would be now instead, debt free and making money."

"The year 2003 was the best thing that ever happened to you," my CFO said

"What are you talking about? Why do you say that?"

"You would have never changed your business model, going from kiosks to big retailers, if you didn't have that horrible year. You would have run that product through those kiosks a couple of years maximum. Then what? You'll probably make a lot more money this way. What's valuable is not so much this product; it's those channels of distribution it's penetrating. That's where the money is. See all that debt on your balance sheet? You bought those channels of distribution with that debt. Now you have an obligation to keep shoving more and more product through those channels. Keep designing—keep innovating. Keep product pumping into those channels. That's where the value of this company is."

I was going to miss that man. He had admitted to me that he was once just as scared and strapped as I was, and he had a happy ending. Turns out just about every millionaire I ever met had the same story. This man had a company that designed computer software. He told me that I had potential to make more money than he had. Even my millionaire mentor friend told me the same thing over lunch a week later. I was so preoccupied with the past that I never had a minute to look ahead to the future.

The Secrets of Marketing: Creative Tricks for Using Numbers to Your Advantage That Nobody Will Tell You

Do you know how many Wuvits I had to sell in just over a couple of years to make a million dollars? Before my CFO left, he taught me an invaluable marketing tool.

There are two different dollar values to look at when calculating sales: the product's wholesale cost and its retail value in the marketplace.

On the one hand, when I was talking to banks or anybody who was looking at my balance sheet and P & L, I had to report only my wholesale sales. On the other hand, if I was talking to prospective retail customers, I had an obligation to express my sales as the number of units sold times retail value. So even though I ran over a million dollars' worth of revenue through my company, the Wuvit product itself had produced over $2 million in retail sales in the marketplace in a little more than two years! This was a more accurate indicator of sales success for retailers, who measured that number by retail dollars instead of wholesale costs. I would soon be telling everyone I could call that we had done $2 million in *retail* sales in just over two years, knowing that it was the truth.

I got into my car and drove to my bank as my CFO had commanded. I was going to show my banker this P & L with the glorious little highlighted number showing I had made money. I had just sold over $2 million worth of product. I knew she was going to give me another shot. I caught her in her office, but things were dramatically different. Before, she had invited me in, rolling out the red carpet and enthusiastically cheering me on; this time, she came out and met me in the bank lobby.

"Here—look at this. We made money!" I proclaimed, all excited, handing her the statements. "Maybe you can take a look at another loan."

She reviewed my P & L and balance sheet while standing up and within ten seconds said, "Sorry, can't help you." She wouldn't even consider it.

Besides the debacle that resulted in terming out the short-term loan I had taken out in favor of a long-term one, I hadn't missed one payment on her two loans. Still, she wasn't interested in talking to me anymore, and she went even further, telling me it wasn't just her. "No bank will talk to you with a balance sheet like that." She more than anybody understood why my balance sheet had so much debt. She had watched the ship inexplicably run aground and had even told me then that if she had to give me the money all over again, based on the business plan and the data, she would have done so. My husband and I had done what was right instead of what was easy, fighting to pay off debt and save our business instead of going bankrupt and starting all over again. If she wasn't going to cut me some slack, who would?

My cell phone rang as I left the bank. It was the General.

"What are you doing Wednesday?" he asked.

"What aren't I?"

"Well, you're going to go to this presentation by a local group of angel investors. You need to raise serious capital if you're going to go on, and after

WHAT IS A SECOND-STAGE OR MID-TIER COMPANY?

In general, a company is second-stage if it is

- Privately held
- Past the start-up stage
- Facing issues of growth rather than survival
- Employing six to ninety-nine full-time employees
- Generating between $750,000 and $50 million in annual revenue or has that amount of working capital in place from investors or grants

WHAT IS MEZZANINE FINANCING?

Mezzanine financing is not a loan but second-stage investment by individuals, usually secured by equity-based options like warrants, which can be converted to stock. Mezzanine financing is a debt only in the event of a company's bankruptcy, when the investors take priority over original owners in the repayment of debt. Typically a business only pays annual interest on money loaned to it through mezzanine financing until warrants are converted into stock.

In bigger deals, mezzanine financing can be any late-stage investment by venture capitalists or angels somewhere between start-up and going public. Banks do not provide mezzanine financing.

WHAT ARE ANGEL INVESTORS?

Angel investors have to be certified by the SEC to be "high net worth individuals" with minimum liquid assets (cash) of $2 million and minimum average salaries of $250,000 a year. Angels are private investors who specialize in high-growth fields and involve themselves directly in management of the endeavors they fund, usually forming "strategic alliances," where they merge their resources/experience/companies with those of a fledgling company on the cusp of exponential growth, while reaping financial returns much higher than any other traditional investment vehicle typically available. Angels fund thirty to forty times as many companies as venture capitalists every year.

WHAT IS VENTURE CAPITAL?

Private equity—money—that comes from investors willing to risk capital on more speculative ventures. Venture capital is usually reserved for second-stage companies in a high-growth mode or start-ups with an exceptionally strong business plan.

A typical VC investment usually requires sale of 25 percent to 55 percent of the company to investors. Some VC firms have the money, and some are brokers who raise it.

WHAT'S THE DIFFERENCE BETWEEN ANGELS AND VENTURE CAPITALISTS?

- Angels typically have a more patient exit strategy, with a mandate to invest in businesses in their communities to foster economic growth and development. Venture capitalists are concerned with only one thing: the bottom line.
- Sometimes angels and venture capitalists are one and the same, moving from their own personal VC firm to their angel group in one afternoon. Do your homework as well as you can on the individuals you are dealing with. The best way to get information on these people is to talk to your SBDC counselor, who is usually connected to many business leaders in the community.
- Some VC firms don't actually have money but are more like brokers who have the connections and know how to get it.
- Don't expect to get names, business cards, or contact info on individual angels as you would on VC firms. Use every opportunity you have to get face-to-face with angels to your fullest advantage.

. . . .

the last year you're in a pretty good position to do so. There is also going to be a venture capital group there. You're going to have to get the ball rolling with these groups ASAP."

"I just left my bank," I argued, "and she told me unequivocally nobody will want to invest in me!"

"Forget about her! She doesn't know what she's talking about. You need a bank that specializes in second-stage or mezzanine financing. Her bank doesn't do that; they just write SBA loans. You need a big national bank. They're the only ones that provide that kind of funding."

On Wednesday morning I found myself at my local university, in a room full of entrepreneurs eager to get the attention of the one VC group, as well as the angel investor group, there to give their presentation. There must have been at least a hundred of us and only five of them. I didn't waste any time. My SBDC counselor had already given me the names of the key contacts of each group and had spoken to them in advance about me. The room was a very posh meeting space complete with paneled walls, green leather chairs around huge circular tables, and a bar. I went to the bar and ordered a glass of water; my hand was shaking so much as I picked it up, I had to put it back down again to keep it from spilling. To my good fortune, standing right next to me, ordering a diet cola, was one of the key members of the VC panel.

"Hi," I said immediately before I lost my nerve, handing him my business card. "I'm Kim Lavine, president of Green Daisy, Inc., manufacturer of the Wuvit. We've done just under two million dollars in retail sales in the last two years on this great product, selling to the nation's premier retailers, like Saks Inc. I'd love the opportunity to meet with you to discuss our exciting future. Could I please have one of your cards so I can follow up?"

He obviously didn't know what hit him. I could see in his expression that he was decidedly impressed. It didn't hurt, either, that I had a very attractive and feminine business suit on, which displayed my secret weapon in this room of buttoned-up collars and drab suits: cleavage. He, like any man, was powerless to keep from staring as he fished his business card out of his wallet, handing it to me and inviting me to call him.

We were asked to take our seats. I found my way to a table with five other hopefuls, all ready with pens in hands and business plans packaged in slick binders for the opportunity to get some face time with money. The first was another freelance CFO, who wanted to network with the angels and the venture capitalists to help package the financials of all the prospective companies that came before them with hat in hand. He ended up doing this for me. Next was a woman from a nonprofit social service agency who was looking for an alternative source of funding. She acknowledged she had a really low percentage shot at getting money from self-proclaimed capitalists. Another woman, whose daughter was in my son's kindergarten class, ran a capital management company. She was dressed in a very conservative suit and looked as if she could have been on the panel. Next to her was an inventor, who told us he had at least ten patents, though none of them had gone on to commercial production or success, partly because he was just interested in inventing. Then there was a man wearing jeans and a denim shirt, who described himself as an artist with a fantastic new idea that had something to do with painting. He was an ineffective communicator, mumbling just barely audibly. Everybody gave up asking him what it was he did exactly after receiving a garbled response.

The panel before us of four men and one woman looked, smelled, talked, and dressed like money: Symphony Money, Washington Money, Corporate Money, Old Money, and New Money. I eventually came to know each of these individuals personally, but then I could only marvel at how perfectly cast they were for the role of millionaire or friend of millionaire, aka venture capitalist. Speaker Number 1 was Symphony Money, the chair; he was so refined in dress and speech, with such a casual elegance and artistic flair, that I could only think Cary Grant meets James Bond. He introduced Washington Money next, who was a venture capitalist; he looked like he was produced from the same mold that made Ken dolls, with perfect immovable politician hair, of senatorial quality. His partner in the VC firm was Corporate Money, the same man I had introduced myself to at the bar; he was the epitome of sedate business protocol distilled from twenty years as an executive-level banker at some of the biggest East Coast institutions, composed, non-expressive, and always thinking. After that was Old Money, the only woman on the panel. She's still an enigma to me today, but her tight-lipped, buttoned-down, sharp-witted presence would always keep you on your very best behavior. Though everyone else spoke briefly, it was clear that New Money was the star of this show. He would later be described to me as a serial entrepreneur who made his millions again and again, each time more novel than the last. He was a hands-on kind of guy, who had one memorable message to deliver to us with his signature straight-to-the-point confidence: "The idea is only five percent," he proclaimed. Most of us, he reasoned, were probably here with only 5 percent of what they were looking for. The other 95 percent was what most people didn't get or couldn't understand. He didn't explain what the other 95 percent was, but I knew I had more of it than anyone else sitting around the table. I was right, because I received a phone call from New Money himself, inviting me to his offices for a meeting with another previously invisible rich person, Trust-Fund Money.

WHAT QUALITIES ARE ANGEL INVESTORS LOOKING FOR IN A COMPANY?

1. Passionate leadership
2. A strong management team
3. Being lean and mean, with low overhead expenses
4. A proven revenue model that is scalable
5. Strategic alliances
6. A sustainable competitive advantage
7. Cash flow
8. A sales and marketing strategy
9. An exit strategy

How to Successfully Approach Angel Investors and Venture Capitalists

The way I secured this invite is worthy of mention. After the twenty-minute presentation broke up, I dashed to the front of the room and stuck my hand

- -

ANGEL AND VENTURE CAPITAL RESOURCES

These are just a few resources to get you started in your hunt for money. Many groups fly under the radar, so contact your local SBDC and see if they have news about organizations and events for you to participate in.

- **Angel Capital Association** at www.angelcapitalassociation.org features a complete list of all angel organizations broken down by geographical region.

- Sign up with **Funding Post** at www.fundingpost.com to showcase your company online to potential investors.

- **Launchpad Venture Group** at www.launchpadventuregroup.com is a Boston-based investment group.

- **Starlight Capital** at www.starlightcapital.com sponsors a Private Equity Forum regularly in cities across the U.S.

- -

out to every panel member, patiently waiting when I had to, using the same elevator pitch I had used on the venture capitalist at the bar with every one of them. I wasn't going to leave until I had each one of their business cards and they each had one of mine. This was the real value of this presentation, and I didn't see anybody else working the room half as hard as I was to get this information. My time for talking to the other entrepreneurs was over. I was all business. I didn't waste Money's time or monopolize it with rambling pointless conversation. I got in, got out, and got home, where I immediately drafted a short, bullet-driven e-mail of accomplishments, thanking them for their time and asking them if I could possibly meet with them to discuss the exciting opportunities further.

Believe it or not, the invitation from New Money wasn't the first. New Money didn't call me for at least a week, the minute after he learned that I had met with Corporate Money. The key message of the angel investor is that they fund start-up companies when no one else will. They have a relatively patient exit strategy, which means that they do not ride you so hard or so fast for Return On Investment, ROI, that you kill yourself trying to get it to them. Angel investors have a mandate to invest in companies in the specific geographical location that they inhabit, stimulating economic development in their own backyard. Many angel investors I have met have more generous, altruistic streaks than venture capitalists, because they are millionaires themselves. They feel a civic and moral responsibility to give back what they had once received: a hand from above. Angel investors have the money that most venture capitalists are frequently trying to get. Angel investors didn't get rich by giving away money, though, and they'll gladly eat you for breakfast if you show them one iota of weakness or vulnerability in the nine to twelve months it takes them to decide to give you the money.

Corporate Money was a classic venture capitalist. His job was to take inexperienced entrepreneurs like me and make me presentable to angel investors or any other kind of institutional investors he could find. I was surprised to discover that some venture capitalists don't have money! They are like a real estate agent who advises you how to fix up your property to make it the most attractive to the widest variety of people, then puts you on the market, selling you to all the various buyers with whom they have contacts for a commission. You always want to go directly to angel money before you go to a venture capitalist. That's why New Money called me when he found out I was talking to venture capitalist Corporate Money: New Money was already interested in me.

The Dramatic Growth of Angel Investing

The numbers for 2004 are in, and there's never been a better time for small businesses to raise capital:

- According to the Center for Venture Research at the University of New Hampshire, angel investing grew by a whopping 24 percent over the previous year.
- Approximately 48,000 businesses across the country received angel financing in one year.
- Total investment is up from 2003's $18 billion to $22.5 billion, slightly higher than the total amount invested by venture capital in the same year.
- Roughly 225,000 people made angel investments.
- The most popular sectors are technology businesses, including life sciences, software, and health care.

Before I left Corporate Money, I did get an invaluable Business Plan Assessment from him. He had prepared a narrative like an Executive Summary, framing in two pages the nature of the opportunity my company presented, its perceived strengths and weaknesses, and an overall recommendation. This was intended to be a teaser that venture capitalists could give to prospective investors to whet their interest. New Money devoured it with glee.

I had gone from being rejected by my banker to being fought over by angel investors and venture capitalists! What did they see that she didn't?

My son came home that day and asked me a question I'll never forget.

"Are we poor, Mom?"

"What? What makes you think we're poor?"

"My friends think we're poor because our cars are so old."

This kid was seven. What did he know about old cars?

"Our neighbors drive a Yukon XL, with DVD screens in the headrests and a leather interior. They said we don't have something like that 'cause we're poor."

I couldn't believe the words coming out of my son's mouth. Up until that point all he cared about was playing army, looking for turtles in the creek behind our house, and watching *SpongeBob*. Still, I had to ask myself, were we poor? Not poor in the sense of desperate third-world poor, but our house was mortgaged to the hilt and my husband and I drove two aging cars that were obviously attracting the negative attention of my neighbors. How did I explain to my son that we had an intangible asset that was possibly worth millions that nobody could see, touch, or feel? Maybe that's what those millionaire angel investors saw that my banker and my neighbors couldn't. Maybe that's why opportunity is so hard to discern: You can't see it. It's like a keen sixth sense you can only develop through the school of hard work, hard knocks, and eventually success. The harder the work, the knocks, and the greater the success you've experienced, the better and clearer you can see opportunity where others only see failure.

We were still cash poor, asset rich. We had used the revenues from the last year not only to stabilize our business but also to develop new opportunities. Owning a business is much like being a shark—you have to keep moving or die. We were constantly on the search for any new products for any underserved niches that we could sell.

New Money called me, giving me exactly forty-eight hours to appear in his office. He was fast-tracking me to my first initial presentation to his angel group, and he wanted to make sure my PowerPoint presentation was good enough to "hit it out of the ballpark!" Gulp! What PowerPoint presentation?

If I had known the level of sophistication demanded of a PowerPoint slide show at any serious investment presentation I would have hung myself! There's no way I could have produced such a presentation in forty-eight hours without the support of the entire Pixar Studios! Not until I briefly joined the caravan of entrepreneurs hitting the road to look for money at one event after another across the country did I perceive how pathetically underfunded and undermanned I was. Forget about pie charts, bar graphs, and an occasional logo. De rigueur today are animation, splash, and fluttering graphics that try to make the most boring financial information come to life, leaping off the screen and right into the laps of those watching. It's all choreographed with the words of the presenter to be precisely ten minutes long and not a second longer, concluding with some visual of a billion-dollar jackpot designed to leave investors salivating.

I worked the next forty of forty-eight hours to create the presentation New Money wanted to see. The morning of our meeting, there was a *category four* blizzard. I had worked so hard in two days to prepare that I had literally become sick, almost losing my voice completely. My husband and I drove through whiteout conditions and met New Money and that other new player who had emerged from the invisible ranks of millionaires in my community: Trust-Fund Money. I turned on our laptop, preparing to begin, and New Money burst out laughing.

"Windows 97!" he commented, watching the screen initialize, loading our outdated software. "I didn't think anybody still used that! You guys gotta upgrade!"

"Hey, we're lean," my husband explained, quoting a caveat that New Money had said he was looking for in any business to invest in. "Lean and mean."

Though we had a state-of-the-art desktop computer system at home, all we had on this short notice was the old laptop my husband had used at one of his previous jobs.

"Okay, whatever. You can plug it into this overhead, and we'll watch on this screen."

Gulp. "I don't have a plug for an overhead," I explained.

"Whatever. We'll watch it on the screen then," he sighed, checking his e-mails on his BlackBerry.

I inserted the CD of my presentation into the drive, pushed start, and—nothing happened. I did it again, and again, nothing happened. The entire slide show had inexplicably disappeared. It was there before I left—I tested it more than once. I couldn't understand it.

"Just tell us . . . whatever then," New Money sighed, very politely reining in his complete exasperation. I had to do the best I could, salvaging some slides I had made on the hard drive and giving a narrative of my business plan with a voice that sounded and felt like broken glass. In my defense, I was doing everything I possibly could with every minute and every dollar I had. There wasn't one thing I could have done better to prepare for this meeting. I had worked forty hours, using all of my skills, on the best equipment I could afford. If I could start out so disastrously and so humbly and succeed, so can you.

THE ANGEL EVALUATION PROCESS

Every group might be a little different, but this is how it worked for me.

PHASE I—Application: Submit an application with the usual financial information, including balance sheet and P & L, along with a business plan. If you get past this, you move on to the next step.

PHASE II—Preliminary Review: A committee of angels reviews your application to determine if there is interest. If they like what they see, you get invited to a Pre-Screening Meeting, where you meet with one of the committee members, probably your "quarterback," who sees how you do in person and is responsible for shepherding you through the process. If they don't like what they see, you'll get your application back. If you are lucky, they will provide comments about what you need to fix.

PHASE III—Screening Meeting: After you met with your quarterback and you've presented a strong enough opportunity for investors, you'll be asked to present to a select group of the angels, anywhere from ten to twenty people. These are members who have expressed advance interest in your concept and want to consider the opportunity before it gets to the whole group. If you make it past this gauntlet, you will be asked to present detailed financials for preliminary due diligence, which means a lot of CPAs and CFOs will be rifling through your books and tax and financial statements to make sure everything you've done since fifth grade has been correct, drafting all kinds of crazy Sources and Use documents. You'll learn more about Sources and Use documents soon. Don't worry—having a lot of debt is not necessarily a bad thing. Just make sure everything is 100 percent accurate, because they'll find out if it isn't.

PHASE IV—Screening Checklist Review: Believe it or not, they're just now getting serious! If you've survived exposing every financial detail to their scrutiny, brush up your PowerPoint presentation, because you're about to go before a whole ballroom of them.

PHASE V—Full Presentation: I didn't get this far, which was a good thing—although I thought it was horrible at the time! Keep reading about what to expect and how to prepare.

PHASE Va—Post-Presentation: After you make your pitch, the group is polled, which might mean that your quarterback goes back to his office and starts calling people, trying to rally the troops to come to a consensus. This can be compared to catching mercury; you'll never know how hard your quarterback works for you during this process until you close the deal, so be really, really nice to him while you're taking him to the mat.

PHASE Vb—Deep Dive: Okay, now you start your second course of due diligence. They will look at your intellectual property, contracts, sales contacts, credit card statements, bank accounts, maybe even make you take a physical—before they get interested in something else and wander off.

PHASE VI: Everything you've done up to this point has been easy! Your quarterback has enlisted interested investors. A Term Sheet is drafted, outlining the general terms of the investment opportunity being offered. Active negotiations are conducted determining every little aspect of how the business will be run, from its corporate structure and the makeup of its Board of Directors to what you will be paid.

• •

I got home and immediately wrote New Money a thank-you e-mail, telling him how much I appreciated him taking the time to meet with us and how excited I was to be presenting to the rest of the group at the once-a-month Screening Meeting, just two days away. I was shocked when he reiterated his invitation, confirming my time. Obviously he still discerned some raw opportunity. It took me at least another six months of hard study to understand what commodity he was after.

I put together my game plan for the next opportunity I had before the angels: the Screening Meeting. For the most part, we stuck to the preceding schedule, but there were some significant episodes where the train went off the track. Don't expect this to go as planned. It looks like a smooth process on paper, but when it comes to going to the mat with them for equity, control, and leverage, all bets are off. Phase VI is probably the most significant, most time-consuming part of the process.

Every entrepreneur needed a quarterback to take them through this process, and New Money was apparently my quarterback. The quarterback is the point man who qualifies you and takes you before the whole group, making sure you know what to do and when to do it. New Money asked me to his office to make sure I knew what I was doing in advance of the Screening Meeting. Most investor groups offer formal Screening Meetings. My group of angels did so the first Monday of every month, giving three different young companies the opportunity to make a ten-minute presentation, followed by ten minutes of questions. The one hard-and-fast rule of these presentations is never to exceed the time allotted for your presentation or your question answering. Angels have no tolerance for anybody who can't effectively and passionately express everything they need to know about their company in twenty minutes. Expect to have the power cut off on your PowerPoint presentation if you run a second too late and to have your words stopped in mid-sentence in the question-answering round if you go over your allotted time. Don't waste a word! Get in front of a mirror and time your presentation to conform to their particular rules exactly.

We went to Symphony Money's law offices for our presentation to the Screening Committee. Imagine a big conference room with a big table, around which were seated fifteen men and one woman who represented the power elite of money in my geographical region. I wanted to get face time with each in order to extract a business card to find out with whom I was dealing, but that would not be allowed. No business cards would be given to you if you asked, which I foolishly did. This was a secret society, after all, formerly known as the "Old Boys' Network." They were giving me a test run to see if I could measure up to their standards of nerve, fortitude, risk taking, and perseverance. There were people in that room worth up to $200 million!

Up first, I was determined not to fail as miserably as I had the last time. My group of angel investors maintained an office staffed with administrative employees, and they provided me with an outline for my presentation. I succinctly addressed each question in a PowerPoint slide. My presentation was better, but it still wasn't good; I wouldn't see what good looked like for another month. Everybody got a custom-made press kit or presentation kit and a Wuvit. I was clipping along, fielding good questions, when one of the key people stood up, looked at his watch, and said loudly, "How long is this going to go on for?"

I was summarily excused, issued out along with my husband and my assistant, checking out the other two presenting groups who waited in the lobby behind me. I had no clue how I did, but I would be told by the group's secretary that it was the best presentation she had ever seen. Just a few months later, someone who joined the picture late told me that New Money felt I bombed once again. Despite bombing twice, with pathetic equipment and resources, selling a product for which some of the attendees could not hide their disdain, I was invited to participate in the next step in the process: the Full Presentation.

I was golden. I had, despite all odds, successfully made it through a process that had sunk most of the entrepreneurs who had come before me. How was it possible that I could be on the brink of failure and the brink of success at the same time? This was a question that would drive me crazy for the next ten months. I didn't have time anymore for petty jealousies or squabbles or school mom gossip, and I totally gave up caring about what others thought about the kind of car I drove. On a scale of 1–10, these considerations were a 1, and I was now living at 10. So this was the process one used, I determined, to get ice water running through your veins. I was going to need it.

PRESENTATION MUST-HAVES

These are standard if you're presenting to angels, venture capitalists, or at any other funding event where organizers sponsor venues for entrepreneurs and investors to come together:

1. **Cover:** Business-positioning statement: What are you selling to whom?
2. **Market:** How many billions of consumer dollars are spent on your market already?
3. **Solution:** What's your product, how does it solve a problem or fill a need, and is any of it proprietary or patented?
4. **Competitive Position:** Who are your competitors—you do have some—and how are you going to protect your market from them?
5. **Marketing/Sales/Support:** How many people are going to be needed to sell and support your marketing plan, and how much do they cost?
6. **Business Strategy:** How do you plan to grow beyond launch, or how soon will you become profitable?
7. **Financial Projections:** What is this market worth and what percentage of it can you sell to?
8. **Funding Sought:** Amount, comparables, use of funds. Here comes the dreaded Sources and Use spreadsheet. Just don't ask for a dollar more than you actually need or they'll eat you alive.
9. **Management:** Nobody asked to see my résumé ever, but they sure cared that I was passionate and driven, with kids to feed at home. They love enthusiasm. Lacking that, if you have a good résumé, make sure you feature it.
10. **Milestones:** For example, product launch, next funding event, when you will break even; again, you'd better be right! Don't build in any "blue-sky" scenarios, where you overproject and underdeliver.
11. **Exit Strategy:** Are you going to sell in an IPO and go public or sell to a strategic partner? These investors want to know how long it's going to be before they see cash money return on their investment, so don't leave this out.

Just weeks after being told I was on a collision path with failure, I put on my own version of a "go-to-hell" outfit to make my presentation to a society of millionaires, whose sole purpose in life, I thought, was to hand out money. A go-to-hell outfit is a manner of dressing that only the very rich or the very eccentric can dare to wear. For the person who taught me this concept, it was the loudest most obnoxious bright green plaid golf pants, which he wore to the links, his country club, *and* the fanciest restaurants, along with the required navy blue jacket and tie. His explanation: "I've worked so hard to make my money, I don't give a damn what anyone thinks of me anymore. If they don't like what I'm wearing, they can go to hell! That's why I call these my go-to-hell pants."

I hadn't made my money, but I thought I was invincible enough at this point. I shunned the de rigueur dark business suit, put on a hot pink linen blazer over a hot pink shell and a knee-length black wool crepe skirt, with my favorite over-the-top green daisy crystal jewelry, and marched into the elegant university ballroom where the millionaires were having lunch around dozens of white-linened round tables, to make my case.

What? Was I early? Nobody was there. My husband and I arrived when we were told to, only to discover a single table of five men waiting for us, some of whom had been at the Screening Meeting. New Money was there as always, furiously checking e-mail on his BlackBerry as always. This wasn't what I expected. What was going on?

"We wanted to meet with you before the presentation," Symphony Money explained. "There are a number of investors who are already interested in you, and if possible, we'd like to keep this among us at this point, instead of offering it to the entire group." I looked around and saw place seats for at least fifty. I had a private audience with five of the key decision makers prior to the general meeting, further evidence, in my mind, of just how golden I was. I had only met this group six weeks ago, and here I was, about to close the deal. Symphony Money asked me to recap my brief presentation for the benefit of the few new members there, and I gave it, in a glib, confident manner, convinced that I had something they wanted to buy and, if they were lucky, I would sell it to them.

I looked at my watch. My presentation took exactly ten minutes. Time to open it up for questions, something that I almost instantly regretted.

"Are these the financials? You call these financials?!" one of the new angels barked at me, thumbing through the documents that I had prepared with the help of my SBDC counselor and shaking his head in disgust.

"Where's the forecast? I need a cash flow for at least the next five years!" another agreed, practically shouting. *Five years?* I thought. *Who does cash flows for five years?* I was about to find out that the answer was any entrepreneur looking for money.

"I need better research than this!" the third argued, louder than the last. "You mean to tell me you're going to do these kinds of sales in the next couple of years? Who's your competition? What's their market share? How are you going to take it away?"

"There is no competition," I answered.

"No competition!" he shouted, with the other two new members agreeing with him, shaking their heads and throwing up their arms with exasperation. "Everybody says that! Do you realize that every entrepreneur who comes in here says that? You're either naive or stupid—which one is it?"

I thought I was golden. My research was light; I'll admit it. But if it was such an issue, why didn't somebody raise it before I got to this point? This was my third meeting with them. I was already doing everything I could to manage this business as it was, working sixty hours a week. Did they actually expect me to do a five-year cash flow and have at least MBA-level research, too? Yes, they did! I had gotten myself to this point on ego and enthusiasm, but I ran into a major roadblock when it came to writing the check. These guys weren't stupid. They weren't going to open their wallets for a fresh-faced entrepreneur. People like me, I would soon see, were a dime a dozen.

"What is all this credit card debt?" one of them gasped, running a finger down my balance sheet.

I felt as if a stake went through my heart. I hated that it was there, too, and I only had a precious few seconds to explain the debacle that was 2003.

"You obviously can't run your business. You expect me to give you my money to pay off your debt? Is that what you're going to do? Pay off your debt with my money?!" one of the most impassioned investors yelled, standing up inflamed, tearing up my business plan and throwing it on the table before me before stomping his way out of the room.

Did he just tear up my business plan and throw it in my face? I couldn't believe it. I looked at New Money for some help. He was furiously checking his e-mail on his BlackBerry. He was ignoring me. I felt like I had run head-first into a Mack truck. The other members of the group packed up their stuff and prepared to leave without so much as a word of good-bye. Symphony Money was the only one who would look me in the eye.

"Each one of these men," he consoled me, "was just like you at one time. So broke that he didn't have two nickels to rub together."

"What?"

"Oh sure, even I was. I remember sitting in my office worrying how I was going to pay my employees, or even my rent."

In my mind I had already spent the money they were going to give me. New Money had told me at my first meeting with him that the six figures I was asking for was "peanuts." I thought it was a done deal. I had put off creditors for months and used every dollar I did have to develop new moneymaking opportunities in anticipation of this deal closing. Now I had to scramble and find another plan. How could I have had so many good meetings for it to end so disastrously?

I was looking crisis in the face all over again. I needed $20,000 just to meet my monthly obligations, and I didn't have it. I was asked to leave because the General Meeting was about to convene and I was not going to be allowed to present. I saw the VC team of Corporate Money and Washington Money. They were going to get a shot showing off the three companies they were shopping around. I wished that I were under their expert stewardship and not running through this frightening gauntlet alone. At least they knew how this game worked and knew the players. Corporate Money looked me right in the eyes from across the room and knew exactly what had happened.

My husband led me out of the room and down to the lobby. We sat there feeling sorry for ourselves for about twenty minutes, thinking of every possible scenario there was to raise the working capital we so desperately needed to stay in business. I wouldn't understand for months that my presentation was terrible, as were my financials, and I deserved what I got. The angels were demanding things of me that I didn't know yet. I hoped they would be patient enough to allow me to learn. My banker had told me I had written the best business plan she had ever seen. But these guys were a thousand times more sophisticated than my banker, and their demands were a thousand times greater. The good news was that they were offering me a thousand times more than my banker could.

Every millionaire's business has hit hard times as mine was doing then.

Knowing that hard times are part of the deal and realizing that the hardest times usually precede the best times, when your success has grown to the point that it demands extreme infusions of capital, expertise, and infrastructure to take it to maximum velocity, is what angel investing is all about.

Thomas Edison observed that "many of life's failures are people who did not realize how close they were to success when they gave up." This is when seasoned business leaders, who are used to eating stress like yours for breakfast, who have confronted every possible scenario of crisis and faced it down with courage and ingenuity to arrive at millionaire status, can see opportunity so far in the distance that you haven't even thought of yet, that they'll pack the trunk of your car with money and accelerate you into the fast lane of millionairedom by taking the wheel and driving it there personally.

I learned that in this process the angels want to see if you can handle the demands of working with a dozen Donald Trumps more virulent than anything you've ever seen in his TV boardroom. If you don't break down in tears, self-pity, or anger, or can move forward with them with a smile pasted on your face as you get past your own emotions and to the work they're demanding of you, you may just get lucky and get money! And free money at that, or as close to free as it comes!

I had an ulterior motive. I was going to wait for Corporate Money to come out after his presentation so that I could beseech him for any kind of help I could, including taking my company back as one of the businesses he was shopping around. Sure enough, he came out alone; Washington Money was nowhere to be seen.

"Do you have a minute?" I asked him, heading him off. "Can I buy you a cup of coffee?"

"Sure, okay," he said, sitting down.

"I don't know what just happened to me," I admitted. "Do you?"

"Well, it can be a tough process. Don't fool yourself."

"But what do you think? Am I down? Am I out? Do I have a shot? You know these people. You know how this process works. What's next?"

Washington Money showed up, put his hand on Corporate Money's shoulder, and squeezed it, as if to say, *Stop talking to her immediately!* Corporate Money said good-bye and disappeared within seconds. I was even more bewildered. It was a very strange end to a very strange day.

15

THE IMPORTANCE OF ATTITUDE

Believe in yourself; never stop having faith in yourself or your vision or your product, even if other people tell you you're crazy!

Just days later the phone rang. It was Symphony Money, calling to see if I could make it to a meeting in two weeks with the interested angels who wanted to make me an offer. I couldn't believe it. I had taken the advice of the General to heart—"apply subtle pressure relentlessly"—and had sent them regular group e-mails, informing them of each new lucrative national prospect I was talking to. I was so relentless that New Money gave me a backhanded compliment on my undisputed e-mail prowess at this very next meeting. Anybody else probably would have given up, but I wouldn't even think about it: *No sissies, no cowards, no complainers, no criers, and no quitters. Especially no quitters.*

My CFO, though now in San Francisco, was still communicating his enthusiasm and knowledge to me from the West Coast via e-mail, phone calls, and occasionally even a chance visit.

"Go after sales!" he was urging me, trying to rouse me from feeling sorry for myself.

"Go after sales? I don't even have the money for production!"

"Don't worry about that," was his advice. "Get the sales; the money will follow. As long as you have sales, you'll always have the opportunity to find money. No sales, no money. Get the sales."

Get the Sales; the Money Will Follow

My CFO's philosophy was "build it, and they will come." He thought the angels were too hot a prospect from which to walk away. Fail once? Ha! That's nothing, I've learned! By this time I was used to picking myself up, dusting myself off, and trying to figure out *why* I failed so I could fix it the next time. Failure was inevitable. I was done beating myself up for failing. Not facing failure—my own shortcomings, my arrogance, my ignorance, or my self-defeating attitude—then coming back to try to fix what I had failed at? Now that was something to be ashamed of. In the end, those who have succeeded are those who have failed and conquered their failures.

All you need to do is succeed one more time than you fail to become a millionaire.

I was beginning to understand that with every failure I was calling upon newer and deeper personal resources of courage, ingenuity, and responsibility to find success. It was as if I was becoming a more realized person every day. I was using every single capacity God had given me—physical, mental, emotional, spiritual—to the utmost limit. I started to see providence in little as well as big events in my daily life. I was a hundred percent alive, feeling every emotion on the spectrum every day. I was becoming addicted. In a way, I was already part of this secret society that I was so desperately trying to join.

I took my CFO's advice and went after sales with a new relish. My husband had done what he done before, mysteriously pulled money out of nowhere. There was $25,000 left in our 401(k) that only he and God knew about. We took it out, paid the creditors we needed to pay, buying ourselves another month of time. In addition to that, we had been faced with disposing of the very last asset that we had in the world: a rental property that was almost entirely leveraged with our second SBA loan. My husband had bought this house right before we got married, and we had kept it as an investment. Our tenant, after ten years of renting, had become seriously delinquent. We put the house on the market, making the monthly mortgage payments, and hoped that our money wouldn't run out before the house sold.

When we got an offer, our banker threatened to take every dollar from the proceeds, in excess of the $75,000 we owed her, because she had a blanket lien on our assets secured by the first SBA loan of $75,000. There was an additional $25,000 to be had from its sale, after we paid our realtor, and we needed that money to keep our business afloat. Our banker was going to take it anyway, even though our primary residence still secured the $75,000 of the first loan, and even if it meant our business would fail. My husband decided to play hardball. He called up the realtor and told him to cancel the closing, that we were going to look for a new tenant instead, then called our banker and told her he had done so. She relented, realizing that now she might not even get her $75,000. We didn't know till the closing was over whether she was going to swoop in at the last minute to take every dollar.

I had discovered that my successes in 2004 were not going to go unrecognized. My product had indeed achieved momentum in the marketplace as my VC mentor had prognosticated, and I had my hands full juggling prospects, hoping to roll out to major retailers across the nation for the holidays.

Making sales cost money. I had a major trade show in New York just a month away that I needed to attend if I was going to stay in business. That would set me back $10,000 minimum, which I didn't have. If I didn't go, I might as well shut down the whole operation. If you don't have the money to support your sales functions, the lifeline of your business, you truly are in trouble.

At this time, my son Dylan was determined to be really smart and was put into an advanced class at school. However, my other son, Ryan, was struggling through kindergarten. GameCube had become for him some kind of addictive drug; he was extraordinarily good at it, beating kids twice his age while mastering the most difficult cognitive and fine motor skills it demanded. The drums were beating relentlessly at school that he had autism, particularly Asperger's syndrome, which had very quickly become the catchall for anything that could remotely be confused with the most high-functioning symptoms of autism. Even the most educated school professionals and psychologists were telling me he had it. My argument was, how could he demonstrate such advanced skills in video games if he was autistic? Their reply: because he's autistic! They wouldn't be satisfied until they sent me on an exhaustive odyssey of pediatric neurologists and psychologists, subjecting the kid to every single test known to man. I began to understand the value of health insurance and that most people took it for granted, including Ryan's teachers. Health insurance has become so outrageously expensive, my husband and I could barely afford to keep our family covered, let alone employees. We had the bare minimum coverage necessary to ensure that if any of us were catastrophically hurt in an accident or handed a potentially terminal disease diagnosis, we were covered. Everything else, including all these specialists and all their tests, was out-of-pocket. The nurses on the other side of the desk when we registered would always look at me totally aghast when they asked the usual question: "Insurance provider?" "None," I would answer, to their utter shock. With all my other bills, the mounting medical costs totaling into the thousands were something I couldn't avoid. My husband and I found ourselves asking the question, "Can we afford to do this?" The answer always was, "Can we afford not to?" Ryan was at a critical growth stage and he needed to be diagnosed. I'll never take health insurance, or the employers who pay for it, for granted again. Regardless of the insurance, there were days at this point, even weeks, where the hardest thing I had to deal with had nothing to do with work or money; it was all about worrying about my son.

The Hard Work of Raising Money

Symphony Money wanted me to bring along a Sources and Use document for this meeting, so that the angels could understand the exact itemized cash needs that I had in the short term to keep my business running. This document, of all the documents I've listed, was the one that caused me the most agony in the months that ensued. Its exact use was not well understood by anyone, including bankers, accountants, CFOs, and even my SBDC counselor. Our combined limited understanding produced a finished product that never failed to disappoint. By the time I was in final stages of negotiation with the angels, they had looked at so many different Sources and Use documents produced by so many different people with so many different purposes in mind that they thought I was even more of a financial mess than I actually was.

My angels wanted to know how much cash I needed short-term to keep my business from going under—forget about paying off long-term debt like credit cards and SBA loans—and how specifically I would use those funds. My husband and I did our best to prepare this, then got all dressed up again to drive an hour to meet with the angels. This was my fifth meeting with them in the fifth location. I was cautiously hopeful that things would go well, but after the last ambush, I didn't know what to think.

We were escorted back to an office, where Symphony Money, Old Money, New Money, and a new person, henceforth known as Bad Money, were waiting to meet with us. While New Money furiously checked his e-mail on his BlackBerry, Symphony Money told me what he wanted me to do.

"We've decided we're going to invest in Green Daisy," said Symphony Money.

You could have knocked me over with a feather.

"We're concerned that your financials aren't exactly in order, and we don't know if we have time to complete due diligence before these critical time and money deadlines you're facing pass," said Old Money.

"I need to make product to deliver to these big retailers, who I'm closing now," I said. "I also need to go to New York just weeks from now for a major show. If I don't go to that show, I'm going to miss serious opportunities. I have leverage in the marketplace, that I've earned from selling Saks Inc. twenty-five thousand Wuvits in just five months in 2004, and I need to capitalize on it—now!"

"Exactly," said Bad Money. "Did you prepare your Sources and Use document?" he asked.

"Yes," my husband responded. I noticed we needed a pathetic $25,000 in the near term to fund our million-dollar operation. The number we had previously been discussing for investment with the group was in the six figures, depending on how much infrastructure the angels wanted to grow and how fast. I was used to functioning on a shoestring budget, which is a quality that endeared me to them. There was just no way they could get a better value than by buying part of a company with more than a million dollars in revenues in just over two years, with an energetic and inspired president who was creating all kinds of new award-winning products to shove through those valuable channels of distribution every day.

"There is a lot of money here," Symphony Money said almost unconsciously to himself and to the others, seeming to consider an invisible pile of cash on the table before him. I couldn't even see the money he was looking at then. He was exponentially more skilled, perceptive, and accomplished at seeing opportunity and turning it into money than I was. Seven hundred million dollars a year to be exact, I would later find out, as the past president of a huge national brand. He had met an artist with drawings on paper twenty years ago and created a business empire from them, licensing the art into every conceivable item of merchandise known to man, from collectible figurines, to books, pajamas, cartoons, Bibles—you name it! He had secured one license worth a hundred million dollars alone. When I would meet the current president of the company—the same one who was making regular appearances on QVC, shipping container loads each month from China—he characterized Symphony Money's accomplishments perhaps better than anybody else. "I'm the car, sitting in the garage, of the house that he built."

"It's clear we need to apply life support," said Bad Money. "We want to get you some cash to take care of these immediate and critical needs, which will keep you growing and headed in the right direction until we put the whole deal together."

"What happened to the six figures?" I asked. I could not have known then how impossibly naive this question was at this time. Most angel deals, I would later learn, take a minimum of a year to complete. I was only on my second month. Due diligence alone, I would later find out, took a full eight weeks. Nobody told me this then, and I had absolutely no clue, but I thought the idea of giving me money in the short term while we put together the long term sounded like a good idea.

"What kind of credit do you have?" asked Bad Money, ignoring my question. "I mean, if I called your banker right now, what would she say about you?"

"She'd say that we have two loans with her, of which we've never been late on a payment once in two years. She'll tell you that we're about to pay off one of those loans in full, worth seventy-five thousand dollars, when we sell our rental property in the coming month. She'll tell you that we've had an account in good standing for over ten years at her bank, never once bouncing a check. She'll tell you that, despite our business's financial difficulties, we've managed to maintain an exceptionally good credit score by making all of our payments on time and negotiating with our vendors for terms on the rest," I told him, knowing it was all the truth.

"What's her number?" he suddenly demanded of me very brusquely. "Her name and number—I need it now!" I opened my day planner, all flustered by his urgency, and read off the name and number as he wrote it down. He took his piece of paper, got out his phone, and immediately left the room while dialing.

Just a few minutes later, he came back into the room, all in a huff. "I just called your banker," he proclaimed to the group. "She told me that you're a big credit risk and that all the things you just said to me aren't true!"

I knew my banker had lost all interest in me, and she was many things, but she wasn't a liar. She would not compromise her job, her career, or her professional standing to say something that was untrue about me just to scuttle my business.

"Could you please leave the room for a few minutes while we work this out between us?" Bad Money asked.

My husband and I left the room in a state of bewilderment. I didn't like pressure being applied. I hadn't asked to come there; they had asked me! All of my senses started to beep: *Warning! Danger!* I called my banker to ask her if she had indeed said these things. Her secretary answered; I couldn't talk to my banker because she was on vacation. She wasn't even in the office. "Had somebody else said these horrible things?" I asked. Her secretary assured me, "I've been sitting next to this phone for the last half hour, and it hasn't rung once."

This plan was once again going to hell before my eyes. I was suddenly in a cash free fall without a parachute. My survival instincts instantly kicked in. My husband and I were waiting to be summoned back into the room when two men came in, looking and smelling like money. They were checking in with the receptionist to let her know they were there for their three o'clock meeting with the angels.

I was really hoping they were venture capitalists, here to shop their pet businesses to them. I wasn't going to wait to find out. "Hi, I'm Kim Lavine, president of Green Daisy, maker of the Wuvit—over two million dollars in sales in the last two years at the nation's premier retailers, including Saks," I said, introducing myself. "I heard you have a meeting with the angels." I needed venture capital, and I needed it now! "We're meeting with them, too. Can I get your card?"

"Sure," one of them said, stunned and impressed at the same time. I know this is an effective tactic, so use it fearlessly.

"What do you do?" I asked.

"We have a life-sciences company," one of them explained. "We specialize in nanotechnology. Do you know what that is? You know, very small elements of matter . . ."

Yes, I was a woman, I had blond hair, and I *did* know what nanotechnology was. "Oh sure," I assured him. "So you're here looking for funding?" I didn't know it then, but I was looking at cookie-cutter high-tech life-sciences entrepreneurs. They would become painfully obvious to me in the next months. They always showed up looking for money, ultra-casual, dressed in short sleeves, sometimes even shorts, never a tie, and always had a shiny, full-of-themselves self-assurance that bordered on smugness. They couldn't help it, after all. Life sciences was the absolute darling of VC and angel funding of the moment, picking up all the slack from high tech, which had sustained critical damage from the late-nineties dot-com bust. Money was falling all over itself to find the next big life-sciences thing. Compared to that, Wuvits weren't very sexy. Still, I like to remind everybody that Wal-Mart is the biggest corporation in the world, not Microsoft, not Apple, bigger even than the Big Three automakers put together, and certainly bigger than any medical device or drug company that I know. But all the smart money is in life sciences.

Bad Money suddenly appeared from the conference room, shaking the hands of Life Science. "Doesn't anybody wear a suit anymore?" he asked them. "Where's your tie?" He definitely wasn't pleased with their short sleeves. *Great way to make a first impression,* I thought, secretly agreeing. "Go on in," he said, directing them into our meeting room. "I'm going to finish up with these people, and I'll be in in a few minutes.

Even More Bad Things That Only Happen to Women

I'm not even going to tell you what happened next. Just think of this as a cautionary tale. I'm going to put it in a nutshell. A bad offer was made to us by Bad Money, one that we rejected on the spot, and again, over the phone through our attorney, who told me it was a bad deal. Bad Money had perceived weakness and vulnerability in our situation, and had highjacked the process. He was new to this discussion; he didn't know me, and he underestimated me. All he saw was a woman with blond hair and a short-term need for $25,000. A year later, I would learn that playing "good cop, bad cop" like this was an expected part of the game. I found myself walking away from a table piled with money the second time in just weeks. What was I going to do?

I Love New York!

I was going to go to New York! That's what I was going to do! I had waited to the eleventh hour for the cash I needed to go to the show, and it didn't come. I want to make it very clear right now: You obviously need money from venture capitalists and angels or you wouldn't be asking for it in the first place. You have to protect your leverage at all costs. I never sold my "critical demise" to Money; I always sold my "critical opportunities" to them. After two years, I realized I would no doubt find a way to make ends meet. My husband would magically pull $20,000 out of thin air. I would persuasively convince a vendor to not only not cancel my credit but instead triple it. I began to understand that crisis is constant. That fear and anxiety were part of the territory. I needed to learn to manage crisis and accept fear as a motivator. Nothing got me out of bed in the morning like fear. I started to see that there was no crisis that I couldn't solve. Crisis was just another challenge that had to be conquered through either hard work or innovative thinking. My Reiki Master would later put it all into perspective for me: Everything beautiful, strong, and worthwhile comes out of intense work, patience, time, sometimes even painful suffering. "You only need to look at your children to see that that's true."

This trade show in New York didn't accept credit cards—only cash. I took four thousand dollars out of our business checking account, packed my truck up with my set, and drove to New York. The show management had never seen anything like it; I called one day to see if I could get in, arrived the next with a complete set, and managed to have such a strong presence there that they photographed my booth. It was so last-minute, I didn't have anyone to work with me.

An attractive and smart woman came up, introduced herself, and asked if I needed help for the show. This had never happened to me before, and I had never needed it more. She turned out to be an incredible saleswoman, and her efforts contributed to what was perhaps the best show I ever had in my life. We wrote thousands and thousands of dollars' worth of orders, but more important, we took business cards from some of the nation's biggest retail chains, which turned into orders across the U.S. just months later. From this show alone, the number of potential doors—or individual stores—we added to our prospect list was over 1,500! This could turn into a million dollars in revenues annually very quickly if we launched correctly!

Try not to let exciting developments create stress. Spend less time worrying and more time being happy.

I had other business to do in New York. It looked like the angel deal was dead. I needed to find a way to fund my Chinese production for Holiday 2005 to all these new national retail accounts I had just picked up. I had come to this show as beat-up and tired as anyone could ever be. In just forty-eight hours, my entire situation was transformed to one of unbelievable excitement and opportunity. I couldn't believe that I had thought about not coming to this show. I was suddenly red-hot. A *New York Times* business reporter came to my booth to find out what all the excitement was about. I didn't need those angels after all. I called up my Chinese MBA, who lived just across the river in New Jersey. Before I knew it, he was at my booth with three of his business partners, watching in amazement as we wrote orders, talked to big retailers, international importers, national catalogs, reps for QVC and HSN, and distinguished press, while the show management sent over a camera crew to take pictures of it all!

"Luck is preparation meeting opportunity." Luck is an illusion. Nobody ever "lucks" into entrepreneurial success. They first had a vision, then positioned themselves to be on the receiving end of opportunity.

Remember, I met this Chinese MBA in a mall a year and a half earlier, when he offered to buy me a cup of coffee so he could ask me some questions about how he could set up his own kiosk. Just months after that, he had gone to China on my dime to source potential manufacturers. That seemed like an eternity ago, in both time and circumstances. Since then, he had partnered with another Chinese immigrant as well as a Middle Eastern man, who were both experienced in international importing; they used their contacts in the Orient, the Middle East, and Pakistan to buy handmade Oriental rugs dirt cheap, importing them into the U.S. and wholesaling them to fine retailers across the country. Business was so good, they were on a major capital expansion campaign, planning to open up to seven of their own retail stores in some of the country's most affluent cities, including Washington, D.C.

My Chinese MBA definitely wanted a piece of my action. He saw in me exactly what he lacked, and I saw in him the same. I needed Chinese manufacturing sourced, managed, and delivered by someone with contacts and experience. Not only did he have an MBA, but he also had done supply-chain management for some of the biggest Fortune 500 companies. With me, he saw access into thousands of prime American retail channels of distribution. He saw expert design, marketing, and sales functions already in place, headed up by a figurehead, in his limited cultural vernacular, of Martha Stewart caliber. I would learn a lot from him in the next couple of months, most importantly insights into the Chinese industrial mind.

The Real China, as Told to Me:
What We Have That They Want

After the show wrapped, I spent a half a day in New Jersey with him before I headed home. He had developed a relationship with one of the factories he had made contact with when he went to China on my behalf. Its name was Angel. According to him, some of the Chinese factories were growing tired of being America's workshops. They wanted to penetrate America's markets with their own goods to get the margins that the American companies, for whom they were manufacturing, were getting. Despite China's massive industrial complex, they didn't have a single national brand. China was a country in search of a brand. Since there was so much American money in China, there were unlimited reserves of capital to fund any kind of production we wanted. He reiterated his assertion that China loved cash, valued only cash, and that the people he knew who owned the factory had millions of dollars, perhaps as much as $10 million. He proposed we plug his Chinese contacts with their manufacturing and capital resources into my highly functioning and successful design, marketing, and sales machine. We could fund all our production and use their millions as a huge rotating credit line with very generous payment terms—he had already negotiated it. He would handle all the sourcing and supply-chain management, while I continued to do what I did.

China, he explained, was radically in love with all things American. It was a culture in extreme transition. The Chinese were having a love affair with all things Western. They wanted to be American, look American, talk American, and, most important, use American products. (If you're not laying the groundwork for selling your products in China now, get busy. According to him, it's the next big consumer culture.)

Since I looked like such an archetypal American—blond hair, blue eyes—I had an instant cachet, which he claimed would earn me their respect and their business commitment; I would be an easy sell to them. He explained that they desperately wanted to get inside the American aesthetic, a complete and total mystery to them. If they could only unlock it, understanding what American markets demanded and creating their own products, the opportunity for reward was mind-boggling. We struck a tentative deal: I'd give him 10 percent of my company in exchange for him securing a line of credit from his Chinese manufacturing sources. It all looked so good on paper.

I drove home in a state of euphoria. I had already seen evidence that sometimes the worst things that happen to you can turn out to be the best. Maybe the deal with the angel investors was meant to fail. I looked at my day planner on the seat next to me. It was bursting with business cards from prospects worth millions of dollars, including Gottschalks, Von Maur, and Bed Bath & Beyond—all interested in carrying my product. I had already taken three calls from the HSN rep I had met at the show. She had me booked for an on-air appearance already! In addition, I had the beginnings of an international corporation ready to be launched. And best of all, it looked as if I had money, up to $10 million of it, to fund my overseas production. All I really needed was money to fund my production—nothing else. The framework of a business that I had created so painstakingly these last three years had become an extremely valuable commodity. Now I understood what those angels were after. I was a successful company! I had become a Mommy Millionaire!

I prepared to get ready for my upcoming show in Atlanta in a big way. We had been awarded a license from the Collegiate Licensing Company (CLC) to apply the logos of certain universities to our Wuvits just before the holidays and had delivered our first collegiate Wuvits to Parisian, where they blew out of the store like a hurricane. I was doing a Demo Event in a store in Alabama and we had four Alabama Wuvits at 10:00 A.M. at opening. By 10:30, all had sold. I actually had to referee a fight when one shopper got mad that the woman before her bought the last two and wouldn't give her one of them to buy for her husband. This was huge! The minute my license was granted, I got a call from one of the VPs of the biggest rep group of collegiate merchandise in the U.S. "Do you know that this license could be worth ten million dollars alone?" he practically shrieked. "This opportunity is so big, you can't even see where you're going with it!"

Where had I heard that before?

My million-dollar opportunities were turning into snowballs that were rolling down the other side of the mountain on their own momentum, getting bigger and bigger every day.

I understood then, and have seen it a hundred times since, that having ideas and opportunities is the easy part; the hard part was finding money.

Raising money is the hardest thing an entrepreneur has to do, and nobody anywhere is teaching anybody how to do it.

I had been on the hot trail of money for about six months, and though it kept eluding me, I had a very good shot at bringing it down. I felt like the better and bigger my opportunities got, the more likely investors would buy into the deal. *Build it and they will come,* I said to myself as my assistant and I got in the car and drove to Atlanta.

"We have to come up with a new product to sell Parisian," I told my assistant as we drove. "We're already selling our product in the intimate apparel departments of all their stores. Is there anything else we could possibly segue in? What about pajamas? I noticed in all my travels to all their stores during the holidays that everything they have is so outdated—all those silly pastel floral patterns that only grandmas wear. I hate them! Do you wear them?" She admitted that she did not.

We looked at each other and said, "Let's sell Parisian pajamas!" We understood that there was an underserved niche glaring at us and somebody had to exploit it with fresh and fun pajamas featuring design excellence in fabrics and body. "These aren't your mother's pajamas," I said. I called our buyers and asked them if they could meet us at dinner the next evening in the same restaurant where I had once sat with my former employees, plotting my million-dollar empire.

Five Smart Women and a Bottle of Wine

The next evening we were at a table with another group of women, selling another million-dollar concept, in an event I like to refer to as Five Smart Women and a Bottle of Wine. We all knew each other fairly well at this point. I had the utmost gratitude and respect for the buyers, for not only buying my product in such abundance and launching it into the national retail marketplace but also for so generously allowing me to demonstrate it in their stores across the country. They liked me, because I had gone out and worked hard to generate sales and drive revenues through their stores, regardless of whether it immediately made me more money or not. We had come to regard each other warmly, inevitably talking about kids, dogs, husbands, and boyfriends, which we discussed for two hours and fifty minutes. The last ten minutes were spent talking business. When my assistant and I floated the idea of making them pajamas, they all practically gasped in unison in response: "We're dying for some fresh, updated pajamas! Can you launch a new line of pajamas?"

I went right back to the hotel and sent every one of the angels for whom I had an e-mail address an update saying we had just secured another million-dollar revenue stream! *Get on board now, because this train is about to leave the station,* I implied. If it wasn't them, I'd no doubt find somebody else to fund my production. The very next day I got a call from one of Symphony Money's friends, making an appointment with me at the show to introduce himself, along with his own Chinese manufacturing contacts, who flew in all the way from China just to meet with me. This was Chinese manufacturing I could see, touch, smell, and shake hands with. They had seven factories doing just about everything possible, along with their own contacts throughout the Pacific Rim, including Cambodia. This was before the cotton quota had been lifted in China, limiting export of cotton clothing to the U.S. to certain quotas. I was walking back to my booth after our impromptu business meeting in the show's aisles and ran into a fellow exhibitor I had last seen in New York at the Extracts Show at the Javits Center. His ingenious new product—a paraffin hand treatment that heated itself in its own gloves—had won the best new product in show then. He told me he was scheduled to debut it on QVC, and that he was also raising capital to fund his growth. He was selling 1 percent of his company for $100,000, and already had numerous shares sold. He had his own license to sell securities, so he had handled all his own paperwork, calling up every rich doctor in his town to make the offer to. I was shocked and wondered what made his company worth so much—with almost no sales and no channels of distribution—and mine worth comparatively so little, except for his confidence, and his expertise. He didn't even own the patent—he just had an exclusive right to distribute in the U.S. Obviously, there was a better way to do this that I didn't know about.

In response to Saks's question, we would design, sell, and launch a new line of pajamas in less than six months to major retailers across the U.S. We were so successful at listening to what they wanted and adapting it with our own vision that the pajamas would be featured on the cover of Parisian's store sales circular going to over 7 million homes! Who has ever heard of a small company like us, selling a product most people laughed at, launching a brand-new product line at major retailers across the U.S., featured on the cover of a sales circular going to 7 million homes? Again, we went to all forty of Parisian's stores—no test—and major retailers across the country gasped, asking us with incredulity, "They're sending you to all their stores? You're not even testing? I've never heard of that!"

One of those retailers was Gottschalks, a sixty-store chain on the West Coast. We went out right before Christmas to meet with the intimate apparel buyer to show her sketches on paper of our new line. We sold her this line without even a prototype, without even a product sample. All we had was drawings on paper and a passion for design excellence that resulted in our getting a personal invitation to Macy's as well while we were there, whom we had cold-called again. Just weeks later, we met Von Maur in Davenport, Iowa, whom we had cold-called, too! That is four major retailers, representing over 2,000 doors or individual stores, that we were walking into to show product on the virtue of one phone call, and a cold call at that! Wuvits had just launched to all of Gottschalks's sixty stores, again no test. We decided to do a massive marketing blitz to support the rollout, with my assistant and me traveling to nine stores in just over three days. We'd sell twenty Wuvits in two hours, except for when we sold thirty-six in twenty minutes. We showed the Wuvit to a shopping customer in Fresno, who was looking for presents for a doctor's office staff; she saw the Faith, Hope & Love Wuvit and decided that was it; she had to have them for all her oncology nurses. Our work was done, we thought, leaving after only twenty minutes. We made a point of visiting with the buyer of Wuvits for Gottschalks while we were meeting the intimate apparel buyer. "The only reason you guys got your product in here," he told us as we sat in his office visiting, "is your passion and persistence. Nobody could say no to you guys."

We got home and received a call from Bed Bath & Beyond. They wanted our product and wanted it ASAP! We had spent every dollar we had developing the pajama opportunity, as well as paying the advance royalties to the Collegiate Licensing Company for our university licensing deal, and didn't have the cash to turn around and deliver Bed Bath & Beyond's order, which we had been trying to land for over a year. Can you believe it? A big order from a major retailer and no inventory to fill it? Time for my husband the hero again. We started to make the product, talking our manufacturers with whom we had termed out the loan into sewing them. Our promise was that we would pay for half of the order the day it left the warehouse if they gave us sixty-day terms on the balance. They agreed to it.

There Is Always a Negative and a Positive Side to Everything That Happens— Choose to Look at the Positive

It's amazing to me that up until that moment I couldn't even see my success. All I saw was crisis, challenge, struggle, and stress. I suddenly realized that there was always a negative and positive side to everything that happened to me on a daily basis and I had been trained like everybody else to only see the negative. I see people like me just starting out now, and the most important advice I can give them is this: spend less time worrying and more time being happy.

Everything happens for a reason. Have faith in this; even if the reward isn't immediately or even distantly apparent, it will become so. It took me a year to see that the worst thing that ever happened to me was the best thing that ever happened to me.

Being with my kids is the number-one perk I have in my job. I have a lot of work to juggle, but it isn't day care, babysitting schedules, or nannies. At the end of the day, as long as we're all happy, healthy, and safe, I really don't care how clean my house is and what kind of car I drive.

My success as a mother wasn't measured anymore by how clean my house was or how well decorated it was, but by how happy my children were.

16

SHOW ME THE MONEY

I had so much opportunity in front of me, I didn't know what to do. I was almost giddy. I was still angry with the angels, but I recognized this was an opportunity that was scuttled by the actions of one individual. *Why couldn't I put everybody together?* I thought. The angels, besides bringing money, were also bringing talent and experience of a caliber that I would never be able to afford to pay for.

I was thinking about this when the General called.

"What are you doing Tuesday?"

"What aren't I doing?"

"You're going to Venture Tuesday; that's what you're doing. The first Tuesday of every month, the university sponsors an event where three businesses looking for capital present to a panel of investors, venture capitalists and angels. It looks like your angels are going to be there. You gotta go."

Indeed I did, I thought. If for no other reason than to flaunt before them all my recent successes. I was still angry at this time, and in retrospect, this was a foolish waste of my time. Anger is a counterproductive emotion that brings no value. I can honestly say, that after everything I've been through, I almost never get angry anymore. (Not counting at my husband, of course. We live and work together, and I'm his boss!) Anger clouds your ability to see problems and their solutions clearly. This angel situation was still a problem for me, and until I got rid of the anger, I didn't see the solution.

I dressed myself up in my lucky suit, the one that managed to look very professional while displaying the absolute limit of politically correct décolletage, and put on all my best over-the-top green daisy crystal jewelry. I drove the hour and a half to this university's event and found my way to a crowded room filled with at least a hundred people, all focused on a panel before them made up of three individuals. The first can only be described as the most buttoned-down, formidable-looking Master of the Universe I had ever seen in my life—bow tie, spectacles, and all! If you looked up "Prestigious East Coast Cash Money" in the dictionary, his picture would be there.

Out of all the Money there, he was Smart Money. Next was Old Money her-self, sitting on the panel and receiving the fawning attention of the three en-trepreneurs there waiting to present. Third was a person who was the second-generation founding family member of a major pharmaceutical company, William Parfet of Upjohn, recently purchased by Pfizer, for which I once briefly worked. They had brought out the big guns. There was another group of investors sitting at a table to their right. I turned around to see that the VC team of Corporate Money and Washington Money were there, too.

CRITERIA FOR PRESENTING AT CAPITAL-RAISING EVENTS

Large Potential Market: For most of these events you have to be talking about a minimum $200 million market, of which you would forecast a percentage of sales, with profitability in three years.

High Anticipated Growth Rate: Projected annual sales growth of 25 percent or more.

An Experienced Management Team: Key people who have been there, done that.

A Competitive Advantage: A "distinct" advantage in performance, price, et cetera, compared to the competition.

Barriers to Entry: Economic means to discourage or beat competition in the field, including proprietary technology or patent.

A Clear Strategy for Commercialization: A realistic and well-thought-out plan to bring product to market.

Scalability: A substantial likelihood that the business can grow exponentially once the product is launched.

Proof of Concept: Ideally, a product or service that clearly fulfills a need and has achieved some level of sales or sales commitments.

A Business Model Anchored in Reality: Management has thoroughly assessed its market, product development costs, ongoing operating expenses, and overall funding requirements.

The usual introductions were made, but this was a group that wasn't about wasting time. There weren't going to be any compulsory lame jokes or sleepy personal narratives about the events of their drive there today. Time was money, and these people were all about money. The panel was introduced; Smart Money, turns out, had his own capital investment firm, was involved in the late-nineties Silicon Valley IPO madness as a senior VP for a major investment firm. And he was a first-round investor in Google.

The room went dark, the overhead projector was turned on, and Presenter Number 1 hooked up his laptop and started the PowerPoint show. I could tell right away he was in life sciences. His short-sleeved shirt—no tie—and sandals gave him away. He was a certified genius—he was a Nobel Prize laureate—but he had no idea of the step-by-step mechanics of how to ask for and close a sale. I listened with rapt concentration for the ten minutes he was allowed to make his pitch, laboring to understand just what he was talking about. The second the precious ten minutes expired, the panel moderator stood up, cutting off the power supply to their laptop, ending their dazzling PowerPoint display preemptively. He asked the audience, "Anybody here understand what they're selling, raise your hand!"

I had to admit that I did not, along with most of the room by evidence of the scant hands raised in answer to the rhetorical question. How could it be possible that such an accomplished and learned group of scientists could come this far in the evaluation process of capital funding without understanding the rudimentary basics of asking for a sale? They had succeeded in dazzling the audience with their unfathomable and recondite knowledge of life sciences and some baffling new technology they had discovered in their labs at Cal Tech and MIT but had completely failed in expressing what and when its practical application and financial benefit would be to the group of investors gathered there who were concerned with only one thing: the bottom line.

This exercise in vanity was rewarded with ten minutes of passionate criticism from the group of investors—or bad guns—who spared no ego as they tore apart the business plan and its ineffective presentation. The stunned entrepreneur presenter stood staring like a deer in the headlights, helpless to avoid the truck that was rolling over him, while the room of observers sat in stunned silence, witnessing the carnage with self-satisfaction, thinking they would say the same things if only they had the chance or the courage. This guy was a Nobel laureate, and he was being eaten alive! *Guess my angels treated me with kid gloves, after all,* I thought.

Next was a company selling fuel-cell technology. I could hear the fear in the presenter's voice as he started. He had flown in from California for this opportunity to present. He spent a few minutes explaining how airport security had stopped him, wanting to confiscate his fuel-cell prototype, and how he almost didn't get it there. This was a very bad decision, because he burned up two of the ten minutes of his presentation time, and he found his

PowerPoint slides cut off a full two minutes early. He didn't even get to show them the money at the end. Didn't matter. One member of Bad Guns was so knowledgeable about the most arcane details of fuel-cell technology that he appeared to know more than the presenter. He didn't mince any words. "I know more about this technology than you do, and that prototype you're holding is worthless! Your technology is already obsolete!" Yikes! *I* was scared, sitting in the audience. This same man would later check out my cleavage and smile at me with a big friendly "hello" at the break, more proof that breasts can tame the savage beast.

The third and final presenter was from another life-sciences company; he had the charisma of a board, and I lost interest one minute into his presentation, remembering only one thing he said: "We have a burn rate of forty thousand dollars a month." I listened long enough to hear that burn rate meant how much money you went through with all your fixed and variable expenses each month, or your negative cash flow. It presented a sort of thumbnail for potential investors to understand what your capital needs were. This company was researching a cure for cancer, so they had laboratories, scientists, and all kinds of technical expenses. They needed money as soon as possible, he explained, if they were going to continue their work. Everybody here, including Nobel laureates, was in a state of Code Red when it came to money, apparently.

. . . .

BURN RATE

The amount of negative cash flow per month that a company goes through. The burn rate indicates how long capital raised will support operations until a company shows profitability.

. . . .

The presentation was over and the three panelists Old Money, Smart Money, and Drug Company Founder were besieged with people from the audience, anxious to present their own opportunities. I was one of them. I dashed up to the front, waited in a very short line for my turn, then made my pitch first to Drug Company Founder. "Sounds very interesting," he replied politely, "but I only invest in life sciences." Next I was on to Smart Money. I put my low-cut-décolletage suit in front of him along with my pitch. Within seconds he gave me the direct contact information for the president of Old Navy in San Francisco, including her direct dial phone number. I later found out that taking cutting-edge technology out of MIT and commercializing it into start-up businesses was something he did in his free time. I got his business card and burned his e-mail address and telephone number into my memory. It wouldn't be long before we were talking regularly.

I was walking away when I bumped into Corporate Money. He hadn't gotten around to pitching the panel, and I didn't know if he would. He was shopping a whole new company and wanted to know how I was doing. I told him I was working with a Chinese MBA with experience working in supply-chain management for Fortune 500 companies, who was right now working to set me up with an unsecured line of credit in China to fund my overseas production. "This will allow me to manufacture and source unlimited product at Wal-Mart costs, with a huge revolving credit line," I explained. In addition, as Plan B, I was working on a contact I had made on my recent trip to New York with an Israeli bank that specialized in Purchase Order factoring, which could give me the money to fund any production I needed based on the Purchase Orders I secured for it from the major retailers I was working with. I could read the shock and awe in Corporate Money's expression. Though he had had a former career in banking on the East Coast, he admitted to me that didn't even know this resource existed. Maybe I didn't need venture capital after all, I thought. I seemed to be doing a pretty good job working every possible angle on my own, with a passion that he or anybody else could never approximate. This process would later be given an appropriate analogy by my soon-to-be New Best Friend—my new banker. "Act like a duck," he would urge me. "What does that mean?" I asked. "Just like a duck, on the surface of the water, all you see is a calm bird gracefully gliding away on smooth water, while underneath he's paddling like crazy for his life."

My impatience had reached critical mass. I had two options, both of them angels, and I had to force both of them to show their hands. I looked at all the entrepreneurs around me bowing and scraping for funding in a very wrapped-up, stilted, and formulaic environment and thought, *Nothing is going to happen here unless I make it happen. This is obviously all-out war! I saw it in this room today, and I saw it just weeks ago in a back room.* I went out into the hallway and called my Chinese MBA.

"Do we have a deal?" I asked him. "I need to know, because I'm standing in a room with a bunch of investors right now, and I have to decide my course of action."

"We have a deal," he promised me. "The deal is done."

My next call was to my attorney.

"Can you put this deal together?" I asked him. "Chinese MBA has a Limited Liability Corporation in New Jersey, which we plug the Chinese company into. So essentially, I don't have a deal with China; I have a deal with him and his LLC, and he has his own deal with China. I've already done a background search on him. He gets ten percent for this amount of a credit line. Am I nuts? I met this guy at a shopping mall a year ago!"

I was violating one of my cardinal laws: Don't expect your attorney to be your business counselor or give you expert advice.

"You gotta trust somebody sometime," was my attorney's advice. Turns out it was the only good advice he would ever give me. "No business relationship begins without a certain degree of trust. You can't know everything about anybody; just do your due diligence, and then make a decision based on your gut. It doesn't matter if you met him in a shopping mall or a McDonald's. A lot of great business relationships start with casual encounters."

"Make it happen," I told him. I should have asked what it was going to cost first. But I had too many other things on my mind. I had a feeling in my gut that this was a day I was going to remember for a long time. I was right.

The minute I got home I wrote a thank-you e-mail to Smart Money, very short and to the point, featuring bulleted highlights of the last few weeks. I attached to it the business plan assessment that Corporate Money had prepared for me at the very beginning. He called me five minutes later. He spent fifteen minutes asking me penetrating questions, no doubt sizing me up. I asked him if he heard of my Israeli bank in New York. He had and asked me if I was talking to the very woman I had been. He was for real.

In the meantime, my attorney was at work drafting a legal tome structuring the deal with my Chinese MBA. Suddenly I was talking to a junior attorney in his office who was asking me the same questions I had answered two phone calls earlier with my number-one attorney. My attorney, who told me he knew what he was doing, was way out of his league. I knew something was wrong when I received by e-mail a copy of a fifty-plus-page document that he had forwarded to my Chinese MBA without even giving me a chance to look at it first! He probably figured I wouldn't understand it anyway. "This deal is going to die!" I practically shrieked into the phone to him when I opened my e-mail and saw a copy of the legal document he had forwarded without my review. "This is still in the delicate, formative stages. We can't bludgeon him with paperwork! We're still handling this with kid gloves! I was thinking of a two- or three-page document summarizing the details of the deal." I would later learn that there was indeed a document for just such purposes, and it was called a Term Sheet.

A Term Sheet is a document usually five to ten pages long summarizing essential terms and conditions of an investment opportunity.

The deal died just like that. The nail in the coffin was the paperwork my lawyer generated and forwarded without a phone call to either me or my Chinese MBA. With that overdose of legalese, all the good faith that existed between us dried up. I called up my Chinese MBA to see if I could salvage the relationship.

"I don't know what this document is," he said to me. "It would cost me at least ten thousand dollars in legal fees to have an attorney review this. I don't want to spend that kind of money. This kind of paperwork is worth nothing in China. This means nothing to them. They would never sign this stuff! How am I supposed to explain a seventy-five-page legal document to them? They don't even speak English! I can't bring this to them. This deal is dead!"

I received a $10,000 bill for this piece of work from my attorney. Weeks after sending the document, my attorney was no longer at the practice anymore and they didn't know where he was or what he was doing. This was a lot more about people management than it was about legal knowledge. Smart, careful people balancing leverage and personalities would ultimately put together the very fragile, precarious deal, then turn it over to lawyers to hope that they didn't totally screw it up. The best lawyers understand this fluid dynamic and work with it. I suddenly understood that I was operating at a rarefied altitude where only Top Guns flew. I could only think of one whom I knew—Smart Money.

"My Chinese MBA deal just went south," I told him over the phone. "He says he's got five million dollars in available credit from Angel in China."

"I can tell everything I need to know about a person by looking them in the eye. I'll get on a plane and fly to meet with him in New York tomorrow," he said. And he did. He reported his findings to me over the phone the very next day. Smart Money turned out to be the shrewdest person I've ever met in my life. He subjected every single detail of a person's appearance, attitude, and behavior to his sublime intellectual machinery.

"He was late. I didn't like that. I flew in from Michigan and was on time; he only had to come across the river from New Jersey. He wasn't dressed appropriately. He should have had a suit and tie on, and he didn't. He had a curious lack of composure that concerns me. We only have his word right now. Can he deliver? Right now, all you have is trust, and I believe that trust is broken."

I didn't want to hear that. Apparently all the information went into his machine and came out marked "defective." If only I had listened to him.

Chinese MBA had met Smart Money, and suddenly it was a whole new ballgame. He called me the very next day and wanted to resume discussions. Smart Money was that impressive. I started to understand that I had latched onto a veritable force of nature that I could use to my own benefit. He not only looked like smart money, but he talked, thought, and acted like smart money. He was the real thing, and when he walked into a room, everybody paid attention. He brought an instant legitimacy and credibility to me that a young company like me lacked. And he was working on behalf of me to secure my interests! I wasn't even paying him anything. Yet.

I had to go to New York on business just a week later. I asked Chinese MBA to meet me there. He was still telling me that he could deliver up to $5 million in Chinese credit. I couldn't ignore that. We planned to have lunch in Manhattan and put the seal on the deal. I waited a half hour past the time he was supposed to meet me before I called him on my cell phone.

"Where are you?" I asked.

"I'm not going to be able to make it."

"What?! I came all the way from Michigan. What do you mean you're not going to make it?"

I spent more than an hour on the phone with him as he backpedaled on everything he had ever said. It was exciting to talk about all these grand ideas, but when it came time to deliver, he was nothing but a poser. Not showing up for a meeting in his own backyard delivered the final blow. If he couldn't make it to lunch, how could I trust him to deliver credit and manufacturing in China? It had all looked so good on paper. Smart Money's pronouncement weeks ago was right. Regardless, Chinese MBA would be an invaluable piece of leverage I would use in my ongoing discussions with all the new and different kinds of Money I would soon be talking to. Back to the drawing board. It was time to call Symphony Money, which I did the moment I got home.

"Oh, I'm so glad you called," said Symphony Money to me over the phone, in his singularly urbane and gracious style. "It's so unfortunate how things ended with us. I've thought about it so much since then with regret. I don't know what happened."

The very next day I was sitting in Symphony Money's law office, on the top floor of a huge building, with a panoramic view of the city. There were towers of papers stacked two feet deep on his desk, on the floor, on the table. Each stack was orderly, with flagged annotations and "sign here" stickers protruding everywhere.

I sat across the table from him and engaged in a sympathetic mind meld for one hour. He was a big-picture, blue-sky person. "You don't even know what I have in mind for you," he said. He was as enthusiastic as a kid at Christmas about the other young companies that he was shepherding; one was a team of artists who came up with some very interesting cartoon characters and a unique concept, and the other was some kind of thermal box company. "I have $250,000 into this box company," he almost lamented, "and we've sold forty boxes. I know this is going to catch on!" he said, really meaning it.

Why Investors Really Invest, or More Proof That Money Ain't All It's Cracked Up to Be

"Why are all you people investing in risky start-up companies?" I asked, unable to get over the shock at hearing he had a quarter of a million into a company that hadn't "made" a dollar yet.

"Oh, we're all addicted to it. It's exciting! We're certainly not doing it for the money, if that's what you mean. People aren't satisfied with the money once they make it. They realize it's the game they love, not the money. None of us can get it out of our blood. That's why we're always looking for something new."

I couldn't believe it. Some of these people were making millions, and instead of going to a Caribbean island where they could retire for life, they were looking for the next exciting start-up to back, just to keep themselves from nodding off in total boredom. This was my second clue that money wasn't all it was cracked up to be. I asked myself, *Would an excess of money really make my life different?* The answer was a shocking and disconcerting, *No!* Did I really have everything that I wanted and not know it? I controlled my own destiny, had financial independence, and saw an immediate and valuable return on the equity of my work; plus I could spend whatever time I wanted whenever with my kids—does it get any better than that?

I didn't need to fill any gaping holes anymore in my heart, mind, head, or self-esteem with things that I could buy. They were all filled up doing satisfying, challenging work that was directly rewarding. I couldn't believe how just two short years ago having the biggest and most beautifully decorated home, the nicest car, and the husband with the best corporate job was of such incredible importance to me in measuring my self-worth. I couldn't believe that, up until now, what my neighbors thought of me was the yardstick I had used to measure my self-worth. Looking back, when I ostensibly had it all, I couldn't believe how many holes I had that I needed then to fill up with all things material. Instead I had discovered that I had filled them all up with gratitude, faith, and love. I had filled up my hole of fear with self-confidence. I had filled up my hole of not having enough with a complete appreciation and gratitude for every little thing I did. I had filled up my hole of a lack of faith with a daily appreciation of God's providence and grace in my life. I had filled in my hole of not being thin enough or beautiful enough for Hollywood standards with a new understanding of my power as a real and self-confident woman in a world with a critical shortage of them. I had filled up negativity and anger with a positive faith in myself and a commitment to choosing happiness wherever and whenever possible on a minute-by-minute basis. Most important, though, I had filled in that aching black hole of being away from my children not by choice but because of a job, with an unlimited ability to be with them along with an understanding that everything they did, said, messed up, or broke was given to me as a special gift from God to make me laugh, cry, and love in new and more profound ways every day. Even if I failed, I figured, I'd never be the same.

As I left Symphony Money's office, the phone rang. It was the General.

"What are you doing Wednesday next week? I'd like you to meet this new banker. I've already met with him and gave him your story. He really wants to work with you."

On Wednesday I was sitting in the new banker's office. He was a VP in corporate banking for a national bank. A former entrepreneur himself, he understood every challenge I was faced with every day, particularly when it came to cash. He was on a mission for his bank to secure new business clients, with only one caveat—they couldn't be in the automobile industry. The Big Three were taking a big hit in Michigan, where the state economy was driven almost exclusively by the auto industry and tourism. It was time for the bank to hedge its bets. He knew I was hot on the trail of angel money and he wanted to put the deal together. After the rejection from my first banker, here was a guy possibly more excited about my prospects than I was. I had just come back from the trade show in Atlanta, where I had had a three-hour dinner with my Saks buyers, who gave me the green light for a whole new line of pajamas. When I told my banker and his assistant about the new pajama line, the banker said, "I can't believe the incredible things you've done with the limited resources you have! I've never seen anything like it!" He continued, "Just imagine what you could do if you were properly funded! It's amazing that you've come this far on your personal financial resources alone. It's amazing that you could even afford to do over a million dollars in sales in two years, using just your home equity. And how you managed to launch a new line in top retailers across the country—I just don't know how you did that. That is certainly a personal testimony to who you are and how you present yourself to your customers. There are companies who have been in business for twenty years who would kill for that opportunity, and you got it on a new line! You should be very proud of yourself."

The Myth of Overnight Success:
Nobody Does It Alone

I was so busy chasing opportunity down, I didn't see what I had. I had created unrealistic expectations for myself and my business. Nobody does this alone! Nobody does this without going through crisis! Nobody does this without risking every single dollar they have and coming close to losing it all! Nobody does it without investors, stakeholders, family support, and angels of every variety possible. It was almost like undergoing cancer treatment. They have to bring you to the doorstep of death with radiation and chemicals, just so you can have a hope of surviving. I couldn't keep beating myself up for coming perilously close to dying anymore. The clouds had parted; the sun had come out. I was going to survive!

I never knew these perilous conditions were part of the territory. If I had, I probably wouldn't have been so hard on myself along the way. I read the countless entrepreneurial magazines published each month, the sole purpose of which seems to be to tout the "overnight" successes of other businesses. The articles made me feel inadequate, because I hadn't achieved these astonishing feats of sales, or exponential growth, "overnight." The magazines seemed to cut out all the hard work and just sell the success, because success sells and everyone is buying it. In all my years of briefly scanning articles of particular relevance my husband had torn out for me, read while I was locked in the bathroom while the boys pounded on the door for my attention, I only saw one reference to the personal downside to entrepreneurial success, from no less than a pre-dot-com-buster who had made millions on his IPO. He admitted that he had to self-medicate with a combination of ibuprofen and alcohol to relieve the stress and anxiety enough to go to sleep at night. If a pre-dot-com-buster, who made millions on an IPO rendered worthless just months later after the bust, felt stress, surely I wasn't suffering alone. Ah-haa! So I wasn't alone after all! This kind of stuff comes with the territory, and it has a beginning and an end! And I was at the end!

The Most Exclusive Club You Can Join

"Listen," said my banker. "You've got to close this deal with the angels."

"How do I do that?" I asked. "I've been trying to put pressure on them. Believe me, I know how to do pressure."

"I know; it's like herding cats. They're all successful, powerful people with their own minds and schedules. They're the hardest to herd. But you can't give up. Tell them I'm your banker and whatever they put down in cash I'll match with an equal line of credit with their personal guarantee."

I told him about Smart Money's offer to help me get the job done. My banker was even more impressed, hearing that I had someone of Smart Money's caliber willing to come and work for me.

Later that day, I told Smart Money about my conversation with my banker. Smart Money asked for his contact information, and soon the two of them would be talking, too, trying to figure out a way to put all the pieces together.

I continued to work on Symphony Money for weeks, if not months. I knew I was getting somewhere when he asked me to go to lunch with his wife, no doubt part of the critical evaluation stage. The thing about angels, I learned, is that they won't do business with you unless they like you as a human being. After all, they're granting you admittance into their secret society, formerly known as the Old Boys' Club. They want people who value their family, their spouses, their community, and their place of worship. They want people who value their role in society, in supporting charities, in championing education and issues affecting families, and they want to make sure that when it's time for you to take the mantle of stewardship, you'll not only invest your money in the next round of entrepreneurs, but you'll also invest your time and mentorship. In a way, it's probably one of the most exclusive clubs you could ever join.

I called up Smart Money and asked him, "What can you do to help me close this deal?"

"Oh, I can close it all right. It's going to be a lot of work. I'll do it only if you agree to compensate me with an equity stake in Green Daisy. In return, I'll work for you for a period of two years." Did I just hear Smart Money, a first-round investor in Google, a former senior VP with a major East Coast investment banking firm, who commercialized new technology out of MIT and drove some of the IPO madness in Silicon Valley in the late nineties, offer to come to work for me? He was no doubt the shrewdest, most experienced financial mind I had ever known. I already had a man who had built a $700 million brand from the ground up, an expert in brand management and licensing, interested in working with me. Now I had a big-picture Executive Officer who could guide our ship to exponential growth through stock offerings and a priceless knowledge of corporate law and taxation. Could this get any better?

"You need somebody like me," Smart Money said. "You just can't do this alone. I tried twenty years ago, and I got beat up so bad by a group of savvy experienced investors, I still hurt. I mean, they really screwed me. This is dangerous business. Since then, I've put together deals like this for at least twenty companies. I don't do it for just anybody. Believe me, I get a lot more offers than I accept. In your case, I believe in you. I always bet on the jockey and not the horse. You're the reason this company is going to succeed, and I'm willing to invest two years of my time to see it through."

"Okay," I said. "Let me think about it and get back to you." Can you believe I said this? This was very appealing to me, but it didn't solve my immediate critical problem: I needed cash! I was convinced at this point that giving away part of my company would only make that solution harder to attain. What did I know?

I called him back a few days later and tentatively agreed to his offer, giving him a very small percentage of my company in the event that he was able to do what I was not able to do: successfully close the deal. *Nothing ventured, nothing gained,* I thought.

How to Herd Cats

Still, I needed all the help I could get. The angels felt no urgency to do anything, so I had to create urgency any way I could, by putting marketing, production, and sales deadlines before them weekly, letting them know that opportunity was slipping away with inaction. I wasn't going to let any opportunity get by me, but I was willing to let them believe that I might. Part of the delay resulted from the fact that they were all busy running their own businesses; part of it, I believe, was the result of a deliberate attempt to allow me to continue to sink all my capital resources into developing the opportunities, so they didn't have to. I told my banker how frustrated I was. He called me the very next day.

"I'm having a meeting at two thirty today in my office. Can you make it?"

"Today? Kinda short notice, isn't it?"

"I know. It's important. Can you be here? I've asked two of the angels to come meet with me. They just wanted to talk generalities, but it's time to talk specifics. Are you ready for this?"

I didn't have a choice. When I got there I saw Old Money and a new member of the angel party, recruited just to qualify my financials, Mr. CFO. I sat down and was startled when my banker picked up a speaker line on the telephone on the conference table and called Smart Money.

"I'd like to introduce everybody to everybody," he said. The angels wondered who was on the phone and why were they talking to him. Smart Money was just as shocked as we were to find himself talking to any of us. He spent ten minutes going through his list of achievements as a way of introducing himself, at my banker's request. The angels were definitely impressed but curiously silent.

To the angels, Smart Money had been up to that point a shadowy figure, another possible investor, who was working to put together a deal with my Chinese manufacturing connections.

"Are you an investor?" Old Money asked Smart Money pointedly. "What kind of money are you bringing to the table?"

"No, I'm not bringing any money. Ms. Lavine has agreed to give me an equity ownership stake in her company in exchange for working for her for two years."

My heart skipped a couple of beats. There was at least thirty seconds of dead silence in the room. How could I give away for free to this man what I was selling to them? After all, Cash was King, and I needed cash! Did I make a mistake? Was this going to torpedo the deal? My banker was grinning as if he knew exactly what he was doing. I wasn't so sure.

"So you're not bringing any cash," Old Money reiterated, making sure she got it right.

"That's right; I'm not."

"We're going to discuss this and get back to you," Old Money said. With that my banker hung up the phone; I definitely had some explaining to do.

"How'd you get this guy on your team?" said Mr. CFO with the enthusiasm of a televangelist. "I don't know how you did it, but it is the best thing you could have ever done. In fact, I want that guy's deal, too!" he said, practically shouting and bringing his fist down on the table for emphasis.

What had I done? Would anybody want to give me cash when they could get it *free*? Was this the beginning of the end all over again?'

"Let's see if we can come to some agreement," my banker interceded.

"We're going to have to discuss this and get back to you," Old Money said again.

That didn't sound good. I was crushed as I followed them out to the parking lot. I needed to get a sense of what Old Money was thinking.

"I'm sorry this came up so unexpectedly," I said. "What do you think the angels will think about this? How can I afford to give Mr. CFO an equity stake, too?"

"You'd better worry about how you can afford not to. Nobody is going to give you any money unless they have somebody like him onboard making sure it's managed wisely."

"You mean the investors won't mind giving me money when I'm giving part of my company away?"

"Are you kidding? That's the best thing you could have possibly done in there. How you got somebody of that caliber to offer to come and work for you is nothing short of amazing. That isn't going to make the investors mad; it's going to make them happy. If they can get executive-level management like that at no cost other than equity, they'll have so much confidence and security in this venture that they'll give you more cash. Like I said, you'd better worry now about bringing on capable financial management."

Obviously, Mr. CFO was in the driver's seat. I had already been through a total of two CFOs and one banker before him. All of them had bowed out for being too busy or too disinterested. By this time, my books were a mess. Everybody had rifled through them, imprinting them with their own incomplete work, and consequently nobody understood them anymore, including us. My CFO in San Francisco couldn't even be reached. We needed help.

By the time I pulled into the driveway, Mr. CFO had e-mailed me his résumé and called. I found myself interviewing him for the job of chief financial officer for Green Daisy! Me—interviewing him! He was almost as accomplished as Smart Money, who took one look at his résumé and said, "You'd be lucky to have this guy work for you. Did you look at his résumé? He's amazing!"

The next day I was calling his references. One of them was an international greenhouse grower based in Colorado. They told me that he was almost single-handedly responsible for leading them from the brink of bankruptcy to record profits, hedging both euros and natural gas futures to squeeze every penny out of every dollar possible. I thought he could handle Wuvits.

Mr. CFO wanted an equal equity share to that of Smart Money. I started to add up the equity and worry a lot about what was going to be left for cash to buy. I asked Smart Money what to do. He advised that I negotiate with Mr. CFO.

Mr. CFO told me how excited he was to be working with me. I started to negotiate, and by the time the phone call was over, I had him down to what Smart Money gave me as a best-case goal.

The next morning there was an e-mail waiting for me, calling a halt to Mr. CFO's participation. He was in revolt, and he was taking the whole deal with him. The angels agreed. This ship was sinking. The money was within reach and was slipping away again. I called Smart Money, who made the first of what were no doubt thousands of mediating phone calls as he cautiously blended and balanced the volatile personalities and combustible financials. He put together the delicate framework of a deal, before turning it over to a lawyer, who he hoped wouldn't screw it up. How could I have trusted my lawyer to do this job before? Smart Money was about to do two years' worth of work for me in the next four months. I wouldn't have believed it unless I had seen it. This was definitely something better left to professionals. I don't think there are many people in the U.S. capable of this task. One of them was working for me—for "free."

Smart Money called Mr. CFO and, after some amount of massaging, managed to put him back in the deal. It turned out Mr. CFO didn't like negotiating with a woman, especially a woman who was looking for cash, over which he held the control. Smart Money knew just how to spin this, and Symphony Money laughingly agreed: "If she can negotiate that tough with you, just think what she can do with everybody else. It's a good thing!"

I woke up the next morning with a sobering revelation. I had an experienced executive management team, including invaluable brand manager who had already created one empire out of nothing. In addition, I had secured an enthusiastic banker who wanted nothing more than to see me succeed so that he could bank the $20 million of sales he forecast for me in the next five years. Things were about to get even better, as well as unimaginably difficult.

It was time for the Bed Bath & Beyond order to go out. I was tired of spending every dollar I had to develop opportunities at great costs while the angels dragged their feet, consumed with making their own businesses profitable. It was time to show me some money. We needed to come up with the lump sum of cash we had promised our manufacturers to ship the order. It was a tough choice—stop all my pajama manufacturing and developing to ship Wuvits, jeopardizing a potential million-dollar account, or stop Wuvits and ship pajamas, another multi-million-dollar opportunity. My husband had had enough of this. We weren't going to expose ourselves to any more risk, he decided. It was time for somebody else to pony up some money.

He called up Symphony Money and within hours had a $15,000 check from him! As I've said, my husband is the King of Schmooze. Your results may vary. My husband had had enough of spending every dollar he had worked so hard for his whole life. The angels had spent so much time talking to us, he just figured it a foregone conclusion anyway. If the deal didn't work out, we could consider it a loan and he would pay Symphony Money back. My husband and I were supporting all our sales and the growth and development of all these million-dollar opportunities with our home equity alone. If they expected us to deliver the moon, they'd better be prepared to pay for it. Symphony Money still scratches his head to this day, bemused that he had so willingly written this check when we didn't even have a deal and at how he could have possibly been talked into it. But that's my husband, my hero. Super Money Man.

My banker called and asked if I could come to his office to meet with another investor he knew.

"He's a friend of mine, and he manages the family estate. He's also a CFO, if you find that you need another one. Two P.M., my office. Just give him the ten-minute spiel; he's already onboard."

I came; I met Estate Money; I sold him. He not only wanted to invest, he wanted to work for me, too, and he e-mailed me his résumé to prove it.

The CFO I had met at the original angel presentation called me to see how I was doing; I filled him in and he said, "Put an ad in the paper and see if you can shake any more investors out of the woodwork." I did, and I got two phone calls. Turns out one of them had been watching my progress from a distance since my very first kiosk. This was an embarrassment of riches.

The time had come to put the cap on the deal. There were so many interested players by this time, I had to find out who was for real and who wasn't. I learned to qualify potential investors by asking them to sign a complex NDA before I showed them the business plan. Those who weren't for real never would. My list of players was long: Smart Money, the angels with all their complicated individual personalities, Mr. CFO, my banker, Chinese MBA, Estate Money, and a motley crew made up of strategic manufacturing partners and vendors, investors I picked up from the newspaper, and—last ditch—family members. My banker had another caveat: "Don't ever put all your energy behind one plan. You gotta have a Plan B and Plan C if you can. It isn't a deal till it's a signed deal." I was working every possible angle. I met with my manufacturing partners, with whom I had a substantial personal guaranty loan, and asked them if they would trade it for stock. They were definitely interested.

How to Find a Business Broker

I called up my millionaire mentors and asked them to put me in touch with the business broker who sold their business. They had put their business on the market after nine years with a broker based in Philadelphia; in just months they had an offer worth millions. There are at least a hundred things to negotiate in the sale of a business, including earn-outs, so get a good broker and check his references. To find a good broker visit the International Business Brokers Association online at www.ibba.org.

Before I knew it, I was talking to a very bright and aggressive business broker from Philadelphia, who very much wanted me to put an end to the angel deal as soon as possible so he could work on creating a structured buyout with a strategic partner, much like my millionaire mentors had done. For a moment, I thought of stopping everything to go down this road. His plan would have provided me with a very easy exit strategy that could have solved all my debt problems, while compensating me handsomely for all my years of hard work.

A year earlier, this would have been my first choice: take the money and run! I would have been happy with a million dollars cash. But the angels were throwing around the hundred-million-dollar number as if it were nothing. My banker and Mr. CFO had gotten together and done that five-year Cash Flow Spreadsheet, forecasting $30 million in revenue in just five years. I thought about what Symphony Money had said, about my not even being able to see the road ahead he already had mapped out. I knew he built a superhighway himself to $700 million. I looked at the wealth of talent I had put together, the Dream Team. Would I really turn down the opportunity to work with this group of Masters of the Universe for a million dollars? Was money the endgame? Or was the journey the reward? I already knew the answer.

How to Do a Deal

It was time to get everybody in a room and see what happened. I called up Symphony Money and asked for a meeting, including him, Old Money, Mr. CFO, Smart Money, my husband, and me. On the phone would be Chinese MBA, who was still calling me regularly, and the current president of the company Symphony Money created, who wanted to source all my manufacturing in China, as well as handle all the shipping and EDI logistics through his various warehouses. This resource appeared with just a phone call from Symphony Money. He could call up anyone, from Maine to Florida, and ask in his urbane, gracious style if he or she would be interested in getting behind a young mother and entrepreneur who he thought was not only just good people but also someone who deserved a hand up. "Oh, you would? That's great!" With his one phone call, I was meeting days later with people who had flown in all the way from China, anxious to do business with me.

Symphony Money had taken on the unofficial role of quarterback. New Money was nowhere to be found anymore. I thought I had embarrassed myself and him so badly that I would never see him again. I was wrong. Smart Money was connected with him in the Old Boys' Network. "Nobody anywhere wants you to succeed more than him," Smart Money reported after a phone call to him. "He's just really busy. These investors have an obligation to their community and its economy to see you succeed." There was a greater good than just my success involved here.

The moment of truth came. Smart Money made a special trip from the other side of the state. The angels had decided just the day before that Chinese MBA did not have "the right stuff" to be invited to participate by conference call. My manufacturing partners didn't make the cut, either. Exceptionally high business, professional, and moral standards were being applied.

About ten seconds of niceties were exchanged before we went straight to business. Smart Money had sworn to me prior to coming that he wasn't leaving the room until a deal was done. Symphony Money sized up Smart Money, and vice versa. It was their first meeting and I could tell they both liked what they saw. Symphony Money was the very picture of urbane and cultured suaveness; Smart Money looked and talked exactly like a Master of the Universe should. Five minutes into the discussion, the only sticking point was the valuation of my company. How could anybody understand what their money bought if we didn't all agree on the value of the stock?

"I'm not here to make Kim happy, or the Angels happy," Smart Money confessed. "In fact, I'd consider my job well done if you both felt like neither of you got exactly what you wanted. I'm just here as an impartial and fair person to make a deal happen."

Valuation: The Real Art of the Deal

Mr. CFO threw out his valuation. It was unbelievably low. Still, he insisted that it was what the strict numbers told him. Nobody disputed the EBITDA figure, or Earnings Before Interest, Taxes, Depreciation, and Amoritization; the variable was what factor you multiplied them by. Was it a multiple of two, which the angels wanted, or a multiple of five, which we wanted?

"We're selling our future, not our past," my husband reminded them.

"You can't put that in the bank," Mr. CFO quipped.

There was about fifteen minutes of animated discussion, Smart Money versus Mr. CFO, one high, the other low, till we realized that we had come to an impasse.

"Let's take this into the back room," Smart Money suggested, walking out with Symphony Money and Mr. CFO while my husband and I waited in total bewilderment. Just ten minutes later they were back. They obviously had enjoyed some secret ritual of their secret society, because they were laughing, acting as if they had been best friends all their life.

"Get up and shake the hands of the new shareholders of Green Daisy," Smart Money urged us. "We have a deal."

That statement would mark the beginning of what would become all-out war.

THE END OF THE BEGINNING

I went home and sent everybody an e-mail, asking for brief bios so I could draft the press release. I was too inexperienced to know that with this shaking of hands a cannonball had been fired across my bow, warning me that we were about to engage in battle. Everybody knew this but me. Everything up to this point had been easy. The hard work was about to begin. Smart Money was about to *really* earn the money I wasn't even paying him!

Looking for Money: A Full-Time Job

All we had agreed on at this meeting was the value of the company. This accomplishment cannot be underestimated, as it is the most critical part of the process. Without an agreement on valuation, all the other discussions that followed would never have taken place. I had been discussing valuation for at least three months, and they never made one move past a very low figure that they had proposed at the very beginning. Smart Money did in five minutes in a back room what I couldn't do in months. He was an expert at valuation—having done it for dozens of other companies before—and they knew it, so their extremely conservative interpretation of EBITDA got them nowhere. He had already earned his shareholder stake, but he would go on to earn it at least a dozen times more. He had in mind a business plan he had recently seen presented at the Michigan Business Challenge held at the University of Michigan. A start-up business, founded by a graduate business student, had managed to raise over a million dollars in nine months, on a business plan that proposed selling printed sweatshirts and athletic gear featuring high school logos. If they could raise this kind of money with an untested business model and absolutely no sales experience or history behind them, then my company, with over $2 million of sales, a constant stream of new creative products distributed through the nation's top retailers, and an experienced, passionate president, was worth more. I don't know where I would have been without him; my banker agreed.

My husband and I went to lunch with Smart Money after the meeting, and he filled me in on some of the backroom details. Symphony Money, Mr. CFO, and Smart Money would all get a stake in the company in exchange for working for it for two years, at no cost. In order to make the deal work without taking too much of an equity hit on my end, Smart Money had lowered his percentage, getting the others to make similar concessions. Because the angels had asked that I get a reverse vest just like them, meaning that no one would get any shareholder stake in the company until they had actually worked two years, Smart Money got them to throw out that condition for me as long as it applied to them, too. I knew this was a symbolic concession on my part, since I had no intention of taking a reverse vest myself, or having to work two years to legally get the ownership I already had; I had no doubt that they would do the work, but unless you have similar confidence in your shareholders, I wouldn't recommend giving away equity until people actually do the work. In addition, Smart Money worried that new tax laws would penalize us severely if we took our equity two years from now, when the company would be worth a lot more, rather than if we took it at the front end. This must have put everybody in a very generous spirit, because they agreed to the high valuation, allowing me to raise the capital I needed while still retaining ownership of 65 percent of my company, including the shareholder stakes. I was about to find out that owning a majority of your company's stock meant almost nothing when it came right down to controlling it, or even getting paid!

Next a Term Sheet had to be drafted. I was confident and relieved to put the details of this enormous task in the hands of Smart Money, Symphony Money, who was a lawyer, and no fewer than two attorneys in his office. Smart Money wasn't going to let just any attorney handle this. He wasn't going to go to all the trouble of balancing volatile personalities and combustible financials to craft a deal equal to any work of art and turn it over to a lawyer who would mess it up. This wasn't going to be cheap; $15,000 from beginning to end is considered to be extremely economical, with $40,000 not unheard of. Fortunately, this gets built in right up front with the amount of capital raised.

I got the Term Sheet by e-mail from Smart Money, with the directive that I sign it as soon as possible. He was not only good at making deals, but he was also good at closing deals. The pressures he brought to bear on everybody to keep the deal moving along in a timely manner were extreme. The angels suffered almost as much as I did. I went over the Term Sheet in detail with him; he had done the best that he could after much negotiation, but there were still two items that were going to need my immediate and urgent attention. Even though we had come this far, I was suddenly confronted with two absolute deal breakers. And just like that, I was contemplating the possible death of this deal for the third time.

- -

ANATOMY OF A TERM SHEET

Each one of these items were addressed in my Term Sheet, which specifically spelled out all the details in a paragraph for each:

- Type of security
- Investors
- Amount raised
- Use of proceeds
- Closing
- Capitalization
- Corporation structure
- Term of payment
- Terms of conversion
- Warrant coverage
- Security
- Protective provisions
- Board of Directors
- Indemnification of Board of Directors
- Management and information rights
- Investor participation rights
- Guaranty of investors
- Proprietary information, inventions, and noncompete agreements
- Documentation
- Conditions to closing
- Nonbinding terms
- Exclusivity
- Confidentiality
- Legal fees and expenses
- Expiration

- -

A Cautionary Tale

There was going to be a five-member Board of Directors, initially made up of the other three shareholders, my husband, and me. The voting rights of this board were what was in question. The investors wanted to reserve the right to elect three of the five board members, which meant that they would always have a controlling voting interest, regardless of the fact that I owned 65 percent of the company. I trusted all of the board members to represent my interests but I didn't know how long they'd be around. I had to protect not only my short-term interests, but my long-term interests as well. If we were extremely profitable in just years, I could have the control of my company taken away from me in such an arrangement with a simple vote of the board.

This had just happened to someone in our community, in fact, and it was the talk of the town. He had built an empire of outlet shopping malls across the U.S. worth tens of millions; he brought in some investors with the same board arrangement, in which the investors had a controlling interest. Within weeks after the closing, they fired him without cause, just because they could. He hadn't negotiated a favorable employment agreement. He had a noncompete for five years, so he couldn't even get another job. Though he owned a majority of the stock, he couldn't convert it into cash, because his severance arrangement wouldn't force the investors to buy it in the event he was terminated or quit. Though he had stock worth millions, he couldn't sell it, couldn't get a job, and was literally left penniless. Within two years he was filing bankruptcy.

He had gone into the deal saying he had trusted his partners, but he should have protected himself against every eventuality.

This was a cautionary tale at the very moment I needed it. It could happen to me. I first demanded that I be allowed to select three of the five board members, one of them being my husband. That didn't work because they wanted to select three of the five. I then tried saying that no majority could carry unless I was one of the majority voters. This didn't work, either, so we finally agreed that I would elect two board members, the investors would elect two board members, and together we would elect the fifth. Whew! Next crisis!

The next item was a deal breaker for them. It involved intellectual property. Enough can't be said about the value of IP to a company. Too many people don't do enough to protect IP because they don't understand that it is the most valuable asset that your company owns. From the very beginning I had trademarks, copyrights, and patents on just about every thought that ever came out of my head. Some of them were the property of Green Daisy, and some were not. The ones that were not were potentially lucrative. I was going to go to the mat on this. One shareholder went so far as to say the deal was dead unless I ceded not only all of my current IP but all of my future IP as well, whether it had anything to do with Green Daisy or not. Their fear was that I would create some other new, exciting concept and abandon Green Daisy in favor of it.

· ·

THE RECAPITALIZATION OF A COMPANY: A DOCUMENT LIST

This is an itemization of every document that was included in the hundreds of pages of my deal. Before you sign them, each one of these documents should be reviewed in painful detail by experienced business attorneys who specialize in just this.

- Restated Articles of Incorporation
- Amended and Restated Bylaws
- Joint Consent Resolutions of the Board and Sole Shareholder
- Articles of Organization
- Operating Agreement
- Membership Interest Transfer Restricted Agreement
- Initial Resolutions—Organizer
- Initial Resolutions—Members
- Initial Resolutions—Managers
- Subscription Agreements
- Membership Interest Transfer Log
- Form SS-4
- Term Sheet
- Note Purchase Agreement
- Promissory Notes
- Warrants
- Security Agreement
- UCC-1 Financing Statement
- Form D Notice and Sale/Filing Letter to the SEC and States Securities Administrators
- Employee Proprietary Information and Invention Assignment and Noncompete Agreement
- Debt Conversion Agreement
- Stock Certificates
- Shareholders Agreement
- Indemnification Agreements

· ·

In the heat of negotiation one solution was proposed: I get to keep all the revenues from the IP, but the corporation and its shareholders would hold the legal rights to it, including any copyrights and trademarks. My attorney made a very good observation, though. "If you don't own the car, don't assume you get to drive it." In this arrangement I would get to drive the car only at the pleasure of the board, over which I wasn't guaranteed to have any control. This time I was killing the deal, though I worked it out in a diplomatic way with an element of compromise by talking directly with Symphony Money. I understood that they were afraid that as a very creative person I might be distracted from my job as president of Green Daisy by a new idea. They didn't want to keep me from being creative or from financially benefiting from it. There were very technical legal considerations that prohibited them from bifurcating IP rights, so they agreed that Green Daisy would own the IP and license me certain exclusive rights to it, which we negotiated.

I signed the renegotiated Term Sheet and thought the deal was done. Again I prepared to write the press release and pushed for a closing date. In return, I was emailed a 250-page document, laying out the real meat and potatoes of the deal. In contrast, the Term Sheet was only eight pages.

I had to hire a new attorney of my own, only after Smart Money marginally approved him. This took another month to go through and cost me another $5,000. I was playing hardball and chicken at the same time. Everything was on the table: control, my salary, IP, noncompete agreement, severance package—thirty-six points to be exact, which my attorney and Smart Money and I uncovered in the 250 pages, that needed to be fixed, mediated, or just thrown out. The potent mixture of money, egos, pressure, and deadlines had to explode. Soon people were yelling at each other, mostly in e-mails.

I was working on not only Plan A but Plan B and Plan C, too! In what I thought was a confidential e-mail, I said that I considered the deal finally, irretrievably dead. Note to self: don't ever say in an e-mail anything that you don't want the whole world to read for posterity. This e-mail got forwarded to every one of the investors! I thought this was the worst thing that could possibly happen, but it turned out to be the best, and Smart Money knew it. I received frantic communications from the other side. They had to confront the possibility that the deal was dead and it brought them back to the table with a renewed seriousness to close the deal. New Money called up Smart Money and demanded: "What the heck is going on there?!" Smart Money answered him: "Intense and serious negotiations."

Dangerous Business: How to Protect Yourself

This was indeed dangerous business. I had never confronted anything so complicated that demanded such a sophisticated patience and understanding before in my life. If it was possible, I cultivated an even greater appreciation for the skills of Smart Money. When other people around me were melting down with anger, worry, and negativity, he persevered, shining his light of reason on us like a beacon guiding us in. I came to understand that my tendency to make negative suppositions about people, their motivations, and the situation was a personal shortcoming I needed to conquer in order to go on. A person will achieve success in direct proportion to their ability to let go of negativity in favor of all that is positive. Being negative is easy; being positive is what's hard.

Be a positive, big-picture person, always striving to work for the highest good of all parties involved, and you can't help but succeed.

Since then I've understood that I've never encountered one successful person who didn't have this quality. No sissies, no cowards, no complainers, no criers, and no quitters. Especially no complainers.

I understood this was a big chess game with all kinds of players who needed to sense risk and imminent fear of losing in order to keep making progress forward. I could bring those pressures to bear, threatening that the deal was dead and that I was going to walk, without ever really feeling them. This was a game, and emotions were the just the playing pieces, not the players. Suddenly I was pulling strings, applying pressure, and threatening to walk, not meaning one word of it. Whatever it took to get the job done.

The last battle was for my salary. I had with some compromise gotten everything I wanted, but I as of yet hadn't gotten what I needed. Nowhere else did they have any chance of leverage against me but here. I wasn't working for myself anymore; I was working for a company, with responsibilities to my investors. The value of what I had wasn't going to be immediately seen in my wallet; it was going to be seen in my stock and in my future. We volleyed this back and forth. On the day I successfully launched Green Daisy's brand-new pajama line, getting commitments from major retailers across the country and effectively selling out the very next day, I called Symphony Money and did on the phone what nobody could do via e-mail: came to agreement on all the remaining terms. It was time to bring everybody under the proverbial Big Tent as a team—and for due diligence.

Final Due Diligence—What Is It Really?

The person elected to do due diligence on my company was Mr. CFO. I asked my millionaire mentors what their due diligence process was like. They only explained that it generated paperwork an inch thick. The paperwork generated on my deal was more than two feet thick!

First there were the financials. This had been so scrupulously investigated by this time already that a lot of the work was done. Still, Mr. CFO would ask for every one of my husband's and my personal and business credit card statements for the last three years, and he would review them to understand what exactly was business debt and what exactly was personal. Unfortunately, we had been forced to use personal credit cards to secure business debt in the debacle of 2003. Mr. CFO separated them out and confirmed that all the business debt was accurately recorded in our Shareholders Accounts Payable. Shareholders Accounts Payable is a number on your books that represents owner's equity in a company. This is any personal cash or personal debt that you invested in order to start and grow your business. Besides our personal credit card debt, our $125,000 IRA contribution was recorded here. Eventually, the idea is that once the company becomes profitable enough, it will pay you back this money you borrowed. Can you believe it? I was going to get every penny back that I ever invested in this company! Why didn't anybody tell me this at the beginning? I would have worried a lot less about all that debt.

- -

SHAREHOLDERS ACCOUNTS PAYABLE: WHAT IS IT AND WHY DO INVESTORS CARE SO MUCH?

This is a number on your balance sheet that represents the amount of money you've personally invested in your company, which you expect to get paid back and have recorded as a loan, or a Shareholders Accounts Payable.

Every investor group wants to see detailed evidence that you have absorbed much of the risk of start-up by investing your own money, including 401(k) funds and even credit card debt. The more you've invested of your own cash, the more confidence they'll have in the company.

The good news is that all that money you've put in your company to get it to this point to get all these investors interested is going to come back to you as cash or future equity. You can even negotiate an annual interest rate be paid to you on this loan from the corporation.

- -

Next was all the intellectual property. This included all of my trademarks, my patent, and my copyrights. IP attorneys looked at each legal document in penetrating detail, ensuring that my rights were secured and transferable to Green Daisy, Inc. I had registered everything in my own name at the beginning, because it was the easiest, least-complicated legal process to do so. Then there was the legal documentation, including my Articles of Incorporation, all my business registrations, my EIN, my state tax ID, and every other document in my three-tier filing cabinet. After that came verification of all my sales prospects. They wanted personal contact info for each and every buyer I had ever worked with in the years I had been in business, confirmed by reams of e-mails detailing the correspondence. They wanted to see Purchase Orders for my pajama line and proof that I had the manufacturing in hand well enough with vendors on whom I had done my own due diligence. In addition, they wanted to make sure I had a clear health history. Because of my commitment to breast cancer awareness, they wanted to know my genealogical history on this terrible disease. I had to explain that it was my mother-in-law and her sisters who were decimated by breast cancer and not my mother; otherwise there was risk there that had to be considered. They made it a condition that I take out a million-dollar insurance policy on my life, payable to the corporation and its investors, in the event that I should die. I'm sure they also did a personal background check on my husband and me to make sure we didn't have any criminal histories. By the time they were done they knew everything there was to know about me, past and present, that was conceivable, including what I spent on groceries on a weekly basis. They were onboard to ride the Green Daisy train.

The Momentum of Success, or When the Boulder Rolls down the Other Side of the Mountain

Other people started to rush to work for me, lending their formidable talents without any pay or firm commitment of employment. They saw a ground-floor opportunity and were willing to invest their time and work to get in. One of them was my new designer: She went to the prestigious Rhode Island School of Design, studied in Switzerland through Yale's graduate program in fine arts, then went on to get her MFA at Michigan. Her designs could already be seen nationally in museums, catalogs, and retailers across the country. She was so ahead of her time that major retailers were knocking them off a full two years after she made them. Add to this an International Sourcing Manager who had been in the business for more than twenty years, with contacts across the world, with experience as a buyer at some of the nation's biggest retailers, and it was like pouring gas on the fire.

The people I had assembled were all uniquely talented and synergistic:

Symphony Money: His experience was the stuff legends are made of. He was so well connected, he could call captains of industry up on the phone and get them to invest in my company in five minutes. When I finally saw the investors he had assembled for me, I was dumbstruck. It was only at the closing, when I signed more papers than I had ever signed in my life, that I understood how diligently Symphony Money had worked to call in all the favors that brought me the capital that I needed to go on.

Smart Money: His past experience was epic. His future role would be to continue to lead us through every incarnation our growing company would demand, using his formidable talents and experience for structuring offerings, eventually taking us all the way to public, if that's what we wanted.

Mr. CFO: In addition to getting his shareholder stake, he had put up his money, too. This man was definitely my toughest audience, and he believed in me. His world-class experience handling the most complicated financial management issues would not only steady our ship toward a course of exponential growth but would also instill the investors with the confidence necessary to give us their money to get it done.

My banker: Bankers are the most conservative skeptics on the face of the earth, and this banker believed in me almost more than I did. He believed in me when others would not. He believed in me enough to invite me to participate in a roundtable of fast-growth second-stage business leaders through the PeerSpectives Program, created by the late Ed Lowe to break down the walls that existed between entrepreneurs, who often labored tirelessly under the extraordinary demands I've detailed in this book in anonymity and without peer support. He did this under mandate of the governor of the state of Michigan, who recognized in these daring, hardworking risk takers the future of employment for thousands of her state's residents. And so I had come full circle, from being hopelessly unemployed to being an employer upon whom the governor pinned her hopes.

The Definition of Success

I looked at this Dream Team that I had assembled with little more than an idea and passion. What was important wasn't the money; it was the people! Money was just the machinery that made ideas work. The passion of the people was the commodity that was precious. With the culmination of three years of hard work, I had found much more than I had even been looking for—way more than money. I had found my purpose, my daily gratitude, and the affirmation of my love for my family on a hourly basis. I had learned to rely on the inner resources of strength, hope, hard work, and faith to bring me the things I really needed in my life, instead of a reliance on material possessions to fill up all the holes where these qualities were missing. I had started out an imperfect person, and I had come out whole. I finally, only at the very end, saw what these investors were after in me. The person and their passion, I learned—their conviction, their ideas, their belief in themselves, hard work, and insistence on doing what is right and not what is easy—is the commodity worth millions. With that, everything is possible.

BECOME YOUR OWN MOMMY MILLIONAIRE: HOW TO BECOME PART OF THE MILLIONAIRE MENTOR CLUB

The Entrepreneur Revolution

There's a revolution going on, flying just under the radar of the nation's consciousness, about to explode.

But this revolution isn't a political revolution, it's an economic revolution.

It's not a woman's revolution—it's a family revolution.

It's not a technology revolution—it's a communication revolution.

America is in the midst of the largest entrepreneurial surge this country has ever seen. In 2006, a record number of Americans started companies, including women, college students, seniors, corporate refugees, and recent immigrants, who in 2005 started 25 percent more companies per capita than U.S. residents. According to the Small Business Administration, more new companies were created in 2005 than at the height of dot-com hysteria in 1996. Investment of private equity in new businesses in the form of angel and venture capital is growing exponentially each year, bringing unprecedented capital resources within the reach of even modest business models. It's time for those of you sitting on the sidelines to take advantage of this unique time in history and start your own business. Fortunately it's never been easier with the Millionaire Mentor Club.

It's not just that these numbers are revolutionary. It's the social conditions behind them that are driving this sea change where the real revolution lies. According to a recent poll by Oprah, out of 38 million women with children in the United States two-thirds of the working moms who responded said they would quit work and stay home with their kids if they could. Among the stay-at-home moms, more than one-third wished they worked outside the home. The truth is, the technology of the twenty-first century is changing our daily lives in new and revolutionary ways, radically transforming the 9-to-5 workday and family world. Fed up with the corporate world, women are taking their destinies into their own hands and following their dreams in record numbers.

A New Cottage Industry

Fortunately, it's never been easier to follow your dreams. This revolution isn't based on new technology; it's based on a revolutionary ability to communicate with every individual in the world from your own home. The Internet is a relatively new invention that is revolutionizing the way people do business—and live their lives—around the world. The Internet has leveled the playing field between small entrepreneurs and big businesses, giving both an equal opportunity to speak to consumers directly and sell products and services without a middleman, whether it's in Detroit or Dubai—provided you have an understanding of the tools of this new communication revolution to do so, something I call "The New Grassroots." This is giving rise to an exploding "new cottage industry" era, where people can find the means and opportunity to supplement their family's income and fill their entrepreneurial and creative ambitions without compromising family life. Some entrepreneurs I know are doing $500,000 or more in annual sales from Web sites they run from their home—without investor money or headaches—while making their family their number one priority.

Hopes, Dreams, and Aspirations

In my experience, as I traveled across the country this last year talking to entrepreneurs at books signings, speaking events, on the radio and TV, or via e-mail or the www.mommymillionaire.com forum, people aren't starting businesses for the money as much as they're starting them for hopes, dreams, and aspirations. Maybe it's a hope for a better life for their kids, or for their spouse to escape the pressures of an unrewarding and demanding job. Sometimes it's about giving themselves permission to believe in a dream they've had for themselves for years, but didn't know how to act upon. Or it could be an aspiration to rise above a difficult childhood, an abusive marriage, or some personal tragic setback that has left them questioning the emptiness of a culture focused on consumerism, with a need instead for finding greater personal fulfillment through experiences of faith, love, and family. In the end, as I've watched these people come together spontaneously in communities, whether it was after a book-signing event, on our message board, or after a speaking event, I've recognized that entrepreneurs crave community, and given just a few tools, will find the means to support each other in their pursuit of a better life for themselves and their family.

That's why I've created the Millionaire Mentor Club and am offering the tools necessary to begin your journey and support its progress online at ww.mommymillionaire.com.

All Great Journeys are Begun on the Strength of Just One Individual and Their Dream

I asked my ten-year-old son the other day if he knew what an entrepreneur was. He answered: "Somebody who follows their dreams." I asked him who his hero was. He said it was me. I asked him why. He said it was because I follow my dreams.

If you look up the word in the dictionary, the definition of entrepreneur is simply "one who organizes, manages, and assumes the risks of a business or enterprise." Funny, it doesn't say "hero" anywhere. I don't see the word "dream" either, but I think the definition would be just as true if you replaced the words "business" or "enterprise" with "dream."

I've spent a good portion of the last year listening to the best and brightest from the highest levels of state government, business, and academia, trying to figure out how to turn people into entrepreneurs, because our economy is desperately in need of risk-taking idealists who have some irrational passion coupled with a visionary idea that could just as easily be qualified as crazy—to start new businesses.

The opinion of all these very smart people was that being an entrepreneur has more to do with growing up in affluent homes, with access to lots of information and resources coupled with great private educations, than not. If that's true, why are a stunning percentage of people who are starting businesses in America today born in countries other than the United States? Nobody's living large like Americans!

The truth is, entrepreneurs aren't born—or born into conditions that make you entrepreneurial. **Entrepreneurs aren't born—they're made**. And it's really simple.

Entrepreneurs are optimistic—but we're born into a pessimistic world. Being optimistic is not natural in this world, it's a learned response. The Millionaire Mentor Club program will teach you to be optimistic. That's the secret in a nutshell. It's a lesson straight out of *Mommy Millionaire*: "A person will achieve success in direct proportion to his ability to let go of negativity in favor of all that is positive. Being negative is easy; being positive is what's hard. Be a positive, big-picture person, always striving to work for the highest good of all parties involved, and you can't help but succeed."

Entrepreneurs are risk takers—but nobody is born wanting to take risks. Risk-taking is a learned response. The only way you can evaluate risk is to evaluate reward. The Millionaire Mentor Club program will teach you to see reward. To see it in the morning when you get up, and in the evening when you go to bed. See it when you look in your kids' faces at 2 P.M. on a school day for a school party, see it in your business plan's exit strategy, see it as the hope, dream, or aspiration that reward is for you—not just money— every minute of your workday.

Entrepreneurs are passionate—but you're not born passionate. Being passionate is a learned response. The Millionaire Mentor Club program will give you the tools you need to follow your passion. This world is jealous of passionate people. We're taught early to go to school, get good grades, get a good degree, then a good job with a good title in a good career track. Becoming an entrepreneur means learning to value ideas and passion over degrees and job titles. It means stepping out of everything you were taught and redefining success in your own terms. It means boasting unapologetically about your ideas, about your kids, and it means not being afraid to be enthusiastic when the whole world is telling you you're crazy.

Entrepreneurs are courageous—but you're not born being courageous. Being courageous is a learned response. We're taught in this world early that to get along, you've got to go along. We're taught to measure our value as human beings by the size of our houses and SUVs and not our hearts. We're taught to equate success with material things and not freedom: freedom to control our own destinies, freedom to reap reward in direct proportion to our efforts, freedom to fail trying, freedom to succeed—freedom to follow our dreams without sacrificing our need to be a great parent. Life is short. The Millionaire Mentor Club program will teach you that courage requires only one easy step: believing in yourself and your capabilities to face a challenge.

Don't only be these things—teach these things! Teach them to your kids, and to your friends and fellow entrepreneurs. Be optimistic, passionate, and a courageous risk taker, and teach your kids to be positive, big-picture people who are smart and confident enough to redefine success on their own terms. Learn how to see opportunity all around you to make the world a better, or prettier, or kinder, or easier place and learn how to develop the courage and the passion to face the challenge and get it done. *Remember you're human*—not superhuman—and you need encouragement and affirmation, too. So the next time you're feeling down in your daily battle to pick yourself up, call up a group of friends and get together to form your own Millionaire Mentor Club, where the focus is on defining, believing in, and supporting each other in the pursuit of individual dreams, whether they're to make a million dollars, or to take your community service mission into the stratosphere, or to revolutionize school lunch programs across the country. All you need to do to get started is go to www.mommymillionaire.com, where you can learn how to get involved with the Millionaire Mentor Club program, where you will be provided with not only the inspiration, but the detailed business reference you need to turn your vision into a reality. Complete with detailed checklists, invaluable templates, empowering exercises, and winning strategies, the Millionaire Mentor Club provides a road map to success for anyone who has a dream. Go there today to learn how you can get started.

Turn your dream into a reality—today!
Since I've begun my journey I've met many people who have reminded me of the incredible transforming power of dreams. Those who haven't read my book are surprised to know that I get discouraged just like you. No matter where you are in your journey, every day will surely bring new challenges to your dream that only faith, hard work, and an unremitting belief in yourself will get you through. Join a Millionaire Mentor Club to help you enjoy the journey with supportive friends, because in the end, the journey is the reward. Treat your dream the same as you treat your kids, laughing, crying, getting mad, showing patience, failing one day, succeeding the next—taking it one day at a time instead of waiting for the day they leave for college or the day you bank a million dollars—and you'll do just fine.

Many of my "Daddy Millionaires" have written to me lately to remind me how they're part of this revolution, too. As we lead this revolution across the world, let's make sure we focus on substance, not image; on detailed resource, not the promise of information; on inspiration and support, and not an impossibly high standard that only a few gifted with exclusive educations and career choices can attain. Let's not only talk about success, but also talk in detail about every important step along the way that got us there, showing the reality behind the myth of "overnight success" that demoralizes and exasperates the rest of us, creating false expectations and images of perfection that none of us can attain. Let's come together in Millionaire Mentor Clubs across the United States to support each other with hope, honesty, and faith. There's enough success for everyone to go around.

Follow your dreams.

Be a hero.

To join the revolution and learn how you can join a Millionaire Mentor Club, log on to www.mommymillionaire.com today.

"Everything begins with a search for something better—a dream, an idea, the courage to face a challenge, and the passion to get it done.

You can do it.

Believe in yourself.

Change the rules.

Join the revolution."

AFTERWORD

Can you believe things have gotten even more exhilarating, fascinating, and challenging since I finished this book? Green Daisy has developed in unexpected ways I could never have anticipated at the beginning of my journey, leading me to the edge of unimaginable frontiers. The events detailed here were the chronicle of a business's start-up phase. Now that Green Daisy has graduated to second-stage company status, I'm doing things I never even thought were possible just a year ago, learning priceless lessons from real Masters of the Universe, with whom very few people have the opportunity to work.

To follow all the exciting developments that are going on with Green Daisy and my continuing journey as a Mommy Millionaire, log on to www .mommymillionaire.com, "your home on the Web for creating the life you really want."™

To learn more about or purchase any of our family of Green Daisy products, visit our Web site at www.greendaisy.com.

I look forward to meeting my readers as I travel the across the United States, and I wish you every success in your journey toward creating the life you really want.

Your friend in the business,
Kim Lavine

INDEX